The Literature of Cinema

ADVISORY EDITOR: **MARTIN S. DWORKIN**
INSTITUTE OF PHILOSOPHY AND POLITICS OF EDUCATION
TEACHER'S COLLEGE, COLUMBIA UNIVERSITY

THE LITERATURE OF CINEMA presents a comprehensive selection from the multitude of writings about cinema, rediscovering materials on its origins, history, theoretical principles and techniques, aesthetics, economics, and effects on societies and individuals. Included are works of inherent, lasting merit and others of primarily historical significance. These provide essential resources for serious study and critical enjoyment of the "magic shadows" that became one of the decisive cultural forces of modern times.

Instructional Film Research 1918-1950

Charles F. Hoban, Jr. and Edward B. van Ormer

ARNO PRESS & THE NEW YORK TIMES

New York • 1970

Reprint Edition 1970 by Arno Press Inc.
Library of Congress Catalog Card Number: 76-124015
ISBN 0-405-01621-2
ISBN for complete set: 0-405-01600-X
Manufactured in the United States of America

NAVEXOS P-977
TECHNICAL REPORT NO. SDC 269-7-19

INSTRUCTIONAL FILM RESEARCH 1918-1950
(RAPID MASS LEARNING)

The Pennsylvania State College

Instructional Film Research Program

December, 1950

Project Designation NR-781-005

Contract N6Onr-269, T.O. VII

SDC Human Engineering Project 20-E-4

Report Prepared by: Charles F. Hoban, Jr. and Edward B. van Ormer

Sponsored Jointly by Department of the Army and Department of the Navy.

FOR THE PENNSYLVANIA STATE COLLEGE:

Dean M. R. Trabue
Responsible Administrator

C. R. Carpenter
Program Director

FOR THE SPECIAL DEVICES CENTER

Reviewed for Human Engineering Branch:

J. Gaberman, Project Engineer
Head, Applications Research Section

C. P. Seitz, Head,
Program Branch

L. S. Beals, Jr.
CDR (MC) USN, Director
Human Engineering Division

Submitted:

B. G. Eaton
Technical Director

Approved:

for T. B. Haley, Captain, USN
Commanding Officer and
Director

3ND-P&PO-1979

FOREWORD

This report constitutes one of a series of technical reports prepared by the Instructional Film Research Program at the Pennsylvania State College. This research program is jointly sponsored by the Department of the Army and the Department of the Navy.

The purpose of this report is to bring together, in one source, the findings growing out of the many and widely scattered investigations in the area of training through motion pictures. Historically, the report covers a period of about thirty years.

Many of the studies contained herein admittedly fail to meet the highest standards of research design. They are, nevertheless, included, since no better information is available at this date. In spite of their limitations, the results of these studies can serve as valuable guide lines in the practical situations of training film planning, production and utilization and in the planning and design of new research.

J. Gaberman
Head, Applications Research Section
Human Engineering Division
Special Devices Center

AUTHORS' NOTE

In presenting this report, we are endeavoring to meet a long-standing need for a major review of experimentation in the area of the instructional film. To meet this need we have undertaken to summarize, evaluate and integrate three decades of research to which we have ventured to add our own interpretations and a tentative statement of principles of film influence. We hope that this work may have both theoretical and practical significance. Specifically, we hope that the report will be helpful as a guide for (1) predicting the results of film instruction more accurately; (2) improving the planning and production of instructional films; (3) increasing the effectiveness of film utilization procedures. If this report serves also as a stimulus and guide to continued inquiry into the basic, theoretical, and practical problems of film communication, another of our goals will have been realized.

In carrying out this arduous and tedious task, the authors and their assistants have worked, when time permitted, for over two and one-half years. In a cooperative project of this nature involving many individuals, it is almost inevitable that some errors, misstatements, and perhaps incorrect interpretations have been made, despite our efforts to avoid them. To assist in preparing possible future revisions of the report, the authors will greatly appreciate having any such errors called to their attention.

We are indebted to the several faculty members and graduate assistants who, under the supervision of the authors, prepared systematic abstracts of research reports. Among the persons rendering this valuable assistance were: Edward Abramson, Philip Ash, Theodore Blau, Irving Jacks, Nathan Jaspen, James Gallagher, Marjorie Mertens, Joseph Murnin, Clare Robinson, Abram VanderMeer, and Jeanette Walter.

For their careful reading of the entire manuscript and their many valuable suggestions, the authors are indebted to C. R. Carpenter, Arthur A. Lumsdaine, Leslie P. Greenhill, A. W. VanderMeer, and Edward McCoy.

Edgar Dale and Seerley Reid furnished valuable bibliographical lists.

At the beginning of the project, the U. S. Office of Education supplied an extensive set of unpublished short abstracts which served as an initial annotated bibliography.

The Yale Motion Picture Research Project, under the direction of Mark May, supplied this Program with a duplicate set of its card file of references to research studies. The main results of several unpublished studies conducted by this project were furnished through the courtesy of Arthur A. Lumsdaine, who was the assistant director of the Yale project.

Special acknowledgement is due Jean Wilson, who, for two years, was in charge of the Information Center of the Instructional Film Research Program. During the summer of 1949, she was secretary to the authors.

Special credit is due Mary Catherine Welch, research assistant during 1949-50, for her valuable bibliographical work, expert typing, and the collation and proofreading of manuscript during the summer of 1950, when she served as secretary to the authors.

Allen L. Edwards, visiting professor of psychology during the summer of 1951, gave valuable assistance in the preparation of the glossary.

The critical, untiring, and meticulous work of Leslie P. Greenhill, research associate, and Edward McCoy, research assistant, in the final reading of the manuscript and in reading of the proof, is greatly appreciated.

Charles F. Hoban, Jr.
The Catholic University of America

Edward B. van Ormer
The Pennsylvania State College

The Instructional Film Research Program

The Pennsylvania State College

October, 1951

TABLE OF CONTENTS

CHAPTER I

INTRODUCTION

PART I.   DEVELOPMENT OF THE REPORT

Need for the Report

Over two hundred experimental and survey studies have been made in the past thirty-odd years on the educational influences and effectiveness of motion pictures. With the rapid growth of television, research data dealing with the projected picture and voice may have an increased practical, as well as theoretical, importance. From an educational point of view, it is important to know what kind of research has been conducted on the effectiveness of the projected picture and sound in promoting learning, what valid conclusions can be derived from the mass of accumulated research data, and which of the prevalent beliefs about the effectiveness of motion pictures are supported by controlled observations and empirical data.

This information is needed by both the sponsor and the producer of educational and training films or television programs so that planning and production may be more efficient in terms of process and end-product. It is needed by users of these channels so that best results can be obtained in mass instruction, training, and public information. Research workers in motion pictures and television need this information to avoid unnecessary repetition of previous studies and to help in the better formulation of problems and the better design of new experiments so that systematic knowledge of the principles of visual communication can be extended and refined. Theory is, in the final analysis, a very practical thing for practical people.

The purpose of this report is to present such a summary of the film research published prior to June 1, 1950. The report is largely, although not exclusively, confined to experimental studies which report the observed effects of motion pictures on human behavior.

Plan of the Report

At least four major elements must be taken into consideration in an adequate discussion of the educational effectiveness of motion pictures:

1. The end-purpose, or objective, for which the film is produced or used; that is, the particular changes in the motor skill, knowledge, attitude, or motivation that the film is intended to help in bringing about.

2. The characteristics of the audience or of individuals in the audience which impede or facilitate the intended reaction to the picture, and, hence, affect the degree to which the film objectives are realized.

3. The content and structure of the film itself, which in many or most sound films, is a combination of pictures, language, music, occasional graphs and charts, and the particular cinematic or instructional treatment of the combination of communications media.

4. The context in which the film is presented to the audience. This includes the related instructional experiences, the teaching procedures that accompany the presentation, and the physical and social circumstances of the presentation.

The data reported in film research studies are organized and discussed in this report so as to (1) emphasize the above four factors: objectives, audience characteristics, film techniques, and context of presentation or utilization; (2) summarize the available data on each of these factors; and (3) formulate the conclusions from these data into a series of operational principles which can be employed to increase the educational and instructional effectiveness of films.

Since much of the research data applies to learning results (achievement of various educational objectives), rather than to audience characteristics, film techniques, or use situations, this report necessarily contains several chapters of varying length dealing with the effectiveness of films in achieving the several objectives of instruction for which they are used in military and civilian education and training. A separate chapter is devoted to the effectiveness of films in comparison with other instructional media and procedures. The remaining chapters are devoted to audience characteristics, and to production and utilization techniques. In the final chapter, a statement of tentative principles of motion picture communication and their implications for producers and users is presented.

In order to meet the needs of the busy film maker and film user who are interested in conclusions and have little time to study the detailed data from which the conclusions are drawn, a summary is provided at the end of each major part of each chapter.

In addition, psychological and statistical terms which occur from time to time are explained in a glossary which appears at the end of this report.

Method of Procedure

The question to which this review of research studies is addressed is: What do we know with reasonable certainty about the influence of motion pictures on the behavior of people? In other words, what do these research studies add up to? Our task is that of analysis, interpretation, and creative synthesis.

More than two hundred of the available research studies on the influence of motion pictures (including masters' theses* and doctoral dissertations) published or reported in English were examined with a critical regard to experimental design and the reliability of the data from which conclusions were drawn.

All significant research reports not published in book form, i.e., all periodical articles and bound manuscripts, such as graduate theses, were abstracted** in such a way that the experimental problem and procedure were stated in concise form, the crucial data were condensed, and only the conclusions which were supported by the experimental evidence were stated.

Most of the studies, both those abstracted from manuscripts and those published in printed form, were briefly summarized by the authors of this report. This summary consisted of a one-page condensation of (1) the

problem, (2) experimental variables, (3) experimental design, (4) conclusions supported by the evidence, (5) indices of the statistical reliability of the data, and (6) educational or psychological significance of the results. Reliability is used in its usual statistical meaning; psychological significance is defined in terms of the magnitude of differences and their practical educational or social importance.***

These summaries were then classified under: (1) type of behavior, such as attitudes, motivation, conceptual learning, and perceptual-motor learning; (2) factors in audience response; (3) production techniques; and (4) methods of use. A given study was classified under each area to which it contributed relevant data.

In summarizing the data from available reports of research, we have attempted to relate the research findings to basic principles which may be useful in predicting the effects of motion pictures, and in improving the production and use of films in order to increase their effectiveness. The virtue of experimental and survey research lies in the verification, rejection, or reformulation of principles, postulates, and hypotheses on the basis of careful observation of behavior under carefully controlled conditions. The collection and systematic arrangement of these principles constitute the beginning of a theoretical system from which procedures may be developed to obtain, with greater predictability, the desired results in audience reaction.

The interpretations which we have made from the data reported in the experimental literature are necessarily somewhat cautious, but we have tried to temper caution with some imagination and insight. After our examination of the experimental literature, we are impressed not with how much we have learned, but with how little we know with reasonable certainty about films and their influences, and we are impressed with how little discrimination has actually been developed with reference to the various factors or processes that influence audience behavior by means of

* Available lists of masters' theses were examined for studies whose titles suggested some special approach to this area. Such theses were obtained, if possible, and abstracted if they contributed something to the present survey. Many of them were found to fail to meet the criteria for inclusion herein. Their titles will be found, however, in the comprehensive bibliography at the end of this report.

** The abstracting was done by the authors and by assistants working under the authors' supervision. These assistants had received graduate training in experimental procedure and statistics. The material was recorded on specially prepared, four-page folders, with an additional sheet of tables inserted where necessary. This type of abstract furnishes sufficient information for another investigator to evaluate a study without reference to the original report.

*** There is some precedent for this distinction. Cf., Peters, C. C. & VanVoorhis, W. R. Statistical procedures and their mathematical bases: 1935, 332-333; 1940, 452-453; McNemar, Q. Psychological statistics. 1949, 82-83, 86, 234. Statisticians have pointed out that statistical significance, or reliability of differences or changes, is not the same as the size of the change or its importance educationally or socially in changed behavior. All too many research workers make statistical significance and importance synonymous.

films. As a result, we are in the difficult position of discussing a medium of communication which has been subjected to very little discriminating analysis, even though the medium contains many variables that can be arranged in a variety of combinations in any specific motion picture on any specific subject, for any specific audience, for any specific purpose. On the other hand, progress has been made in determining the general effects of the medium and some of the factors which appear to determine this result.

Criteria of Study Suitability

The specific investigations to be mentioned in the various chapters of this survey include the majority of those studies which meet three out of four of the following criteria:

1. The study adds significantly to our knowledge of some factor involved in the effects of motion pictures.

2. The experimental design was of such a nature that the experimental variables investigated were actually variables, and the experimental variables were the only variables which could exert a pronounced influence upon the results.

3. The experimental results were psychologically or educationally significant, and were reliable in terms of well-known criteria of statistical reliability.

4. Even though results were not "highly reliable" statistically, useful insights were suggested or gained from the data.

PART II. EDUCATION, INSTRUCTION, AND ENTERTAINMENT

Education

Since the experimental data deal with educational, instructional, and entertainment films, it is necessary to define these three processes. Historically, education has meant directing or guiding an individual's learning so that he will develop socially useful forms of behavior. This might be called formal education or instruction. It has become increasingly obvious that, in a complex society, much of a person's "education" occurs outside the formal direction of the school, and is strongly influenced by such institutions, groups, and media as the home, church, companions, reading, motion pictures, radio, travel, and, now-a-days, television. Thus, education, in a broad sense, refers to all those experiences, both planned and incidental, which the individual encounters and which contribute, in a large or small degree, to the modification and growth of his knowledge, abilities, attitudes, and other aspects of self-development. These experiences, interacting with his hereditary and natural potentialities, result in his being the kind of person he is now.

Instruction

Education may be thought of as the broader or generic term which includes the more specific term, instruction. Instruction means a pre-planned, deliberate selection and arrangement of situations so as to stimulate learner interaction. The result of this interaction is experience, which is intended to help the individual change his patterns of response in a predetermined, prescribed direction considered desirable by those responsible for the instruction. In the broad meaning of education, educational influences of films may occur somewhat independently of, and at times, even contrary to the intent for which the film was produced or exhibited.

Instructional influences of films, to be most effective, thus require a high degree of pre-planning and directional intent in both production and use. It is in this sense that the terms instruction and instructional film are used throughout this report. So defined, the term includes films produced and used for information and propaganda as well as for teaching and training.

Relation of Entertainment to Education

A brief digression into the relationship between entertainment and education appears desirable, since we shall deal in this review with the influence of films produced for many types of purpose and use. Some of these were produced to provide entertainment in the theater, others for instruction in the classroom, and still others for instruction in the theater. In addition, a few of these films were produced by entertainment-film personnel for instructional use.

One of the major premises of the motion picture, radio, and television industries is that their primary function is to provide entertainment for the mass of the American people. By implication, at least, education is regarded as the function of the school and college. Thus, education and entertainment are postulated as being distinct from each other, and, in the popular mind, almost antagonistic.

This line of reasoning involves a confusion of process and product, and considers education, in the narrow sense of formal education or instruction. Actually, the function of the school and college is to provide instruction and other educational experiences. The intent of the instruction is educational in very specific ways, but sometimes the product or outcomes are not necessarily educational in the manner intended. The educational outcomes that result from instruction are necessarily the direct product of the learner's activity, not of the teacher's activity. The teacher does not and cannot do the learning for the student. The teacher infuses the instruction with a "contagious" personal quality, and attempts to arrange the environment in a way that will stimulate the learner to efforts and activities, which, if continued, help the learner progress in the acquisition of knowledge, attitudes, skills, and habits, and help him to develop socially and intellectually.

Entertainment, so-called, places considerably less responsibility for effort and activity on the members of an audience, and increases the responsibility of the "entertainer" (at least for outward activity) for holding and occupying the attention of the audience. On the other hand, in instruction, the individuals of the audience expect to be required to recall and apply the material or actions presented. Consequently, an "instruction" audience frequently puts forth more effort than an "entertainment" audience. But the social and intellectual activity of the audience may at times be highly stimulated by entertainment. A person who attends an entertainment function expecting only to be entertained, may and often does abstract, absorb, analyze, and conserve his experience, rather than molt it or drop it at the theater exit.

The Learning Process

When an individual has particularly pleasant or unpleasant experiences, and these are related to the means for satisfying his basic needs for acceptance, respect, achievement, prestige, and self-fulfillment, he is likely to retain them and make them part of his perceptual, conceptual, and motivational structure. When experiences derived from motion pictures and other environmental situations, (which may or may not be intentionally instructional), are integrated, especially through further thought and, or discussion, into such structures involving the basic drives and needs of the individual, these experiences become involved in changes in the individual's way of looking at his private world and of behaving in response to the world around him.

We call this process, learning, or education in a broad sense, and the resulting change we call an educational product. It is immaterial whether entertainment or instruction was uppermost in the minds of those in charge of the medium or in the minds of the audience. From an educational point of view, a hard and fast distinction between education and entertainment is not acceptable because the distinctions are misleading. It is true that many of the techniques used in instructional films differ from those used in entertainment films, but regardless of the producer's intent, films produced for instruction or for entertainment may have an educational effect.

For these reasons, all research studies, whether on films produced to entertain in the theater, to train

in the military services, or to teach in school or college, are included in our review of experimental literature on instructional films.

PRACTICAL VALUES OF FILM RESEARCH

One of the difficulties of film research is attempting to generalize from any one experiment or from a series of repeated experiments in order to predict the influence of a given film on a given audience, where experimental evidence is lacking. The problem of applying research to film production is very much like the problem of Professor X in choosing a wife. He had reached early middle age, but had not yet married. As a scientist, he approached the problem "scientifically." He studied the variables which had been experimentally demonstrated as relevant to the behavior of the wife of a college professor, and constructed a scale for measuring the candidate population on these variables. He administered the scale to the available sample of the population parameter, and then ranked the candidates in order of high and low scores on the scale. He found one subject to be significantly superior, with a probability less than .001, on all criteria. On the basis of his scientific selection of his bride-to-be, Professor X proceeded with his version of the ritual of courtship appropriate to his station in life. His entire procedure worked successfully, except for one thing--Professor X did not like the lucky lady!

Perhaps one of the virtues of research in an applied field, such as that of the instructional motion picture, is that judgments involved in each step of the process can be "educated" judgments. Such judgments, formed on the basis of experimental and testimonial evidence, (though with an awareness of alternatives and "hunches"), are more likely to lead to the production of more effective instructional films and to a more effective way of utilizing them. But, just as in the case of Professor X, scientific research offers no guarantee that the ideal marriage between knowledge and application will be consummated.

Regardless of the difficulties of predicting the influence of a particular film on its audience, that process can be facilitated and improved by the existence of a body of experimentally established information about instructional films, and by a systematic theory of the dynamics of film influence. Sometimes the research evidence is fragmentary or subject to qualification in the light of later evidence, but the research efforts of the past thirty years have produced some consistent evidence upon which many of the generalizations and implications in this report are based.

The report is, unfortunately for the reader, quite lengthy. In this, the reviewers had little choice if they were to present both the evidence and the conclusions and interpretations warranted by the evidence. We have, regrettably, been unable to find the royal road.

CHAPTER II

MAJOR FILM RESEARCH PROGRAMS IN THE UNITED STATES

INTRODUCTION

Film research began in the United States around the time of the first World War and has continued since in a series of major studies and individual research projects. The major studies, and the trends of film research, will be discussed briefly in this chapter.

The first large scale research on the educational effectiveness of motion pictures was undertaken in 1919 when a grant of $6600 was made by the United States Interdepartmental Social Hygiene Board to the Psychological Laboratory of Johns Hopkins University "for the purpose of assisting the laboratory in 'investigating the informational and educative effect upon the public of certain motion pictures used in various campaigns for the control, repression, and elimination of venereal diseases.'" (K. S. Lashley and J. B. Watson, 1922, p. 3). The work was carried on under the general supervision of an advisory board consisting of Adolph Meyer, S. I. Franz, and R. S. Woodworth, and the study was conducted by Karl S. Lashley and John B. Watson, both were then psychologists of some distinction and later achieved considerable recognition.

The report of the Lashley-Watson research has lain dormant for at least two decades. By way of apology to the experimenters and to the reader for omission of the data of the Lashley and Watson study from subsequent chapters of this review, it may be said that the present reviewers did not learn of this study until early in 1951, after the manuscript of this review had been prepared and submitted to the Instructional Film Research Program. Partly to initiate the reader somewhat more quickly into the actual research on film influence, and partly to compensate for our oversight while this review was in original process of writing, the Lashley-Watson study will be briefly summarized here.

The film selected for study was entitled, Fit to Win, a six-reel 35mm film prepared for general public exhibition from the original wartime version, Fit to Fight. The original version had been produced for exhibition to military populations during World War I. The treatment of the subject was primarily

dramatic, featuring consequences of venereal disease and of continence on the various characters in the drama. The setting was World War I. The characters were personnel of the U. S. Army. In addition to its dramatic content, factual information on venereal disease was also included in the film. The primary appeals of the film were to fear, to the desire for social acceptance, and to parental hope and affection.

In the experiment, the film was shown to approximately 5000 people. Results were tested by questionnaires on informational and emotional effects of the film, and by interviews with 35 men from six to 18 months after the film showing. Pre-tests on venereal disease information were obtained from approximately 425 individuals, and post-tests were obtained from 1230 members of the various audiences to whom the film was shown in the experiment. The experimental population included a medical group, an executive and clerical group, a group of literary club women, a mixed audience of male and female youths and adults, and separate groups of male streetcar company employees, merchant sailors, and soldiers.

In general, the film was found to be effective in conveying information on venereal disease, although, in some respects, the informational effects were inadequate for an essential understanding. No adverse emotional effects were detected after the film showings. In general, there seemed to be an immediate reaction of fear of venereal disease and a temporary resolution of continence. No effects on inhibition of exposure to venereal disease were found to follow the film showing. In other words, the film was not effective in inhibiting sexual exposure to venereal disease. A few infected men sought medical advice after seeing the film. Some individuals seemed to be educationally motivated, or to be motivationally reinforced, by the film and requested additional showings of the film, related pamphlets, and other propaganda materials on venereal disease.

The small amount of data on retention of information obtained from the film suggests that the main facts were well remembered up to five months after the film exhibition, but no enduring effects on behavior with reference to the source or prevention of venereal disease infection were discovered by the experimenters.

The results of the Lashley-Watson study are consistent with the findings of later experiments on film influence which indicate that motion pictures are most effective as an instrument for the wide-spread dissemination of information. There is little evidence in this or subsequent research that a single motion picture is effective in restructuring conduct or habits related to primal desires, or that the information presented in a film will, because it is presented in a film, inhibit or modify behavior immediately or later on.

There are many interesting observations in the Lashley-Watson report on the reactions of various types of audiences to the film, and on the effect of various situations of exhibition on audience reaction. These observations are, on the whole, in accord with the data reported in our subsequent chapters dealing with later research on film influence, and with the postulates and principles which we derived out of the later research data. A tendency toward exaggerated expectation of the influence of a single film on behavior is as apparent in the report of this study made over 30 years ago as it is in the expectation of film influence evident today among film sponsors and film producers.

One cannot view some of the lengthy propaganda films produced behind the Iron Curtain of International Communism without developing some respect for the probable influence of motion pictures on attitudes, opinions, and, perhaps, actual political behavior of the individual, especially when these films are reinforced by the strong compulsive social pressures of Party dominance over the individual and the community. It is evident, however, that the theory of single causation, coupled with the concept of the determinism of the motion picture as a medium of social influence, is without support in the experimental evidence on the influence of the kinds of motion pictures whose effects have been studied experimentally in the English-speaking world.

Before examining the results of the film research studies, which form the substance of this report, we will turn our attention, briefly, to the major research programs in the United States* which have supported or inspired much of the experimental work in the area of instructional films.

INDIVIDUAL RESEARCH

Many of the individual film research projects have been conducted by students in connection with their graduate studies. Among the earliest experimental studies of the influence of motion pictures upon learning were those by D. R. Sumstine of the Pittsburgh (Pennsylvania) public schools, reported in 1918, and by J. V. Lacy, in two New York City schools, reported in 1919. The chief value of these studies was to raise questions and to stimulate further research.

One of the pioneer experiments in visual education was J. J. Weber's (1922) study of the comparative effectiveness of several visual aids. In this study, which he undertook as his doctoral research at Columbia University, objective measures and statistical procedures were extensively and carefully used. Weber introduced pictorial tests in his study of motion picture influences and thus was among the first and one of the relatively few investigators to measure the results of learning from a pictorial medium by other than purely verbal tests.

Some of these individual research efforts produced results which add significantly to our information about films. For instance, L. L. Ramseyer's (1938) study of films and attitude formation at Ohio State University has provided information and insights in this area.

A. W. VanderMeer's (1943, 1945) Chicago University study was the first experimental study of the contributions made by films in speeding up industrial training on a mass basis. By and large, however, adequate research on the motion picture puts the individual unsubsidized research worker at a serious disadvantage. One conclusion that seems evident from the available research literature is that progress in the discovery of principles that govern motion picture communication is aided by the coordinated teamwork of a well-trained, full-time research staff and by continuity of research activity over long periods of time.

COMMONWEALTH FUND STUDIES

The first coordinated team studies were conducted by F. N. Freeman (1924) and a research staff which he assembled at the University of Chicago. This study, aided by a small grant from the Commonwealth Fund, investigated such areas as perceptual-motor learning, motivation, various methods of film use, types of verbalization, and film content. It also compared the teaching effectiveness of films with that of other instructional materials and procedures.

---

* For a survey of the major research programs concerned with educational motion pictures conducted in Great Britain see the historical summary for 1922 to 1947 in the bulletin of the Scottish Film Council and Scottish Educational Film Association, entitled, Sound Films in Education: An Interim Report by the Advisory Committee Dealing with the Place of the Sub-standard Sound Film in the General Provision for Visual Education in Schools (Scottish Film Council, 1948). Where these studies, and two or three British and Australian studies not mentioned in the Scottish summary, contribute to the formation of conclusions they are mentioned in the present report.

Some of these Commonwealth Fund studies contributed basic insights which have been substantiated by later research, and introduced into film research some experimental variables which were ignored in the studies conducted during the next two decades. For example, in one study an experimental film was produced. The production of experimental films is now recognized as an effective method of controlling the experimental variables in motion picture research. In another study, the technique of stimulating pupil responses during the showing of a film was utilized. The technique of having the audience respond during the exhibition of a film, known today as "audience participation," has been demonstrated as a factor which facilitates learning from films with some types of audiences and some types of learning tasks.

EASTMAN STUDIES

The Eastman Kodak Company produced one of the first comprehensive libraries of (silent) motion picture films for instructional use. Research funds were given to B. D. Wood, of Columbia University, and F. N. Freeman, of the University of Chicago for an extensive investigation of the contribution of these films to instruction. The Wood and Freeman (1929) study involved a large and perhaps unwieldy teacher and pupil population. Extreme care, (almost to a fault), was taken to avoid biasing the experiment to favor the influence of films over that of other teaching materials and procedures. Wood and Freeman's major conclusion was that "the film gives the child clear-cut notions of the objects and actions in the world about him" (p. 221). This matter-of-fact observation has been borne out by subsequent research in informational and conceptual learning from motion pictures. Learning is especially aided when the film is designed to convey the material clearly through the picture, or visual medium, and not overload the verbal medium (the titles in silent films or the commentary in sound films).

YALE UNIVERSITY STUDIES

At about the same time that the Eastman Kodak Company was producing silent motion pictures for instruction in geography, science, health, etc., Yale University produced a series of silent instructional motion pictures known as the Chronicles of America Photoplays. Not only were these photoplays historically accurate in fine details, but they also involved a compromise between the text-book type of film organization and the plot-type of dramatic organization of entertainment films. The dramatization of incidents within a discernible story thread in the Photoplays involved the peculiar style of acting that was characteristic of silent entertainment films. The advent of sound films, with their radically changed acting style hastened the technical obsolescense of these films for elementary and junior high school use.

D. C. Knowlton and J. W. Tilton (1929), of the Yale faculty, undertook to discover experimentally the contributions of the Chronicles of America Photoplays to the objectives of history instruction at the seventh-grade level. With unusual insight, Knowlton and Tilton's experimental design provided for the study of various types of conceptualization involved in responses to the films (knowledge of historical relationships, time relationships, and historical personages, etc.).

Ten years later Yale University sponsored another study of the influence of these films. This study, conducted at the senior high school level, was reported by H. A. Wise (1939), and was a valuable supplement to the Knowlton and Tilton investigation.

CARNEGIE FOUNDATION STUDY

The Yale studies of the Chronicles of America were the last of the major researches dealing with silent motion pictures. In 1928 sound motion pictures were commercially exhibited in theaters, and shortly thereafter, instructional film makers also began to concentrate on sound films. Among the first serious attempts to produce sound films for classroom use was that of the Harvard Film Foundation.

The contribution of sound films to instruction was investigated by the Harvard Film Foundation and the Harvard Graduate School of Education, in a study financed by the Carnegie Foundation for the Advancement of Teaching and conducted by P. J. Rulon (1933). It was undertaken with full recognition of the previous research and dealt with the contributions of films and textbooks, which, except for two films, were specially produced to include a predetermined selection of subject content, and, presumably, to meet specified instructional objectives. This study added to our knowledge about the increase in informational and conceptual learning that results when films are used in combination with textbooks, and introduced some reliable evidence on both initial learning and retention.

PAYNE FUND STUDIES

Despite the fact that motion pictures developed as a medium of entertainment rather than instruction, and still enjoy greater popular support in the theater than in the school, no serious investigation of the influences of entertainment motion pictures was undertaken until 1929, and few have been undertaken since. The entertainment film industry is one of the few major industrial enterprises in America that continues to manufacture a product without continuous organized research in product improvement, although such research has been undertaken sporadically.

At the recommendation of the Motion Picture Research Council, the Payne Fund subsidized an investigation of the effects of commercial entertainment motion pictures on informational and conceptual learning, attitude development, conduct, public morals, emotional excitement, and sleep. These studies, supervised by W. W. Charters of Ohio State University, were made by professors and their associates from the University of Chicago, the University of Iowa, New York University, Ohio State University, Pennsylvania State College, and Yale University.

The results of these studies were summarized by Charters (1933), and separate reports of each study were published. A "popular" and somewhat propagandistic summary was written by H. J. Forman (1933) under the title of Our Movie-Made Children. A vigorous criticism of the studies was written, presumably in rebuttal, by M. J. Adler (1937) of the University of Chicago under the title, Art and Prudence, and was popularized by Moley (1938). Adler's criticism is answered by Cressey (1938).

The results of these studies of the influences of entertainment films are included in this summary of the educational influences of motion pictures, since the educational effects of motion pictures, as has been pointed out, do not result solely from the intent of the producer, or from the circumstances under which they are exhibited. As P. J. Rulon (1933) has pointed out, designating a film as "educational" does not make it so and by the same logic, designating a film as "entertainment" does not make it entertaining nor prevent it from being educational in its effect.

The Payne Fund studies were designed to explore a comprehensive pattern of problems. They have provided data on factors in films which exert an influence on audiences, and the kinds of effects that motion pictures conceivably have on people; although the advances in statistical procedures and the more rigorous experimental requirements of the intervening years may lead one to a re-evaluation of some of the results. The Payne Fund studies appear to have had little direct influence on the thinking about the role and use of motion pictures in organized instruction, although they apparently did affect public opinion and the thinking of motion picture producers about the need for censorship and for a more careful consideration of the content in entertainment films offered to the general public.

AMERICAN COUNCIL ON EDUCATION STUDIES

Three years after the publication of the results of the Payne Fund studies, the American Council on Education undertook the evaluation of motion pictures used in general education under a grant from the General Education Board. Some 1500 films produced or released for the schools were used in classrooms throughout the country under teacher observation, and from this list some 500 films were selected as educationally worthwhile on the basis of the judgments of teachers and pupils, and, in some cases, panels of "experts." An encyclopaedia listing and describing these "experience-tested," worthwhile films, and appraising them in terms of educational level, purposes, unusual strengths or weaknesses, and quality of production, was published by the American Council on Education in 1942 under the title, Selected Educational Motion Pictures.

Descriptive accounts of the methods of using these films and of the results observed from this use were written by selected teachers from several experimental centers. One of these studies was conducted in the Santa Barbara (California) public schools and has been reported by R. Bell, L. F. Cain and L. A. Lamoreaux (1941).

As another facet of the Santa Barbara study, F. W. Noel (1940) summarized experience in the practical problems of projecting instructional films.

The experimental production of films was undertaken in the Denver public schools to meet local curricular needs. This project which involved high school students in both the planning and production of the films, has been reported by F. E. Brooker and E. Herrington (1941).

Another descriptive study of the use of films in a modern curriculum, throughout all twelve grades in this case, was made by the staff of the Tower Hill School, Wilmington, Delaware (Tower Hill School Staff, 1940).

A series of experimental studies on the influence of motion pictures in instruction was conducted at the General College, University of Minnesota. Reports of the Minnesota experiments were prepared in manuscript form by C. J. Potthoff, L. C. Larson, and D. O. Patterson, (1940), E. C. Wilson, L. C. Larson and F. Lord, (1940), and L. C. Larson, (unpublished). These various experimental studies were in the fields of biological and social science at the college level and were concerned with the relation between educational films and changes in information, interest, attitudes, and resistance to propaganda.

Some of the reports of the American Council studies are descriptive and others experimental, and in some cases evaluation was made on a subjective rather than a statistical basis. Nevertheless, these studies have increased our understanding of the influences of motion pictures, and particularly of the factors in audience responses and in the areas of informational learning, attitude formation, and methods of using films. The experimental studies were conducted with attention to factors which might conceivably modify behavior (as many as seventeen variables were used as a basis for matching groups and in analyzing responses to films), and rather complicated statistical procedures were used in the treatment of experimental data.

COMMISSION ON HUMAN RELATIONS STUDIES

At the same time that the American Council on Education was conducting its film research program, the Commission on Human Relations of the Progressive Education Association (1939) conducted a study under the direction of A. V. Keliher. This study assisted by a grant from the General Education Board, dealt with the experimental use of some 60 specially selected and edited excerpts from full-length entertainment films in stimulating discussion among young people on the problems of behavior in everyday, personal, and social relationships. As a means of studying the attitudes of a group which had just viewed one of these films, a stenographic record was made of the rather free discussion which followed. In 1939 Keliher said, "We have experimented with The Human Relations Series of Films for two years. . . .in all parts of the country. We know from our records of discussions and from our surveys of attitudes that students can learn to see the causes that lie back of human behavior and see what can be done about them" (Commission on Human Relations, 1939, p. 11). The results, however, have not been published in comprehensive form and therefore could not be included in this report.

U. S. ARMY STUDIES IN WORLD WAR II

During World War II, extensive use was made of motion pictures by the Army and Navy for training and morale purposes. It has been said that, whereas World War I gave great impetus to the development of group measures of abilities, World War II provided a similar impetus to the development of films and other training aids.

Three series of research studies were undertaken by various Army agencies. Two of these dealt with the effectiveness of films in bringing about various learning outcomes, and the third, with the organizational factors which influenced the extent of film use in training situations.

Studies conducted by the Experimental Section, Research Branch, Information and Education Division of the War Department were reported by C. I. Hovland, A. A. Lumsdaine, and F. D. Sheffield in Experiments on Mass Communication (1949). Brief and separate reports of various studies had previously been published through War Department publication facilities. The problems investigated include opinion and motivational effects of orientational films, factors in audience response, effects of alternate methods of presentation, of audience participation, etc. Hovland, Lumsdaine, and Sheffield's report is of major value because it clarifies some areas in which the previous research evidence was conflicting, and contributes important findings in previously unexplored research areas.

Their report contains an unusually comprehensive discussion of the various hypotheses which might account for observed behavior, and the accompanying analyses of data to support or refute these hypotheses. It contributes many hypotheses which make additional research necessary, particularly with reference to production techniques and procedures. The research of the Army's Information and Education Division may well mark the close of a phase of motion picture experimentation that was concerned almost exclusively with broad categories of research on effectiveness of films (e.g., films vs. usual methods, films plus usual methods vs. usual methods, sound vs. silent films,

etc.). It may set the stage for a second phase of film research which discriminates to a greater degree the variables within films and in their utilization which, separately or in combination, contribute to the effectiveness of motion pictures in influencing specific behavior. This second phase is already evident in the experimental work of the Motion Picture Association of America studies at Yale University, the Instructional Film Research Program at the Pennsylvania State College, and the Human Resources Research Laboratories of the United States Air Force.

Another phase of Army research in motion pictures during World War II was that carried on by the Psychological Test Film Unit of the Aviation Psychology Program of the Army Air Forces, located at Santa Ana Army Air Base, Santa Ana, California. The work of this unit originated from its effort to utilize the motion picture medium for psychological testing and examining of Army Air Forces personnel. The motion picture medium seemed particularly adapted for giving various sorts of group test of visual recognition and for testing the spatial perception abilities of persons moving in space. It appeared that motion pictures might also be capable of simulating many of the conditions encountered in flying, which is characterized by motion, and which is continuous and possesses tempo. The film has a number of unique advantages for measuring the non-verbal aptitudes and perceptual abilities required for flying.

The most important research objective of the Psychological Test Film Unit was, therefore, the construction of motion picture tests for aircrew classification. By an extension of its original research, the Unit came to be concerned with additional problems, such as the representation of three-dimensional space by pictures, effective perceptual learning, general problems of obtaining more effective instruction by means of projected pictures, and films, and problems relating to the physical conditions of the projection of films to groups. Some of these problems are of general interest to educators and others interested in instructional films. The work of the Psychological Test Film Unit was directed by J. J. Gibson. The report of this work, edited by Gibson (1947), is made in AAF Aviation Psychology Program Research Report No. 7, entitled Motion Picture Testing and Research. Studies of more general interest in this report, such as audience participation in pictorial learning, effect of room illumination and of viewing angle, will be discussed in Chapter VIII. Gibson's interesting and valuable report increases our understanding of the factors which probably contribute to the effectiveness of the motion picture, and offers numerous suggestions for future research.

The third series of Army film research studies was conducted at the Signal Corps Photographic Center and dealt with patterns of film supply, print utilization, and film library adminstration. Results of these studies were incorporated in a report by C. F. Hoban Jr. (1946) on motion picture developments for instructional purposes during World War II. These studies serve to underscore the necessity for trained personnel and organized promotion of film utilization, if films are to reach the audiences for which they are intended.

The first of these three series of studies, the one conducted by the Experimental Section, Research Branch, Information and Education Division of the War Department, involved quite a few studies of the effects of orientation films upon information, opinion, and motivation. As a background for understanding some of the problems and results of this first series, the Army orientation program and the nature of the Why We Fight films will be outlined briefly. The results of the research studies are presented mainly in Chapter III on informational learning and in Chapter V on motivation, attitudes, and opinions.

A. Army Orientation Program

During World War II, the staff agency within the War Department known as the Information and Education Division had the responsibility for the ideological aspects of troop morale. This was a morale area separate from those presumably affected by entertainment movies, organized sports, recreational reading, regimental bands and the like, by military events and circumstances, and by shared experience and characteristics of leadership in military activities.

As Hovland, Lumsdaine, and Sheffield (1949) point out, the Army's orientation program, of which the Why We Fight films were an important element, rested on two basic assumptions. It was in terms of these assumptions that the effects of these films were studied:

"The first assumption was that giving men more information about the war and its background would give them more favorable opinions and attitudes toward our participation in the war. The second, related assumption was that improvement of opinions, attitudes, or interpretations about the war would lead in some measure to higher motivation in terms of greater willingness to accept the transformation from civilian to Army life and to serve in the role of soldier" (p. 72).

Three major communications programs were used by the I and E Division in its morale mission: (1) Yank Magazine, published in several versions to conform to overseas locale of American troops; (2) the Armed Forces Radio Service, which arranged for overseas broadcasts of commercial radio entertainment and news in almost all theaters of operation; and (3) motion pictures, including: (a) the Why We Fight series and related films, (b) the Army-Navy Screen Magazine for exhibition in post theaters along with commercial entertainment films, and (c) the G-I Movies which had a semi-entertainment, semi-informational intent, and were exhibited on 16mm circuits domestically and overseas.

In the course of the war, a large number of other films of an informational, orientational, and motivational character were produced under the sponsorship of the Army Service Forces, the Army Ground Forces,

Army Air Forces, the General Staff, and overseas commanders. Among these were: The Film Bulletins, reporting on new developments in weapons and other military developments; the Fighting Man series dealing with specific combat attitudes, motivations, aversions, and combat skills; and films dealing with military security and resistance to interrogation, etc.

This brief review is presented to give the reader a perspective of the broad field of communications employed by Army agencies during World War II, and the relative importance of the Why We Fight films which were evaluated for their influence on information, opinion, and motivation.

B. The Why We Fight Films

Within this context, the Why We Fight films acquired a somewhat unusual prestige. Their production was directed and supervised by Frank Capra, Hollywood film director, who held the commission of Colonel in the Signal Corps during the war. He was attached to the Information and Education Division, together with a full production team, while the first four of the Why We Fight films were in production.

1. Distribution

A War Department directive required the showing of the Why We Fight films to all military personnel. The usual procedure for this exhibition consisted typically of an hour-by-hour scheduling of the films in post theaters before large assemblages of troops. The camp-to-camp circuit was generally arranged by the Information and Education Division, but the detailed scheduling of troop audiences was a prerogative of field commanders. The camp-to-camp circuit of each of the Why We Fight films was arranged with the least possible delay. After the initial circuit had been completed, 35mm prints were deposited in Replacement Training Centers, and 16mm prints could be scheduled by troop commanders directly from New York distribution headquarters.

This system of distribution and use of the Why We Fight films differed from that used with training films and orientational, informational, and motivational films produced for Army agencies other than the I and E Division. The usual procedure for these other films was to deposit 16mm prints in training film libraries on all large Army posts and Service Command headquarters, so that the films were constantly available for use as appropriate to the training schedules of the troop units at the Army training camps and in overseas theaters of operation.

2. Production

As to the Why We Fight films themselves, four were evaluated for their effects on information, opinion, and motivation: (1) Prelude to War, (2) The Nazis Strike, (3) Divide and Conquer, and (4) The Battle of

Britain. Each of these was approximately 50 minutes in duration, and as their titles indicate, they dealt with events leading to World War II and the progress of the war up to and including the air invasion of Britain.

The films consisted primarily of motion picture footage assembled from existing newsreel stock, captured enemy films, feature films produced by America's allies, and any other available, appropriate and accessible sources.

Production of the Why We Fight films involved examining the accessible film footage, selecting the appropriate material from this available stock, editing it, composing and performing a special musical score, and writing and recording the narration.

To achieve their objective, these films had to "sell themselves," since their style was largely documentary. In short, these films let the facts speak for themselves. Brilliant combinations of production techniques were employed. The visual presentation was held together by background music and a running commentary which told the story and explained or interpreted the scenes. "Production" shots, using actors and English narration with "foreign accents," helped to integrate the documentary scenes. Animated diagrams and montages, accompanied by a skillful use of sound effects and music, contributed to vivid and dramatic presentation.

3. Experimental Limitations

These production facts impose the first limitation on Hovland, Lumsdaine, and Sheffield's studies: while the films were especially produced for use in the orientation program of the I and E Division, the selection of the pictorial content of the Why We Fight films was limited mainly to films already produced and available for the producer's use.

Another limitation of the study was that the Experimental Section of I and E's Research Branch (consisting of experimental psychologists), was requested to undertake the evaluation of these films after they had been completed and released. Hovland, Lumsdaine, and Sheffield and the other psychologists who conducted the evaluation studies had no opportunity to introduce experimental variables in either the pictures or the sound track which might conceivably have influenced the effectiveness of the films. Thus, it became difficult for the research staff to generalize its findings on motivation and opinions beyond these four particular films and the particular measures of effectiveness used in testing the influence of these films.

It is regrettable that the research on the motivational and combat conditioning effects of motion pictures used in World War II was confined to the Why We Fight film series, rather than extended to the Fighting Man series and other films which were more specific, in their content and treatment, to these important objectives.

MOTION PICTURE ASSOCIATION OF AMERICA STUDIES

Following World War II, the Motion Picture Association of America allocated funds to the Commission on Motion Pictures in Education of the American Council on Education for a series of studies on the need for instructional films and for the preparation of educational specifications and recommended treatments of content for such films. These materials have been made available without cost to educational film producers. The studies were conducted at Yale University and were reported by M. A. May, (1947).

Also at Yale University, a series of research studies dealing with film techniques and film treatments was conducted with funds allocated by the Motion Picture Association of America and Teaching Film Custodians. Some mimeographed summaries of these studies have been prepared, but thus far only one preliminary report has been published (Yale Motion Picture Research Project, 1947). This report deals with the relative effectiveness of audience participation, motivation, and repetition in film learning (see Chapter VIII).

In 1946 the Motion Picture Association appropriated funds for a pilot film project, that is, for the production of several experimental films in which alternate versions were to be made and tried out in schools. This production project was under the general management of A. L. Mayer of New York City, but was interrelated with the Yale projects. The experimental tryouts were conducted in schools by Yale personnel (May, 1947). Unfortunately, the production of experimental versions was curtailed by lack of funds, and was limited to alternative versions of one film prepared later by the Yale Project.

NEBRASKA MOTION PICTURE PROGRAM

In 1946 a program of research was proposed to study the contribution of films to the enrichment of instruction in the rural high schools of Nebraska. The project was officially named, The Nebraska Program of Educational Enrichment Through the Use of Motion Pictures. A grant of funds was obtained from the Carnegie Corporation and from the Motion Picture Association of America, through Teaching Films Custodians, and the cooperation of several producers and distributors of instructional films was obtained (May, 1947; Scott, 1949; Alexander, 1950). This program, under the joint direction of the University of Nebraska and the State Department of Public Instruction, has conducted a series of experiments on the effect of films upon informational and attitudinal learning through vitalizing existing school courses and through adding, by the use of films, important information not provided in the existing courses.

An over-all report of this program has not yet been published; but a report of one phase of the study, made by H. E. Wise (1949), has been published and is included in this review. At least three doctoral theses, apparently as yet unpublished, have resulted from the study (Scott, 1949; Alexander, 1950; and Peterson, J. A., 1950). Scott's and Alexander's studies are mentioned in this review. Peterson's thesis has not been available to the reviewers.

INSTRUCTIONAL FILM RESEARCH PROGRAM

Extensive research on influences of motion pictures is currently being carried on by the Instructional Film Research Program at the Pennsylvania State College. This program was supported originally by the Special Devices Center, Human Engineering Branch, Office of Naval Research, Department of the Navy (Carpenter, 1948), and is now sponsored by both the Department of the Navy and the Department of the Army.

This present report has been undertaken as one of the studies of the Instructional Film Research Program. The authors of this report acknowledge that the content of their summaries and interpretations of previous research has been considerably influenced by the findings of the Instructional Film Research Pro-

gram studies. Moreover, the staff of the Program has contributed many insights which have been incorporated in the organization of this report and its theoretical basis.

U. S. AIR FORCE PROGRAM

In 1949, the U. S. Air Force established an Audio-Visual Research Division in its Human Resources Research Laboratories. This Audio-Visual Research Division is conducting a program of experimentation dealing with variables in the production and utilization of training films. At the time of writing the present review, no reports of this research had been published.

In this brief summary of motion picture research activity, many individual studies have been omitted, particularly those of individuals working alone in the field. Individual studies which have contributed significantly to the information or theory about motion picture influences, are incorporated in subsequent chapters, or listed in the bibliography. If some studies are not discussed, the omission arises from the need to confine this report to a reasonable size.

CHAPTER III

INSTRUCTIONAL OBJECTIVES:
IMPARTING A KNOWLEDGE OF FACTS

INTRODUCTION

Importance of Facts as an Instructional Objective

Facts are the building blocks of human knowledge and activity. In the American culture, free, intelligent behavior is valued as a more powerful creative tool than externally disciplined obedience and ignorance of alternative courses of action. Because an adequate knowledge of relevant facts is the basis for intelligent behavior, the imparting of factual knowledge is an important concern of education, and hence an important instructional objective.

Role of Facts in Human Behavior

The attainment of the more complex objectives of instruction, which are described in later chapters, depends upon a knowledge of facts (more formally, the "cognitive content of experience"). A knowledge of facts, even though incomplete or inaccurate, is made part of the complex pattern of activity that arises from behavior involving motivation, attitudes, opinions, and perceptual-motor performance (commonly called a "motor skill"). On these levels of behavior, probably the principal value of a knowledge of facts lies in the ability of the individual to apply, or use, the facts. Nevertheless, it is possible to deal with a knowledge of facts without considering the ultimate use of the knowledge, and much of the research on motion pictures has been conducted on this basis.

Levels of Acceptance of Facts

To say that an individual has a knowledge of facts implies that he perceives things in a way that conforms with their reality. As discussed in Chapter V, this conformity may be on either of two levels: (1) the individual may merely be acquainted with the facts, or (2) he may accept them. But even on the level of acquaintance with the facts, the individual may acquire or use his knowledge (a) by methods based on rote and rule, or (b) by processes involving reflective or analytical thinking.

Experimental Bias in Film Research

In the majority of studies on the effectiveness of motion pictures as an instructional medium, little distinction has been made between the possible methods of acquiring and using facts, or between acquaintance with the facts and acceptance of them. Perhaps the failure to preserve these distinctions during the design and conduct of experiments may account for the apparent differences in the effectiveness of motion pictures in achieving various instructional objectives. The influence of motion pictures on motivations, attitudes, and opinions is in contrast with their influence on factual knowledge. For example, L. L. Ramseyer (1938) found little relationship (r = .053) between an increase in information resulting from government propaganda films and positive attitude changes, and that these informational gains persisted longer than the attitude changes.

PLAN OF THE CHAPTER

This chapter describes the effectiveness of motion pictures as a medium for imparting factual knowledge. The inquiry is divided into three phases: the extent to which factual information can be acquired from films, including the kinds of information best adapted to the process; a comparison of the long-time and short-time effects of film learning; and the ability of films to contribute to the learning of concepts.

A number of studies, selected largely from the research programs described in Chapter II, are used to furnish data on the various phases of the problem. Experimental techniques, conclusions, and other significant features of the studies are discussed wherever appropriate. At the end of the chapter is a summary of the conclusions and postulates drawn from these studies. The summary emphasizes those conclusions deemed of special interest to film users, film producers, and others concerned with the techniques of conveying factual information.

PART I.   IMPARTING FACTUAL KNOWLEDGE BY FILMS

HOLADAY AND STODDARD STUDY

One of the best known studies of films which relates to knowledge of facts is that of P. W. Holaday and G. D. Stoddard (1933). The study, pursued from 1928 to 1930, inclusive, was conducted as a part of the Payne Fund studies of the effects of entertainment films on children and youth.

Experimental Design

In this extensive study, responses were analyzed on 17 entertainment films, of which ten were silent and seven were sound films. Approximately 3000 children in grades 2, 3, 5, 6, 9, and 10, and 200 graduate students and young faculty members constituted the experimental population. The subjects were divided into four age groups: second- and third-grade children, fifth- and sixth-grade children, ninth- and tenth-grade children, and adults. There was an aggregate of "20,000 testings with approximately 813,000 items attempted" (p. 2). During the first year of the study, the experimental population was selected from the University of Iowa, including the University's elementary and high schools; during the second year, the experimental population was selected from various types of communities and schools in Ohio, West Virginia, and Mississippi.

For purposes of measuring both immediate and delayed responses based on film experience, groups were matched in age, intelligence, and reading ability. Three matched groups were used and rotated.

Responses on all films were analyzed in terms of (1) ten categories of scenes portraying such elements as emotion, humor, crime, etc.; (2) types of action; (3) kinds of background; and (4) items essential, nonessential, and incidental to the plot.

In reporting results, Holaday and Stoddard used the term "retention" rather than learning. Responses to specific film item tests were not considered as indications of learning film material because pretests could not be given. By retention, therefore, they meant that the experimental population recalled information and concepts related to the contents of the movies.

Findings

The following conclusions, among others, were reached:

1. The general information of children and adults is increased to a considerable extent by informatio correctly shown in motion pictures.

2. General information presented incorrectly by the pictures is frequently accepted as valid unless the incongruity is quite apparent. The content of a picture is accepted as authentic by a large percentage of the audience unless the errors contained are glaring.

3. Retention of the specific incidents of motion pictures is high. Children, even very young ones, can retain specific memories of a picture with a high degree of accuracy and completeness. The second-third grade group retained on the average nearly 60 per cent as much as the group of superior adults.

Evaluation

The performance of lower-, middle-, and upper-grade children, as compared with that of "superior" adults, appears to involve some statistical exaggeration in favor of the younger children. Four elements in experimental measurement may have influenced this possible exaggeration.

Ceilings of Learning Response Varied

First, the same tests were used from grades four through "superior" adults, with the possible result that the ceiling of learning response for adults, while not exactly zero, was, at best, somewhat low. Elsewhere in this report, the relationship of film response to intelligence is discussed, and the conclusion appears warranted that responses to films are correlated with intelligence in a general population. This general finding is difficult to reconcile with the conclusion that second- and third-grade children "retain" nearly 60 per cent as much in perceptual response as the group of "superior" adults. One of the factors involved in the measurement of retention of specific responses is the perceptual discrimination involved in viewing a motion picture. The great differences in intellectual development between second-third grade children and "superior" adults should, theoretically, be evident in perceptual discrimination in viewing motion pictures, and these perceptual responses would be expected to differ to a greater degree than Holaday and Stoddard's data indicate.

Second-Third Grade Results Were Least Reliable

A second element that enters into a possible statistical exaggeration is the number of items in a test on a given film. While the number of items in the specific and general tests is not given, it may be inferred that there were approximately 40 items in the specific test, and perhaps approximately the same number in the general tests. Odd-even correlation, stepped-up by the Spearman-Brown formula, gave reliability coefficients for specific tests varying from .10 to .94, with median reliability coefficients varying from .56 to .90. The lowest values here were for the second-third grade group.

Test Populations Were Small

In the third place, the populations used in measuring the influences of various films were frequently as low or lower than 30, although lumped data populations were sometimes as large as 700.

Tests Varied in Difficulty

A fourth factor may be mentioned. The film tests administered to the second-third grade group were considerably "easier" than the tests used for the other populations, and they were administered orally.

Performance of Younger Children Was Overstated

Added together, these elements of experimental measurement seem to indicate that the reported relative proportion of retention (involving perceptual discrimination) of younger children selected from a general school population as compared with a selected university population is over-optimistic.

These do not necessarily invalidate the general conclusions of Holaday and Stoddard, but they conceivably may reduce the predictability of their conclusions, and they tend to weaken the significance of the data reported on the behavior of pupils in the second and third grades.

HOVLAND, LUMSDAINE, AND SHEFFIELD STUDY

One of the primary objectives of the Why We Fight films, which were an important phase of the Army's orientation program in World War II, was to add to the factual knowledge about the events leading up to the war and the progress of the war. While the effectiveness of these films in changing a soldier's opinions and motivations was not strikingly evident, their effectiveness in influencing his knowledge of facts appears to be clearly established.

Findings

Three different studies by C. I. Hovland, A. A. Lumsdaine, and F. D. Sheffield (1949) showed that these films had a sizable effect on increasing the factual knowledge of Army trainees concerning the background of the war, the Nazi strategy, and the events of the Battle of Britain. Measurements were made approximately a week after the trainees had been shown one or more of these films. The table below, quoted with some modification from the published report (p. 55) summarizes this effect.

Educational Level Affected Results

It is pointed out in Chapter VII that the increase in factual learning from these orientation films depended greatly on the educational level and the intelligence of the men - a conclusion that is brought out when the results are compared on the basis of grade school, high school, or college groups.

ORIENTATION FILM EFFECTS ON FACTUAL KNOWLEDGE

Orientation Film	Average Percentage of Groups Checking Right Answers[1]			Range of Difference Between Film and Control Groups on Individual Test Items
	Control Group	Film Group	Avg. Diff.	
	Percent	Percent	Percent	Percent
Prelude to War[2]	34.8	49.3	14.5	1 to 52
The Nazis Strike; Divide and Conquer[3]	32.8	52.0	19.2	-3 to 46
The Battle of Britain[4]	29.4	51.4	22.0	3 to 57

[1] In the case of each film the average is based on a test of ten or more items about factual points covered in the film.

[2] Equated samples from three different camps, half experimental and half control. Total N used: 1678.

[3] Sample contained 1140 cases, half experimental and half control.

[4] 1200 cases from one camp and 900 from another camp, divided equally into experimental and control groups.

KNOWLTON AND TILTON STUDY

<u>D. C. Knowlton</u> and <u>J. W. Tilton</u> (1929) made a study of the contributions of the Yale Chronicles of America Photoplays to teaching historical facts.

Experimental Design

Ten of these silent films were used in addition to the usual teaching materials in the experimental classes. The results were compared with those of control groups which were taught with usual materials and procedures only. The study involved the material covered in one semester of teaching.

Findings

Knowlton and Tilton reported that the scores of the groups that received film instruction in addition to the regular instruction exceeded those of the groups that received the regular instruction only. The test results for the film groups, given in terms of percentage of superiority over the mean scores of the non-film groups, are shown in Fig. 3-1. The mean differences

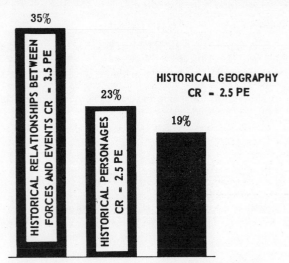

Fig. 3-1. Percent superiority of scores for regular-instruction-plus-film-instruction groups over mean scores for non-film groups. (Knowlton & Tilton, 1929)

on which these percentage gains are based approached high reliability (CR = 3.5 PE's) in the case of historical relationships only. Reliability for knowledge gains in the other two categories were each 2.5 PE's.

On the other hand, there is some evidence to suggest that these Photoplays interfered with the teaching of time relationships, or at least did not facilitate the development of this type of understanding. Film groups were ten per cent inferior to non-film groups in their learning of historical time relationships, but the difference had low reliability.

Evaluation

Small populations, as low as 17, were used in the experimental and control sections, possibly reducing the reliability of over-all differences between film and non-film groups. The reliability of tests used to meas-

ure learning was low in some cases. Split-half correlations of the pretests varied from .16 to .42, and for the reliability of the whole tests (presumably stepped up by the Spearman-Brown formula) varied from .28 to .59. Split-half correlation for all pretests combined was .85 and when stepped up was .92 for the whole test. Reliability indices for learning gains and retentions were, on the whole, considerably lower.

The Knowlton and Tilton study, conducted with seventh-grade pupils, is most valuable because of the insights it affords into the kinds of facts and concepts that <u>may</u> be learned from specific kinds of films. It does not offer conclusive proof that learning <u>will</u> take place in a predictable manner when such films are used under the same conditions that prevailed during the experiments.

WISE STUDY

In a second Yale Photoplay Study, <u>H. A. Wise</u> (1939) studied the effectiveness of the Yale Chronicles of America Photoplays in teaching history, using eleventh-grade pupils for his experimental subjects.

Experimental Design

As in the Knowlton and Tilton study, the experimental groups received instruction from ten silent Photoplays used with the usual teaching materials and procedures. The control groups were taught with the usual teaching materials and procedures only. The study measured learning from one semester of teaching.

Findings

Wise's findings confirm those of Knowlton and Tilton in that the groups receiving regular instruction plus film instruction showed reliably greater gains in historical knowledge than groups receiving regular instruction only. Per cent superiority for the film groups over the mean gains of the non-film groups, are illustrated in Fig. 3-2. In measures of time relationships, Wise found some superiority in favor of the film groups (11.8 and 7.8 per cent) which was of rather low relia-

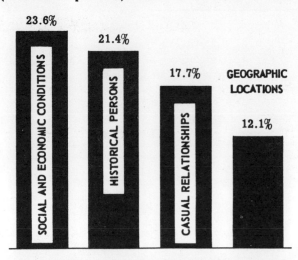

Fig. 3-2. Percent superiority in historical knowledge for groups receiving regular instruction plus film instruction. (Wise, 1939)

bility (CR = 2.00 and 2.28 PE's). This latter finding seems somewhat at variance with that of Knowlton and Tilton. However, the two studies agree that it was more difficult to teach time relationships by means of these films than it was to teach certain other knowledge outcomes.

Wise also found that on the Columbia Research Bureau's American History Test, administered at the beginning and end of the experiment, the film group was slightly (3.51 points in mean gain) and reliably (6.61 PE's) superior to the non-film group. The percentage of superiority of mean gain for the film group was 18.3. In the Knowlton and Tilton experiment, the Van Wagenen Information Scale C-2 was administered at the beginning and end of the experiment to samples of the film and non-film classes. A very slight superior gain (three per cent) was noted for the film groups on this test.

Evaluation

It may be significant that the standardized (Columbia) test used by Wise correlated above .60 with each of the unit tests developed by him to measure specific unit outcomes. Thus, it would be expected that superiority of the film group in tests on specific items taught would be reflected to some degree in the standardized test. It may be presumed that no such correlation was to be found between the topical tests used by Knowlton and Tilton and the Van Wagenen standardized test they also employed.

With regard to the learning of time relationships, the slightly reliable superiority of Wise's film group might be attributed to the fact that 11th-grade pupils were used in Wise's study whereas seventh-grade pupils were used in the Knowlton and Tilton study.

DAVIS STUDY

There is collateral evidence in many film research studies which indicates that the influence of films on factual knowledge is specific. For instance, H. C. Davis (1932), in her analysis of a sample of essay tests used in the Wood and Freeman (1929) study, found that the groups taught with films were superior in mentioning items shown in the film, while the control groups taught without films were superior in items not shown in the film.

WISE STUDY

H. E. Wise (1949), in reporting on part of the Nebraska study of the enrichment effects of motion pictures in rural schools, found that, on informational tests directly related to the content of the biological science films used in the study, film groups were reliably superior to non-film groups. But, on a standardized test administered before and after the semester's teaching, the slight superiority of the film groups did not meet criteria of statistical reliability.

SCOTT STUDY

Another, more extensive study from the Nebraska Program, by G. Scott (1949), adds much support to this concept of the specificity of factual learning from films.

Experimental Design

This study was concerned with the learning in three different science courses and four social studies courses, in each of which six to 14 films were used. Students from 25 to 35 high schools were the subjects for the experimental and control groups.

Findings

Scott found that the influence of the films tended to be specific to the areas covered by those films and was less evident in a standardized test of achievement in the year's work. The superiority of the film groups on the specific area tests was reliable and appreciable in all seven subjects. On the other hand, in only two of the six subjects where standardized tests were given was there a reliable difference in favor of the film groups.

PART II. INFLUENCE OF FILMS ON CONCEPTUAL LEARNING

It is frequently assumed that when films are used in instruction, the reaction of the audience is passive. Film instruction is likened to pouring water in an empty pitcher: the film learner, like the water pitcher, can give out only what has been poured in. In other words, motion pictures are generally assumed to be an undesirable instructional medium because they require no effort from the learner, and, by consequence or coincidence, they dull thinking.

RULON STUDY

To investigate the influence of films on "rote" and "eductive" learning, P. J. Rulon (1933), at Harvard University, studied the effect of adding eight sound films to usual methods of instruction.

Experimental Design

The study involved a six-week period of instruction given to a ninth-grade class in general science. Rote learning was measured on the tests by means of rote items, which required only recognition of the facts. Eductive learning was measured by eductive items which required the application of a concept or the inferring of one fact from others. He says, ". . . all knowledge may be classified as factual, and . . . differences among the thought processes involved are largely differences in the manner of acquiring or using the knowledge. If the fact is learned by rote and applied by rule, mainly memory is involved; if the fact is educed from other facts, or applied to the solution of a new problem, then 'thinking' has been called into play" (pp. 62-63).

24.1%

14.8%

ROTE ITEMS CR = 3.0 SE's

EDUCTIVE ITEMS CR = 5.9 SE's

Fig. 3-3. Percent superiority of text-plus-films groups over text-only groups in immediate learning. (Rulon, 1935)

The experiment was based on a six weeks' unit of instruction entitled The Earth and Its People. Eight topics were covered: The earth's rocky crust; the causes of land erosion; the function of water; plants and their functions; animals and their functions; plant growth; animal growth; stimulus and reaction in living organisms. A film was used with each of these topics. Six of the films were produced by the Harvard Film Foundation and two by Erpi, which has subsequently become Encyclopaedia Britannica Films, Inc. As can be seen from their subjects, three of the films dealt with physiography and five with biology.

In this experiment, the films were used in close integration with the textbook. With the exception of the two Erpi films, Growth of Plants and The Frog, both textbook and films were specially produced to conform to an outline of subject-matter content. The 127-page textbook with 100 illustrations was of typical general science text format and was more discursive and extensive in its coverage than the films. Care was taken to prevent having the films portray any topic not dealt with in the text. The construction of tests was based entirely on textbook content. Thus, the unusual and perhaps highly desirable situation was developed whereby films and text were both produced to meet the same subject-matter criteria and to supplement each other, although the textbook was produced so that it could be used independently of the films.

Findings

The tests were scored separately for rote and eductive items, and it was found that the pupils taught

by text plus films excelled the text-only pupils by a larger margin on the eductive items than on the rote items. Figure 3-3 shows a comparison of the superiority (in per cent) of the text-plus-films group in immediate learning tests for rote and eductive items. Figure 3-4 makes a similar comparison in the superiority of the text-plus-films group in retention of information three and one-half months after the instructional period.

In regard to the greater superiority of the text-plus-films pupils on eductive items than on rote items, Rulon reports that performance on eductive items "can be predicted more accurately from a knowledge of mental ability and previous achievement [in general science] than can performance in terms of Rote Items" (p. 105). It is a conceivable hypothesis that the film presentations in some way appealed to the science interest and reasoning of the students, thus increasing the text-plus-films group's performance more on the eductive items than on the rote items.

Differences between rote and eductive items were in the same direction as differences between verbal-test items and picture-test items, which Rulon reported as meaning that his "picture tests measure eduction to a greater extent than do the verbal tests" (p. 105).

41.0%

33.4%

ROTE ITEMS CR = 3.8 SE's

EDUCTIVE ITEMS CR = 6.2 SE's

Fig. 3-4. Percent superiority of text-plus-films groups over text-only groups in retention of information after 3½ months. (Rulon, 1935)

Evaluation

From Rulon's study we may tentatively conclude that, when certain films, constructed as were his, are used within an instructional context, and when the objectives of instruction are measured with both pictorial and verbal tests designed to sample reasoning and application as well as simple factual knowledge, there is no evidence that films as such interfere with thinking and the ability to apply to new situations the concepts presented in the films. Furthermore, we may tentatively conclude that when film and text teaching are mutually reinforcing, (not merely repetitious), their effectiveness, when compared with text teaching only, is even more pronounced in retention than in immediate learning.

VERNON STUDY

Additional evidence on the effectiveness of motion pictures by themselves in aiding conceptual learning (understanding of facts presented) comes from a study of motion pictures and filmstrips in World War II.

P. E. Vernon (1946), a British psychologist associated with the Senior Psychologist's Department of the British Admiralty during World War II, reports a study of the use of a sound film and a silent filmstrip in training British seamen to take soundings with a lead line and a Kelvin sounding machine. Despite certain inadequacies pointed out by Vernon, this study was productive of several useful insights into the role of films and filmstrips in informational and conceptual learning.

Vernon reports that "this experiment is now regarded by the Admiralty training authorities as 'classical,' and that neither the particular film and filmstrip employed, nor their method of application, should be regarded as typical of present-day naval instruction" (p. 150).

Experimental Design

In a sense, Vernon's study involved somewhat deviant experimental variables. The filmstrip contained 140 frames of photographs or captions taken, or adapted from, the film. Instructors of extreme ratings were used, the best and poorest. The experimental population was drawn from a general trainee population of "distressingly low standard of literacy," (p. 154) and half the population was "semi-literate." The experimental population consisted of 732 men taken from 22 classes.

On the basis of a test of knowledge of facts ("memory items") and of principles ("comprehension items") regarding the sounding process, comparisons were made between "normal instruction" without film or filmstrip and the following other variables:

1. Film alone shown twice (no other instruction)

2. Film twice, filmstrip once (no other instruction)

3. Taking notes on filmstrip

These comparisons were made in various classes of above and below average intelligence and with the best and poorest instructors. An analysis of covariance was used to establish the reliability of the differences obtained from various experimental variables.

Findings

The following variables were found to be reliably most effective in instruction (one per cent level of confidence): (1) the filmstrip, (2) the film, (3) good instructors, and (4) high intelligence.

Vernon pointed out, among other things, that the addition of the film to the usual instruction and also to the groups having usual instruction aided by the filmstrip, was beneficial to both groups. In the case of the latter group, the benefit was chiefly an increase in the comprehension scores. He suggests that apparently the memory for details tested by the memory questions was already fixed by the filmstrip; but that the film aided better understanding of the comprehension questions.

No striking differences were noted between the film and the filmstrip in effectiveness, but the film plus filmstrip with no other instruction compared with the film alone (no other instruction) produced 14.6 per cent improvement in memory for details and 53.7 per cent improvement in comprehension scores. These were the highest percentages reported; but Vernon is inclined to discount this surprising result since the film-plus-filmstrip group was only one class.

Evaluation

The comprehension measured by Vernon was apparently of a relatively low order by academic standards. The filmstrip added to the film alone aided comprehension more than memory for details, and the addition of either the film or the filmstrip to usual teaching increased comprehension scores more than the memory scores. However, the effect on comprehension tends to be maximized by the relatively brief test, on which a small difference in actual score produces a disproportionate difference in percentage of effectiveness.

The significance of this study is that either the film or the filmstrip increased the learning of detailed facts, but also, and probably to a greater degree, increased comprehension, or learning on the conceptual level. The combination of filmstrip plus film appeared to materially increase this conceptual learning.

GIBSON, ET AL., STUDY

A significant experiment conducted by Gibson and others has been reported from the Psychological Test Film Unit of the AAF Training Command (J. J. Gibson 1947).

Findings

In this study it was found that aviation cadets learned and remembered more about the system of position firing from a training film than they did from either classroom teaching or study of a manual. Both of these latter methods made use of good visual aids, slides with the lecture and illustrations in the manual, and were judged to be as effective as they could be made.

An analysis of the test items and the film showed that the items in which the film did its most superior teaching were "dynamic" items dealing with a sequence of events or with the variations of one thing with another. For example, the concept of a "rad" was more clearly comprehended by the film group since they had seen how it was used and had <u>vicariously</u> experienced the process of sighting a .<u>50</u> caliber machine gun.

PART III. LONG-TIME RETENTION OF KNOWLEDGE FROM FILMS

HOLADAY AND STODDARD STUDY

One aspect of the <u>P. W. Holaday</u> and <u>G. D. Stoddard</u> study (1933), (which is part of the Payne Fund study), is concerned with the amount of long-time retention of factual information from films. This study is particularly interesting since it reported long-time effects of films on factual knowledge different from those reported in previous studies of learning. While some deterioration of responses, both of a specific and of a general nature, was evident over a period of from one to seven months after the movie experience, there was evidence of an unusual persistence in the retention of response, and in some cases evidence of increments of response to the films some weeks and months after they were seen.

Experimental Design

As described on page 3-2, the experimental population was divided into four age groups: second- and third-grade children, fifth- and sixth-grade children, ninth- and tenth-grade children, and adults. To test the amount of long-time retention of scenes from motion pictures, one-third of each group was not tested until three months after the showing of each picture. Their scores were compared with the scores of equated groups at each age level, which were tested on the day after the picture was shown.

Findings

Holaday and Stoddard reported that the retention of specific scenes remained high over a long period of time. Their findings for the amount of retention by the delayed-test group, expressed as per cent of the average scores of the immediate-test groups, are illustrated in Fig. 3-5.

On some individual test items and occasionally on entire tests, an age group had a higher average retention on tests a month and a half or three months after the picture than it did the day after the picture. This situation occurred most frequently in the second and third grades, but it was common with all three of the older groups.

Evaluation

An evaluation of the Holaday and Stoddard conclusions about the effectiveness of films in inducing short-time factual "learning" is given on page 3-2. There it was pointed out that a statistical exaggeration in favor of the younger children may have been introduced into the results because of four elements in the structure of the experiment. These elements were: (1) the fact that the same test was used for all groups from the fourth grade through the "superior" adults may have produced a low ceiling of learning response for the adults; (2) on the basis of odd-even correlation, stepped up by the Spearman-Brown formula, the second-third grade group had the lowest reliability coefficients and the lowest median reliability coefficient of all groups; (3) the populations used for measurement frequently consisted of 30 or fewer individuals; (4) the film tests given to the second-third grade group were administered orally and were considerably

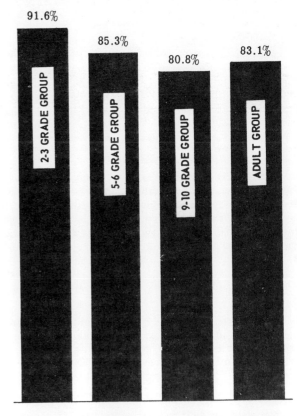

Fig. 3-5. Long-time retention of specific incidents from films, expressed as percent of scores on immediate tests. (Holaday & Stoddard, 1933)

"easier" than similar tests for the other groups. These findings on the comparative ability of the various age groups to retain information over longer periods of time may also be subject to a statistical exaggeration from these elements, and should be qualified in the light of the earlier evaluation of the Holaday and Stoddard results.

HOVLAND, LUMSDAINE, AND SHEFFIELD STUDY

In their studies of the effectiveness of the Why We Fight films, C. I. Hovland, A. A. Lumsdaine, and F. D. Sheffield (1949) present data on the amount of long-time retention of factual information from films.

As part of their study, Hovland, Lumsdaine and Sheffield made a comparison between the short-time and long-time effects of The Battle of Britain. Three film companies and three control companies (900 men) were given the questionnaire five days following the film showing. Two other film companies and two other control companies (500 men) were not given the questionnaire until nine weeks after seeing the film. This was the longest time period during which the investigators could retain the experimental population under war-time training conditions. It is to be noted that equivalent groups of men, not the same men, were used for the long-time testing, in order to avoid the practice effect on test results from a second administration of the test to the same population.

Findings

In this study of "long-time" retention of the factual learning from the film, it was found that the mean score advantage on the fact-quiz after nine weeks was slightly less than half as great as the short-time advantage (22.6 per cent vs. 11.1 per cent). Thus, the increment in factual knowledge attributable to film experience was reduced by 50 per cent in nine weeks. Six of the ten fact-quiz items showed decrements with the passage of time; the remaining four either showed no decrement, or an unreliable change. These four items were the ones which had shown the smaller short-time effects. In no case does an item fail to show some advantage for the film group, even at the nine-week interval (p. 185).*

KNOWLTON AND TILTON STUDY

The D. C. Knowlton and J. W. Tilton study (1929) also provides information about the amount of long-time retention of material learned from the Yale Photoplays.

Findings

The findings indicate that the contributions of films may be greater in immediate learning than in retention of material learned, but superior to non-film instruction in both. The major exception to this was the learning of historical relationships other than those of time. Here the difference between immediate scores and retention scores was reversed. The film groups were 43 per cent superior in retention of material learned and 35 per cent superior in immediate learning to the non-film groups. The critical ratio of the mean gain in this case was 3.5 PE's.

RULON STUDY

In his study of the comparative effectiveness of films in producing "rote" and "eductive" learning, P. J. Rulon (1933) furnishes data about the relative persistence of information gained from instruction by the combined use of text plus films and that gained from instruction by text only.

Findings

Rulon found that, although some forgetting took place, the superiority of the text-plus-films group over the text-only group was greater three and one-half months after the film than it was immediately afterward. Thus, contrary to results reported by Knowlton and Tilton, the persisting differential benefit of instructional films reported by Rulon becomes greater after a lapse of time, rather than smaller.

This advantage in favor of the text-plus-films pupils becomes more evident in Rulon's analysis of test results. Rulon contrasted the scores of the experimental groups on items covered only in the text with the scores obtained on items covered in both text and films. He found that on text-only items the initial superiority of text-taught pupils disappeared in three and one-half months, and the two groups had the same retention scores; on the test items included in both film

---

* The critical reader may wonder why factual learning was measured by a quiz of only ten items. It should be borne in mind that the measurement of factual learning was only one of the functions of the study, as indicated above; and that the effect of this type of documentary film (exhibited in the course of routine training, without preceding or follow-up discussion) upon interpretations, opinions, and "morale" was the major area of concern. For this purpose the investigators felt the men should not realize that an experiment was in progress or that the film was being tested.

The test of factual knowledge, interpretations, and opinions was given as a War Department survey to a platoon at a time, under a "leader" selected from the enlisted personnel, and stressed anonymity of answers. The fact-quiz items were placed at the end of the questionnaire, so as not to influence answers to opinion items coming earlier, and were distributed among an equal number of "camouflage" fact questions unrelated to the film. Even with these precautions, a certain amount of specificity was sacrificed to prevent suggesting the film. Yet, in spite of all these "obstacles" to measuring what the men "recalled" from the film, evidence of sizable factual learning was obtained.

and text, the text-plus-film pupils were 56.4 per cent superior to the text-only pupils on the delayed tests.

It appears reasonable to conclude that where there was overlapping of subject content between film and textbook, pupils taught by both instructional media were definitely superior in retained learning to those taught by text only. The critical ratio of this superiority is 8.6 SE's, indicating high reliability. The immediate learning superiority of the text-plus-films group on film-text items was 39 per cent (CR = 10.3 SE's).

SUMMARY

The main purpose of this chapter is to survey the extent and kinds of factual knowledge which are acquired from motion picture films. It is not the intent here to compare learning from films with learning from usual teaching methods or from other instructional media, except incidentally, in showing that there is a considerable amount of learning from films. In Chapter VI a detailed comparison will be made between learning from films and from other media and usual teaching methods. Lest the reader may assume that learning from films is always more effective than from other media, a number of studies with contrary findings are reported and analyzed in some detail in that chapter. However, from the studies cited in this chapter, there are many indications that factual learning can result from film instruction.

1. FACTUAL LEARNING FROM FILMS

Films Convey Factual Information

The research studies of the effects of motion pictures on knowledge of facts indicate that films can be good communicators of information that can be presented visually. When the instructional objective is to impart factual knowledge about people, places, conditions, and interrelationships, the motion picture can be a very effective medium. However, film presentation may at times result in the distortion of some facts, such as time relationships, during learning.

Incorrect Information is Often Accepted

The effectiveness of films in imparting factual information is further illustrated by a postulate suggested by the Holaday and Stoddard study, i.e., unless some other influencing factor is operative, information presented within a plausible context in a film tends to be accepted as fact, even though the information may be objectively incorrect.

Factual Learning Occurs Over Wide Range

The Holaday and Stoddard study suggests also that there is, for entertainment films, considerable overlapping in the amount of factual learning within a wide range of age and abilities. This finding seems to be borne out for the orientation type of film by the Hovland, Lumsdaine, and Sheffield study, although both studies (and others mentioned in Chapter VII) also contain data which show that the amount of factual learning from films is associated with the age, educational level, and intelligence of the audience.

Variation in Acquisition of Different Facts

The Hovland, Lumsdaine, and Sheffield study indicates that the immediate influence of films in communicating specific facts varies widely from one item of information to another within a given audience.

Contribution of Films is Specific

It appears that, insofar as the effectiveness of films may be attributed to their content alone, specific information contained in the film contributes almost entirely to the specific information of the individual, and little to his general information. Thus, the effectiveness of films depends on the specific relationship of their content to the instructional objective. No general factual knowledge may safely be anticipated. However, it is possible that films which will have general effects can be produced using radically new methods.

2. CONCEPTUAL LEARNING FROM FILMS

One of the arguments often levelled against instructional films is that learning from films is "passive." The implication of this argument is that learning from films somewhat resembles a state of hypnosis. The audience "drinks in," so to speak, but does not "give out." Hence, the "passivity" of this way of learning. Research does not bear out the notion that film learning is passive, at least not to the extent that instructional films impede the application of what is learned to somewhat different, and in a sense, new situations.

Films Aid Conceptual Learning

Rulon's, Vernon's and Gibson's studies indicate that the contribution of good instructional films to the comprehension or understanding of facts (conceptual learning) is greater than their contribution to the rote memory of details presented in the films. The contribution of films to understanding has been widely assumed without experimental validation, and it is encouraging to know that certain well-made films, contrary to some opinions, not only do not interfere with thought processes involved in the application of knowledge, but on the contrary appear to facilitate such thought processes.

3. RETENTION OF INFORMATION FROM FILMS

In the light of developments in experimental design and measurements, the Holaday and Stoddard study appears inadequate in some respects. Nevertheless, the study suggests some important conclusions about the long-time effectiveness of films. It indicates that the force of motion pictures in communication is of such nature that the influence of certain films on factual knowledge may persist over a long period of time. Confirmation is furnished by the findings of the Hovland, Lumsdaine, and Sheffield study, which suggest that, although there may be some forgetting of learned information from films, the learning may be evident two or three months later, even though the film did not present the facts as instructional material to be learned (e.g., entertainment, documentary, and orientation films).

Consideration of the Hovland, Lumsdaine, and Sheffield data leads to the additional conclusion that the stability or performance of the effect of the film-learning of specific facts varies widely from one item of information to another within a given audience, and is not necessarily dependent upon the size of the initial effect. Even though the initial influence of a film upon the learning of a specific fact may be rather widespread, this influence in some cases may lack stability, with a resulting greater decrement of film influence over a period of time than is found for other items. A somewhat similar phenomenon occurs at times in connection with a film's influence upon attitudes (see Chapter V).

4. SPECIFICITY OF FILM INSTRUCTION

Film Effects Are Specific

The photographic content of motion pictures is necessarily specific, and hence the perceptual experiences it stimulates are of a specific rather than a general nature. Broad, general effects do not result from a single motion picture as a medium of communication, and general effects on factual learning should not be anticipated from the use of a few instructional films alone. Thus the effectiveness of films depends on how well their content is related to a specific instructional objective. There is nothing in a motion picture presentation, per se, that guarantees better learning. Some films do not add to the effectiveness of usual methods of teaching, and some may even be worse than the usual methods. Merely to use any film or any filmstrip does not make a better teacher, or insure more learning by the pupils. The instructional value of a given film depends upon many factors, some of which we shall endeavor to analyze in the light of research in the chapters to follow.

Maximizing Film Effectiveness

If films merely repeat material that is usually presented by the instructor or the text, they may contribute little or nothing additional to the learning (see Chapter VI). On the other hand, the facts seem to show that when the film and text, or film and class teaching are mutually reinforcing and supplementary, and not merely repetitious, learning does take place. Moreover, when films are used to supplement usual teaching methods, their effectiveness is more pronounced as an aid to retention than to immediate learning.

Significance to Film Producers

The evidence that the influence of films on factual knowledge is specific and closely related to specific film content has important implications for the sponsor and producer of instructional films. The specific nature of the effect of a given film or given series of films implies that, in the planning and production of instructional films, the film content should be selected and treated in a way that directly relates to the desired effect. To do this the sponsor must first define the specific effects he intends to bring about. With the objectives defined in terms of the specific effects desired, the producer and sponsor can then turn to the production of the film with greater assurance of its instructional effectiveness.

CHAPTER IV

INSTRUCTIONAL OBJECTIVES:

TEACHING PERCEPTUAL-MOTOR SKILLS

INTRODUCTION

Importance of Perceptual-Motor Learning

Another major objective of instructional films is training individuals to develop perceptual-motor skills, that is, to coordinate body movements with sensory impressions. These skills are a basic part of many characteristically American sports and recreational activities. More important, the industrial supremacy of the American culture and the ability to maintain it depend to a large extent on the abundance and variety of motor skills. For these reasons perceptual-motor learning is an important phase in the education and training of most individuals.

Importance of Film Research to Such Learning

During World War II many films devoted to teaching perceptual-motor skills were produced by the armed forces and the U. S. Office of Education. Such films have particular application in times of national emergency, when mass training in perceptual-motor skills is necessary to meet expanded industrial and military requirements.

Despite the hundreds of wartime films produced, surprisingly little experimental research has been conducted on the effect of these films on perceptual-motor learning. In his description of the World War II film production program of the U. S. Office of Education, which was concerned with teaching industrial crafts and skills, F. E. Brooker (1946), reports that, on the basis of subjective evaluations, films were very helpful as a training medium. He considers it unfortunate that the wartime emergency prevented more objective evaluation and study of the effectiveness of such films. Fortunately, the films produced during the war provide a rich source of experimental material, and Brooker urges that this source be exploited through research to increase our understanding of the factors involved in teaching perceptual-motor skills by motion pictures. He states that the production program was a pioneering one in that it introduced untraditional variables in various films, thus furnishing available raw material, or at least suggestions, for further research and study. Examples of such variables are: "stream-of-consciousness" self-identification commentary in films on pattern making, the intimate commentary in films on

aircraft maintenance, the pattern of organization followed in the nursing films, the introduction used in the elementary wood-working series, etc.

An immediate problem for investigation is the extent to which motion pictures aid in teaching perceptual-motor skills. This problem is being broadened to include the degree to which the instructional process itself can be mechanized, that is, to what extent motion pictures alone can be used to guide perceptual-motor and other types of learning.

PLAN OF THE CHAPTER

This chapter is concerned with the effectiveness of motion pictures in promoting the learning of perceptual-motor skills. The problem is discussed in two parts. In Part I the evidence from a number of studies is surveyed to ascertain whether film presentation can be used to teach perceptual-motor skills. The skills under consideration lend themselves to three broad classifications: "academic" skills, or the skills usually taught as part of an academic curriculum; athletic skills; and industrial, or mechanical, skills. Whenever feasible, the techniques used in making the studies are described to aid in understanding and evaluating the experimental results.

The studies in Part I suggest that under certain circumstances, learning which improves motor skills does occur from films. This conclusion prompts the question, "What process is involved in the viewing of a film demonstration of a motor skill, which results in subsequent improvement in the skill itself?" Part II investigates some of the steps apparently involved in the process and attempts to relate them to the immediate problem of film effectiveness.

The chapter concludes with a summary of the conclusions and interpretations drawn from the various studies on film effectiveness and the learning process. As will become evident in the course of the chapter, many areas of the problem of perceptual-motor learning from films are yet to be fully explored. These limitations in our knowledge are pointed out to emphasize the need for continuing and, if possible, expanded research.

PART I.   PERCEPTUAL-MOTOR LEARNING FROM FILMS

SECTION 1. ACADEMIC TRAINING

McCLUSKY AND McCLUSKY STUDY

In an early study, F. D. and H. Y. McClusky (1924A) conducted two experiments with 350 pupils in the fourth, fifth, and sixth grades. Their objective was to measure the relative effectiveness of a film, teacher-demonstration, stereographs, and slides in training the pupils to make a reed mat in one experiment, and a pasteboard box in the other.

Findings

In both cases, the teacher-demonstration was superior to all other methods when effectiveness was measured by scoring the finished mats and pasteboard boxes on a quality scale. In the pasteboard box experiment, the order of effectiveness was (1) demonstration, (2) stereographs, (3) film, and (4) slides. In the mat experiment, the order of effectiveness was (1) demonstration, (2) film, (3) slides, and (4) stereographs. All methods were somewhat effective, but consistent differences were found among the several small groups used in the study. No measures of statistical reliability of differences were reported, so that the practical significance of the differences among methods cannot be estimated.

HOLLIS STUDY

In another early study, A. P. Hollis (1924A) investigated the relative effectiveness of films, teacher-demonstration, and oral instruction in teaching 28 eighth-grade pupils to cook an omelet. No conclusive evidence on the effectiveness of these two methods was obtained.

FREEMAN, SHAW, AND WALKER STUDY

F. N. Freeman, L. A. Shaw, and D. Walker (1924) in a third early study, investigated the effect of a film plus regular instruction in teaching handwriting position and performance to 1528 students in the fourth through eighth grades.

Findings

Films were found to be consistently superior in bringing about improvement in the handwriting position, but not in improving the quality of the handwriting. No reliability data were reported.

The authors stated that an opportunity for the individual to evaluate his results was the most influential factor in helping him to improve his performance, regardless of the medium of instruction used. This psychological factor is of prime importance in producing improved methods of instruction, and failure to employ it imposes limitations on any medium of instruction.

SENGBUSH STUDY

G. A. Sengbush (1933) made a study which, though not based on films, shows the possibilities of a good film in demonstrating various typewriting operations to beginning students. This is an important pioneer study, suggesting the possibilities of film or filmstrip demonstrations for teaching the parts of a machine and its operation where an actual demonstration to a large group is difficult.

Experimental Design

Sengbush compared (1) a method involving the use of pictorial and textual slides accompanied by the use of a pointer plus the answering of pupils' questions, but with no demonstrations, with (2) the traditional method of demonstrations and explanations used in teaching beginning typing both to first and second semester classes in junior high school. The groups were tested on both information and performance.

Findings

Slides Facilitated Factual Learning

In both first and second semester typing classes the slides facilitated factual learning about the operation and parts of the machine. In the first semester comparison (after eight weeks of instruction), however, the slide group and the traditional method group did not differ in rate of typing.

Slide Group Increased Typing Speed

In a typing comparison during the second semester, the slides were not only beneficial in factual learning, but also helped increase typing speed. At the end of the eighth week of this semester, there was a reliable and significant difference* in the rate of typing and this difference was in favor of the slide group despite an IQ superiority on the part of the traditional-method group.

---

* The author gave no means and SD's, but presented raw scores, so that the present reviewers were able to calculate means and SD's and critical ratio, the latter being 2.92. The difference was .74 of the SD of the distribution of the traditional method group.

SECTION 2. ATHLETIC TRAINING

RUFFA STUDY

E. J. Ruffa (1936) investigated the influence of specially produced regular-speed and slow-motion silent films supplemented by several films showing prominent track stars in action, in teaching athletic skills (football throw, 100-yard dash, high jump, broad jump, and shot-put) to tenth-grade boys.

Findings

He found some evidence (difference of .27 SD's of distribution and CR of 1.23) which suggests that when these films were shown without demonstration, required practice, or oral instruction, the results were equivalent and perhaps slightly superior to those from the combination of oral instruction, demonstration, and practice, the same amount of time being involved in both cases. It is reported that the film group did more voluntary practicing than the other group. It may be that part of the influence of the film was to motivate more of this type of practicing.

PRIEBE AND BURTON STUDY

R. E. Priebe and W. H. Burton (1939) studied the effects of films in teaching tenth-grade boys the high jump.

Experimental Design

The investigators used slow-motion and normal-speed films of three champion high jumpers, plus slow-motion films of the experimental subjects during their third week of practice, in teaching a new high jump technique, the "western roll." Thirteen pairs of boys were carefully matched in intelligence, leg spring, first scissors jump, age, height, and weight. The experiment extended over six weeks of the regular track season.

In the second week of the experiment both groups were introduced to the western roll technique in the usual way. In addition, the film group was shown the films of the champion jumpers, which were run, re-run, and discussed. Both slow and normal speeds were used. The film was stopped at crucial points for comments. During the third week, slow-motion films of the boys in the film group were made and shown to them with analysis of good and poor form. During the fifth and sixth weeks both sets of films were shown to the film group again. The control group was taught by demonstration, oral instruction, practice, and individual criticism, in the usual way.

Findings

The group taught with the additional aid of the "champion" and "diagnostic" films was superior to the control group after the six weeks of instruction. The mean gain of the best western roll jump over the first scissors jump was 4.58 inches higher for the film group.

(No reliabilities of differences are given by the investigators, but the present reviewers, taking account of the correlation between the matched pairs, have calculated the standard error of this difference, and find it to be 1.18. The t-value is 3.88, reliable at the one percent level. It is significant that all 13 of the film group jumped higher by western roll than they did in their original scissors jump, but five of the 13 in the nonfilm group did not even equal their original scissors jump when using western roll, even after six weeks of practice.

Film Group Had Less Trial-and-Error Behavior

The superiority of the film group showed up in the first test given at the end of the third week and was maintained throughout the remaining three tests, given at weekly intervals. The authors report the observation that the films seemed to eliminate to a large extent the initial trial-and-error behavior found in the western roll jumps of the control group. This observation is borne out by the statistical fact that eight of the 13 boys in the control group showed greater variability in the heights of their poorest and best western roll test jumps than did their pair-mates in the experimental group.

The general observation was also made that more boys could be handled per unit of time by use of the films, and that the film group showed more interest in learning the jumping.

It may be pointed out that "diagnostic films," i.e., films showing performance of the learners themselves, are widely used by collegiate football coaches in team training throughout the football season, and are coming into use by track coaches.

BROWN AND MESSERSMITH STUDY

A similar study, involving the teaching of tumbling to college freshmen, was reported by H. S. Brown and L. Messersmith (1948).

Experimental Design

Brown and Messersmith conducted their experiment during 15 instructional periods with two freshmen classes of 36 students each at Southern Methodist University. The groups were equated on the Metheney revision of the Johnson test of muscle educability.

Each class met three times a week, during the five weeks of the experiment. The instruction consisted of orientation in tumbling, demonstration and practice, and review (for the control group only). During the fifth class session, the experimental group was shown a film on expert tumbling, while the control group reviewed the stunts which had previously been taught. During the eighth class session, the experimental group was shown slow-motion, silent films of their stunt performance, while the control group practiced mat stunts. The slow motion film was shown twice, with further repetition of selected scenes. During the showing, the instructor commented on the performance shown in the film. Results were tested by use of a rating scale which was applied to the individual performance of ten stunts by students in both groups. (The correlation between the scores awarded by two judges was .85 ± .04 PE.)

Findings

The experimental group, taught with demonstration and diagnostic motion pictures, was superior to the control group taught without the films, but this difference was not highly reliable statistically. The mean score of the film group was 135.5 and that of the group taught without films was 125.9. The mean difference between film and non-film groups was 9.4, and the CR, 1.24. Incidentally, the non-film group was slightly, but not reliably, superior to the film group on the equating measure of muscle educability.

ADAMS STUDY

T. Adams (1939), in a study which the reviewers have not been able to obtain*, investigated the effectiveness of teaching the serve in tennis by methods similar to those used in the Priebe and Burton study, that is, with "champion" and "diagnostic" films. From the abstract it is not clear whether this was an experimental, or merely and experiential, study.

Findings

Adams reported that the slow-motion picture was of superior value in comparison with verbal instruction or demonstration. He estimated that good films can cut the learning time 50 per cent.

LOCKHART STUDY

J. B. Lockhart (1942), studied the effects of a specially prepared silent film on bowling used with the "regular method" or instruction in teaching college-freshman women to bowl.

Findings

She found that with the addition of the film the learning progressed more regularly in its early stages and reached a higher level sooner. But the study, in which the procedure and controls are poorly described, reports that, after six 30-minute practice periods spaced over two weeks, the mean scores on the ten first balls for the experimental and control groups were the same.

SECTION 3. INDUSTRIAL TRAINING

VANDERMEER STUDY

A. W. VanderMeer (1943, 1945) reported the only extensive study, other than those undertaken by the Instructional Film Research Program, of the influence of motion pictures on the learning of perceptual-motor skills of the type required in modern industry and in the armed services. Prior studies on athletic skills, and mat and pasteboard box making, though informative, do not apply to the skills required to manipulate modern machines.

Experimental Design

Eight U. S. Office of Education films were used by VanderMeer in his study on the training of lathe operators during six 40-hour weeks. Control groups were trained by demonstration, practice, and individual instruction. Film groups were trained with films, some demonstration (demonstration time was reduced to compensate for the demonstration effect of the films), and were given the same amount of practice and individual instruction as the control groups.

Performance was measured by (1) time required to complete twelve jobs within specified tolerance limits, (2) the frequency of "rejects," i.e., performance outside tolerance limits, and (3) factual information on machine operation. In judging the effectiveness of any particular medium or method, the complexity of the performance and the elimination of errors, as well as the quality of the resulting product, are factors which enter into the evaluation.

Findings

Film Group Cut Working Time

In over-all performance in terms of time, the mean sigma score of the non-film group was -.333, and of the film group, +.433, with a mean sigma score difference of .766. This difference was highly reliable (CR=6.55).

In seven out of the twelve comparisons, the working times of the film group, as measured by the standard deviation of the time scores, were more uniform than those of the non-film group. In these seven comparisons the CR was at least greater than two, and in five of the seven comparisons the CR was greater than three.

---

* Information regarding this study has been obtained through the courtesy of the National Education Association, whose abstracts of literature dealing with audio-visual aids were made available to the Instructional Film Research Program.

Film Group Had Fewer Rejects

After the first three of the twelve jobs, the average number of rejections was consistently smaller for the film group than for the non-film group. VanderMeer interprets this as indicating "that the use of films reduced the period of trial-and-error activity typical of motor learning. In other words, the greater number of individuals in the film group approached their maximum efficiency more closely during the instructional period." (1945, p. 83).

Film Group Gained More Factual Information

The film group gained twice as much information on machine operation, as measured by the Purdue Test for Machinists and Machine Operators. This gain was highly reliable (CR=6.61).

Evaluation

Films Appear Helpful in Teaching Complex Skills

Reliable evidence was thus found by VanderMeer that the use of a series of instructional films over a prolonged period of instruction and practice, results in substantial time saving, consistent reduction of unacceptable product, and increased information on job operations. As measured by both reduction in the amount of training time required and the greater efficiency in reaching a successful performance, films appear to be of value in teaching complex perceptual-motor skills. VanderMeer suggests that films are perhaps more valuable in teaching the more complex skills than the simple ones.

BECK AND LUMSDAINE STUDY

A less extensive study related to industrial training with films was conducted by L. F. Beck and A. A. Lumsdaine for the Army Pictorial Service, and has been reported briefly by Hoban (1946).

Experimental Design

The purpose was an exploratory comparison of two methods of teaching the assembly and disassembly of a portable radar station, (1) with a film, and (2) with a competent instructor using a scale model. Four inexperienced teams of nine men each were taught to assemble and to disassemble the equipment. In two of the four groups, the assembly procedure was taught by the film and the disassembly procedure by the instructor. In the other two groups the teaching process was reversed: the instructor taught the assembly, and the film instructed in the disassembly.

Findings

In terms of the time required to complete the assembly or disassembly, the parts of the procedure taught by the film were completed, on the average, in slightly less time than was required when the process was taught by the instructor demonstration; the difference, however was quite unreliable.

Film Preferred to Average Instructor

The men were interviewed as to their opinion of the relative effectiveness of the film and the instructor. Half thought that the film was better; a third thought the instructor demonstration was better; and the remainder were of the opinion that the methods were about the same. These exploratory results suggest that this particular training film was at least as effective as a comparable lecture-demonstration by an instructor, who was judged by the experimenters to be highly competent. As one of the men suggested, if the instructor had been average or poor, as is likely in a normally distributed population of instructors, the film method would probably have been the much more effective.

Film Increased Teamwork and Efficiency

Two further observations or impressions of a non-quantitative nature were reported, which may be significant beyond the narrow limits of perceptual-motor learning: the men who received film instruction (1) appeared to the experimenters to perform more as a team than did those to whom the films were not shown, and (2) appeared to require less additional on-the-job instruction.

Evaluation

Films May Help Solve Many Community Problems

The observations that the films fostered teamwork and reduced the amount of instruction time necessary, if substantiated, may be of great importance. Films showing student or community groups working together to solve common problems of health, inter-racial cooperation, education, recreation, or management and labor relations, might prove to be an important medium for teaching some of the fundamentals of community living. At least several avenues of research must be explored. To what extent can motion pictures teach the important attitudes and habits of teamwork, or cooperation in school, in industry, and elsewhere? Again, the problem of the direction and reinforcement effect of the environment arises.

If the groups taught by the films need less on-the-job instruction, then there is more independent learning by the film groups and less dependence on the instructor for help and suggestions. If these tendencies could be clearly demonstrated, and shown to be applicable to the various elements of social behavior, it would be extremely significant. The person who is doing more independent learning is likely to develop more self-confidence and self-reliance, and a greater willingness to explore new and broader areas of activity.

FILM RESEARCH PROGRAM STUDIES

Problems of perceptual-motor learning from motion pictures have been investigated in studies of the Instructional Film Research Program (Jaspen 1948, 1950; Roshal 1949; Zuckerman 1949). These studies are concerned with determining the best combination of film variables for producing learning of perceptual-motor tasks, as well as with measuring the effectiveness of individual variables. Because they relate largely to variations in production technique, the studies are discussed in detail in Chapter VIII.

One outstanding finding which relates directly to the present discussion was obtained in one of N. Jaspen's studies (1948). He found that 98 per cent of a large group of Navy trainees were able to assemble the breechblock of a 40mm antiaircraft gun after a single showing of an experimentally produced film.

In the Roshal study experimental versions of a film were designed and produced to teach Navy trainees to tie three knots of graduated difficulty. Among the trainees who did not see some one of the film versions, only seven per cent could tie the bowline; three per cent the sheetbend, and none the Spanish bowline. The best experimental versions taught 59 per cent of the trainees to tie the bowline, 35 per cent the sheetbend, and 26 per cent the Spanish bowline, after one showing of the film. The best versions were shot from the "subjective," or performer's-eye-view, camera angle and involved motion of the hands rather than static sequences in tying the knot.

Zuckerman, using the films produced for Roshal's study but with modified commentary, studied, among other things, the effect of level of verbalization (number of words per minute of film) in learning to tie the three knots. The definition of the levels of verbalization varied somewhat with the difficulty of the knots. The low level of verbalization ranged from 62 to 80 words per minute, the medium level, 89 to 125 words per minute, and the high level, 120 to 176 words per minute. He found the medium level of verbalization superior to either the low or high levels. This finding is also in accord with Jaspen's second study of learning breechblock assembly, in which a medium level of verbalization (97 words per minute) was superior to both a low (74 words) and a high (142 words) level of verbalization in film versions which also included a slow rate of development and the showing of errors to be avoided. As was mentioned, more details of these studied are presented in Chapter VIII in the discussion of production techniques.

PART II. IMPLICIT PRACTICE AND VERBALIZATION IN LEARNING A MOTOR SKILL

The foregoing studies showing the value of demonstration films and slides in teaching motor skills raise the question: What is the process whereby a learner views the film material, listens to the instructional commentary, and, having had little or no chance to practice the skill overtly, (or physically), shows an improvement in this motor skill when tested?

This question involves the problem of "participation" or "practice" in film learning, and of the possible equivalence to, or superiority of, this type of "participation" or "practice" over more overt practice in other instructional situations. We need to know more about implicit and/or symbolic practice* of a motor skill during film instruction, the kinds of activities most suitable for this type of practice, the conditions under which it is efficient, and the limits of its efficiency.

SECTION 1. IMPLICIT PRACTICE

1. WHAT DOES THE LEARNER DO?

M. A. May (1946), in an article on The Psychology of Learning from Demonstration Films, has speculated on how film learning occurs. He points out that the learner must grasp the meaning of the performance, try to fix mental pictures of how the machine or performer looks in each step of the process, and perhaps most important, formulate silent verbal directions for the steps or sequences in the process. The learner may also make slight imitative movements of arms, hands, or legs which constitute an abbreviated immediate imitation or practice of the task or skill.

Responses to Demonstrations Vary Widely

Great individual differences in the use of these different types of response to demonstrations or to demonstration films undoubtedly exits, as May suggests. Some persons can mentally "photograph" and retain a "motion picture" of the performance which they later run off mentally as a guide to the correct

---

* For this symbolic and possibly implicit practice, the term, "mental practice," has come into the literature, as the two studies, soon to be mentioned, indicate. Though not the most widely accepted term, it is probably the one most suitable to describe this phenomenon.

process. May thinks such ability is rare. Most people's visual imagery of this type is probably rather vague and unreliable because other images are formed between the time of viewing the film and the actual practice of the skill. Some learners have excellent capacities for verbalizing (putting into words) the sequence of operations or movements observed in the demonstration or in the film. These verbal statements then serve as cues to guide them in the performance of the skill. Such verbal formulations seem to greatly facilitate learning from demonstrations, at least for some individuals.

2. SOME EVIDENCE ON "MENTAL PRACTICE"

Two rather surprising studies on "mental practice" in perceptual-motor learning have recently been reported. Though not concerned with learning from films, they have a direct bearing upon the problem of learning from demonstration films. These studies were carried out with rather small groups and the findings should be considered as tentative until supported by findings on a large number of subjects and other motor skills.

VANDELL, DAVIS, AND CLUGSTON STUDY

Experimental Design

R. A. Vandell, R. A. Davis, and H. A. Clugston (1943) studied the relationship between mental practice and learning athletic skills. Two groups, junior high school boys and freshman college men worked at dart throwing; another group, senior high school boys, worked at basketball foul shooting. At each grade level the subjects were divided into three experimental groups of four boys each. All subjects were tested on the first and 20th days of the experiment. One experimental group had no directed practice of any kind. Another experimental group had daily directed practice on the 18 intervening days. In the case of the dart throwing, directed practice consisted of throwing 25 darts per day; in the foul shooting, it was 35 free throws per day. The third experimental group was simply instructed to sit (or presumably stand, in the case of free throws) at the throwing line and to imagine throwing. For the junior high school group this mental practice lasted 30 minutes per day, but for the other two groups it was 15 minutes.

Findings

In terms of group scores, the mental practice appears to be as effective as actual physical practice under the conditions of this experiment. No measures of variability or individual scores are reported, so that the reliability of the results cannot be calculated. The description of the instructions given for mental practice are very meager. Thus, the need for further investigation is obviously indicated.

* Computed from the raw data by the reviewers.

TWINING STUDY

Realizing the need for a more complete study, W. E. Twining (1949) made a study of mental practice involved in the motor skill of ring toss. (This activity consists of throwing six-inch Manila hemp rings at a stake, one-foot high and an inch in diameter, placed ten feet from the subject.)

Experimental Design

The subjects were 36 college men, assigned at random to one of three groups. Every person in each group threw 210 rings on the first and twenty-second days. Group I "practiced no more for twenty-one days" (p. 435). In Group II, each subject threw 70 rings per day for twenty days. In Group III, the subjects "were instructed to mentally rehearse their initial test, trying to visualize all of the sensations that they went through. They were cautioned to perform no overt movements but to actually 'mentally throw' rope rings at imaginary targets" (p. 434).

The investigator reports that "The mental practice period was usually spent in actively 'mentally picturing' the entire ring-tossing procedure" (p. 435).

Findings

Prolonged Mental Practice Was Difficult

"Occasionally subjects reported attempts at working out new 'theories' of tossing in hopes of improving performance. Several such 'theories' were unsuccessful during the final test, forcing the subject to revert to his original style" (p. 435). Introspective comments of the subjects indicated that the mental practice was effective for only about five minutes of the fifteen-minute practice period; after the first five minutes, concentration became difficult. The physical-practice group threw the 70 rings at each practice, taking an average of 7.5 minutes.

Mental and Physical Practice Were Both Effective

The mental-practice group, which was considerably better than the physical-practice group at the beginning, gained 33 per cent.* The physical-practice group, which showed the poorest performance to begin with, made a gain of 137 per cent of their initial score. In both these groups the improvement is statistically reliable, using small-sample statistics. Twining concluded that both physical and mental practice under the conditions of his experiment are effective in facilitating the learning of a simple motor skill.

Implicit Muscular Activity or Action Currents Possible

The reasons for the benefit from mental practice, he points out, are obscure. Implicit muscular activity during mental activity has been demonstrated by

G. L. Freeman (1931) and others. Twining suggests that possibly coordination was improved by such implicit muscular activity during "mental practice." Other investigators have shown that frequently, and possibly always, when an individual thinks about specific movements, action currents, if not implicit muscular tensions, are created in the muscle groups which would perform these movements. Possibly this neural innervation is in some way beneficial in establishing a pattern of neural activity which later shows up in overt improvement.

3. POSSIBILITY OF KINESTHETIC IMAGERY

Neither of the two preceding investigations definitely mentions the possibility of kinesthetic imagery (the way the muscles feel when they make the movements) as a factor in mental practice. Twining told the subjects to "visualize all of the sensations that they went through (p. 434) in the first physical practice period, but instead of "visualize," he probably meant, "get the feel of it, imagine how it felt." The possibility of kinesthetic imagery raises a number of questions for further research, both with and without demonstration films. For example, would the effectiveness of mental practice vary if the instructions were to "picture your movements," or "try to imagine how your muscles would feel if you were going through the motions?"

PHILLIPS STUDY

B. E. Phillips (1941) reported findings that seem to bear out the involvement of kinesthetic imagery in perceptual-motor learning. He found that, of his various kinesthetic perception tests, certain tests were most useful for predicting, in the early stages, the rate of learning of two perceptual-motor skills, (putting and driving golf balls). In these "best" tests the subject was required to reproduce, blindfolded, the movement which he had just gone through. The movements made during the "best" tests were much like the movement actually made in learning the two skills. This repetition of movement would seem to require the temporary retention of kinesthetic images to serve as a basis of comparison with the new kinesthetic sensations.

SECTION 2. VERBALIZATION IN MENTAL PRACTICE

RUGER STUDY

The process of verbalization is another aspect of mental practice. Forty years ago, in his study of adults solving mechanical puzzles, H. A. Ruger (1910) discovered the importance of verbalization in the solving of certain perceptual-motor problems.

Experimental Design

There was no demonstration in the Ruger experiment. When a subject took a puzzle apart, the experimenter put it together again behind a screen and returned it to the subject for another trial. Scores were computed for time required to take the puzzle apart on numerous successive trials.

Findings

Verbalization Aided in Decreasing Solution Time

In introspective reports from his subjects after each trial, Ruger found that the decrease in time was definitely connected with a verbalization of the process, that is, with the subject's ability to put into words, partially at least, his insight into "how" the puzzle came apart. His most skillful learners, instead of spending all of their time in manipulating the puzzle, did a large part of this "manipulating" verbally in an effort to set up certain assumed relationships that would aid them in actually solving the puzzle.

THOMPSON STUDY

May, (1946), in his article referred to on page 4-6 cites an unpublished experimental study by L. Thompson (1944) on the role of verbalization among fifth-grade pupils learning to assemble two mechanical puzzles.

Experimental Design

Six different groups of 25 subjects, matched in intelligence and spatial arrangements tests, were given demonstrations in assembling the puzzles under varying conditions:

1. The pupils were required to count out loud by two's while watching the puzzle being assembled.

2. The pupils were asked to give a description of what the demonstrator was doing.

3. The pupils were silent and the demonstrator gave an incomplete verbal description of the process.

4. The pupils were silent and the demonstrator gave a complete verbal description of the process.

5. The pupils were asked to describe the demonstrator's acts. The demonstrator did no talking except to correct the pupils' verbal errors.

6. The sixth method was the same as the fifth, except that the pieces had numbers pasted on them to indicate the order of assembly.

Findings

Ability to Verbalize Increased Learning Speed

The best methods were the fifth and sixth, with a slight tendency for the sixth to be better than the fifth in the case of the harder puzzle. The poorest method was the first one. Since it involved counting aloud, this method was expected to interfere as much as possible with inner verbalization.

Thus, May points out in his article, the pupils learned most rapidly when they were "encouraged and aided in making verbal discriminations between the parts of a model to be assembled and in formulating adequate and accurate verbal descriptions of the operations to be performed" (p. 6). Individual differences in speed of learning among pupils taught by the same method correlated with their verbal abilities. The verbal deficiencies of slow learners were very evident in the sound recordings made of their efforts to formulate adequate descriptions of the assembly process in the fifth and sixth methods.

May gives ten suggestions for planning and producing a demonstration film. His suggestions are based on logical application of learning theory, and, as he points out, not on any experimental evidence that a film can effectively produce this type of learning. A number of these and other principles relevant to demonstration films are now being tested by the Instructional Film Research Program at the Pennsylvania State College.

SUMMARY

1. PERCEPTUAL-MOTOR LEARNING FROM FILMS

From the relatively small amount of experimental evidence available, the following conclusions about the influence of films on perceptual-motor learning are indicated. These conclusions are not supported by the studies on films produced in the early 1920's, but rather, are based on the films produced since 1930, when improved techniques of presenting instructional material came into use:

1. Learners benefit from observing certain motion pictures that illustrate the performance of certain motor skills. As reported by VanderMeer (1943, 1945), the learners who watched films were able to develop their skill more rapidly during the practice periods that follow than others who watched the traditional types of demonstrations.

2. With the more complex skills, such as certain athletic activities and lathe operation, which require prolonged instruction and practice, suitably produced films add significantly to learning when compared with the usual methods of instruction.

3. The training time required to master the more complex perceptual-motor skills may be considerably reduced by the use of films.

4. Film instruction seemed to induce increased teamwork in the attainment of a common objective. This finding in the Beck and Lumsdaine study, if verified by further research, may be of great importance because it suggests a means of developing a cooperative spirit, not only in training, but also in the more fundamental area of human relations.

2. ROLE OF MENTAL PRACTICE IN LEARNING

There is some evidence to indicate that while watching the demonstration the learner engages in mental practice, involving, perhaps, visual imagery, silent verbalization, implicit muscular activity, and neural stimulation. Moreover, the rate of learning appears to be connected with the occurence of mental practice.

Mental Practice May Replace Some Actual Practice

The studies on mental practice suggest that, in the early stages of training, further viewing of the film after a period of actual practice may be almost as effective in aiding learning as additional actual practice, an important practical consideration when facilities are inadequate to permit overt practice by large groups. Moreover, as suggested by the Priebe and Burton study, film viewing combined with actual practice may even be superior to the traditional demonstration and practice procedures.

Mental Practice Poses Additional Research Problems

Before the potentialities of films in reducing training time and increasing the rate of learning can be fully realized, a number of problems, such as the process by which mental practice occurs and the extent to which mental practice can supplant actual practice, must be investigated. Most important for its immediate significance, is the problem of the type of instructions to be given so that the learner can secure the most effective mental practice while he views the film. For example, should he be told: (1) to get a mental picture of the motions or operation; (2) to imagine himself doing the task and how his muscles feel as he does it; (3) to make up some words and phrases which will guide his performance later?

Perhaps a combination of these three types of observer activity might be more effective than any one of them alone. It is entirely possible that the most productive type of mental activity for observing the demonstration film will vary for different types of individuals. If different types of observation can be demonstrated as more effective for different types of observers, perhaps the commentary should suggest this variation and tell each one to do what aids him most, or pretests should be used to group the learners into special classes, each with its own specialized film commentary. This whole problem of the nature of the commentary demands further research and enlarges the concept of audience participation, which is discussed in a later chapter.

The reader is reminded again that further studies of perceptual-motor learning from films are reported in Chapter VIII, where comparisons are made of the influence of different combinations of film variables in demonstrating certain motor tasks.

CHAPTER V

INSTRUCTIONAL OBJECTIVES:
INFLUENCING MOTIVATION, ATTITUDES, AND OPINIONS

INTRODUCTION

Before reviewing the research studies on the effectiveness of motion pictures in achieving the above instructional objectives, it is desirable to sketch in brief form some of the concepts regarding the nature of motivation, attitudes and opinions.

MOTIVATION

Definition

The concept of motivation involves a pattern of personal activity which may be described by:

1. The desire, urge, or less conscious need of the individual for a condition or state, physical or psychological, which will result in at least temporary satisfaction, adjustment, or relief of the need (or needs) aroused.

2. The identification of a course of action, precise or vague, as a possible means of achieving or of eliminating a threat to the achievement of satisfaction of the aroused need.

3. The release of energy into channels of behavior patterned in accordance with the course of action chosen as the means of satisfying the need.

Motives

Motives, so called, are the starting point of the need-means-goal chain of activity. Motives include any state or event in the individual which initiates and regulates his activity in relation to a goal. Such terms as psychological drive, urge, need, impulse, desire, wish, interest, attitude, purpose and ideal are frequently used to describe types of motives.

Motivations of Human Conduct

At the core of all motivation is the self, or person, and the need of the individual to satisfy his urges.

There are four basic motivations of human conduct:

1. <u>self-preservation:</u> biological or physical needs

2. <u>self-realization:</u> satisfaction of the ego by means of achievement, group recognition, and affection

3. <u>self-identification:</u> achieved through sympathy ("feeling with," or sharing the reactions and responses of a group or another person), or through empathy ("feeling into," or having insight into a situation, another person, or group)

4. <u>self-regard:</u> the maintenance of self-respect

One or more of these needs may lead to co-operative and helpful behavior of an altruistic nature.

Each individual lives to a great extent in his private world of perceptual experiences, concepts, feelings, urges, attitudes, and values. His life consists of the development of his private world and his expansion of the <u>meaning</u> of, and <u>means</u> for, satisfying the above needs. When these needs are satisfied in harmony, the individual is well integrated and psychologically healthy. If these needs are not satisfied in harmony with each other, the individual experiences conflict and varying degrees of maladjustment.

Reorganization of Motivation

Reorganization of motivation involves a reorganization of the personality structure. As a result, new situations and courses of action are perceived as the means of bringing about the condition or conditions which the individual identifies with the satisfaction of his dominant needs, or as the means of eliminating obstacles or threats to such satisfactions. The conditions which the individual associates with the satisfaction of his needs, that is, the conditions for "happiness," appear to be defined to a large extent by the cultural environment of the individual.

Motivation in the American Culture

In the American, and generally in the western European, culture, which have been influenced by the Hellenic-Judeo-Christian ethos (or system of morals and ideals), the prime conditions for the attainment of "happiness," or psychologically harmonious self, are (1) the preservation of the integrity of the individual, and (2) the development of individual potentialities to the fullest extent. This ethos, which values the preservation of the integrity and full development of the individual, is in contrast to that of the super-state, super-race, or super-economic unit.

Most Americans believe that they are endowed with inalienable rights to life, liberty, and the pursuit of happiness. It is therefore difficult to convince Americans that personal martyrdom and loss of personal dignity and freedom are the means to the attainment of happiness. Within the ethos of American culture, and within the concept of motivation sketched above, the reorganizing of an individual's motivation so that he will accept contrary values, is a difficult undertaking. Even in time of war, inducing American young men to increase the value they place upon loss of personal liberty, dignity, possible loss of life or physical wellbeing, and inducing them to choose these conditions freely, are extraordinarily difficult tasks.

Films as a Motivational Influence

Films have been produced with the intention of influencing religious, economic, industrial, political, and other social attitudes, as well as motivations of conduct. Even so, except for studies on the modification of verbal attitudes and other verbally-expressed motivations, the majority of studies on the effectiveness of films in motivating actual conduct have been made in the areas of academic motivation and social conduct. Without an adequate comprehension of what is involved in motivation, and of the cultural values assigned to the worth of the individual, it is easy to overestimate the possible effectiveness of films in military motivation, and to underestimate their effectiveness in motivating academic activity and social conduct.

Some of the motion pictures produced and used by the American armed forces in World War II were designed, to some extent, to modify the motivation of military personnel so that the hazards of battle would be accepted more willingly and freely. There is little agreement among social scientists and psychologists that films could have modified the motivational structure of American troops in this way, and some of the research evidence suggests that the Why We Fight films, produced for this purpose, were not successful in doing so.

On the other hand, instructional motion pictures, produced apparently without deliberate motivational intent, have been found to increase academic motivation. Possibly the reason is that behavior such as increased classroom participation, increased voluntary reading, and similar academic activities results in improved status of the individual in school and in the family group. In accordance with our cultural ethos and concept of motivation, the reward of improved status makes it considerably easier to influence academic motivation than some other types, notably military motivation, and there is increasing likelihood that films can be effective in influencing motivation for school learning.

SOCIAL ATTITUDES

Definition

The term, "attitude," is usually reserved for tendencies which are aroused by social situations, and accordingly are referred to as "social attitudes." "Attitude" has been defined in various ways, but common to most definitions, as Quinn McNemar (1946) has pointed out, is the concept of "readiness or tendency to act or react in a certain manner" (p. 287). Writers have tended to follow the thinking of G. W. Allport in developing their concepts of an attitude. The following description of "attitude" would probably be acceptable to many students of this topic.

An attitude is a tendency to feel (and often act) consistently in a certain positive or negative way toward a certain class of events, objects, or persons. This tendency develops largely as a result of experience. The arousing of the tendency is usually accompanied by an emotional response of varying degree. Sometimes the attitude involves a considerable amount of understanding and appreciation, but this is not essential and frequently is not true. Attitudes are more passive, and frequently more generalized, than interests, desires and other motivations. When an attitude is aroused, it functions as a "set," or determining tendency, so that associated activities are facilitated and unrelated activities are inhibited. In effect, an attitude is one of the structures through which the process of motivation operates.

Postulates About Social Attitudes

With or without this structural concept of an attitude, there is likely to be general agreement on several of the following postulates concerning social attitudes:

1. Social attitudes to a large extent are learned; they are not developed, as in hunger behavior, out of very specific and native tendencies.

2. Social attitudes frequently are organized in terms of classes of people, ideas, objects, or situations.

3. Social attitudes involve <u>affective</u> responses (feelings and emotions), <u>conative</u> tendencies (striving toward or away from goals), and <u>cognitive</u> processes (perceptions, beliefs and concepts).

4. Social attitudes vary in strength and modifiability, probably in accordance with how closely they relate to one or more of the four basic motivations previously postulated, i. e., self-preservation, self-realization, self-identification, and self-regard.

5. Social attitudes are usually learned gradually rather than suddenly. The developmental experiences are generally serial rather than single, and "trivial" rather than traumatic. However, an attitude may occasionally develop as the result of a single, intensely traumatic or emotional experience, such as cruelty, either experienced or observed.

6. The motivation, enforcement, and reinforcement of social attitudes are strongly influenced by the necessity for the individual to conform to the social norms, or ethos, of the primary group with which he identifies himself. Non-conformity is penalized, whereas conformity results in acceptance, status, and attendant buoyance of the individual.

7. Strong attitudes frequently operate without the guidance or control of critical analysis and reflective judgment.

OPINIONS

No Rigorous Definition

As McNemar (1946) has pointed out in his extensive discussion of opinion-attitude methodology, some writers use the terms "attitude" and "opinion" synonymously or very nearly so, and with the connotation of a tendency to action. He says, "Since the terms are so frequently used synonymously, and since what one investigator calls an opinion study might be called an attitude study by another, and vice versa, we shall not attempt herein to adhere to any rules about the non-interchangeability of these words. A useful, albeit somewhat artificial, distinction can be made on the basis of techniques: <u>The typical attitude study involves a scale or battery of questions for ascertaining attitudes whereas the typical opinion, particularly public opinion, study leans heavily on a single question for a given issue</u>" (p. 290).

Differentiation Is Desirable

The interchange of the terms, "attitude," "opinion," and even "belief," is somewhat unfortunate. The concept of attitude has been defined to include the tendency to feel, or act, in a certain positive or negative, favorable or unfavorable, way. On the other hand there are opinions and beliefs which do not necessarily imply any favorable or unfavorable tendency. For example: Do you believe that women are more emotional than men? Whatever your opinion, you have little tendency to feel strongly or to act upon it. Or, who will win the Harvard-Yale game? As a non-alumnus you may care little about the outcome. (If placing a wager, however, your opinion will influence your action.) On the other hand some opinions may conceivably lead to real motivational attitudes. The Quakers' belief in non-resistance and international goodwill seems to be a strong motivating factor in their refusal to bear arms. Instead, they extend their energies in relief and rehabilitation work.

A distinction between specific opinions and motivational attitudes, or "general orientation toward an issue," is found in the U. S. Army studies of orientation films in World War II, discussed in this chapter. To the present reviewers, it seems that opinions, used in the sense of <u>specific beliefs and notions about which one is none too confident</u>, do differ from attitudes as defined above. Such opinions are likely to be somewhat more transient, more easily modified, and less intimately related to the basic motivations: self-preservation, self-realization, self-identification, and self-regard. Some critical analysis and reflective judgment probably come into play more frequently when the individual expresses his opinion than when he expresses an attitude, although opinions are by no means necessarily logical or rational.

PLAN OF THE CHAPTER

The influence of films on motivations, attitudes, and opinions are the subjects of inquiry of the three major parts of the chapter.

In Part I three areas of motivation are considered: social conduct, academic motivation, and military motivation. The possibilites of modifying these motivations by the use of films--notably entertainment films, classroom films, army orientation films, and documentary films--are surveyed, using the available experimental evidence. In the final section the possibility of modifying military motivation is further investigated through the medium of several elaborate studies on the effectiveness of the Army orientation program, of which the orientational films were a single, though important, phase.

Part II presents a number of detailed studies on the effects of both entertainment and documentary films on specific attitudes (closely related to the film content) and on general attitudes (only indirectly related to film content). As in Part I, the studies are considered in terms of not only the information they contain, but also the larger problem of modifying attitudes through the use of films.

Part III contains the research findings (principally those of the U. S. Army Studies) on the likelihood of modifying specific and "general" opinions by means of films. Differences in specific and general effects, as well as in long-time and short-time effects, are stressed to emphasize their experimental and practical importance.

A summary section at the end of each major chapter division presents the conclusions and problems suggested by the data in that section.

PART I.   INFLUENCE OF FILMS ON MOTIVATION OF CONDUCT

SECTION 1. EFFECTS OF FILMS ON SOCIAL CONDUCT

SHUTTLEWORTH AND MAY STUDY

In the Payne Fund studies, F. K. Shuttleworth and M. A. May (1933) investigated the reputation, conduct, and attitudes of "movie-going" children in grades five through eight as contrasted with those of "non-movie-going" children.

Experimental Design

The study surveyed differences in these characteristics between a group made up of children that attended movies most frequently, and another group of children that attended least frequently. Specifically, it compared the behavior of the ten to 15 per cent of the individuals at the upper and lower ends of a movie-attendance-frequency scale. The extreme deviation between these two groups is emphasized by the fact that 98 per cent of the age group and community group in the study attended movies at least once a week. These group differences are an important basis for interpreting the two general results reported by Shuttleworth and May.

Findings

Shuttleworth and May presented data which indicate that children who are somewhat habitual abstainers from entertainment movies tend to be "good" boys and girls in school, judged by the school's standards of behavior and reputation. Further, habitual movie-goers, although better known and more frequently chosen by their classmates as friends in "Guess Who" tests, were found to be considerably inferior in reputation, achievement, and behavior in school. These two extreme groups did not differ, however, in tests of honest behavior outside of school, nor in tests of persistence, suggestibility, and moral knowledge.

However, persistent abstainers from movie attendance among fifth to eighth-grade children were superior to persistent movie-goers on several reputational and behavioral characteristics. The abstainers had higher deportment records, better scholarship records, and better reputations among their teachers and classmates. In addition, they were more co-operative and self-controlled, slightly less deceptive in school situations, slightly more skillful in judging the most useful, helpful, and sensible thing to do, and slightly more stable emotionally.

Evaluation

One is struck by the notion that this list of superior behavioral characteristics of the persistent movie-abstainers includes many items involved in social status. In A. B. Hollingshead's study of Elmtown's Youth (1949), a coefficient of contingency of .54 for boys and .48 for girls of high school age was reported between frequency of movie attendance and social class status.

Movie Attendance Habit May Be Learned

The greatest difference between persistent movie-goers and persistent abstainers among children was found to be in the movie-attendance habits of their parents. The fathers of movie-going children attended the movies four times more often than the fathers of non-movie-going children, (3.4 times a month as compared with 0.9 times a month, a difference which is 17 times as large as its probable error). A similar, though smaller difference was found to exist between the mothers. This fact suggests the possibility that the movie-attendance behavior of the children was learned, at least in some degree, from their parents. It is possible that the parents of the two groups may also have differed in other characteristics, and it is also possible, in this event, that some learning of these other characteristics may have taken place among the children.

If these suppositions are correct, a substantial case could be made for the fact that characteristic differences in school-rewarded behavior between movie- and non-movie-going children arise from a factor or factors other than the children's movie-attendance. Further, a case could be made for the belief that, movie-attendance itself may be a behavioral outgrowth of other factors.

Behavior Not Attributable to Movie Alone

There is no evidence in Shuttleworth and May's study to justify the conclusion that movie-attendance habits result in either socially superior or inferior behavior. In other words, there are no grounds for attributing the characteristics of non-movie-goers to the fact that they do not attend movies, or the characteristics of movie-goers to the fact that they do attend movies.

Thus, even when substantial and reliable differences in general reputation and conduct characteristically rewarded in school are found between movie-going and non-movie-going children, no general effect may safely be attributed to the single and simple fact of their movie-attendance.

THRASHER STUDY

In his study of movie attendance by children in a congested area of New York City, F. Thrasher compared the advancement in grade level of children who attended movies habitually (four or more times a week) with that of children who attended once a week or less.

Findings

He found that, in the habitual-movie group, there were twice as many children retarded and half as many accelerated in their school curriculum as there were in the less-frequent-attendance group. Similarly, among delinquent boys, the percentage of habitual movie-goers was higher than among the non-delinquents. However, from the data of these studies, it is not possible to establish causal relationships between movie attendance and the rate of advancement in school or juvenile delinquency.

BLUMER STUDY AND BLUMER AND HAUSER STUDY

H. Blumer (1933) reported extensive autobiographical accounts of high school young men and women on the effects that entertainment movies had on manners, social behavior, day-dreaming, emotions, life patterns, etc.

H. Blumer and P. M. Hauser (1933) reported similar data from delinquent populations. The data are difficult to interpret except in terms of general concepts. It seems evident that, insofar as the data are trustworthy, effects of entertainment films appear to vary with individuals. Even in homogeneous groups, such as sexually delinquent females, roughly half report arousal of erotic appetites by "passionate" movies, and roughly half report no such effects.

Blumer maintains that, for the individuals, "In a sense, motion pictures organize his needs and suggest lines of conduct useful for their satisfaction" (p. 195). The power of entertainment films he attributes in part to "emotional possession."

The data reported by Blumer seem to substantiate that when certain patterns of behavior, presented in films, are perceived by various individuals in the audience as means of gratifying unsatisfied "needs," these individuals will imitate or copy the patterns presented. The data seem to indicate, and this is a purely hypothetical interpretation, that specific motion pictures are perhaps more effective in stimulating or reinforcing existing motives than in reorganizing them or arousing new kinds of motives. Whatever reorganization may be involved appears to be in conduct patterns directly related to existing "needs" and motivational structure. It appears that under certain conditions not well known at this time, entertainment movies provide opportunities for learning patterns of conduct which are directly related to the satisfaction of existing motives. In a strict sense, movies probably serve little function in organizing the needs of the individual; rather they appear to help the individual to perceive the means for satisfying his needs. While it is somewhat difficult to document without a wide search of the literature outside the experimental field, popular anticipation of, and belief in, the motivational influence

of motion pictures on delinquent and criminal behavior appears to have been exaggerated beyond the facts reported in research studies.

LASHLEY AND WATSON STUDY

In a very early study mentioned previously, Lashley and Watson (1922) reported on the effects of the film Fit to Win on sexual behavior.

Findings

While they found that the film immediately influenced members of the audience to "resolutions of continence," there was no actual effect of the film on sexual behavior as measured by (1) venereal disease frequency and prophylaxis frequency and (2) information collected from interviews with doctors, clergymen, and social workers who were in close contact with the test populations. There was some indication, however, that the film did influence behavior of venereal disease-infected audience members in the direction of seeking prompt treatment.

FREEMAN AND HOEFER STUDY

F. N. Freeman and C. Hoefer (1931) investigated the effect of classroom films dealing with care of the teeth on (1) daily brushing of the teeth, (2) diet, and (3) dental care.

Findings

The results were inconclusive, for which several reasons might be advanced: the small margin for improvement in diet and use of the toothbrush; the unreliability of the index records of these activities; and, failure of the experiment to take adequate account of socio-economic status.

BELL, CAIN, AND LAMOREAUX STUDY

A preliminary inquiry into the effect of National Tuberculosis Association films was supervised by R. Bell, L. F. Cain, and L. A. Lamoreaux (1941).

Findings

The use of the films was followed by a higher percentage of children submitting to the skin test than during the previous year when films were not used. However, materials other than films were used for instruction, and comparison was made between years rather than between groups. Consequently, no unique effect can safely be attributed to the films as such, nor was any attempt made to do so.

SECTION 2. EFFECTS OF FILMS ON ACADEMIC MOTIVATION

Interest Used as a Measure of Motivation

In studying the motivational effects of classroom films, the majority of investigators have used "interest" as a measure of motivation. "Interest" apparently is used to denote a degree of involvement on the part of the individual pupil in the curriculum. This involvement is indicated, in part, by such activities as reading, reciting, constructing, making reports, bringing clippings to class, etc. In general, such activities imply voluntary behavior and independent activity, that is, activity beyond the minimal requirements of the curriculum which are traditionally enforced by rewards and punishments in the school and the family. Motivational influences of films may be inferred from the voluntary nature of the activities.

POTTHOFF, LARSON, AND PATTERSON STUDY

C. J. Potthoff, L. C. Larson, and D. O. Patterson (1940) investigated the effects of the use of films in the course in human biology at the General College, University of Minnesota. The experimenters pointed out that the student population in the human biology course was not of high scholastic ability and apparently had an aversion toward science course.

Findings

It was found that the use of films resulted in an increased number of students enrolling for advanced courses in biology over the number enrolling from classes taught without films. Potthoff, et al., report that "in this experiment, where we dealt with a class that included many pupils of indifferent or worse mind set toward science courses in general, the film heightened interest and, apparently, favored the other desired outcomes. Aside from any other values films may contribute, this finding alone justifies film use, (pp. 29-30), since, as the authors point out, people enrolled in science classes are likely to learn more science than similar people not so enrolled. Incidentally, no reliable difference in academic achievement on tests of course material was found between film and non-film groups.

Evaluation

Films Stimulate Academic Motivation

Potthoff, et al., present evidence which seems to indicate that the films measurably aided in motivating the students to enroll in additional courses of a subject which is normally regarded with considerable indifference and some apprehensiveness among "nonacademic," or "low status," college students. If choosing to continue study of science courses is an index of the strength and direction of educational motivation, then it may be concluded that the films used in an introductory and general course in college science

tended to reinforce and perhaps reorganize the pattern of educational motivation in a given stratum of a college student population.

This interpretation of the data of the Potthoff, et al., study is stated conservatively for two reasons. First, as previously indicated, the motivational values generally attributed to films appear to have been exaggerated. Second, this study is one of the very few, if not the only, study that introduces this type of experimental evidence on the motivational effects of films, that is, in terms of the election of an academic program which previously had been accepted somewhat under compulsion and without expressed enthusiasm.

With reference to other manifestations of "interest," which can be interpreted as manifestations of motivation in that they involve directional and voluntary expenditure of energy, other studies generally are in agreement that the use of films is accompanied by increased reading, participation in classroom recitation, and the like.

SHUTTLEWORTH AND MAY STUDY

F. K. Shuttleworth and M. A. May (1933) investigated the possible influence of movie attendance on the reading habits of children.

Findings

Movie-goers Read More

They reported that boys and girls who frequently attend entertainment movies read more than those who seldom attend. While the difference in percentage of each group reading five or more books during the previous months was small (48 per cent vs. 44 per cent), the difference was statistically reliable. The favorable difference in number of magazines read was greater. Two or more magazines read the previous month were reported by 57 per cent of the frequent movie-goers and 40 per cent of the non-frequent attenders.

Reading Material Was of Lower Quality

When the magazines read by both groups were analyzed for "quality," a higher percentage of the boys and girls who seldom went to the movies reported reading such magazines as Scientific American and Popular Mechanics, and higher percentages of the boys and girls who frequently go to the movies reported reading such magazines as True Story, Love Story, Liberty, and adventure, western, and air story magazines. The Shuttleworth and May studies were made prior to the advent of comic books in their present form and popularity and, thus, no data were gathered on the relation of movie-attendance and comic book reading.

LAZARSFELD AND KENDALL STUDY

P. F. Lazarsfeld and P. Kendall (1948), in their analysis of adult communications habits, report data on adult reading and movie-going.

Findings

Adults who are moderate movie-goers tend to be moderate readers, whereas adults who avoid movies tend also to avoid books and magazines. This is in accord with the May and Shuttleworth comment that "there is no evidence of impoverishment as to amount of reading but rather the contrary" (p.66) as far as movie-attendance, as such, is concerned.

WOOD AND FREEMAN STUDY

B. D. Wood and F. N. Freeman (1929) investigated the value of the silent instructional films produced by the Eastman Kodak Company.

Findings

The teachers reported that films increased student "interest," as manifested by reading and bringing clippings, cartoons, etc., to class, but no quantitative data on actual behavior were reported.

KNOWLTON AND TILTON STUDY

D. C. Knowlton and J. W. Tilton (1929) studied the contributions of the Yale Chronicles of America Photoplays (silent versions) to teaching history in the seventh grade. In this experiment film instruction was used not exclusively, but in addition to the usual instructional materials.

Findings

They report a ten percent increase in pupil participation (recitation) among classes taught with films over classes taught without films. An increase of 40 per cent in voluntary reading in the classroom, with an increase in the percentage of pupils reading and in the amount read, was reported for the film-taught groups.

There was no evidence in the data collected by Knowlton and Tilton to show that the amount of library reading or out-of-school reading was affected by the use of films, or that the film group had a greater preference for history in relation to six other school subjects than the non-film group.

HIRSCH STUDY

R. S. Hirsch (1949) reported a study of the value of films in changing attitudes toward literature.

Experimental Design

He studied the effect of three motion pictures upon the attitude of eleventh-grade pupils toward Shakespearean literature. These films were: Hamlet, produced by J. Arthur Rank and starring Laurence Olivier; a 40-minute, edited version of MGM's Romeo and Juliet, distributed by Teaching Film Custodians, and a 20-minute excerpt of the funeral oration in Julius Caesar, released in the United States by the British Information Service. An experimental group and a control group, of 25 students each, were equated on intelligence and sex distribution. In both groups, two plays, Romeo and Juliet and Macbeth, were read and discussed; Hamlet was not. In addition, the experimental group saw the films. The same teacher taught both groups.

Findings

Film Group Had Greater Shift in Attitude

The control group was somewhat, but not reliably, more favorable to Shakespearean literature than the experimental group at the beginning of the experiment. At the end of five weeks of study, the experimental group was slightly, but not reliably, superior in favorable attitude. When the amounts of attitude change, measured by pre-tests and post-tests, are compared on a Thurstone-type scale (0 to 11 points), the attitude shift is more pronounced. The mean score of the control group shifted .25 in a more favorable direction (CR, 1.04), whereas the experimental group shifted 1.25 in a more favorable direction (CR, 5.45).

Boomerang Effect Occurred in Non-film Group

Significantly enough, in the control group, which read and discussed the two plays but saw no films, seven of the 25 students shifted attitudes in a less favorable direction during the period of study. On the other hand, in the experimental group, which read and discussed the plays and saw the three films, only one student shifted attitude in a less favorable direction. No student in either group was unaffected in attitude.

Although the mean for the control shifted slightly in a favorable direction, the rather alarming implication of Hirsch's data is that the instructional procedure followed in the control group, i.e., reading and discussion of the two plays, was accompanied by a boomerang effect: 28 per cent of the students had a less favorable attitude toward Shakespearean literature after instruction.

Evaluation

The results reported by Hirsch cannot be attributed entirely to the addition of movies alone to usual methods of teaching, since neither group read nor discussed the play Hamlet. The only formal contact of the students with Hamlet was that of the experimental group, which saw the full theatrical film version of the play. Of the three films, Hamlet is unquestionably the most satisfactory from a literary, artistic, or filmic point of view. It is conceivable that the critical effect of the films can be attributed to this film alone, and that, had Hamlet been read by both groups, attitudinal effects of either group or both groups might have been modified. Nonetheless, Hirsch introduced evidence that the three motion pictures added to the amount of reading and discussion, and reliably increased favorable attitudes toward Shakespearean literature, whereas reading and discussion of two Shakespearean plays alone did not result in a sizable or reliable increase. More studies of this type might well be carried on in the field of literature teaching to document the presumed value of film realism in this area.

SECTION 3. EFFECTS OF FILMS ON MILITARY MOTIVATION

The influencing of military motivation through changes in the ideological aspects of morale was an important objective of the Information and Education Division of the War Department in World War II. The Army Orientation Program, which implemented this objective, was the subject of an extensive report by C. I. Hovland, A. A. Lumsdaine, and F. D. Sheffield (1949). An important phase of the orientation program to which the three devoted considerable attention, was the Why We Fight films. The orientation program including its film phase provides some unique opportunities for studying military motivation. It was discussed in some detail in Chapter II.

In Chapter II certain aspects of the Why We Fight films were pointed out as imposing limitations on the experimental value of the Hovland, Lumsdaine, and Sheffield study. Briefly these limitations were: (1) the film content consisted mainly of excerpts from films already produced and available to the producer; and (2) the evaluation of the films was undertaken by personnel who had had no opportunity to introduce or control the variables that might have influenced the effectiveness of the films. As a consequence, it is difficult to generalize the findings on motivation and opinions beyond the Why We Fight films, and beyond the measures of effectiveness used in this particular study.

HOVLAND, LUMSDAINE, AND SHEFFIELD STUDY

Hovland, et al., (1949) investigated the motivational influences of the Army's orientational film, The Battle of Britain, in terms of verbal statements relating to: (1) willingness to serve as a soldier, (2) insistence upon unconditional surrender, and (3) resentment against the enemy.

Experimental Design (1)

Two questions were asked to determine the influence of The Battle of Britain on the troops' acceptance of their role as soldiers. The first question involved a choice between domestic and overseas duty after training. The second question investigated whether the men felt more helpful in winning the war "here in the Army" or "in the job you had before you came into the Army."

Findings (1)

In replying to the first question less than half the men in the control group and in the film group indicated a preference for overseas duty after training. The acutal percentages are illustrated in Fig. 5-1.

In replying to the second question, as in the first, less than half of the control group and the film group expressed preference for their role in the Army (see Fig. 5-2). The differences in favor of the film group were three per cent on the first question, and four per cent on the second question, neither of which is reliable at the one per cent level of confidence.

Thus, slight but statistically unreliable differences were consistently found in favor of the film groups. Little evidence was found to indicate that a substantial increase in military motivation occurred, or that it could be attributed to The Battle of Britain.

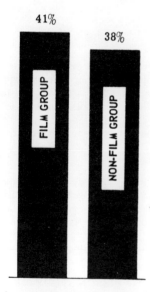

Fig. 5-1. Percent of personnel indicating choice for overseas duty. (Hovland, Lumsdaine & Sheffield, 1949)

48%

44%

FILM GROUP

NON-FILM GROUP

Fig. 5-2. Percent of personnel believing their contribution greater as soldiers than as civilians. (Hovland, Lumsdaine & Sheffield, 1949)

Experimental Design (2)

In an analysis of questionnaires used with the film, Prelude to War, Hovland, Lumsdaine, and Sheffield identified four attitude and belief areas which showed a correlation with expression of the desire to "get into the real fighting soon": (1) a conviction that war was inevitable, (2) a belief that we should seek freedom for all countries, (3) resentment toward the enemy, and (4) respect for enemy strength.

Findings (2)

The greater the degree of conviction in each of the first three areas, the greater the percentage of men expressing a desire to get into the fighting war soon. The fourth area, respect for enemy strength, correlated negatively with the desire to get into the fighting war; that is, the stronger the respect for enemy strength, the smaller the percentage expressing the desire to get into the fighting (pp. 73-75). This fact is consistent with the theory of motivation within the American culture discussed in the introduction to this chapter.

Evaluation

Remoteness May Be Factor in Results

It should be borne in mind that this experiment was conducted among troops who had recently entered the Army from civilian life, and that it was conducted in April, 1943, before American troops had engaged Nazi troops in North Africa or Europe. Thus, there was a geo-psychological remoteness from the events

of The Battle of Britain and the other events, military and otherwise, that led up to the European war.

It should further be borne in mind that The Battle of Britain stressed civilian participation in the war effort. However, similar responses regarding acceptance of the role of soldier were reported from the other films. For this reason, the failure of The Battle of Britain to strongly affect the trainees' acceptance of their role as soldiers should not be attributed to the stress placed on the prestige assigned the role of civilian in the film.

Films May Have Reduced Motivation

Of some significance may be the fact that The Battle of Britain reliably increased respect for enemy strength. This result was indicated by the percentage who rated German Air Forces and Ground Forces as one of the two strongest among the five chief combatants - Japan, Germany, Britain, Russia, and the United States.

As Hovland, et al., point out with specific reference to Prelude to War, it is also possible that The Battle of Britain may have reduced the trainees' motivation for a choice of overseas duty by contributing to their respect for the enemy. Note that the instilling of such respect was consistent with one stated orientation objective to obtain "a realization that we are up against a tough job" (p. 24).

This raises a question of the validity of the psychological structure of the orientation objectives as conceived when the Army orientation program was established, and of the psychological assumptions that presumably were basic to the orientation films (pp. 72ff).

Experimental Design (3)

Another set of data reported by Hovland, et al., with reference to the relation between military motivation and specific attitudes and opinions, has a direct bearing on the rationale of films and motivational changes.

Findings (3)

On a series of ten opinion items concerning such subjects as U. S. participation in the war, integrity of America's allies, etc., a marked relationship was found between favorable opinion on these ten items and preference for the role of soldier over civilian, among 13,000 trainees. Of those with most favorable opinion, 54 per cent preferred the role of soldier, and of those with least favorable opinion, 18 per cent preferred the role of soldier (p. 76).

Evaluation

These data tend to suggest that the trainees' preference for the role of soldier over that of civilian is related to an integrated set of opinions about the desirability of military cooperation among the United States and its allies.

In a review of the influence of films in changing behavior, the nature of this relationship is a question of more than academic interest. Its applications are important because they involve the employment of films as elements of the ideological environment that is potentially able to bring about a change in motivation by changing opinions. Presumably, if a change in ideological opinion can effect a change in stated military motivation, and if a given motion picture or series of motion pictures can potentially influence specific ideological opinions, and, in the long run, bring about stable changes in some more or less general opinions or attitudes, then they can reasonably be presumed to influence actual motivation, and this influence might presumably be somewhat stable.

SECTION 4. EFFECTS OF ORIENTATION PROGRAMS ON MILITARY MOTIVATION

HOVLAND, LUMSDAINE, AND SHEFFIELD STUDY

The nature of the relationship between opinions and motivation can be studied by observing how a change in one variable is associated with change in the other variable. In a study of orientation programs (not just the effect of films) between April and August, 1944, Hovland, et al., investigated this relationship by measuring the change in opinion score resulting from a regimental orientation program, and by comparing the quantity and direction of change in opinion with the quantity and direction of change in preference for the role of soldier over that of civilian.

Findings

Motivation Decreased Independently of Opinion Change

It was found that all changes in opinion, regardless of the direction of the change, were accompanied by negative changes in the preference for role of the soldier over that of civilian. Zero change in opinion was accompanied by a 12 per cent negative change in acceptance of the role of soldier; any negative change in opinion involved a 22 per cent negative change in acceptance of the soldier's role. Moreover, a change of plus one on a ten point scale involved a three per cent negative change in acceptance, while a change of plus two or more in opinion involved an eight per cent negative change in acceptance of the role of soldier.

Evaluation

Decrease Occurred During Orientation

These results seem to indicate that in all categories of opinion change, the shift in motivation was negative; that is, during the period of the orientation program more of the men shifted away from the alternative, "could do more for my country as a soldier," than shifted toward it. Apparently there was a general tendency for men to become less highly "motivated" (in the sense of saying that they could do more for their country as a soldier than as a war worker*) with increased service.

Decrease Smaller When Opinion Shifts Were Positive

On the other hand, this deterioration was less for men who had a positive opinion change in the area of the orientation objectives. Thus, the investigators say, "A tendency is shown for 'improved' opinion to be correlated with increased motivation" (p. 77).

At the close of their discussion of this particular point, Hovland, et al., offer an extremely cautious but debatable conclusion:

"On the basis of these considerations it can only be said that the foregoing correlational analyses incline the balance in the direction of indicating that motivation is directly related to the opinions stressed by the orientation program. Thus it seems likely that if a more effective method of changing opinion had been available, improvement in motivation might have been produced, despite the fact that with the type of information program actually employed little over-all effect was observed on either opinion or motivation" (p. 79).

STOUFFER, SUCHMAN, DEVINNEY, STAR, AND WILLIAMS STUDY

The conclusions of S. A. Stouffer, E. A. Suchman, L. C. DeVinney, S. A. Star, and R. M. Williams, Jr., (1949), may be applied to the hope expressed by

---

* A comment regarding technique may be apropos. The statement used to measure "willingness to accept the soldier role" reads: "If it were up to you to choose, do you think you could do more for your country as a soldier or as a worker in a war job? (Check one)

As a soldier

As a war worker

Undecided" (p. 76)

Yet the authors in the text discussion and in their charts call this, "would rather be a soldier." It is conceivable that part of the deterioration in "acceptance of the soldier role" which was found could be due to the phrasing of the question and the possible effect that may have had upon men trained in skilled trades and in more advanced technical ways, who were having no chance to use such skill or technical training in their military assignment.

Hovland, et al., --that certain opinions might be changed by more effective methods and that such changes would influence the motivation of soldiers to accept their role. Their conclusions are based on the extensive study of the opinions and attitudes of the American soldier during Army life, and included studies of the orientation program in this country and overseas.

Experimental Design (1)

Taking a cross section of 2000 soldiers in the United States, Stouffer, et al., asked a number of questions to investigate the feeling of personal commitment in the war. Three of the items were (1) feeling of greater contribution as a soldier, (2) willingness to fight overseas, and (3) desire for real fighting soon.

Findings (1)

Strong Convictions Aid Esprit

The authors say, "There was never much doubt as to the fact that men with strong convictions about the war not only tended to have a stronger sense than others of personal commitment, but also that they were more favorable on other attitudes reflecting personal adjustment" (p. 459). To support this statement they present data showing that those who said they never had doubts about the war being worth fighting had more personal esprit and a greater feeling of personal commitment in the war. On the three items listed above, the group that had no doubts about the objectives of the war was more favorable than the other group by the following percentages: Item 1, 13 per cent more; Item 2, 14 per cent; Item 3, 10 per cent. Further, the men with no expressed doubts were more satisfied with their status in the Army, as indicated by their response to eight items.

Cause-Effect Evaluation Often Misleading

Stouffer, et al., point out that the results of studies reported by Hovland, Lumsdaine, and Sheffield were somewhat disappointing for those specialists who believed that information media would have a marked effect on attitudes toward war and that the change in attitude would affect personal commitment. They stress that the experimental evaluation of the orientation films illustrates "...how extremely dangerous it is to translate a correlational finding into a system of causation" (p. 461); and the same point is made by Hovland, Lumsdaine, and Sheffield (pp. 73-150).

Experimental Design (2)

Stouffer, et al., state that films constituted only a part of the orientation efforts of the I and E Division and that the institution of orientation courses (weekly discussion groups conducted in small units) both in the overseas areas and in this country, was an important part of the program. They compared two equated groups of Army units in the European Theater in April, 1945; one group had discussion sessions during the three months prior to the study, and the other had no discussions during that period. Over 100 items were used in this analysis.

Findings (2)

Few Opinion Changes From Orientation Program

In none of the attitude areas in which the items were grouped (information about the war, worth-whileness of the war, attitude toward Army, attitude toward personal participation, attitude toward home-front, etc.) "...were any significant consistent differences found as between men in units conducting an orientation program and men in the other units" (p. 473).

Evaluation

Program Objectives Were Difficult

They point out that the orientation program was operating against great difficulties, and that it is not surprising, under the circumstances, if the enlisted men took the orientation "with a large grain of salt." They stress that even under the best of conditions, the remolding of basic attitudes is a gigantic task, and that when one considers the long years of pre-military experience that shaped some of these basic attitudes, one could hardly expect one hour a week of information and discussion, however ideal, to do much in reversing cultural trends.

Stouffer, et al., believe that the orientation program served the useful purpose of reassuring men regarding their knowledge about affairs in the world and reduced somewhat their feeling that the Army was not concerned with the welfare of the individual. They conclude that there is some reason to believe that, given the pre-war intellectual history of these men and precluding any further galvanizing experiences like Pearl Harbor, no increase in personal commitment to winning the war could have been produced, even by a frankly propagandistic program of indoctrination instead of the "appeal to facts" upon which the Army sought to depend.

Lack of Difference May Reflect Other Variables

In a comparison of a "model" and a "typical" orientation program in two regiments in training in the United States from April to August 1944, referred to previously from Hovland, et al., it was found that both regiments made "small but significant gains in information and in attitudes toward the war ....." (pp. 477-478). They further point out that the few differences between the two regiments are so slight as to make any interpretation ambiguous. Stouffer, et al., conclude that the results could mean that the two programs ("model" and "typical") were equally effective, or it could be that the changes found "are not attributable to the orientation program but to influences not under consideration" (p. 478), (underscoring by present reviewers). They point out that the three questions on personal zeal did show changes, but in opposite directions. Increased willingness to go overseas, decreased acceptance of Army values, are ". . .exactly the types of trends in attitude shown . . . to occur as men progressed from new recruits to trained soldiers, and the data probably reflect this process rather than an effect of the orientation program" (pp. 478-480).

Instilling Convictions Is Important Objective

They hasten to add that it would be dangerous to conclude their discussion of orientation ". . . by leaving the inference that convictions about one's cause are of negligible significance" (p. 284). The rela-

tionships, mentioned above, between belief that the war was worth fighting, personal esprit, personal commitment, and satisfaction with Army status, are not to be ignored merely because specific efforts to improve personal commitment by improving information and opinions about the war were not successful to any great extent. They go on to say that ". . . given other historical contexts, it is possible, indeed probable, that convictions about a war would play a still greater role than among Americans in World War II" (p. 484). John Dollard's study (1943) of the veterans of the Abraham Lincoln Brigade, made up of Americans who volunteered to fight in the Spanish Civil War, presented a situation where ideological convictions appeared to play a much more powerful role than in the American Army, Stouffer, et al., contend.

SUMMARY

1. INFLUENCE OF FILMS ON ACADEMIC MOTIVATION AND BEHAVIOR

Some evidence exists that both entertainment and classroom films exert an influence on behavior which is valued academically. Furthermore, there is no evidence that motion pictures reduce academic motivation, that is, that they result in less voluntary reading, less voluntary participation in classroom recitation, or greater avoidance of a specific course of study.

Theoretically, at least, such influence as films may have on academic motivation is likely to arise from the nature of motion pictures and the context of instruction. Pictures are perceived in much the same way as situations and actions are visually perceived, that is, with no intervening intellectual skill, such as reading, operating either to facilitate or to obstruct perception. The experience derived from a motion picture facilitates further communication in the same general content area. This facilitation enables the individual to behave in ways which are socially approved in school and college.

Movies Offer Means of Attaining Goals

Academically approved behavior is reinforced by social approval of the middle-class family, which constitutes an appreciable majority in the American social structure. To the extent that the individual accepts academic (and intellectual) achievement as a condition of self-realization and to the extent that social approval enhances his self-regard, motion pictures which facilitate intellectual activity and enable the individual to behave in socially-approved ways are a useful tool in the attainment of basic goals, and in the approach to a culturally defined condition, or state, of happiness.

The relationship between entertainment movie attendance and reading noted by May and Shuttleworth

(1933) and by Lazarsfeld and Kendall (1948) may be viewed in somewhat this same light, except that, in this case, self-realization and self-regard are probably increased when the individual projects and identifies himself with the protagonists and situations in the movies and the magazines. In either case, movies appear to be a means to the gratification of personality needs, and appear to be positively correlated with the amount, and probably the kind, of reading. There is no evidence in research studies that movies take the place of reading, assuming that reading and movies serve somewhat the same functions for the individual.

2. INFLUENCE OF FILMS AND OTHER MEDIA ON MILITARY MOTIVATION

The studies cited point up the difficulty of modifying military motivation within the American culture. There is little exact evidence that films, as a medium of communication, can modify actual conduct motivations, if the desired motivations are contrary to those presumably developed by personal experiences and the vicissitudes of daily living.

Some of the evidence does indicate that films tend to reinforce motivations which are consistent with the milieu of daily life and with the aspirations of the individual or the social group of which the individual is a part.

Thus, we have, as a very moot and open question, the problem as to what extent one can hope, by using information and attempting to work upon the opinions of recruits, to bring about rather sudden changes in their motivation concerned with accepting the role of a soldier, which, in itself, is not highly valued in the American culture. There is no warrior cult in the United States.

PART II. INFLUENCE OF FILMS ON SOCIAL ATTITUDES

Distinction Between General and Specific Attitudes

In this review of research data on the effect of motion pictures on social attitudes, a somewhat arbitrary distinction is made between specific attitudes and general attitudes. This distinction does not involve a sharp dichotomy, since it is based on how closely the attitude to be influenced is related to the content of the film. This review also makes a distinction between films produced for entertainment and those produced for instruction and for propaganda.

SECTION 1. EFFECTS OF ENTERTAINMENT FILMS ON SPECIFIC ATTITUDES

THURSTONE AND PETERSON STUDY

The "classical" studies of the effects of motion pictures on social attitudes are those conducted by L. L. Thurstone and R. Peterson in connection with the Payne Fund studies (1933).

Experimental Design

The studies by Thurstone and Peterson included measurement of the effect of then-current entertainment films on attitudes toward Negroes, Chinese, Germans, crime, and criminals. The effects of single films, the cumulative effects of more than one film, and the persistence of these effects were studied.

In measuring attitudinal effects, Thurstone and Peterson used specific attitude scales, constructed by one or both of the experimenters, and which were adapted to the vocabulary levels of the populations tested. In general, the audiences used in these attitude studies were "unsophisticated," in the sense that they frequently were drawn from communities in which, at that time, motion pictures were exhibited relatively infrequently. This audience characteristic may or may not have had some effect on the results obtained.

Findings

Film Produced Unfavorable Attitude Toward Negroes

The most striking influence of motion pictures on attitudes was reported in the study of the effect of D. W. Griffith's Birth of a Nation. This film, originally produced as a silent film, was revived in 1931 with the addition of a sound track. This film has been described as "anti-Negro." It was one of Griffith's most spectacular productions from a theatrical point of view and one of the most controversial motion pictures produced for public exhibition.

Thurstone and Peterson reported that Birth of a Nation produced a modification of attitude toward the Negro in an unfavorable direction, and that this modification had the greatest magnitude of all effects observed in their studies of attitudinal influence of entertainment films. A mean change of 1.48 scale points on the attitude scale (which extends from 0.0 to 10.6), with a critical ratio of 25.5 PE's, was found among the 434 students from grades six through twelve immediately after the film was shown. This change persisted, in diminished magnitude (.95), five months after the film was exhibited.

Film Modified Attitudes Toward Chinese

Favorable attitude changes were reported by Thurstone and Peterson with Sons of Gods, a film "favorable" to the Chinese. A mean change of 1.22 scale points (on a scale of values from 0.0 to 10.6) in the attitude toward Chinese was found immediately after the film experience, with the favorable effect persisting nineteen months later.

A slight, but statistically unreliable, change less favorable toward Chinese was found among high school students following exhibition of Welcome Danger. This film was a Harold Lloyd comedy, involving Tong conspirators and a lawless element of Chinatown. Thus, the element of comedy, the somewhat subordinate dramatic role assigned to Chinese, and possibly other variables were introduced. Whether these variables accounted for the absence of a reliable influence of this film on attitudes cannot be ascertained, since no film variables were considered in the Thurstone and Peterson studies other than the abstract quality of "favorable" or "unfavorable" film content.

Film Increased Favorable Attitudes Toward Germans

Four Sons, a film dealing with Germans and war, was shown to 133 students from grades seven through twelve. After seeing the film, the group was somewhat more favorable toward Germans on the Thurstone attitude scale. The mean difference before and after the film experience was .38 scale points (on a scale from 0.0 to 11.0), and the critical ratio, 5.37 PE's. Preference toward the German nationality shifted from fifth to second position on a preference scale.

The effects on attitude and preference persisted six months after the film experience. The experimental results may have been influenced somewhat by the novelty effect of the film experience, since the experimental population was drawn from a small town in Illinois in which entertainment motion pictures were not regularly exhibited.

Films Intensified Anti-War Attitudes

A slight anti-war influence was noted in connection with Four Sons. The before-after difference was .09 on the Thurstone scale. No critical ratio was reported, and it is assumed that this difference was not statistically reliable.

With both All Quiet on the Western Front and Journey's End, attitudes shifted reliably in an anti-war direction. The differences varied from .33 to .54 on the Thurstone scales. Critical ratios were all above five PE's.

The reliability of these attitude changes increased for those groups which saw both films. There was a significant persistence of effect for two months after exhibition, but this effect was less evident after four months.

Film Effects Were Cumulative and Persistent

High school and college students who saw The Criminal Code were less favorable toward punishment of criminals after seeing the film. The differences were approximately .50 on the Thurstone scale, and the critical ratios, above 11 PE's for both high school and college students. Thurstone and Peterson reported that 88 per cent of the effect persisted after two and a half months, and 78 per cent persisted after nine months.

When three films dealing with crime and criminals, (Big House, Numbered Men, and Criminal Code), were shown to 745 students from grades six through twelve, the magnitude and reliability of attitudinal effects were greatest when the films were shown cumulatively. This effect remained constant after two months, and appeared to increase after four months. Thus, while it was found that an individual film might produce no change in attitude, the cumulative effect of seeing two or three films with similar bias at several-day intervals was observable.

The films, The Valiant and Alibi, had no reliable effect on the attitudes of children, drawn from grades seven through twelve, toward punishment of criminals. Hideout produced no measurable effect on the attitudes toward prohibition and bootlegging of 254 children, from grades nine through twelve. On the other hand, Street of Chance produced a "socially approved" effect, in that 240 children, drawn from grades nine through twelve, on taking a paired-comparison test, were more severe in their judgment of a gambler portrayed in the film, even though the gambler was presented as "an interesting, likeable character" (p. 15).

Evaluation

Audience Stratification Not Reported

Thurstone and Peterson reported no results in terms of audiences stratified by age or school grade, except where high school and college populations were used on the same experiment. The range of school grades, from four through twelve, appears somewhat large and may be an important variable, since, when adult audiences were stratified by educational level in subsequent studies, differences in film effects were reported. In these later studied, age could be held relatively constant in the analyses of the effects of films on populations stratified by education, whereas in the Thurstone and Peterson studies, age presumably varied with educational level. Apparently, in their studies on attitudes, Thurstone and Peterson assumed either that attitudinal effects of motion pictures were not influenced by age or education, or that the age- and grade-groups were too small for reliable statistical analysis.

Social Norms Govern Attitude Changes

While Thurstone and Peterson present no directly supporting data, we may postualte that attitudes will be influenced in the direction of the motion picture bias, provided this bias is not strongly contradictory to accepted social norms on the subject. This postulate may possibly account for the fact that films dealing with bootlegging and prohibition had no or unreliable effects on attitudes toward those activities.

Film Bias May "Boomerang"

We may further postulate, with even less experimental proof, that, when there is bias in a motion picture portrayal of a role toward which there is unfavorable social bias, the attitude, instead of being redirected, will be reinforced in the direction of the community bias. (This often is called the "boomerang" effect.) This postulate may possibly account for the fact that a film, in which the gambler role was apparently presented with some degree of sympathy or attractiveness, had an unfavorable effect on attitudes toward gambling.

Both these postulates are consistent with the basic premises that social attitudes are developed in conformity with group norms of behavior and that they resist redirection. The Thurstone and Peterson experiments merely suggest such interpretations as possibilities, since no directly supporting data are provided. These possibilities indicate the need for research on the effects of films and other means of communication on attitudes, particularly on those attitudes which are consistent with social group norms having various strengths and ethical values, and on those attitudes closely integrated with self-regard, self-preservation and self-realization.

JONES STUDY

V. Jones (1936) investigated the influence of entertainment motion pictures on moral values, standards, or attitudes as part of a large study of character and citizenship training in the public schools.

Experimental Design

Three seventh-grade classes were divided at random into two groups; one of the groups attended some then-recent entertainment films. The films, carefully chosen for their depiction of moral choices of conduct, were Tom Brown of Culver, The Champ, Abraham Lincoln, and Fast Companions. Moral attitudes were measured by tests which were based, in part, on film content. In each test, pupils ranked items in terms of moral values. The effects of the films were inferred from differences in ratings assigned to the items by the pupils who had seen the films and by those who had not. The tests were administered shortly after the films were shown and, again, six months later.

Findings

He found, as did other experimenters in the field, that motion pictures changed the attitudes of seventh-grade pupils "on the test items connected with the pictures in precisely the direction which one would expect from the nature of the films. If an act was condemned, the children became more severe in their judgment of it; if an act was excused or applauded, the children tended to excuse or praise" (p. 359). He also found some evidence that, "somewhat larger changes were found in the direction of lowered or less rigid standards of conduct than in the direction of higher or stricter standards" (pp. 359-360).

Evaluation

Human Values Temper Moral Standards

In his report, Jones was careful to accompany the moral choices apparently influenced by the films with a description of the situations and circumstances in which related moral principles were presented in the films. One can debate whether "lowered or less rigid standards of conduct" as influenced by the films, were actually lowered or less rigid. For instance, one item upon which a "lowered" standard was found was "he steals something to eat if he is hungry." On this item the group which saw the film, The Champ, assigned less moral reprehensibility (1.80 points on a scale of 1 to 15) to the behavior than the group that did not see the film. It is remembered that one of the classics of French literature is based on the motive of hunger and the theft of a loaf of bread, and that the moral turpitude of the theft of food by a hungry person is frequently tempered in the Western mind. It seems that, when moral reprehensibility is tempered with other human values in a film treatment of moral conduct, there is a tendency in a film audience to temper justice with mercy. This, in effect, is a norm of community morality.

Attitude Changes Influenced by Social Norms

Viewed in this light, Jones' study is consistent with the interpretation that the influence of films on attitudes is in the direction approved by the social group. In support of this interpretation, Jones found evidence in his tests of actual conduct (honesty and cooperation) that there were small gains in favor of the film group. He attributes this apparent advantage of the film group to two factors: "first, the transfer effect of the pictures themselves upon the conduct of the children in the test situations; and, second, the transfer effect of other conditions associated with the attendance at the pictures, such, for example, as a more friendly and cooperative attitude on the part of the picture group toward the examiner, who had made it possible for them to go to the pictures" (pp. 361-362).

SECTION 2. EFFECTS OF DOCUMENTARY FILMS ON SPECIFIC ATTITUDES

RAMSEYER STUDY

Experimental Design

L. L. Ramseyer (1938) studied the attitudinal effects of U. S. government motion pictures dealing with soil erosion and with the Works Progress Administration (WPA) program. He used a population of approximately 2000 subjects drawn from seventh grade through college and from the general adult population. The films used included, The Plow that Broke the Plains, and The River, produced by the U. S. Department of Agriculture; and Work Pays America, and Hands, produced by the Works Progress Administration.

Both The Plow that Broke the Plains and The River are historical landmarks in the development of the "documentary" film in the United States. They were produced under the direction of Pare Lorentz, with musical score composed by Virgil Thompson. Their appeal is consciously dramatic. The other two films are more "factual."

Findings

Films Produced Favorable Attitudes Toward WPA

The films, Work Pays America, and Hands, produced reliable attitudinal changes favorable to the WPA among high school students from grades nine through twelve, and among college students. With these groups, critical ratios exceeded five PE's. Favorable changes among the adult population with reference to WPA had a critical ratio of at least 3.16 PE's. These effects persisted for at least two months, but in diminished magnitude.

Films Produced Support for Federal Help in Erosion

The exhibition of both The Plow that Broke the Plains and The River was followed by attitude changes favorable to government help in the problem of soil erosion. On The Plow that Broke the Plains, these changes were reliable from grades ten through college by more than four PE's, and among adults by only 2.2 PE's; on The River, the attitude change was reliable with twelfth-grade students by 5.9 PE's, and with tenth- and eleventh-grade students by 3.5 and 3.3 PE's, respectively. Attitude changes attributed to The Plow that Broke the Plains persisted in diminished magnitude for at least two months after its exhibition. In the case of all films used, the actual changes in attitude were small, although reliability of these changes was frequently high.

All four films were effective, to some degree, in modifying attitudes directly related to the bias of the motion pictures. Furthermore, the favorable effects ostensibly attributable to the films persisted over a period of several weeks.

Films Had Largest Effects on Students

Interestingly enough, in the case of all four films, reliability of the measured changes reached the level of probable certainty in the senior high school and college populations, but was somewhat below this level with adult populations. All the films were ostensibly produced for adult populations, but their propaganda effect appears to have been most reliable among high school and college student populations.

Attitude shifts toward both WPA and government help in soil erosion were of least magnitude and least reliability among children of professional parents, and were most reliable among children whose parents were farmers, laborers, and white collar workers.

Evaluation

The films used by Ramseyer differed from those used by Thurstone and Peterson in at least two respects: (1) They were approximately one-third to one-half the length of the feature film, and (2) the treatment was expository rather than dramatic.

Two qualifying factors emerge from Ramseyer's data on the attitudinal effects of the films used in his study. The reliability of the effects of the films on specific attitudes varied with (1) the age (and correlative educational level) of the population, and (2) the sub-cultural group with which the individual ostensibly identified himself.

Conditioning to Instruction May Vary Effectiveness

We may postulate a certain docility among the population drawn from school and college because of its conditioning to instruction. An adult population ordinarily is not expected to have such a docile disposition. This difference may possibly be reflected in the degree of influence of the films in the adult population as contrasted with the high school and college populations, just as it may possibly have been involved in the school populations used exclusively in the Thurstone and Peterson studies.

Effects Varied with Social Status

Of considerable importance, however, is the differential effect of the films on attitudes of children and adolescents drawn from families of different occupational status. This implies, as suggested in the introductory discussion of attitude development and motivational structure, that attitudes are developed in the context of the social group of which the individual is a member or with which he identified himself, and that the effect of a film or films on an attitude depends, at least in part, on the nature and strength of the individual's attitude prior to the film experience.

Ramseyer's data indicate that the films he studied did not have the same attitudinal effect within a heterogeneous population. His data also indicate that different films vary in their attitudinal effect, even though they are biased in the same general attitudinal direction.

SECTION 3. EFFECTS OF ENTERTAINMENT FILMS ON GENERAL ATTITUDES

SHUTTLEWORTH AND MAY STUDY

The second part of F. K. Shuttleworth and M. A. May's study (p. 5-4) dealt with measurement of attitudes which, sometimes, are attributed to the kinds of entertainment movies that children (and adults) see. These attitudes dealt with the heroes and "boobs" of the movies, national groups, prohibition, criminals, sex, school, clothes, militarism, parents, and escape from danger.

Findings

Films Had Few Effects on General Attitudes

In instance after instance, no discriminable difference was found between movie-going and non-movie-going children on attitude or opinion stereotypes. The differences found were differences on specific items and these appear to lack any high degree of integration. For instance, as Shuttleworth and May report, "While there are no differences in attitudes toward crime and criminals, there is some evidence that movie children believe that few criminals escape their just punishment. On the question of the criminal reforming, a question which indirectly involved sex attitudes, there is evidence showing that the movie children believe that feminine charms are more potent in reforming the criminal than fear of the police. There is evidence that, under certain conditions, the movie children expect the hero to carry the girl off by force or compel her to dance with him. No difference was found in approval or disapproval of such conduct" (pp. 70-71).

With reference to entertainment films seen in the early 1930's by children in grades five through eight, the differences in reputation and conduct between frequent and non-frequent movie-goers are difficult to account for in terms of movie attendance. Such general differences as were found to exist between movie-goers and non-movie-goers cannot be safely attributed to movies as such.

Movies Tend to Reinforce Existing Attitudes

Attitudinal differences were found to be specific, not general, and they lack integration. There is reason to believe that these differences originate in personality characteristics of the persistent movie-going population. Shuttleworth and May conclude their report with the following interesting hypothesis: "We are. . . convinced that among the most frequent attendants the movies are drawing, are children who are in some way maladjusted and whose difficulties are relieved only in the most temporary manner and are, in fact, much aggravated. In other words, the movies tend to fix and further establish the behavior patterns and types of attitudes which already exist among those who attend most frequently" (p. 93).

SECTION 4. EFFECTS OF INFORMATIONAL FILMS ON GENERAL ATTITUDES

The effect on general attitudes of films with an informational, rather than an amusement, intent was investigated by E. C. Wilson and L. C. Larson (1940) in the General College, University of Minnesota, and by L. F. Cain in the Santa Barbara (California) public schools, [R. Bell, L. F. Cain, and L. A. Lamoreaux (1941)]. The effect of training in the identification of propaganda techniques and in "scientific thinking" as factors in resistance to propaganda influences of films was investigated by L. C. Larson (1940) at the University of Minnesota. All three of these studies were part of a larger program of research concerned with the evaluation of motion pictures in general education, conducted under the Committee on Motion Pictures in Education of the American Council on Education (see Chapter II).

WILSON AND LARSON STUDY

E. C. Wilson and L. C. Larson (1940) studied the effects on general attitudes of a series of films dealing with events leading up to World War II. The films were used in the course in current history at the General College, University of Minnesota.

Experimental Design

The attitudinal changes of classes in which films were used as an integral part of the instructional program were contrasted with those of classes in which the film content was presented verbally only. Experimental and control classes were matched on an unusually large number of factors. In this experiment, extending over several weeks of instruction, nine films were used. All films, the majority of which were March of Time releases, related either to the background of World War II or to America's attitude toward neutrality, or both.

Findings

Changes were found in both film and non-film groups on attitudes concerning (1) U. S. entry into war, and (2) war itself, but the differences between the film and non-film group were not reliable on either attitude. In other words, after the several weeks of instruction

in current history, the film group showed no reliably greater change that could be attributed uniquely to the particular films used.

Evaluation

It appears that the attitudes measured in this study approach a degree of generality, although it could be argued, with equal or greater validity, that the attitudes were as specific as those measured by Thurstone and Peterson. Nevertheless, in the sense that the attitude scales used in this study were not constructed with specific reference to course or film content, it may be assumed that the attitudes measured were somewhat more general (less specific) than those investigated by Ramseyer (1938).

BELL, CAIN, AND LAMOREAUX STUDY

In the R. Bell, L. F. Cain and L. A. Lamoreaux (1941) study, the generality of the attitudes measured is relatively clear-cut. They used the Progressive Education Association Scale of Beliefs which covered the subtopics of (1) democracy, (2) economic individualism, (3) labor and unemployment, (4) nationalism, (5) race, and (6) militarism.

Experimental Design

The study involved the cumulative effect of eight March of Time films on specific information and general attitudes when these films were used in an instructional context similar to that studied by Wilson and Larson. Classes in grades five, seven, nine and eleven in the Santa Barbara public schools were used in the study. The films were used as integral parts in the units typically taught to these classes. In order to preserve the "integrated" and "typical" use situation, the units varied in length according to the "normal" pattern of instruction on the various grade levels. The films, which dealt with conservation of the soil and wild life, community planning, consumer protection, and child welfare, were selected because of their relation to the scope and objectives of the Santa Barbara curriculum. Both film and non-film groups were matched on relevant factors, including teacher efficiency. Results were reported in terms of total scale scores.

Findings

Reliable attitude changes exceeding 3 SE's were reported on the Scale of Belief for both film and non-film groups in grades seven, nine, and eleven, but not in grade five. However, the only difference in attitudinal effect between the film and non-film classes which approached high statistical reliability (2.60 SE's), occurred in grade nine. Interestingly enough, no real difference was found in informational learning between film and non-film groups of this grade. Although this is an isolated instance, it does raise the question of the relationship between the general attitudinal and specific informational effects which may possibly be ascribed to film use.

There was a positive difference in informational gains in favor of the film groups in all grades, but this difference was reliable (critical ratio exceeding 3 SE's) in grades seven and eleven only, and most reliable (4.5 SE's) in grade eleven.

In both the Minnesota and the Santa Barbara studies, attitude changes of a general character were obtained after a period of several weeks of organized instruction, both when films were and were not used in the instruction. In only one instance does the evidence indicate that film instruction produced a more reliable general attitudinal effect than did the verbal presentation of the film content.

SUMMARY

1. INFLUENCE ON SPECIFIC ATTITUDES

The following conclusions about the influence of films on specific attitudes (closely related to the film content) are justified from the Thurstone and Peterson study:

1. Specific attitude changes can result from certain motion pictures whose content is closely related to the object of the specific attitude.

2. The effect of motion pictures on specific attitudes can be cumulative for two or more films on the same social theme. The cumulative effect may result even though some films in the sequence may be individually ineffective in reliably influencing a specific attitude.

3. When the initial influence of one or more motion pictures on a specific attitude is large and of high reliability, it may persist for several weeks or months, generally, although not necessarily, with some diminution.

The Thurstone and Peterson study suggests the hypothesis, and Jones' and Ramseyer's data seem to confirm it, that few, if any, specific attitude changes will result when the film bias is strongly contradictory to the social norms. In the case of contradictory influences, film bias may actually reinforce the existing attitude, rather than modify it.

Further, Ramseyer's data indicate that films may not exert the same attitudinal influence within a non-uniform population, such as one in which different occupational, social, or educational backgrounds are represented.

2. INFLUENCE ON GENERAL ATTITUDES

There are several conclusions, largely tentative, which may be inferred from the experimental evidence on the influence of specific motion pictures on general attitudes:

1. The attitudinal influences of a single motion picture appear to be specific, rather than general.

2. The cumulative effect of a series of motion pictures is probably general, but the effect is subject to the following conditions:

    a. The films are all biased in the same direction and are consistent with the general predisposition of the audience.

    b. They are exhibited in a context that supports and reinforces the direction of the bias.

    c. The exhibition of the films is spaced over a period of time.

There is, however, no direct evidence that motion pictures are reliably superior to other media of communication in their influence on general attitudes. Some evidence exists to the contrary. If the conclusions regarding the impact of films on the learning of information could be generalized to attitudes (and there is no evidence to support such generalization), it might be postulated that the force of motion pictures on general attitudes may be greater than that of verbal media alone, when the influence is measured in long-term effects and when conditions required in the development of general attitudes are satisfied. This postulate is somewhat feasible when reminiscent effect is taken into consideration, and when a relationship between specific and general attitude is assumed. However, research is needed on the long-term attitudinal effects of films to substantiate this postulate.

PART III. INFLUENCE OF FILMS ON OPINIONS

HOVLAND, LUMSDAINE, AND SHEFFIELD STUDY

In their studies on the influence of films on military motivation (see Part I), Hovland, et al., (1949) obtained data which describes the effects of these films on opinions.

Findings

Effects Were Greatest on Opinions Covered in Films

Reinforcing the previous findings on the influence of films on general and specific attitudes, Hovland, et al., found that the orientation films used in World War II were increasingly effective in modifying opinions when the opinions were explicitly covered in the content of the films, and that they became decreasingly effective as the opinions to be influenced departed from the specific issues presented in the film. They reported that the films had ". . .some marked effects on opinions where the film specifically covered the factors involved in the particular interpretation, that is, where the opinion item was prepared on the basis of film-content analysis and anticipated opinion change from such analysis. Such opinion changes were, however, less frequent and in general, less marked than changes in factual knowledge" (p. 64).

This finding is consistent with the data reported by S. P. Rosenthal (1934) on the effect of radical-labor newsreels upon the attitudes of 200 college students on a wide range of socio-economic problems. Rosenthal found, among other things, that the effect of the film was greater on items related to film content than on items remote from film content.

Few Changes in Opinions Unrelated to Films

Hovland, Lumsdaine and Sheffield, further reported that "the films had only a very few effects on opinion items of a more general nature that had been prepared independently of film content but which were considered the criteria for determining the effectiveness of the films in achieving their orientation objectives" (p. 64). These conclusions were based on analyses of individual fact and opinion items in the questionnaires administered on all four orientation films, and on analyses of responses to The Battle of Britain. The conclusions also held for several analyses that were based on: (1) all four films, (2) two individual films, and (3) the cumulative showing of The Nazis Strike and Divide and Conquer.

Effects Had Varying Time Stability

In those opinion items which were influenced by the film experience, there was a total score, or general over-all stability of change of opinion, favorable to the British, nine weeks after seeing The Battle of Britain. This over-all opinion change remained favorable, although certain individual items lost some, or all, of the film effect after nine weeks. On the other hand, some items which showed no film effect immediately, showed a reliable influence from the film nine weeks later! Of 15 items significantly affected, either immediately or nine weeks after the film, seven items that had originally been favorably affected lost some of the gain, and two lost practically the entire gain. On the other hand, eight items on which no immediate reliable effect was evident showed a reliable effect from the film nine weeks later (pp. 186-187).

General Opinion Effects Increased with Time

In studying the delayed effects upon the more general orientation objectives produced by The Battle of Britain film, six items related to confidence in the British showed a slightly greater long-time gain than short-time gain (see Fig. 5-3). In addition, results on eleven items of general opinions related to orientation objectives (such as, resentment against the enemy, confidence in home support, etc.), but less relevant to the specific film, showed a similar difference for long-time gain and short-time gain (see Fig. 5-4).

The authors point out that neither of these results is reliable at the five per cent level of confidence if the items are treated as a sample from the total number of relevant items. Yet they feel that the data lend some support to ". . .the hypothesis that changes in opinions of a general rather than specific nature may show increasing effects with lapse of time" (p. 200).

The investigators had assumed at the outset of their study that deterioration of effects with time would be the rule; but apparently this is an unwarranted assumption in the case of some opinions, possibly of a more general nature.

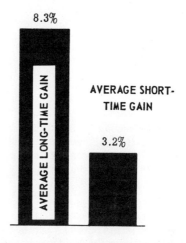

Fig. 5-3. Percent difference between long-time and short-time gains on six general opinion items about the British. (Hovland, Lumsdaine & Sheffield, 1949)

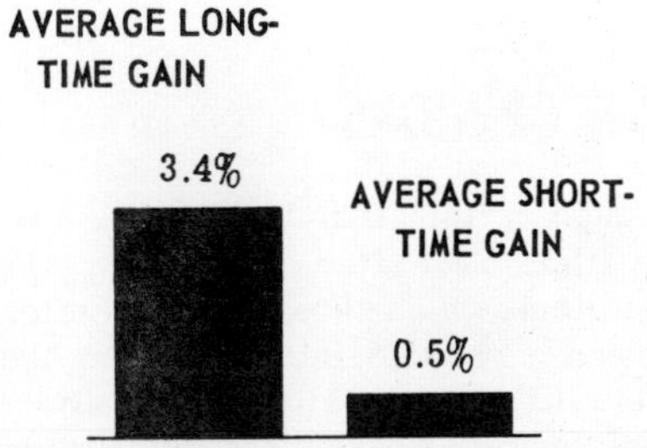

AVERAGE LONG-
TIME GAIN

3.4%

AVERAGE SHORT-
TIME GAIN

0.5%

Fig. 5-4. Percent difference between long-time and short-time gains on 11 general opinion items. (Hovland, Lumsdaine & Sheffield, 1949)

Need More Research on Time Effects

As Hovland, Lumsdaine and Sheffield point out, such findings are important methodologically and theoretically, and suggest the desirability of further research. For example, at which point in time should the effects of a film, or any educational device be measured? The investigators suggest that their findings on short-time and long-time effects on opinion items, may be due to a mixture of two factors; (1) a greater retention of general ideas (or attitudes) as compared with specific ideas; (2) a tendency for slow development, or "reminiscence" effect, in the forming of certain opinions or ideas.

Effects on Opinions Varied with Educational Level

An analysis of the short-time and long-time effects on the eight opinion items showing gains with time was made in terms of four educational levels. Four of the items were found to be "informed" opinions (positively correlated initially with educational level) and the other four "uninformed" opinions (negatively correlated initially with educational level). In the case of the "informed" opinions, the long-time minus the short-time index of effectiveness rose sharply with higher educational levels. In the case of the "uninformed" opinions, this difference rose sharply for lower educational levels. In other words, the "informed" opinions showed greater gains with time among the better educated; and the "uninformed" opinions showed greater gains with time among the less well educated (pp. 190-193).

Retention May Reflect Initial Acceptance

This and other analyses are interpreted by the investigators as favoring a "predisposition hypothesis" to the effect ". . .that degree of retention of opinion changes and the extent to which effects increase with lapse of time is in part a function of initial predisposition to accept the opinion affected" (p. 196).

SUMMARY

Variables Modify Film Influence on Opinions

The data on the influences of motion pictures on opinions appear to be in accord with the conclusions which may be drawn from previous attitude studies. These data serve to emphasize that film influence on opinions can be modified by a number of variables. In general, these variables are problems concerning the difference in effects on specific and general opinions; the length of time the influence persists; the way attitudes change with time; and the nature of intervening processes involved in this change.

Related to the processes involved in opinion changes with time is the predisposition hypothesis of Hovland, Lumsdaine, and Sheffield (they say that retention may be influenced by an initial tendency to accept the opinion).

This hypothesis is consistent with our hypothesis regarding the influences of films on motivation, namely, that specific motion pictures are perhaps more effective in stimulating or reinforcing existing motives than in reorganizing these motives.

Considering the chapter as a whole, the data assembled on the influences of motion pictures on motivation, attitudes, and opinions achieve a consistency when examined in terms of the general concepts briefly sketched in the introduction to this chapter. The general principles which appear to apply to the effectiveness of films in influencing conduct motivation seem also to apply to their effects on verbally expressed attitudes and opinions.

Audience Characteristics Influence Film Effectiveness

In light of the research data and psychological theory, it is becoming increasingly evident that the ability of any medium of communication, including motion pictures, to modify motivation, attitudes, and opinions lies not so much in the medium itself, but in the relationship of the content and bias of the medium to (1) the personality structure of the perceiving individuals, and (2) the social environment of the audience.

Any medium of communication is exactly that -- a medium of communication. In the process of communication the role of a communicator is not to impress his interpretation of experience on an audience. Rather, it involves the reaction of the audience to the communicator's interpretation of experience which he transmits by means of symbols. Hence, the content of communication, the audience predisposition, and the social milieu must all be consistent and mutually reinforcing, if the motion picture is to influence motivation, attitudes, and opinions.

CHAPTER VI

INSTRUCTIONAL VALUE OF FILMS COMPARED WITH OTHER MEDIA AND METHODS OF INSTRUCTION

INTRODUCTION

Differences Between Early and Later Studies

A great many studies on instructional films have been concerned with the amount of informational and conceptual learning that resulted when the films were (1) added to existing methods of teaching, or (2) compared with some other special instructional aid or method.

In considering the trend of the results of studies comparing the effectiveness of motion picture films and other methods of instruction, one should keep in mind that the early films were far below present-day quality and that many of the studies were made ten, twenty, or even thirty years ago. The findings of studies conducted prior to 1929 are based on the use of silent films and, hence, cannot be considered to apply directly to sound films until verified by parallel studies with the newer medium. However, many of the instructional advantages of pictures, and especially of moving pictures, should be common to both silent and sound films. A certain amount of generalization is therefore possible; yet, actually, the final proof must come from careful research.

Deficiencies of Early Studies

The earlier studies were subject to a number of limitations. The samplings of students were, at times, relatively small, but even when large samples were used, the controls in the experimental design were frequently inadequate. Objectives were ill-defined and, consequently, poorly measured. The statistical reliability of the findings was frequently ignored or taken for granted, and published reports do not give enough data to permit a check on reliability at this late date.

Many of the films used in early experimental investigations were produced by industrial concerns for advertising purposes, and instructional efficiency was sometimes subordinated to sales appeal.

Improvement in Later Techniques

Later film research tends to be more nearly free of these limitations. Research objectives are defined more clearly and a greater number of variables are controlled in a particular study. Some studies have extended over long periods of time, permitting several films to be integrated within the units of study, and permitting the measurement of cumulative effects. More studies have measured delayed retention, or the "long-time effects" of motion-picture instruction, as well as immediate results. The retention of learning is a crucial test of effectiveness for, if immediate benefits disappear after two or three months, one may well ask, "Why go to all the expense and bother of making and using instructional films?"

An outstanding characteristic of the later studies is that they have made use of better educational films, such as those produced by the United States Army during World War II. Moreover, within the last decade, studies on the effectiveness of various filmic characteristics have used two or more experimental versions of the same film. This is the direction motion-picture research has taken at Yale University, at the Pennsylvania State College, and elsewhere.

Over-Generalization a Common Research Fault

Because of the differences between the early and more recent studies and other reasons which we will indicate from time to time, there is some inconsistency in the accumulated results of motion-picture research. Some workers in film research seem susceptible to a common tendency among research workers to over-generalize their experimental results and to praise or condemn a given medium or a given technique without regard to the context (student-instructor-subject-environment pattern) in which it is to be used.

PLAN OF THE CHAPTER

Much experimental work has been done comparing the amount of learning from films with the amount of learning from other methods of instruction. This chapter presents many of the studies on the instructional value of films, especially in teaching factual information.

For convenience, this inquiry has been arranged into six parts:

I.   Films combined with usual methods of instruction vs. usual methods of instruction

II. Films alone, or with comments or study guides, vs. usual methods of instruction

III. Films vs. other special illustrative and printed materials

IV. Films vs. demonstrations or lectures, especially in the sciences and military training

V.   Extensive use of films vs. usual methods

VI. Films vs. filmstrips and slides

Part I investigates the amount of additional learning that results when films are added to the usual procedure of instruction. The studies on silent films and sound films are discussed separately.

Part II considers the effectiveness of films when used alone or with comments or guides, as compared with usual methods of instruction.

Part III compares the learning that results from use of films with the learning from special illustrative and printed materials. By "special" is meant that visual-aid materials were used, making the demonstration or lecture more elaborate than the usual form. As in Part I, the studies presented here are segregated according to their use of silent or sound films.

Part IV surveys the comparative amounts of learning (especially in the sciences and in military training) from films and from demonstrations and lectures. The inquiry parallels the one in Part III, but with two major differences: (1) the lectures and demonstrations referred to in Part IV make no use of special visual-aid materials, but consider only "run-of-the-mill" demonstration techniques, and (2) the subject matter taught is mostly in the area of the sciences.

Part V presents the studies which investigate the amount of learning from the extensive use of films. It attempts to answer the question of how successfully a subject can be taught if practically all the course instruction is conducted by means of films instead of by the typical pattern of lectures, demonstrations, and assigned readings.

Part VI compares the teaching effectiveness of motion pictures with that of other film devices such as filmstrips and slides.

A summary at the end of each Part presents the conclusions that we have drawn from the accumulation of published research data. These conclusions, as well as those in the individual studies are discussed with continual reference to the differences between the earlier and more recent studies, emphasizing the difference in experimental techniques and the instructional shortcomings of the early film material.

PART I.   FILMS PLUS USUAL METHODS OF INSTRUCTION COMPARED WITH USUAL METHODS OF INSTRUCTION

By "usual methods" of instruction, we mean the instruction procedure which is usual for the particular teacher or teachers involved in the investigation but excluding the use of films. Usual instruction may consist of some form of the assigned textbook-study and recitation formula, including possible discussions,

demonstrations, and the use of blackboards and other illustrative materials. At times, though less frequently, usual instruction may consist of a more unified project or problem-type of guided learning with the student participating to some extent in the planning.

SECTION 1. SILENT FILMS

WOOD AND FREEMAN STUDY

B. D. Wood and F. N. Freeman (1929) undertook an extensive investigation under a grant from the Eastman Kodak Company to determine the contribution of silent motion pictures used as an integral part of classroom teaching procedure. One of their four objectives was to study the possible increase in factual learning which could be attributed to the films.

Experimental Design

Twenty silent films especially produced for classroom use, including a geography series for the fourth-, fifth-, and sixth-grade students and a general science series for junior high school students, were used in this study. Each film series was used during a ten-week instruction period. Study guides and teacher guides were prepared for the use of both film and non-film groups.

About 11,000 pupils from 12 of the larger school systems in the United States were tested. The subjects for the control and experimental (film plus usual methods) groups were selected by means of a "judicious" randomizing rather than by a matched-group procedure, in order to balance school grade, intelligence, and neighborhood environment. However, preliminary testing showed that the film group had an appreciable initial handicap both in intelligence and knowledge.

Findings

On objective tests of factual knowledge acquired during the instructional periods, it was found that the film group excelled the average of the usual-methods group in both geography and general science. The superiority of the film group on objective tests of factual knowledge is illustrated in Fig. 6-1. As shown in Fig. 6-2, a similar superiority was found for the film group on essay tests of geography and general science.

Here is some evidence that, even with an initial handicap, students in these grades did learn more factual information about these topics when silent instructional films designed for classroom use were added to the usual teaching materials and procedures.

DAVIS STUDY

H. C. Davis (1932) made a study based on data which she took from four of the units of the Wood and Freeman study.

Experimental Design

She analyzed ten per cent of the essay test papers for four units by matching papers from the experimental and control groups on the basis of intelligence and noting differences in the types of informational items mentioned and in the number of irrelevant and omitted answers.

Findings

The film group was superior in mentioning items shown in the film, whereas the control group was superior on items not shown in the film. The film group was distinctly superior on items dealing with action or activity, (the great majority of which were shown in the film), since 61.5 per cent of items in the essay test papers of the film group were of the "action" type, whereas only 22.4 per cent of the items mentioned by the control group were of that type. Here we see an often repeated pattern of response which indicates the specific nature of film influence on learning.

Fig. 6-1. Percent of film group surpassing average score of non-film group on objective tests. (Wood & Freeman, 1929)

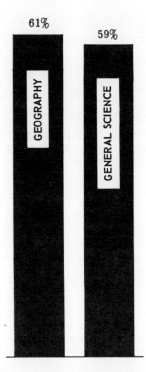

61% 59%

GEOGRAPHY GENERAL SCIENCE

Fig. 6-2. Percent of film group surpassing average score of non-film group on essay-type tests. (Wood & Freeman, 1929)

The control group did not predominantly mention one type of item as did the film group. The highest percentage for the control group, 28.5 per cent, was in the "qualities or characteristics" category. There was no consistent trend in all four units studies for the films to reduce erroneous ideas, although seven of the nine questions for which the film group had fewer erroneous ideas were of the descriptive type.

MOUNT STUDY

In J. N. Mount's study (1931) a comparison was made of the effectiveness of films vs. supplementary reading at the beginning and again at the end of each of five units of study in high school physics dealing with electricity, the units being taught in the conventional manner with this exception. Altogether, 15 films were used. The experimental and control groups each consisted of 24 pupils.

Findings

There was evidence of a slight superiority of the film group in tests measuring factual knowledge. This superiority appeared in only three of five units. (An error in Mount's report makes it appear that no study unit was significantly in favor of the reading group, although, actually, one unit was clearly in favor of the latter group.)

GATTO STUDY

D. Gatto (1933) compared the effectiveness of motion pictures added to other visual aids (such as stereographs and slides) with that of supplementary reading in the teaching of fifth-grade geography classes. The visual aids were used as an integral part of the instruction.

Findings

His results showed that the film group was superior in factual knowledge in both immediate and delayed testing five weeks later. The advantage of the film group was especially pronounced in the delayed testing, in that it gained an additional 11 per cent while the non-film group lost 11 per cent. In the interpretation of geographical materials, such as maps and graphs, the addition of the film was of no benefit.

McCOWEN STUDY

M. C. McCowen (1940) studied the value of 15 silent films in the teaching of two units of seventh-grade general science.

Findings

In the case of his two small groups he found that the group in which films and slides were used gained more than the "non-visual" group. This was especially true in the unit in which 11 films were used as compared with the unit in which only four films were used.

WISE STUDY

H. A. Wise (1939) used ten of the Yale Chronicles of America Photoplays (from the same series used by Knowlton and Tilton (1929) in the junior high school study) in a study of the contribution of these silent films to the teaching of American history in the senior high school.

Experimental Design

Wise felt that his study would add to the Knowlton and Tilton study since it involved senior high school pupils, and that it would be less artificial than their study, since the teachers were not given a specially prepared course of study and were therefore free to use the films when and how they saw fit. He set out to evaluate the films as an accessory to the usual classroom instruction. The teachers were told to keep the work of their experimental and control classes as nearly identical as possible without making it artificially so. Wise felt that the presence of observers and checkers in the classrooms in the Knowlton and Tilton study was an artificial factor, and so he did not use them in his study. In the control classes teachers might use other visual aids and special instructional materials so long as they did not show motion pictures.

Over 800 students in 28 eleventh-grade history classes, taught by nine teachers in five towns representing a cross section of midwestern United States, were originally tested. From this group were selected 218 pairs matched on sex, grade, teacher, IQ, and initial score on a standardized American history test.

Measurement of effectiveness of the ten films used through the semester was obtained in terms of: (1) gains on the Columbia Research Bureau American History Test; (2) objective tests constructed for each of the six units of the semester; (3) an essay test designed to measure factual information; and (4) letters written by the pupils to a suggested personage involved in some event of the historical period studied, to test their ability to re-create the spirit and atmosphere of that period. In addition, to measure the interests developed during the course of the semester, he used: (1) a preference test in which the pupils selected the five most interesting items in each of four lists of 20 items, consisting respectively of personages, groups, places, and events; (2) a ranking of pupils' interest in school subjects at beginning and end of the semester; and (3) the amount of voluntary reading reported during the semester.

Findings

The film groups showed greater mean gains on all six unit tests, varying from .14 to .36 of the sigma of the distribution of gains. The total gain on the tests for the combined units was reliably higher for the film group (diff/PE diff was 10.68), but only 2.78 points higher than that of the control group. This mean gain was .36 of the sigma of the distribution of total gains. It is interesting, as mentioned in the McCowen study just described, that the greatest gain was in the unit in which most films were shown, in this case 13 reels as compared with nine, four, and three reels in other units.

On the Columbia American History Test the film group had a reliably higher mean gain (diff/PE diff of 6.16) of 3.51 points which was .25 of the sigma of the distribution of gains.

On the essay test the film group got reliably higher ratings on both factual information and ability to re-create the atmosphere of a historical period.

On the preference test, (1) the film group ranked the personages of the films reliably higher in comparison with the non-film personages than did the control group, (2) no reliable difference appeared when the film and non-film groups ranked groups of people, (3) the film group showed a reliably higher preference than did the control group for places shown in the films as compared with non-film places, (4) the film group showed a greater interest than did the control group in film-presented events as compared with non-film events.

In the ranking of six school subjects taught during the semester, the film group showed a slightly reliable tendency (diff/PE diff of 1.60) to rank history higher at the end of the semester than at the beginning, as compared with the control group.

In voluntary reading there was a mean difference of 191.6 pages in favor of the film group. This difference was 20.5 per cent of the average mean of the two groups.

In summary, Wise presents evidence that the Chronicles of America Photoplays, consisting of a total of 32 reels, used during the semester as supplementary aids to the regular teaching procedure, produced small, but consistently higher gains in each of the six units of the semester's work. The films resulted in a small, but reliably greater, gain in the Columbia American History Test, which was designed to measure a much broader area than the six units of the semester. In addition, the films increased interest in certain personages, places, and events; produced more voluntary reading; and resulted in a slight tendency to rate history higher among subjects studied that semester.

MONTELBANO STUDY

D. Montelbano (1941) found that 17 teacher-produced silent films were definitely effective in teaching seventh-grade pupils the "informational," "psychological," and "social utility" aspects of mathematics.

Experimental Design

His experimental and control groups consisted of 212 pupils each in four New York City junior high schools. The films were each shown at least three times, though some were shown as many as six times. Several of the films contained problems which the pupils solved; they were then told the correct answers. The films included, for example, problems on paying electricity and gas bills, shopping, planning train trips and reading time tables.

Findings

The film groups showed only a slight tendency to be better in the "computational" aspects of arithmetic as measured by the Woody-McCall Mixed Fundamentals Test. The films were not designed to teach this phase of arithmetic, hence, no great effect in this direction is to be expected, especially since this phase depends so much upon extensive practice.

DUNKERLEY STUDY

G. Dunkerley (1941) studied the effectiveness of four silent films dealing with the blood, the function of eyes, and other physiological topics, with 20 equated pairs of 12- and 13-year old Scottish children.

Findings

He found that the films were effective in producing more learning than were usual methods in a five-week unit on the human body. The superiority of the film group was 16.3 per cent of the mean of the control group on an immediate test and 19.7 per cent on a test seven weeks later. The author claims that test questions were designed to require understanding and application of basic principles and not just recall of specific facts. No samples of the questions are given, however.

* * * * *

Before we turn to the study of the effectiveness of sound films as supplementary aids to usual instructional methods, some studies should be mentioned in which no beneficial effect from the use of the silent films was found.

HOEFER AND KEITH STUDIES

C. Hoefer and E. Keith (1924), in one of the early Chicago experiments, studied the effect of silent films in teaching units on health to upper elementary grade pupils.

Experimental Design (1)

In one study, 691 fifth-grade pupils in 26 different classes were used. Both experimental and control groups received oral instruction based on the film titles and made scrapbooks of picture illustrations of various points of the lessons. The experimental group was shown eight films; the control group used the same amount of time to review material covered.

Findings (1)

The oral instruction group gained slightly more information. The film group showed a slight improvement in some health habits (more milk, less coffee and tea), but the films had no differential effect on hours of sleep, open-window sleeping, or brushing of teeth.

Experimental Design (2)

In another study, 170 seventh- and eighth-grade pupils were divided into experimental and control groups on the basis of intelligence, and were taught health material presented in two of the films used in the previous experiment. The first film, The Knowing Gnome, stressed the need for sufficient sleep, drinking water, the value of milk as a food, and sleeping in fresh air. The general theme of the second film, Mrs. Brown and the High Cost of Living, was the need for a well-balanced diet. The non-film group was taught the principles contained in the subtitles of the films by use of a blackboard. No illustrative material was used. The time devoted to the lessons in the control group was equal to the time required to run the films for the experimental group.

Findings (2)

At the conclusion of both instructional programs, the two groups were practically identical in the information test, the only measure of effectiveness used. The authors state that the films were probably more entertaining than instructive for these seventh- and eighth-grade pupils, thus suggesting the lack of differential effect. After noting the description and sample illustrations from The Knowing Gnome, the present reviewers are inclined to agree.

FREEMAN AND HOEFER STUDY

F. N. Freeman and C. Hoefer (1931) report a study with 207 fifth- and sixth-grade pupils on the effectiveness of two silent films in a 13-day unit on care of the teeth. Groups were matched on intelligence and on an information pre-test.

Findings

It was found that the films produced no greater increase in information. This might have been expected, since, from the description given, these films appear to be primarily motivational. However, 16.7 per cent more of the experimental group reported brushing their teeth daily, and more of this group brought in articles, clippings, and posters related to the topic, thus supporting the assumption that the films were more motivational than informational.

Whether or not the film really affected health habits is problematical, since socio-economic status, which could have a definite influence on daily brushing of the teeth, was not controlled in the experiment. Ninety-nine and ninety-eight per cent of the two groups reported owning tooth brushes, however.

SECTION 2. SOUND FILMS

RULON STUDY

P. J. Rulon (1933), whose experiment was described in Chapter III, studied the effectiveness of adding eight specially produced sound films to the usual teaching of a six-week unit on The Earth and Its People.

Experimental Design

This study was carried out with large groups of ninth-grade general science pupils in three New England cities. Experimental and control groups were equated by a correlation-matching technique on the basis of intelligence and previous knowledge of science.

The film group studied the text for fewer hours, devoting part of the time to viewing the films.

Findings

At the conclusion of the unit it was found that the film group exceeded the control group in total test score by 20.5 per cent, (CR of 5.4). On retention tests given three months later, the difference was even greater, the film group exceeding the control group by 38.5 per cent in total score on the information test items.

Evaluation

It should be noted that six of the eight films had been specially produced to conform to or integrate with a given topic of the textbook which, in turn, had been written specially to serve the purposes of this investigation. Despite this effort to integrate instructional materials, the advantage of the film group, though it appeared large percentage-wise and had a statistically reliable difference, was not excessive. For example, on the immediate test total scores the raw score difference in favor of the film group was only one-fourth of the SD of the distribution of the text group.

ARNSPIGER STUDY

Another one of the earlier and more extensive investigations of the effectiveness of sound films as aids to instruction was made by V. C. Arnspiger (1933).

Experimental Design

Approximately 950 pupils from 32 fifth-grade classes of five cities in three different states were used. Four units on natural science were studied. The topics of these units and their respective films were: butterflies, beetles, amphibians, and growth of plants.

Also, four units of music instruction were studied with seventh-grade pupils, the experimental groups ranging from 462 to 593 pupils per unit and the control groups ranging from 501 to 572 pupils per unit. The schools used in these units were in the same five cities as for the natural science units. The music units and their corresponding films were: the string choir, the woodwind choir, the brass choir, and the percussion group.

Classes assigned to experimental and control groups were matched as closely as possible in intelligence and in initial knowledge in the four units to be taught. This matching was effected fairly well in each of the five schools, and to an even better degree in total scores. In the case of the science units, there was a slight, but scarcely reliable, advantage in intelligence for the experimental groups (CR of 1.88), and in knowledge for the control groups (CR of 1.13) on the pre-tests. In the case of the music units, there was a slight and reliable advantage both in intelligence (CR, 3.06), and in knowledge (CR, 2.90) for the control groups. For music at least, there was a slight "stacking of the cards" against the film groups.

The purpose of this study was to investigate the additional contribution that these films themselves might make to the effectiveness of the usual classroom methods when integrated with these methods. It therefore seemed desirable to eliminate any transfer of teaching method suggested by the films from an experimental to a control class through the teachers. Accordingly the equated-teacher method was used and this required a sufficient number of teachers to balance differences in teaching ability which may have been overlooked by the supervisors who equated teachers for the study.

Both experimental and control teachers were given identical manuals which served as guides in the teaching of each unit and offered suggestions for enrichment of pupil learning. The teachers of the control groups were free to use any instructional devices available except motion pictures. Each unit involved 150 minutes of instruction. The science units each consisted of five 30-minute periods, the experimental groups witnessing three ten-minute picture showings of the same film on the first, third, and fifth periods, respectively. The music units each consisted of three 45-minute periods plus a concluding 15-minute instructional period; the experimental groups saw the film three times, once during each period of the unit. A unit was not taught on consecutive school days, but was extended for as long as two weeks.

Subject matter tests (constructed by the specialists who had developed the units) were used, composed of various types of objective items, including some graphic identification exercises. In these tests, the pupils were required to recognize certain phases of animal or plant life, and in the case of the music units, certain specific elements of the orchestral instruments.

Thus a comparison was made in the amount of learning from the non-film method of instruction and a method using films. Note that, in the film method, teacher-instruction time was reduced by 20 per cent to allow for the three showings of the instructional films.

Findings

In the case of the science units, the film groups showed fairly sizable and reliably greater gains on each unit on the immediate tests; the mean gain in the total science score for the film groups was 25.9 per cent more than the control groups and .69 of the SD of the distribution of gains of the control groups. In the recall test, given four weeks after the completion of the last unit and ten weeks after completion of the first unit, the experimental group was still superior, but to a lesser degree, 15.6 per cent.

In the case of the music units, the film groups were also reliably superior in each unit on the immediate tests; the mean gain in the total music score for the film groups was 26.9 per cent superior to the control groups' score and .96 of the SD of the distribution of gains of the control group. In the recall tests, given four weeks after completion of the last unit, the superiority was still present to the extent of 21.8 per cent.

Evaluation

An analysis of the test items used showed that 60 per cent of the science test items and 69 per cent of the music test items were items given by both teacher instruction and the film. The superiority of the science film group in total score on immediate tests was entirely due to this fact, since this group was 51.9 per cent superior on the film-teacher items, but showed no superiority on the non-film items, which constituted the remaining 40 per cent of the test. In the case of the music groups, the film group was 31.3 per cent superior on the film-teacher items and 15 per cent superior on the non-film items.

It is important to bear in mind that the above benefits of the sound film came as the result of three separate showings of each film on three different days, taking up one-fifth of the time devoted to instruction on the unit.

EADS AND STOVER STUDY

A study of sound motion pictures which apparently antedated Arnspiger's, since he describes it, (but lists it as undated and unpublished), was that conducted by L. Eads and E. M. Stover (1936).*

Experimental Design

One phase of their study on the value of the Erpi film, Individual Differences in Arithmetic, in teaching graduate students about diagnostic work in arithmetic, falls in the category of the present group of studies. They compared the effectiveness of two instructional combinations: (1) assigned reading in an illustrated monograph plus class discussion, and (2) assigned reading, class discussion and two showings of the twenty-minute film.

Findings

The combination of assigned reading, class discussion, and two showings of the film was slightly reliably better than the reading and discussion, in terms of a test given several days later (CR of 1.94).** Apparently they used two film showings in this part of their study because they had previously found that one showing of the picture plus assigned reading was no better than assigned reading alone, whereas two showings of the picture plus assigned reading was considerably better than assigned reading alone.

LAPP STUDY

C. J. Lapp (1939) has reported a study of the value of the sound film, The Molecular Theory of Matter, as a device for reviewing the molecular theory.

Experimental Design

An experimental group of 40 students saw two showings of the film and received comments by the teacher between showings. The control group of 36 students did not see the film, but the report does not make it clear whether they had an oral review or not. Both sections took the same final examination for the semester, which contained 103 items, 29 of which had a bearing on the film material.

Findings

There was a difference (CR, 4.4) in the case of these 29 items in favor of the film group, but on the remainder of the test whose content was not covered by the film, the control group averaged six points higher than the film group. This largely or entirely counteracts the apparent value of the film.

BAKER STUDY

W. K. Baker (1940) compared the effectiveness of ten to 16 sound and silent films with the conventional method of teaching four to five units of general science. Two small matched classes of ninth-grade students were used for each half of the experiment.

Findings

No significant differences were found when the films were used by the instructor at times which he judged appropriate. However, when each film was used as a summary of a unit topic and the students were required to pass in a summary of the film on the next day, the film group was reliably better in three out of four units. Apparently the control group did no writing of a summary paragraph. If it had done so, there might have been no advantage for the film group, although the control group did engage in a teacher-pupil oral summary for the same length of time as that used in showing the film.

BELL, CAIN, AND LAMOREAUX STUDY

R. Bell, L. F. Cain, and L. A. Lamoreaux (1941), studied the effect of eight March of Time films about the role of government in conservation and consumer protection, upon the informational learning of fifth-, seventh-, ninth-, and eleventh-grade pupils.

Experimental Design

The pupils were divided into matched groups of from 58 to 90 pupils each. The film commentaries were used by both experimental and control groups and

---

* The copy of their lithoprinted report available to the present reviewers was so dated. Other reviewers have listed 1932 for an unpublished report of the study from Teachers College, Columbia University. Our copy came from Encyclopaedia Britannica Films, Inc.

** In their report a difference between means is given as 11.16 points, but the calculated difference is only 6.16 points. The CR is calculated correctly.

a mimeographed statement of the content of each film was provided for the control groups. All other supplementary materials ordinarily used in teaching the units were employed.

Findings

The fifth grade showed an increment in favor of the films which was significant almost at the five per cent level. The seventh grade showed a still more reliable difference for the films, well under the one per cent level. The same was true for the eleventh grade, but in the ninth grade there was no difference between the film and non-film groups.

The experimenters were also studying change in attitudes (as mentioned in the previous chapter). It is interesting to note that this ninth-grade group, which showed no increment in information as a result of the films, was the group which showed the most reliable change in attitude as a result of the films.

POTTHOFF, LARSON, AND PATTERSON STUDY

C. J. Potthoff, L. C. Larson, and D. O. Patterson (1940) investigated the use of sound films on human biology with low-academic college students in the General College of the University of Minnesota.

Findings

They reported no reliable increases in information, but measures of interest in human biology were greater for the film group than for the non-film group.

WILSON, LARSON, AND LORD STUDY

E. C. Wilson, L. C. Larson, and F. Lord (1940) studied informational and conceptual learning of current history at the general college level from the use of six March-of-Time-type films on the background of World War II.

Findings

They reported a learning increment reliable at the five per cent level. These films, however, produced no greater shift in attitude than the regular teaching without films. Both film and non-film groups shifted in attitudes in accordance with the objectives of the course.

VERNON STUDY

P. E. Vernon (1946) studied the use of a sound film and a silent filmstrip in training British seamen to take soundings with a lead line and a Kelvin sounding machine.

Findings

He found that, when either the film or the filmstrip was incorporated into the usual instruction, the learning increase, as measured by knowledge of facts and principles, averaged about eight per cent, with the same statistical reliability in both cases.

Using analysis of covariance with his 732 men from 22 different classes, he found that about the same amount of improvement could also be attributed to good teaching as opposed to poor teaching, regardless of the type of instruction used with the group. An improvement of five per cent could also be attributed to above-average intelligence as compared with below-average intelligence, regardless of the type of instruction used. Apparently the film or filmstrip could largely compensate for the weakness of a poor instructor. What the visual medium might add to the increment with a good instructor could not be determined from the data. Apparently the increment from the film was no greater than that due to a good instructor without the film.

HEIDGERKEN STUDY

L. E. Heidgerken (1948) made a study of teaching two units of the course in nursing arts to pre-clinical nursing students in 12 schools of nursing in the State of Indiana.

Experimental Design

The units of instruction were: cardinal signs and symptoms, and therapeutic uses of heat and cold. She compared: (1) the use of sound films integrated with conventional methods of instruction with the conventional methods alone; (2) filmstrips made from the films plus conventional methods with conventional methods alone; (3) films and filmstrips plus conventional methods with conventional methods alone.

The films used were the U. S. Office of Education films, Vital Signs and Their Interrelation, and Therapeutic Uses of Heat and Cold. The two films were designed to illustrate and demonstrate principles underlying certain nursing activities, rather than to teach any specific techniques or procedures.

In each of these comparisons, the use of each medium at two different predetermined times in the unit was compared, for example, films at the beginning and middle of the unit, and films at the middle and end of the unit. Tests measuring response to situations, knowledge of facts and principles, and technical vocabulary were used as pre-tests and post-tests for each unit.

Findings

Using analysis of variance in the treatment of the data, she found: (1) no significant differences between any of the three special aid combinations (films, filmstrips, film and filmstrips) and the conventional methods of teaching these units; (2) no significant differences between the different times of using the special aids.

BENTLEY STUDY

R. R. Bentley (1949) investigated the contribution of audio-visual aids in teaching three units of vocational agriculture.

Experimental Design

The plan of the units of instruction was: a film and filmstrip combined to instruct in a unit on home gardening; a film with a unit on swine production; and, slides combined with a third unit on pasture production. The film used in the home garden unit was, The Farm Garden, and the filmstrip, Gardening for Victory, Parts I and II. Eight different schools were used. Six independent experiments were run on the first unit, four on the second unit, and two on the third.

Bentley reports that the instructional time in each experimental and control group was equal. It is not clear how much additional instruction was given along with the film or the filmstrip, but apparently some additional instruction was given. Analysis of covariance and the Johnson-Neyman technique were used in treating the data.

Findings

The only unit in which the audio-visual aids gave evidence of being a benefit was in the home garden unit, and then, only in part. In the immediate post-test of informational learning, the mean of the experimental group was reliably higher than that of the control group. This advantage did not show up on the second part of the test, the part designed to measure applicational learning. Furthermore, the superiority of the experimental group on the immediate test was not repeated on the retention test, given at some unspecified later date, since the two groups were equivalent.

Evaluation

The article from which this review is written does not state how often the films were shown to the groups. If there was only one showing, then the unit in which the aids were a benefit may have shown such results because both the film and the filmstrip were used, which was not done in the other two units. Using both the film and the filmstrip is somewhat equivalent to two showings of the film; and some studies mentioned above seem to show that two or three showings are sometimes necessary for the supplementary use of the film to produce a learning increment over that from usual methods of teaching.

Bentley's data suggest that with films and filmstrips of the kind used, the effect of several films and/or filmstrips may be cumulative, whereas any one of the films or filmstrips, used alone, might not increase learning reliably. This assumption does not hold entirely, since Bentley used three sets of Kodachrome slides in his pasture production unit without differential results that were statistically reliable.

JOHNSON STUDY

D. A. Johnson (1949) found disappointing evidence of the value of certain films and filmstrips now on the market for the teaching of certain terms and concepts in plane geometry to high school students.

Experimental Design

Twelve schools, all having at least two sections of plane geometry, were selected for the study. Of two instructional units used, the one on circles contained three films and three filmstrips, and the one on loci contained one film and one filmstrip. Experimental and control classes spent the same amount of study time per unit. Excluding the time spent with the film or filmstrip, the experimental classes had the same instruction, the same assignments, the same supplementary projects as the control classes. Guides were furnished the teachers for the experimental classes, describing the use of the film and containing discussion questions and a short test. It is not clear from the article whether a film or filmstrip was shown more than once.

Statistical treatment of the data was made by analysis of covariance and the Johnson-Neyman technique. Some experimental groups saw only films, others only filmstrips, and some groups used both.

Findings

In general, the results were negative because only occasional differences were demonstrated in favor of the film or filmstrip groups. No consistent differences showed up on the immediate tests, but in the retention tests given two months later, the circle-unit group, which had both films and filmstrips, was consistently superior to the control group in all three types of learning measured, namely, informational, problem solving, and applicational. Assuming that a given film was shown only once, then the group which saw more visual material (three films and three filmstrips) benefitted most.

Evaluation

Single Ineffective Films May Have Cumulative Effect

The Johnson study suggests, even more strongly than the Bentley study, that there may be a cumulative learning effect from films or filmstrips that may be ineffective individually. In addition, Johnson points out that training aids, such as films and filmstrips, can be used more effectively if they supplement, but do not markedly overlap, the material presented in the regular class instruction or in the text. Apparently these geometry films, in numerous cases, markedly overlapped the material dealt with by the instructor and the text. He also suggests that instructional films should be subjected to some experimental validation before they are released. On this point, Bentley comments that no hybrid corn is recommended without a careful experimental measure of its yielding ability.

SUMMARY

From these studies of the instructional effectiveness of films plus usual instructional methods as compared with usual methods of instruction, it is possible to draw several conclusions about the amount of increased learning that may be expected from the use of films.

    1.   In the great majority of the studies which can be classified in this section, the addition of films to the usual teaching methods has brought about increased learning.

It should be noted, though, that the showing of a film, any film, is not a guarantee of greater learning. In some studies of the use of films in three or four separate grades of school, or with three or four separate units of study, the addition of the films may aid learning in two or three of the grades, or in some of the unit topics, but, for some inexplicable reasons, the films may be of no benefit in one or two grades or units of the study.

    2.   In a number of the studies of this section in which films were found to be of most benefit, a given film was shown two or three different times under recognized conditions of good utilization. Possibly the lack of repeated showings in some cases may explain the fact that certain films added little or nothing to the learning.

    3.   Some of the studies of this section suggest that where film and text, or film and class teaching, are mutually reinforcing and supplementary to each other, not merely repetitious, the addition of the film is much more likely to be beneficial. In certain cases, the films may have failed to supplement and elaborate the pupil's experience, and thus may account for some of the negative findings mentioned.

    4.   The specific effect of films, noted in Chapter V, is verified in these studies and the dynamics of this effect become increasingly clear. Films transfer only the information they contain, but do not transfer what they do not contain.

In influencing specific information and concepts, motion pictures appear to have a force not ordinarily apparent in other instructional materials. The response to films is less diffused. Actions, people, and situations appear to stand out when they are well presented in films, more so than when presented in comparable textbooks or by other verbal means.

    5.   The influence of effective films added to usual methods of instruction frequently appears in measures of retention, or delayed measures of learning. The superiority of groups taught with films added to other materials, over those taught without films, is often more apparent several weeks or months after instruction than immediately afterward. Sometimes a superiority not evident upon immediate testing shows up later.

Thus, an "effective" film is measured not only in terms of the amount of immediate learning it induces, but also in terms of the length of time the learning is retained. This is a crucial measure of instructional effectiveness. Such findings should be a warning to research workers who are satisfied to give only tests of immediate learning.

    6.   Although films cannot impart factual information they do not contain, they may bring about an increase in motivation (as mentioned in Chapter V) that can spread to other learning.

Two aspects of motivational influence have been noted: (1) In measures of "interest" in the course or in the units being studied, classes taught with the aid of films have frequently been found to excel classes taught without films. (2) Apparently through this motivational influence, an increase in factual learning in classes taught with the aid of films may carry over into a unit in which no films are used. This phenomenon is of some general importance. The same phenomenon was noted in relation to good instructors, i.e., the "morale" of classes taught by good, as contrasted with poor instructors, sometimes carries over into the amount of learning from a given film or filmstrip whether the instructor is present for the presentation of the visual materials or not. It appears that morale has a momentum, and that both the use of films and the use of good instructors have some relationship to academic motivation.

PART II. FILMS ALONE, OR WITH COMMENTS OR GUIDES, COMPARED WITH USUAL METHODS OF INSTRUCTION

In this part, we compare the teaching effectiveness of the film, used by itself, with that of the usual combination of teaching methods. Here, "usual" methods do not include other projected visual media, such as filmstrips or slides. The studies cited here do not evaluate films against one specific medium, such as, lecture, assigned reading, demonstration, or printed booklet. Such comparisons are considered in Parts III and IV.

SHEPHARD STUDY

J. W. Shephard (1922), in one of the early experiments on the effectiveness of films, saw the possibilities of the film alone as a "teacher."

Experimental Design

In the fall of 1919 he started experiments at the University of Wisconsin in which he compared the effectiveness of a 26-minute silent film with that of an average teacher and of a superior teacher in teaching certain topics to small, approximately matched groups of high school students. The instructional procedure favored the superior teacher. The average teacher knew nothing about the experiment, and was only told to conduct the class parallel to the film material. On the other hand, the superior teacher was told about the experiment and was permitted to view the film some days before the teaching.

In his first study the topic was Elements of Map Reading, and a film of the same title was used. The film, produced by the Bray Studios, was described by the investigator as "one of the best educational films to date." The test, which showed Shephard's insight into the testing of film learning, involved three parts. The students were required to draw the things they had learned, apply their knowledge by answering direct questions, and, locate geographical places and interpret parts of maps.

A second study with a different topic and different teachers was carried out. This time, the two-reel film included three topics, The Telephone, Mars, and The Birth of the Earth.

Findings

In the first study he found the film to be almost as good as the superior teacher and slightly better than the average teacher. In the second study he found that the film had a reliable and sizable advantage over both average and superior teachers, with a slight tendency for the superior teacher to be better than the average teacher.

The investigator says, without quoting any further data, that since the above results were secured, the experiment was repeated twice in Oklahoma under varying conditions with practically the same results. The actual data reported in the article are only suggestive, since the number of cases used in the group was so small, but their suggestiveness is significant and fits in with the findings of more recent studies.

Shephard speculates (as early as 1922) about the possibility of using films instead of mediocre teachers to present certain material, thereby making the teaching of large groups of students a more economical procedure. It is significant that a basic problem of current armed-service film research, the use of films for rapid mass education, was conceived and investigated with positive results in 1922.

ROSENTHAL STUDY

N. H. Rosenthal (1945), in charge of visual education for the Royal Australian Air Force, reported a study comparing films and an instructor.

Experimental Design

His experimental population consisted of 275 trainees, divided into groups of about 30 each. One-third was taught a topic by instructor alone, another third by film alone, and the remaining third, by instructor and film. The film used is described as a good, well-edited, sound training film, although the investigator fails to state the exact topic of the film.

Findings

On tests given two weeks after the showing of the film, it was found that of those who were trained with either the film alone or the instructor alone, 76 per cent made scores which could be considered "passing" or better. Of those who were trained with both film and instructor, 90 per cent "passed." The effectiveness of the film was most pronounced in reducing the number of very low scores on the test. Examination of the papers showed that in the case of those who had seen the film, the majority drew diagrams to illustrate their answers, generally showed clearer understanding of the principles, and gave less stereotyped answers. After a period of three months, written answers on the same topic by "students who had seen the film maintained standard, whilst the answers of those who had not seen the film definitely deteriorated" (p. 10).

VERNON STUDY

The study by P. E. Vernon (1946) on teaching British seamen to take soundings has already been mentioned (Chapter III).

Findings

The groups which had two separate showings of the film, but no other instruction, were six per cent inferior when compared with groups which had usual instruction without a film. However, it must be noted that the "normal" groups had three hours of instruction, while the film-alone groups had only 50 minutes of instruction. Also noteworthy is the fact that the film-alone classes were almost as good as the usual classes with weak instructors, but were definitely inferior to classes with good instructors. "Thus an hour's film appears to be as effective as three hours (of) weak oral instruction" (p. 156).

HALSEY STUDY

J. H. Halsey (1936) made a study which did not involve the use of films alone, but which is somewhat analogous.

Experimental Design

One of his experimental groups of ninth-grade pupils was taught a unit on insular possessions of the United States through informal lecture-discussion, based on motion pictures and slides, with no textbook, no homework, and no outside assignments. Three small groups, matched in intelligence and geographical knowledge, were used.

Findings

The control group taught in the usual way gained 90 per cent; an experimental group taught in the usual way, but aided by the use of films and slides, gained 133 per cent, whereas the other experimental group, whose discussion was based on films and slides alone, gained 191 per cent.

CAMERON STUDY

V. E. Cameron (1933) investigated the teaching of high school physics by means of films and usual methods.

Experimental Design

He used 29 pairs of pupils matched on intelligence. In the case of the experimental group, the showing of films, followed by a short question period, replaced the usual lecture-discussion type of class periods. Both groups had the same textbook assignments and four laboratory periods per week. The experimental group saw 70 films during the four quarters of the course.

Findings

In terms of over-all achievement, there was not much difference between the two groups, but there was a slightly reliable tendency (CR of 1.72) for the experimental group to retain more over the entire term's work.

VANDERMEER STUDY

A study by A. W. Vander Meer (1949) for the Instructional Film Research Program was concerned with the use of films as the sole means of instruction. This study, discussed at length later in this chapter, is also pertinent here.

Experimental Design

He studied three matched groups of ninth-grade general science students, using 44 sound films related to four units of science, extending over three months of school. One group simply saw each film twice; another group saw the films twice, supplemented by specially prepared study guides; the control group was taught by the usual methods (without motion pictures).

Findings

On both immediate and three-months' retention tests the films-only group was not reliably worse than either of the other two groups. This films-only group finished the units about four weeks in advance of the other two groups, reducing the instructional time about 20 per cent without a reliable decrement in learning.

SUMMARY

These studies suggest that, for certain topics and for limited objectives in teaching information and concepts, suitable instructional films may be more effective in the instructional process than poor instructors, and at least as effective as average instructors. This generalization is developed further in the next two parts which follow.

PART III. FILMS COMPARED WITH SPECIAL ILLUSTRATIVE AND PRINTED MATERIALS

A persistent problem, of practical importance in terms of both cost and energy, is the relative instructional effectiveness of motion pictures and other visual forms of presentation, such as still pictures, maps, blackboard sketches or illustrations, filmstrips, and the like.

The problems involved here, though fundamental, have not yet been clearly identified. We suggest that the studies on relative film effectiveness involve at least three such problems:

1. The effect on an audience, of the optical projection of a visual form in a darkened or semi-darkened room. This effect enters into the comparison of the effectiveness of motion picture projection with that of blackboard sketches, textbook illustrations, and other modes of visual presentation not involving optical projection.

2. The ability of the audience to "fill-in" or to infer antecedent and subsequent "action" from still pictures presented in some sort of sequence. This ability is involved in the comparison of motion pictures with filmstrips and filmographs (static pictures

photographed on to motion picture film together with a commentary).

3. The amount, kind, mode, and timing of language accompanying any form of visual presentation. This factor is likely to influence the effectiveness of the visual presentation, as has been clearly established in various research studies conducted by the Instructional Film Research Program at the Pennsylvania State College.

Since, as we have pointed out, the components of (1) optical projection, (2) visual inference, and (3) language accompaniment had not been clearly identified, experimental studies of relative effectiveness have been largely empirical, and, in consequence, results are of more "practical" than systematic importance.

SECTION 1. SILENT FILMS

McCLUSKY STUDY

One of the earliest comparisons of films with other visual modes of presentation was that made in the series of experiments submitted as a doctoral thesis by F. D. McClusky (1922) at the University of Chicago. His experiments, which are incorporated in the Chicago studies financed by a Commonwealth Fund grant to the University, are described in briefer form in the report of the Chicago series of studies (Freeman 1924).

Experimental Design (1)

Eight of his 14 experiments would come under the classification of a comparison of the effectiveness of the film with some other illustrative (visual) teaching aid. He used pupils in three different school systems, mostly from the seventh and eighth grades, although, in a few studies, he used pupils down to the fourth-grade level. Results were measured by objective tests and a drawing test. In the latter half of his investigations, retention tests as well as immediate tests were used.

Findings (1)

In the case of a film on French Explorations in North America, he found no difference for two small matched groups between film instruction and oral instruction with maps.

Experimental Design (2)

In another study, two showings of the film were compared with the oral lecture from maps and with an oral lecture which was followed by the film showing. All three methods required the same amount of instructional time.

Findings (2)

In the two different schools in which comparison was made, the lecture from maps or the lecture followed by the film was better than the film alone shown twice. The film-alone group made the lowest map test scores in both schools. Pupils complained that the film went too fast, shifted scenes too quickly, and did not stress the important points sufficiently.

Experimental Design (3)

Using a film containing animated charts describing methods of sewage disposal in two different cities, McClusky compared the results of the film with those from an oral lecture based on the titles of the film and accompanied by charts similar to those of the film.

Findings (3)

The oral lecture with charts was better than the film on both immediate tests and retention tests administered three weeks later, especially for the eighth grade as compared with the seventh-grade groups. The superiority was most noticeable on the chart drawing test.

An analysis of the charts drawn by the pupils showed that the film failed to organize the steps of the two disposal systems as well as the oral method did. This is not necessarily a fault of films in general, but may have indicated a production weakness of that particular film. This suggests that, while a new instructional film is still in the work-print or some earlier stage, it might be desirable to pre-test the film on some classes typical of the intended audience.

Experimental Design (4)

Using a silent film, The Life History of the Monarch Butterfly, in teaching eighth-grade pupils, McClusky compared: the film used alone; a lecture based on six charts copied from the film; and the film accompanied by an oral lecture. Each method of presentation took 12 minutes. Equated groups of 30 pupils were used in each comparison.

Findings (4)

On immediate tests, the lecture and the film plus lecture methods were both, and equally, better than the film-alone method. On retention tests two and a half months later, the film accompanied by the lecture gave the best results, and the other two methods were about equally inferior.

Experimental Design (5)

The effectiveness of the film, The Story of a Mountain Glacier, in which a professional geographer gives a chalk talk on the development and action of a glacier, was compared with that of a chalk talk copied from the film and given by the experimenter in as careful a duplication of content and presentation as possible. This being a silent film, subtitles serve in lieu of the spoken word to accompany the actions of the professor, while in the live chalk talk the instructor gave an oral description as he progressed. The film and the live chalk talk each took 13 minutes. Two equated groups of seventh- and eighth-grade pupils were used. In a repetition of the experiment, another chalk-talk instructor and two groups of fifth- and sixth-grade pupils were used.

Findings (5)

In both experiments, on immediate tests, the live chalk talk was superior, especially with sixth-, seventh-, and eighth-grade pupils.

On retention tests after five weeks, there was no difference between the two presentations, for the fifth and seventh grades, but in the sixth and eighth grades, especially the sixth, the live chalk talk was still superior. It is important to note that, in all four grades, the percentage of loss of the film group was much less than that of the chalk-talk group.

Experimental Design (6)

The same film, The Story of a Mountain Glacier, was compared by McClusky with two other methods of presentation. The first method apparently involved an oral lecture with two wall charts, a blackboard sketch (these duplicated drawings in the film) and, six stereographs. In the second method, five slides were used in addition to the same oral lecture, wall charts, and blackboard sketch as in the first. The slides and stereographs duplicated the scenes from the film as nearly as possible. Since each pupil of the stereograph group had a stereoscope and set of stereographs, all three types of presentation took the same time, 13 minutes. Equated eighth-grade classes of 37 pupils each were used for each type of presentation. Three types of tests were used: short factual questions, drawing a chart, and writing a free composition.

Findings (6)

On immediate tests the groups using the stereographs or slides as part of their instruction were superior to the film group to a large degree in the total score. This was due largely to their performance in the composition part of the tests.

On six-week retention tests, the stereograph and slide groups were still superior to the film group, but to a lesser degree. The groups using the stereographs and slides had equivalent results. As in the previous experiment with the chalk talks and the film, the percentage of loss of the film group was much less than that of the other two groups.

Evaluation

Results such as these several comparisons by McClusky can be interpreted in either of two ways, depending on our concept of the function of an instruc-tional motion picture. If we are committed to the proposition that a film is a teaching aid only, then we may say that a teacher can do as well or better by using another aid or teaching procedure than the particular films of these comparisons. But, if we do not restrict our concept of teaching to a method involving the personal performance of the teacher in face-to-face relation with his class, we may say that these films were slightly inferior, or equal in effectiveness, as the case may be, to teacher presentation of the identical content, and we may qualify such a conclusion in terms of immediate and/or long-range learning effects. Further, we can and must qualify our judgment on effectiveness in terms of the specific learning outcomes measured in the experiment, rather than in terms of all the outcomes that are expected from face-to-face interaction of the teacher and the individuals in the learning group.

FREEMAN, REEDER, AND THOMAS STUDY

Another early comparison between films and visual aids was that made by F. N. Freeman, E. H. Reeder, and J. A. Thomas (1924).

Experimental Design

Facts about railroad expansion in the United States were taught to fifth- through eighth-grade students. The instruction material consisted of maps, charts, and tables which were identical for each type of presentation. The three methods of instruction were: silent film; lectures by teachers using enlarged charts; and reading of material explaining the enlarged charts which the pupil could study during his reading.

Findings

No reliable differences between any of the three methods of presenting the facts contained in these maps, charts, and tables are evident in the investigators' data. The investigators concluded that "the oral lecture, accompanied by maps, tables, and diagrams is superior, both in effectiveness and convenience, to convey information of a more or less general or abstract sort" (p. 274). One might accept the suggestion of convenience, but no objective data are presented to support the claimed superiority of the lecture method.

McCLUSKY AND McCLUSKY STUDY

Another early comparison of films with other modes of presentation was made in the same series of Chicago Studies by F. D. McClusky and H. Y. McClusky (1924A).

Experimental Design

Groups of pupils in the fourth to eighth grades, somewhat comparable in age and intelligence, were taught general science material contained in two films, Lumbering in the North Woods and Iron and Steel. Six methods of presentation were used: (1) silent film,

(2) film plus oral comments during showing, (3) slides with subtitles, (4) slides and oral comments, (5) photographic prints with subtitles, and (6) photographic prints with subtitles and oral instruction. Both the slides and the photographic prints were made from the films. The subtitles on the slides and prints were the same as those on the film. Each method involved the same amount of instruction time. The same teacher taught all groups in a given school.

In the testing technique of this study a variety of measures was used as a basis for evaluating relative effectiveness. Four tests were given each group: a verbal test of the multiple choice type; diagram drawing to show recall of some sequence presented in the film; a picture rearrangement test which required the pupils to arrange a set of small pictures (18 for lumber, 36 for steel) in the order in which they had been viewed in the film; and, a picture identification test.

Findings

No reliable advantage for any of the methods was found. The authors report that "these comparisons show such inconsistent results that the film, slide, and print appear to possess no distinct advantage one over the other as far as these particular experiments are concerned" (p. 257).

JAMES STUDY

Another Chicago Series study by H. W. James (1924) involved a rather careful comparison of silent film presentation with five other methods of presenting the same material.

Experimental Design

These methods were film combined with lecture, "slides,"* oral lecture, reading, film combined with music.

In his main experiment, six films were compared with the other media. The films were: Yellowstone Park, Toads, Lumbering in the North Woods, Through Life's Window (the functioning of the eye), The Mosquito, and Waste Disposal in Cities.

Care was exercised to make the structure and content of the other presentations as similar to the film as possible. The other forms of presentation were limited to the same length of time as the film. Comparable test groups, drawn from the eighth and ninth grades of Detroit schools, were chosen on the basis of the Thorndike-McCall Reading Test scores. Objective tests of sufficient length to have fair reliability were used. Reliabilities of differences were reported in terms of McCall's Experimental Coefficient.

In general, this was one of the more carefully carried out and statistically controlled studies of this early series, yet some of the author's conclusions show a bias favoring films which his statistics do not support.

Findings

For the two films used in comparing films with "filmstrips," James found very slight and unreliable advantages for the films, when scores on two types of objective tests were combined. For one film there was a reliable advantage for the film as measured by the completion test, but no difference on the "yes-no" test. In the case of the other film, the situation was reversed, in that a reliable advantage was found for the film on the yes-no test.

In the one comparison made between a film presentation and reading presentation, a reliable difference was found in favor of the film.

As will be pointed out in the next section, four of James' six comparisons of film and lecture were in favor of the film, while two showed no real difference. His study of the film alone as contrasted with the film accompanied by piano music involved only one film and showed no difference for the groups as a whole. There was an indication, however, that the girls were favorably affected by the music while the boys were distracted by it.

JAYNE STUDY

C. D. Jayne (1944) made a more recent study with silent films in which film presentation was compared with a lecture illustrated with blackboard sketches and diagrams similar to some of the animated drawings used in the films. The subject matter, relativity and petroleum, was presented to ninth-grade general science pupils.

Findings

On immediate tests, the lecture-group gains were reliably and sizably higher than the film-group gains, the differences for five pairs of equated groups being .9 to 1.0 SD's of the distribution of gains.

On retention tests, one pair of equated groups (25 to 30 per class) was used to measure retention after three weeks, a second pair after six weeks, a third pair after nine weeks, a fourth after 12 weeks, and the fifth after 15 weeks. After three, six, nine, and 12 weeks the lecture groups were still superior to the film groups, with differences of .5 to .7 standard score units. Even after 15 weeks the difference in favor of the lecture group was .4 SD's, with a CR of 2.4.

---

* It is interesting to note that the slide series James used in one of his two "slide" presentations was really a filmstrip, as we know it today. Frames representing each scene along with a frame of each subtitle were cut from the film. These were cemented together in the order of their appearance in the film. This strip of film was shown in a projector that allowed moving the film a frame at a time. Apparently this is an early use of filmstrips.

SECTION 2. SOUND FILMS

EADS AND STOVER STUDY

The study by L. K. Eads and E. M. Stover (1936), previously mentioned, is related to our present problem. The reader will recall that they investigated the value of the sound film, Individual Differences in Arithmetic, in teaching graduate education students about diagnostic work in that area.

Findings

These investigators found that: (1) one showing of the 20-minute film was no better than assigned reading in a monograph which contained illustrations of the same apparatus and test materials demonstrated in the film; (2) one showing of the picture plus assigned reading was no better than assigned reading alone; (3) two showings of the picture plus assigned reading gave considerably better results than assigned reading alone; (4) two showings of the picture plus assigned reading was somewhat reliably better than one showing plus assigned reading; and (5) two showings of the film, plus assigned reading plus class discussion gave slightly reliable (CR 1.94) improvement over assigned reading and class discussion combined.

MANEVAL STUDY

R. V. Maneval (1939, 1939A) has reported two studies in which four different units were taught to large matched groups of eighth-grade pupils in general science.

Experimental Design

The teaching method used was either (1) sound motion pictures, shown twice without comments by the teacher, or (2) study sheets, read twice, in which questions were answered by the students. The study sheets are described as consisting of two parts: one part resembled a science text, which presented the material contained in the film commentary with only enough modification to make it understandable without the pictures; the second part resembled a science workbook. The classes which used the study sheets spent the same amount of time on them as the film groups spent in seeing the films twice. Groups alternated between study sheets and film after each unit.

Findings

Maneval's results, in terms of immediate and 30-day delayed recall tests, gave no consistent evidence in favor of either method, although student opinion favored the films. Students reported that they had learned more from the films than from the study sheets.

In the first study, in terms of a 30-day delayed recall test, there was a small, but reliable, difference in favor of the study sheets in one unit; smaller and

less reliable differences in the same direction for two more units; and, practically no difference for the fourth unit. In this study, one film was used with each unit.

In the second study, two films were used with each unit. In this latter case there was a small, but reliable difference in favor of the study sheets for the first unit; the fourth unit showed a very small and slightly reliable difference in favor of the films; on the other two units, no reliable differences were found.

The fact that the pupils using the study sheets answered questions in these sheets may have introduced a practice factor or more active participation (see the discussion of participation in Chapter VIII) which helped to keep the study sheets on a par with or slightly better than the films.

EICHEL STUDY

C. G. Eichel (1940) compared the effectiveness of films with a news leaflet, the Photoreporter, which was specially mimeographed for this experiment and covered the same material as each of the films. Ten March of Time films, each shown twice, were used.

Experimental Design

The same teacher taught a pair of equivalent control and experimental classes, made up from a large group of sixth-grade pupils. Each study unit extended over two periods. The material was presented during the first period, and was reviewed during the second period. Tests were given immediately after the study period, and then ten days, ten weeks, and one year later.

Findings

The film and leaflet groups were the same on the immediate test, but after ten days a very slight difference (1.48 points on 50-item test) appeared in favor of the film groups. A larger difference occured after ten weeks (4.20 points), and for 144 of the original subjects one year later, a mean difference of 6.46 points was found. (No SD's nor reliabilities were given in the article.) Here again, we have evidence of a benefit in retention, which does not show up in immediate test scores.

GIBSON, BORIN, ORVIS, AND GAGNE STUDY

J. J. Gibson, L. H. Borin, C. H. Orvis and R. M. Gagne have reported a significant experiment made by the Psychological Test Film Unit of the AAF Training Command (J. J. Gibson, 1947).

Experimental Design

They studied the effectiveness of three media for teaching the essential facts and principles of a then relatively new system of aerial gunnery, called "position firing." The first, a 15-minute animated (cartoon type) sound film had been produced to present the material in a logical way. The subject matter was presented humorously through the use of a cartoon character, "Trigger-Joe." The second medium was a carefully executed 50-page, pocket-size, loose-leaf, illustrated manual entitled, Get That Fighter, which presented the same material as the film. As the third medium, a half-hour illustrated lecture on the same subject matter was organized around 19 slides made from the same illustrations used in the manual. The instructor memorized the lecture, which included class questioning by the instructor to bring out salient points and used a pointer to explain the slides. Two college teachers judged the lecture to be good face-to-face teaching and not pedantic.

The intent of the experiment was to compare the film with the other two media at their best level of effectiveness. Since 15 minutes used for showing the film was too short a time for adequate study of the manual or for presentation of an adequate lecture, 30 minutes were allowed for the reading of the manual or for the presentation of the lecture.

Four groups of aviation cadets consisting of 100 to 130 men each, were selected at random from the total cadet population at Santa Ana Army Air Base. The first group was instructed by the film; the second by the manual; the third by the lecture; and the fourth acted as the control group and received no instruction. All cadets who had received any previous Army training in gunnery or who had previous information about position firing were eliminated from the study. The three training groups were told in advance that they would be given an examination immediately after the instruction. The test consisted of 25 objective five-choice items, some of them pictorial. All items were selected to measure responses in terms of important phases of the 14 basic points of the gunnery system.

Findings

The results of the objective test showed that the film presentation was reliably superior to the two other methods in producing learning, and that the amount of superiority over both methods was the same. (The superiority of the film-group mean was about 58 per cent of the mean SD's of the two other media distributions.) No reliable difference was found between the manual and the illustrated lecture. After two months it was possible to retest quite a sizable number of the cadets in each group and it was found that the superiority of the film group was maintained over the other two groups, again with no reliable difference between the latter two groups.

A further analysis of the data showed that the film had been of most advantage in raising the scores of the less capable learners. Further reference to this study is made in Chapter VIII in connection with the discussion of production techniques.

RICHARDSON AND SMITH STUDY

A. C. Richardson and G. H. Smith (1947) compared three Disney animated films with three comparable, illustrated Metropolitan Life Insurance Company pamphlets on the same topics.

Experimental Design

The topics were malaria, hook worm, and tuberculosis, and the investigators used equivalent groups of junior and senior high school students. No introduction or follow-up was used with either the films or the pamphlets. The total duration of film showings was 36 minutes, 12 for each film, whereas reading time for the pamphlets was 30 minutes each, or a total of 90 minutes.

Findings

In terms of a retention test after one month, the film method produced definitely higher percentages of gain in both the junior and senior high school groups than did the pamphlet presentation. Superiority was more pronounced in this retention test, which covered all three topics, than it was in the short individual tests given immediately after the presentation of each topic. In the senior high school group the immediate superiority of the film presentation was evident for the tuberculosis film only.

It should be noted that, as in the Gibson study, the animated films produced more learning in less presentation time than did the illustrated pamphlet. It was also reported that the film classes exhibited more interest in the subject matter.

HALL AND CUSHING STUDY

W. E. Hall and J. R. Cushing (1947) compared the effectiveness of three media for teaching a factual topic, a theoretical topic, and a performance topic to college students.

Experimental Design

The three media were (1) the sound films, Malaria: Its Causes and Control (factual), Principle of the Diesel Engine (theory), and Use of the Micrometer (performance); (2) an oral lecture from the film scripts, using enlarged illustrations drawn from the film by a skillful artist; and (3) a mimeographed script accompanied by photographed copies of the illustrations used with the lecture. Three groups of 100 students each, mostly freshman, were matched in "triplets" on the three scores of the American Council on Education Psychological Examination. The groups were rotated for each of the three film topics.

Findings

For the theory and performance topics all three methods gave virtually the same results. In the case of the factual topic, the illustrated reading presentation was reliably better than the other two methods, which were about equally effective. The superiority of the reading method was about .75 of the SD of the distribution of the film-group scores.

A further analysis of results was attempted by correlating the learning scores with the language (L) and quantitative (Q) scores of the American Council Test. The only reliable differences between L and Q correlations were found in the factual and the perform-ance topics. For the factual topic there were some-what reliably higher correlations with L than with Q for the lecture and reading groups. In the case of the performance topic there was a very reliable and size-ably higher correlation with Q for the film group (.24 vs. .54), but not for the lecture or reading groups. The meaning of these correlations is difficult to in-terpret, especially since no differences that were reliable showed up in the theory topic. The rather sketchy description of certain details of the study makes it hard to evaluate its significance.

SUMMARY

Animation may give film advantage over printed illustrations and lecture charts, especially for dynamic content.

It is difficult to summate the results of the studies in which films have been compared with special illus-trative and printed materials for effectiveness in factual learning. Early experiments fail to demonstrate film superiority. However, two of the three later experiments reported here do indicate a superiority for the film as compared with an illustrated leaflet (Richardson & Smith 1947; Gibson 1947). In both of these studies the films contained animation, and were of a cartoon, or partially cartoon type. An analysis of the test items and the film used in teaching "position firing," showed that the items in which the film did its most superior teaching were "dynamic" items dealing with a sequence of events or with the varia-tion of one thing from another. Gibson, et al., point out that they feel that much of the superiority of the film was due to the fact that nearly one-third of it was shot from the "subjective camera angle," that is, from the learner's point of view. Thus, the learner vicari-ously experienced the process of sighting a .50 caliber machine gun.

These two studies suggest that (1) improvement of film treatment, and (2) dynamic rather than static con-tent in the films are basic to the instructional supe-riority of the motion picture over other media and devices considered in this section.

PART IV. FILMS COMPARED WITH DEMONSTRATIONS OR LECTURES ON SCIENCE TOPICS

The content of this Part differs from that of Part III in several respects:

1.   The lectures and demonstrations described in this section are of the type usually given for the particular subject matter, whereas the lectures and demonstrations discussed in the preceding section were supplemented with some special visual aid.

2.   The subject matter in this section is prima-rily in the area of the sciences, and the ac-companying lectures and demonstrations are designed to facilitate factual and conceptual learning. The last few studies in this section involve learning having a military appli-cation.

SUMSTINE STUDY

D. R. Sumstine (1918) in one of the pioneer re-searches on instructional films, compared learning from the film, Farming with DuPont Dynamite, with a lecture covering the same material, and with a com-bination of the film and a lecture read during the film showing.

Findings

His data are inconclusive, especially since groups were not matched, and he wisely makes no claims for significant findings. He gave tests 24 hours, ten days, and three months after the instruction, which shows his insight into the fact that retention of learning is the final criterion of the effectiveness of a teaching medium.

JAMES STUDY

The major part of the study by H. W. James (1924), described in the preceding Part, was the comparison of learning from a film with learning from a lecture.

Experimental Design

The lecture had been prepared to duplicate the film as closely as possible, even to the extent of using the wording of the film titles to supplement the other comments, and requiring the same amount of presen-tation time. The six different films listed in Part III were all studied in this way using as subjects groups of eighth- and/or ninth-grade pupils in the city of Detroit.

In the case of three of the films there was a definite and reliable advantage in favor of the film presentation. For a fourth film there was a somewhat reliable advantage for the film presentation. For the two remaining films, there was no real difference between the two types of presentation. In a preliminary experiment with three other films, he had found an advantage in favor of film presentation over a lecture presentation for two of the three films.

Films Approximate Concrete Experience

His findings lead him to suggest this interesting hypothesis on the circumstances under which film instruction is likely to be advantageous: ". . . when fundamental, concrete experience is lacking, the more nearly we approximate the real experience in instruction, the more effectively is the lack supplied. Conversely, when the presentation deals with material that falls within the experience of the learner, a rearranging of the experience can be secured advantageously through oral instruction" (pp. 222-223).

This hypothesis seems plausible when considered in terms of the topics of the films used in the study. The two films in which there was no difference between the two methods of presentation were Yellowstone Park and Toads. Lumbering in the North Woods showed only a slight advantage for the film presentation. The three in which the film presentation was superior were The Mosquito, Through Life's Window (functioning of the eye), and Waste Disposal in Cities. Obviously, the pupils had less concrete experience in these last three topics with which to apprehend and integrate the oral and more symbolic lecture presentation.

REEDER AND FREEMAN STUDY

E. H. Reeder and F. N. Freeman (1924) in part of their study in the Chicago Series, carried out two short experiments comparing two silent films with an oral lesson.

The teacher who taught the lesson, had viewed the film several times and had studied a copy of the titles. One film was concerned with irrigation and the other with orange culture.

Findings

No difference was found between the two methods when used with 15 pairs of fourth-grade pupils matched in age, sex, intelligence, and initial knowledge.

ROLFE STUDY

E. C. Rolfe (1924), in another Chicago study, investigated the relative efficacy of a film and a teacher demonstration in teaching a lesson on science.

Experimental Design

The subject matter, static electricity, was taught to four section of high school physics consisting of a total of 80 students. Both film and teacher-demonstration groups first spent 30 minutes on assigned reading on the topic. Then, two sections saw the film twice, and the other two sections were instructed by the teacher demonstration and lecture, which required the same length of time as two showings of the film.

Findings

Verbal and laboratory tests both revealed a sizable superiority for the demonstration sections. But it is important to note that speed of development of the topic was uncontrolled, and, on the basis of recent studies, this factor seems to be an important one. The film was shown twice in the same time required for one demonstration, and the slower pace of the demonstration might explain the advantage of the demonstration equally as well as "teaching by a living teacher."

SECOR STUDY

C. T. Secor (1931) compared the usual method of teaching consisting of lecture, discussion, laboratory, and outside assignment with the use of silent films.

Experimental Design

The subject matter was ten four-day units in high school biology. The film group, which saw one film with each unit, received the following instruction: on the first day, it saw the film, which was followed by discussion, but no assignment was made; on the second day, it saw the first two units of the film again, with a discussion following each unit; on the third day, the last two units of the film were shown, followed by discussion. On the fourth day, a comprehensive objective test was given. He used two groups of 46 and 44 pupils each, partially equated in intelligence and rotated from unit to unit.

Findings

Secor found no advantage for either the film or the lecture method. It is important to note that the film group had discussion, but no outside reading assignments in text or supplementary material, whereas the usual-method group did have these instructional aids. Assuming that the usual-method group spent some time on the assignments, then the film and discussion group learned as much in less time.

JAYNE STUDY

The C. D. Jayne (1944) study with silent films, mentioned in Part III, is also pertinent here.

Experimental Design

In this study carefully prepared lectures on relativity and petroleum, using diagrams similar to those in the films, were compared with films in five pairs of ninth-grade general science classes. The film and the lecture took the same amount of time. The lecture was given to all classes by the same teacher, who obtained the lecture material from repeated viewings of the films.

Findings

On immediate tests the lecture groups had reliably higher gains and maintained a superiority on retention tests after three to 15 weeks, although the superiority in retention was only about half that of the immediate test. In other words, again, the film group lost less rapidly than did the lecture group. Nevertheless, the fact remains that this teacher, probably a skillful one, did a better teaching job than these two films.

CLARK STUDY

C. C. Clark (1932) made an extensive comparison of sound films, silent films, and lecture demonstrations prepared in "imitation" of the films.

Experimental Design

He investigated the learning of various science topics in survey courses given at the School of Commerce and Finance, New York University. Three sound films, Radioactive Substances, Liquid Air, and Characteristics of Sound, were used. In addition, three silent films, Electromagnetism, Wizardry of Wireless, and Revelations of X-Rays, were used.

Findings

He found that three sound films in physical science, in which "the sound was a vital and realistic part of the picture," were equally as effective as the lecture demonstrations given by the regular class instructors, in conveying specific information. The three silent physical science films were about equally as effective in this informational learning as their corresponding lecture demonstrations. In the case of one film, Electromagnetism, the demonstration was reliably better, but the difference was only .27 of the SD of the distributions of gains.

On other tests, consisting of four items per film and designed to measure thinking and reasoning ability, or possibly the formation of concepts, it was found that the two sound films and two silent films used, and their corresponding lecture demonstrations were equally effective as media of instruction. Examples of the type of question used to measure reasoning, or concepts are: "Explain with the aid of a diagram, the atomic structure of some one chemical element," and "Just how can liquid air instead of water be used to run a steam engine?"

We are not concerned at this time with Clark's attempt to compare sound films with silent films. This part of his study, though it opened a new area of research, is open to serious criticism.

EADS AND STOVER STUDY

Earlier mention was made of the L. K. Eads and E. M. Stover (1936) study on the value of the Erpi sound film, Individual Differences in Arithmetic, in teaching graduate students about diagnostic work in arithmetic. They compared the effectiveness of a single showing of the film with a lecture, using two small groups of students.

Findings

The film group was superior by a difference which was .44 of the SD of the lecture group distribution, but the critical ratio was only 1.81. This difference probably should be discounted, since the investigators report that the film group was somewhat superior to the lecture group in intelligence. On the other hand, the lecture group was superior to about the same degree in a "psychological survey test." The advantage of the film group is especially suspect because it took two showings of the picture plus assigned reading containing illustrations to surpass the result from assigned reading alone.

LAPP STUDY

C. J. Lapp (1939), in the second of two studies reported in this reference, compared (1) the sound film, Electrostatics, shown twice with intervening comments by the instructor to direct attention to certain points before the second showing, and (2) "a superior type lecture" of 50 minutes' duration on the same material. Both classes (college physics) were asked to read the textbook covering the same material. During the next class session, a 26-item multiple-choice test was given.

Findings

A difference was obtained in favor of the film group which was 10.8 per cent of the size of the predicted mean. This difference, however, is probably not reliable because of the small size of the groups involved, but the investigator does not report enough data to check the reliability.

HALL AND CUSHING STUDY

The study by W. E. Hall and J. R. Cushing (1947), referred to in Part III, investigated the difference between a sound-film presentation and a lecture with enlarged illustrations, in instructing matched groups of college freshmen. Three science topics were taught: malaria, principle of diesel engine, and use of the micrometer. No differences were found.

GIBSON, BORIN, ORVIS AND GAGNE STUDY

The J. J. Gibson, et al., study reported in Part III (Gibson, 1947) is also applicable here.

Experimental Design

They made a comparison between (1) a 15-minute animated sound film, (2) a 50-page illustrated manual, and (3) a half-hour illustrated lecture using 19 slides to teach essential facts and principles of "position firing" to aviation cadets.

Findings

The test given immediately after the instruction showed that the film, which lasted half as long as the other two media, produced reliably better learning, and was about equally superior to the other two methods. After two months' time the superiority of the film group was maintained.

VERNON STUDY

The P. E. Vernon (1946) study, previously mentioned in Parts I and II of this chapter, is pertinent to these comparisons between films and demonstrations.

Findings

In informational test scores, the seamen who witnessed two showings of the film on taking soundings (50 minutes of instruction), were only six per cent below those of groups which had usual instruction lasting three hours. It was also pointed out that "an hour's film appears to be as effective as three hours weak oral instruction" (p. 156).

SMITH STUDY

H. A. Smith (1948) compared a film, a demonstration, and a film plus a demonstration in teaching three general science units to ninth-grade classes in five different schools.

Experimental Design

Each unit extended over ten to 13 class periods. The one film used with each unit was shown at least twice, and in some classes, three or four times. It is not clear whether demonstrations were repeated to match the film showings or not. The three units were: magnetism, properties of water, and simple machines.

Findings

The difference in scores between pre-test and final test was analyzed by an analysis of covariance. In this situation, in which the experimental variable appears to be involved in less than ten per cent of the instructional activities measured by the tests, no reliable differences between any of the three media were found.

SUMMARY

Films Reduce Instruction Time

The conclusion which continually recurs in these studies is that films reduce instruction time with little or no sacrifice of instructional results. In some of the experiments in film presentation, from one-half to two-thirds of instructional time was saved by the use of films in place of lecture or demonstration. There thus appears to be considerable support for the Navy slogan, "More learning in less time," although this may not always be true for all films.

Films Often Equivalent to Good Instructors

A second conclusion that is recurringly supported by the research data is that, in communicating facts and demonstrating concepts, films (or filmstrips) are about equivalent, and sometimes better than superior instructors using the best non-filmic materials at their disposal.

As is pointed out in Chapter VIII, this should not be interpreted to mean that films can eliminate the need for instructors, but as suggesting the following postulates: (1) the effectiveness of instructors of average and below average ability can be improved (and instructional time can be saved) by the use of films; (2) because films can be projected onto a large screen, the size of the group can be increased substantially during film instruction with no loss, and possibly with significant gain, in instructional effectiveness of lesson presentation; (3) films, used alone, can offset a shortage of instructors.

PART V. EXTENSIVE USE OF FILMS COMPARED WITH USUAL METHODS OF INSTRUCTION

The demonstrated effectiveness of films in certain situations leads to the question: How much learning will result if almost all of the instructional material in an entire course is presented by means of films instead of the usual process based on lectures, demonstrations, discussions, and assigned reading? Several studies which relate to this question are presented in this section.

SHEPHARD STUDY

As previously pointed out, J. W. Shephard (1922), although not studying the extensive use of films, speculated that film teaching offered possibilities as an economical method of handling large groups of students and that it might replace mediocre teachers in the presentation of certain material.

CAMERON STUDY

So far as the reviewers know, V. E. Cameron (1933) was the first investigator to test out extensive use of films in a whole course.

Experimental Design

He taught two small high school physics classes matched in intelligence and sex. In the one group, the showing of films followed by a short question period replaced the usual lecture-discussion type of class periods; the other group had the usual lecture discussions. Both groups had the same textbook assignments and four periods of laboratory per week. The experimental and control groups were interchanged at the end of each eight-week period. The experimental group saw 70 films, mostly silent films, during the 32 weeks of the course. Both groups had assigned textbook reading on a topic the day before the film presentation or lecture discussion took place.

Findings

In terms of over-all achievement there was not much difference between the two methods. There was a slightly reliable tendency (CR of 1.72) for the experimental (film) group to retain more of the entire year's work.

SECOR STUDY

The C. T. Secor study (1931), mentioned in Part IV, though not a study of extensive use of films in a whole course, involved the use of ten silent films, one in each of ten four-day units in high school biology.

Experimental Design

The film group had no assignments. In each unit, the film was shown and discussed on the first day; on the second day, the first two units of the film were shown and discussed again; on the third day, the last two units were shown and discussed; on the fourth day, a test was given to both film and control groups. The control group was taught by the usual combination of lecture, discussion, laboratory, and outside assignment.

Findings

No advantage was found for either method, and, as we pointed out before, assuming that the control group spent some time on its outside assignments, the film plus discussion group learned as much with less study time.

MOUNT STUDY

J. N. Mount's study (1931), previously referred to in Part I, involved the use of 15 silent films in five units of high school physics.

Experimental Design

These units must have required at least two months of teaching time and the films for each unit were shown at the beginning and at the end of the unit. The control group devoted as much time to supplementary reading as the film group did to watching the films. The non-film periods of a unit were the same for both groups, involving demonstrations, experiments, discussions, outlining and drill.

Findings

In the case of the two small groups studied, there was a slight superiority for the film groups in three of the five units; the fourth unit was clearly in favor of the supplementary-reading group; the fifth unit showed no significant difference between the methods.

McCOWEN STUDY

M. C. McCowen (1940), as mentioned in Part I, compared the value of (1), 15 silent films combined with slides and the usual teaching techniques with (2), a control group which had no films or slides, in teaching two units of seventh-grade science.

Findings

In the case of his two small groups, he found that the group that saw the films and slides gained more than the control group. The gains were especially pronounced in the unit which saw 11 films, as compared with the unit in which only four films were shown.

MONTELBANO STUDY

D. Montelbano (1941) as mentioned in Part I, studied the effectiveness of 17 teacher-produced silent films when used in combination with usual methods.

Experimental Design

The "informational," "psychological," and "social utility" aspects of mathematics were taught to groups of seventh-grade pupils in four New York City junior high schools. The films were shown at intervals within four units of the course which probably extended over the major part of the semester. Each film was shown at least three times, and some, as many as six times. In other respects, the experimental and control groups received the same instruction, which included printed material, discussion, projects, etc., as well as the same number of class periods.

Findings

The extensive use of films resulted in reliable gains in the film-taught groups in the "informational," "psychological," and "social utility" aspects of mathematics. "Computational" skills were only slightly improved. In other words, the films were effective, but only with reference to their specific content.

VANDERMEER STUDY

The studies cited here have been related only indirectly to the question raised at the beginning of this section. A. W. VanderMeer (1949), in a study for the Instructional Film Research Program, attacked this question and even went beyond it, asking, "What results would come from exclusive film instruction?", that is, with no assignments, post-film discussion, guide sheets, or other aids of any kind.

Experimental Design

He studied three matched groups of ninth-grade general science students, using 44 sound films related to four units of general science that extended over three months of school. One group saw each film twice; another group saw two showings of the films, supplemented by specially prepared study guides which presented questions on the film material to be answered; the control group was taught by usual methods without the use of motion pictures.

Findings

Results of immediate tests failed to show any highly reliable differences between the three methods. The relative effectiveness of the three methods is tabulated in Fig. 6-3. These differences were relatively small and not highly reliable, since the highest CR was 2.73. It should be stressed that the films-only group completed the four units about four weeks in advance of the other two groups, reducing the in-

structional time about 20 per cent. Retests administered after a three month interval gave substantially the same results.

Evaluation

Films Substitute for Instructors in Certain Instances

This initial experiment on the question of whether or not sound films can be employed to carry the full burden of instruction in certain units of subject matter is strongly suggestive, even though the films used were not produced to serve as the sole means of instruction. We have, 28 years after Shephard first speculated that film teaching might eliminate the necessity for teacher presentation of certain material, some definite experimental evidence which shows that it can be done under certain conditions. This research supports, partially at least, the validity of the techniques of mass education used by the armed forces, and their application to civilian education is clearly indicated.

	UNIT 1	UNIT 2	UNIT 3	UNIT 4
1	Films plus Study Guides	Films plus Study Guides	Films plus Study Guides (equal to)	Usual Method
2	Usual Method	Usual Method	Usual Method	Films only
3	Films only	Films only	Films only	Films plus Study Guides

Fig. 6-3. Order of effectiveness of three instructional methods. (VanderMeer, 1949)

SUMMARY

As pointed out in a previous section, the implications of these research data are not that films should replace instructors, but that effective films used exclusively of other training materials are approximately equivalent to an instructor for presentation of facts and demonstration of concepts. Further, these data suggest that films do the job in substantially less time.

The role of the instructor, defined in Chapter I, extends beyond mere communication and demonstration, and involves stimulation of learner interest. The implications of the exclusive use of films in instruction must be viewed in the light of the proper functions of the instructor.

PART VI. FILMS COMPARED WITH FILMSTRIPS AND SLIDES

McCLUSKY STUDY

One of the earliest comparisons of the amount of learning taking place from film presentation as compared with stereopticon-lecture presentation (oral lecture illustrated with slides) was made as a part of

the extensive series of experiments carried out by F. D. McClusky (1924).

Experimental Design

The general nature of his experimental program was described in Part III of this chapter. In one study he compared the effectiveness of the film, The Life History of the Monarch Butterfly, with (1) a stere-opticon lecture using eight slides to illustrate each step in the life-cycle, and (2) an oral presentation illustrated with two still pictures and two blackboard sketches. All three methods took 12 minutes. McClusky used pupils in grades six and eight in one school and pupils in grades seven and eight in another. The pupils were arranged into equated groups of 20 or 21 pupils per school for each of the three methods of presentation.

Findings (1)

His results failed to show any real superiority for any of the three methods.

Experimental Design (2)

In another study McClusky compared a film on the Panama Canal with a stereopticon lecture using 25 slides showing scenes similar to those in the films. His experimental population consisted of pupils in grades four through seven, with nine to seventeen pupils in each grade section.

Findings (2)

He found the slide-lecture better in the upper three grades. Actually the pupils learned very little by either method, especially at the fourth-grade level.

Experimental Design (3)

As mentioned in Part III, he compared the film, A Story of a Mountain Glacier, with a stereopticon lecture using five slides, and with an oral lecture illustrated with six stereographs. It should be noted that the latter two media were supplemented with two wall charts and a blackboard sketch. Each presentation took 13 minutes. Equated sections of 37 eighth-grade pupils were used for each presentation.

Findings (3)

On immediate tests the latter two media were definitely better than the film. On retention tests after six weeks, the stereographs and slides were still better than the film, but to a lesser degree. However, the percentage of loss of the film group was much less than that of the groups taught by the other two media. There was no difference in learning from the slides and the stereographs.

Experimental Design (4)

In another one of his experiments a more exact comparison between the film and still pictures was made by a makeshift device which, in essence, was similar to a slide film or filmstrip. (Perhaps this is where James got his idea of pasting titles and film scenes together to make a "filmstrip.") Using the film, The Steamboat in United States History, a four-minute sequence of action scenes was selected, showing models of early steamboats in action. This section of film was shown as a motion picture to two groups and as still scenes to two other groups. The still scenes were shown by projecting a single frame with the shutter open for the same length of time required for the action scene to run through the projector. In the case of the movie film, an extra time of black screen was added after each title or scene to equal the time it took to run the film through to the next frame in the "still" version. Thus, the actual time of presentation was seven minutes in each case.

Findings (4)

Using equated, separate sections of fifth- and sixth-grade pupils, 19 to 20 per section, he found that on immediate tests, the film was superior for both grades, especially for the sixth grade. On retention tests ten weeks later the film was still superior. However, the still-projection groups lost only 2.7 per cent and 2.5 per cent, compared with the film groups' losses of 6.6 and 14.8 per cent for the fifth and sixth grades, respectively.

Evaluation

McClusky's somewhat awkward projection procedure, necessitated by the lack of a real filmstrip, suggests a research problem. It may be that, if the important points in an instructional film are followed by a short interval of dark screen, during which the learners are instructed to "get this," "hold this," or "think about it," such a technique would be an effective way of impressing important points and preventing interference and retroactive inhibition.

JAMES STUDY

The experiments by H. W. James (1924), mentioned in Parts III and IV of this chapter, involved two comparisons of films with series of slides, one of the latter being a real "filmstrip" made from the film.

Findings

In two comparisons with eighth-grade pupils and using two different films, no reliable superiority for either method was obtained, although there was a slight tendency for the films to be better in both cases.

McCLUSKY AND McCLUSKY STUDY

F. D. McClusky and H. Y. McClusky (1924), conducted an experiment, described in Part III, with fourth- to eighth-grade pupils.

Findings

Using two different films, Lumbering in the North Woods and Iron and Steel, they found, among other things, that slides plus subtitles, but with oral comments, taught the subject matter equally as well as the films.

BROWN STUDY

H. E. Brown (1928) investigated the relative values of the film and the filmstrip for teaching factual information about physiology at the high school level.

Experimental Design

Two experiments were conducted; the second experiment was conducted to offset the limitations of the data secured from the first. In the first study, two groups of 16 high school freshmen, paired on the basis of intelligence test scores, were instructed in the physiology of hearing. The film group was shown the film, How We Hear, and the pupils were permitted to ask spontaneous questions. The filmstrip group saw a filmstrip on the same topic, including still shots from the film that was used with the other group. Pictures were reshown "as often as seemed desirable" (p. 519). Both classes were then given an objective test in which there were eleven possible responses.

In the second, more elaborate experiment, the subject was the physiology of seeing. In this experiment 40 matched pupils were used in each group. In the filmstrip group, "discussion was free, questions were asked both by the examiner and by the people being tested." In the film group, the moving picture, How We See, was projected, and during the projection, important details were pointed out on three occasions. Measurement of results consisted of a test involving 15 multiple-choice and 14 true-false items.

Findings

In the first experiment, it was found that of the 16 pairs, the scores on three were equal, the scores of five were in favor of the film group, and the scores of eight of the filmstrip group were superior. The algebraic total of these scores showed an advantage of four points for the film group.

In the second experiment, of the 40 pairs of students, 27 pupils in the filmstrip group had higher scores than did the paired students in the film group, and ten of the film group had higher scores than did the paired pupils in the filmstrip group. The algebraic score of the filmstrip group was 128 points higher, and the filmstrip group had a net advantage of 17 cases over the film group.

Brown concludes from these data that "we are forced to the conclusion that in this case (the second experiment) at least, the filmstrip, with the greater exchange of comment it allows, proved the better. The differences were so large that I am inclined to believe that they would reappear on a similar investigation" (p. 526).

CARSON STUDY

D. Carson (1947) reported and experimental study conducted by the Scottish Educational Film Association on a filmstrip and a motion picture on the American cowboy.

Experimental Design

The experiment involved four groups consisting of 144 to 157 11- and 12-year-old Scottish pupils per group. The filmstrip used was Cowboy on the Range, produced by the American Council on Education for the U. S. Office of War Information (later, the United States Information Service). The sound motion picture used was, Cowboys, (producer and source unidentified), "which in subject matter approximated fairly closely the filmstrip" (p. 10). The time consumed in teaching with the filmstrip versions was not indicated. The sound motion picture was ten minutes long.

With Group A, the filmstrip was used in its entirety of 102 frames, and the printed commentary supplied with the filmstrip was read to the pupils.

With Group B, an abbreviated version of the filmstrip, consisting of every third frame, but including all title frames, was projected, and the commentary was read. This abbreviated version was used on the assumption that the original version was too long.

With Group C, the sound motion picture was shown.

Group D, slightly lower in mean intelligence score than the other three groups, saw neither film nor filmstrip and served as a control group.

All experimental groups were given a 40-item test, true-false and multiple-choice in nature, immediately after the film or filmstrip was shown. The nature of the investigation was explained to the control group prior to the administration of the test.

Findings

In order of magnitude of mean gain over the control group, the original filmstrip was superior to the abbreviated version, and both filmstrip versions were superior to the sound motion picture in informational and conceptual learning. The superiority of the mean scores of the experimental groups over the control group on the 40-item test is shown in Fig. 6-4. All mean gain differences were statistically reliable, the critical ratios varying from over 3 to 13.

Evaluation

It is not possible in this brief summary to do justice to the report of this Scottish experiment. Perhaps the most interesting and most important data reported are the free-response statements of the pupils of their concepts of cowboys and ranch life in the United States, concepts ostensibly formed from Western movies and stories commercially circulated in Great Britain. Also included are comments from teachers on the elements of the filmstrips responded to by the pupils, and points of similarity and difference noted by the pupils. The report of this experiment is of more than passing interest to agencies preparing informational materials for circulation abroad.

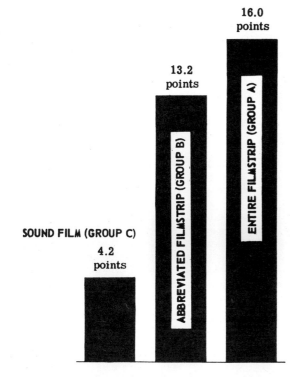

16.0
points

13.2
points

SOUND FILM (GROUP C)
4.2
points

ABBREVIATED FILMSTRIP (GROUP B)

ENTIRE FILMSTRIP (GROUP A)

Fig. 6-4. Mean-score superiority of experimental groups over control group (Group D). (Carson, 1947)

VERNON STUDY

P. E. Vernon's experiment (1946) discussed in Parts I, II, and IV above, compared the use of films and filmstrips in teaching the taking of soundings to British naval trainees.

Experimental Design

A 25-minute sound film was compared with a filmstrip comprising 140 frames of photographs and captions taken or adapted from the film. In Vernon's somewhat complicated experimental design the film and filmstrip were used in several ways: (1) each combined with some amount of usual instruction; (2) one, two or three showings of one visual aid alone; (3) both film and filmstrip used together.

Findings

Either the film or the filmstrip, added to some usual instruction, produced learning increments of approximately the same degree over the learning obtained with the usual methods alone. The groups which had some combination of the film and the filmstrip scored higher than the group which had one showing of the film in addition to the usual instruction. The gains were greater on comprehension items than on memory items.

Evaluation

Vernon argues that the film is better than the filmstrip because it saves time. Moreover, he attributes to the film the increase in comprehension scores, but a careful examination of Table III, p. 160 of his article, does not seem to justify that assumption. The table shows that the highest comprehension scores occurred when the film and filmstrip were used in combination. In two of these cases, the filmstrip was shown two or three times, and the film once; in the third case, in which no instruction was given except one showing of the filmstrip plus two showings of the film, the biggest gain of the whole experiment was obtained. Two showings of the film alone, with no other instruction, gave the poorest results of any of his experimental variations, although it did produce sizable learning.

GOODMAN STUDY

D. J. Goodman (1942) investigated the relative effectiveness of (1) sound motion pictures, (2) silent motion pictures, (3) sound filmstrips and (4) silent filmstrips with printed titles, in teaching four topics of safety in sixth- and seventh-grade classes. The two silent media contained the same pictorial material as their respective sound versions, and had caption frames inserted to present the verbal material. In the case of either the filmstrips or the film slides, (it is not clear, which) this verbal material was identical with that of the sound films.

Findings

In tests of immediate learning he found small, but reliable, differences in favor of the silent motion picture over both the sound motion picture and the sound filmstrip. In addition he found slightly smaller, but statistically reliable, differences in favor of the silent filmstrip over the sound motion picture and sound filmstrip. No differences were found between the two silent media or the two sound media on immediate tests.

However, in delayed measures of learning administered 30 days later, the size and reliability of the difference in favor of the silent motion picture over sound motion picture and sound filmstrip were reduced. The silent filmstrip lost its advantage over the sound motion picture and sound filmstrip, and the silent motion picture was slightly better than the silent filmstrip. No difference was found between the two sound media.

Evaluation

The idea load, or fact density, of his sound and silent filmstrips for each topic was apparently the same, since the text for the slides was recorded on a disc, but no data are reported on the comparative idea load between the film and the filmstrip for a given topic. This is a very crucial matter, as some of the research reported in Chapter VIII on fact density and level of verbalization points out.

It is interesting that of the four safety topics taught: auto, bicycle, fire, and pedestrian, pedestrian safety showed the smallest learning gain in both immediate and delayed tests and for both high and low IQ groups. Goodman reports a tabulation of the number of pictorial and text frames in the filmstrip for each topic. Pedestrian safety had seven to eight more text frames than any of the other three topics and no more pictorial frames than any of the others; in fact, it had six fewer pictorial frames than one of the other topics.

HOVLAND, LUMSDAINE, AND SHEFFIELD STUDY

C. I. Hovland, A. A. Lumsdaine, and F. D. Sheffield (1949) compared the effectiveness of a 43-minute Army training film on map reading with an Army filmstrip which presented much the same content but with some differences in emphasis and treatment.

Experimental Design

Three groups of Army trainees at a Quartermaster Replacement Training Center were equated on both the extent of their formal education and their scores on the Army General Classification Test. The control group received no instruction in map reading. One of the experimental groups was taught by the use of the filmstrip, and the other by use of the motion picture. Results were tested by a 39-item test, half of which involved purely verbal items, and half of which involved maps and diagrams.

Findings

In overall scores, there was a slight (1.6 per cent), but not very reliable (CR 1.3 SE), difference in favor of the group taught by the filmstrip. The learning gains of the filmstrip and the motion-picture groups over the control group were 8.7 and 7.1 per cent, respectively.

The scores of both experimental groups were analyzed in terms of the performance of the more intelligent (Class I and II, AGCT) and the less intelligent (Class III and IV, AGCT) trainees. The difference of the filmstrip group over the control group increased 2.2 per cent for the less intelligent trainees, but the reliability of this difference remained approximately the same (CR 1.4 SE). For the more intelligent group, the difference decreased 0.9 per cent, as did the reliability of the difference (CR 0.7 SE). However, the more intelligent trainees gained significantly more from both the motion picture (10.5 per cent) and the filmstrip (11.4 per cent), than did the less intelligent trainees whose gains on the film and filmstrip were 4.2 and 6.4 per cent, respectively.

The analysis of scores in terms of items dealing with (1) distance and direction, (2) "azimuths," and (3) contour maps and elevations, showed a reliable difference (.01 probability level) of 4.4 per cent in favor of the filmstrip on items dealing with distance and direction. Item analyses indicated that where the method of presentation was more explicit in the filmstrip than in the motion picture, (as was the case for the measurement of distance on a map), the difference in results was pronounced in favor of the filmstrip group.

Similarly, where "the motion picture used a moving viewpoint (from horizontal to vertical) to show how differences in elevation of terrain are projected onto a map in the form of contour lines" (p. 129), the movie was much more effective than the filmstrip. From this analysis, Hovland, Lumsdaine, and Sheffield conclude that "here the large effect of the motion picture appears to be due to the fact that in a movie the object being photographed can remain still while the angle from which it is viewed is progressively altered. Thus, we have the hypothesis that where familiarity with three-dimensional spatial relationships is important in learning the material, movies have an inherent advantage that cannot easily be equalled by filmstrips" (p. 129).

GIBSON STUDY

J. J. Gibson's (1947) study, previously discussed, contained an analysis of concepts and points for which the motion picture showed its greatest superiority over the illustrated lecture and the illustrated manual.

Findings

The analysis indicated that "the concepts which were most successfully taught were those which might be called 'dynamic,' in the sense that they deal with changing events or with the variation of one thing in relation to another" (p. 251), and the "ones which get their meaning from use or human action and which are hard to describe in words or static diagrams" (p. 252).

HEIDGERKEN STUDY

L. E. Heidgerken's (1948) study, previously discussed, sought to find differences between (1) motion pictures alone; (2) motion pictures plus filmstrips; and (3) filmstrips alone, when these media were presented under several different circumstances.

Findings

She found no significant differences between these media when they were presented at the beginning and middle of a unit, at the middle and end of the unit, at the beginning and end of the unit, and throughout the unit. Also, she found no differences between any of these media and usual methods of teaching nursing arts.

Evaluation

The lack of reliable differences in Heidgerken's experiment, in contrast with the Vernon and other studies, may be due to several reasons. The statistical design intermixed several factors, most of which have been demonstrated in other experiments as influential factors in learning response, regardless of the media employed. These factors were: 24 small instructional groups; uncontrolled instructional materials and procedures; and, teacher variability. The experiment involved 28 class hours of instruction, and the use of the visual media consumed approximately ten per cent of the instructional time. Because of the probable influence of these uncontrolled variables, her results probably do correctly represent the complex comparisons studied.

The media themselves (the motion pictures and filmstrips) probably do not exert an important influence in this experiment. Since the time devoted to these media was only a fraction of the total instructional time, it is unlikely that the media could have had a stronger influence on learning responses than the other factors combined.

It is interesting, though perhaps of little immediate importance in terms of specific factual outcomes, that the students rated the instructional materials in the following order of preference: (1) motion pictures, (2) motion pictures and filmstrips used together, (3) filmstrips, (4) neither motion pictures nor filmstrips.

By her experimental design, statistical analysis, and negative results, Heidgerken has done the field of instruction a considerable service. Enthusiasts for motion pictures and filmstrips often behave as though a single medium of communication, such as a few movies, filmstrips, or a movie plus filmstrip, used at some strategic point in the instructional unit, were the answer to all instructional problems. To them such factors as the teacher, the class, the morale of the instructional group, the atmosphere of instruction, and all other instructional materials are unimportant elements in the educational picture.

SUMMARY

Film-Filmstrip Comparisons Involve Many Variables

The results of comparisons between filmstrips (projected still pictures) and motion pictures are not easy to generalize. Filmstrips and motion pictures are difficult to compare because they have the pictorial medium in common. Presumably, the filmstrip and the motion picture are forms of the same communications medium, except that the motion picture simulates motion within the picture, whereas the filmstrip does not. Nevertheless, a specific comparison between films and filmstrips involves many other variables which have been identified as influential factors in audience learning.

Content and Pictorial Technique Vary in Both Media

A picture (including a motion picture) always has a "content." This content may vary from a rather simple, visual form to some intricately related actions and interactions, photographed from many different points of view. Furthermore, within a filmstrip or motion picture, either photographs or line drawings may be used. In the filmstrip, this illustrative material is shown "still," but in motion pictures, it may be shown in either "still" or animated form. Thus, in comparing a filmstrip with a motion picture, still photographs may be compared with cartoon animations in which motion could be an important variable.

Rate of Development Varies in Filmstrip

In addition to the variability of content and of picture technique involved in a comparison of the filmstrip and the motion picture as media of communication, such a comparison must usually consider rate of development and level of verbalization. As shown in Chapter VIII, both variables influence learning reactions. In a motion picture, the rate of development (the time devoted to the presentation of successive facts or ideas) is fixed in the editing stage, and is not ordinarily varied in projection. But for a filmstrip, although the number of pictures included is fixed at the editing stage, the rate at which the pictures are shown to the audience can be varied during projection, and almost always is from one audience to another. This variation in rate of development may occur not only for the entire filmstrip, but also for the individual pictures in the filmstrip.

Level of Verbalization Varies in Filmstrip

The level of verbalization (the amount of language) and the kind of verbalization (the content of language) are variables which become fixed in the sound track of a sound motion picture. In a filmstrip, short titles are frequently printed on the individual pictures, or may be omitted entirely. But when the filmstrip is shown, there is likely to be considerable variation in the amount of verbal explanation, direction, description, or discussion of any single picture, or throughout the entire filmstrip.

Despite the many possibilities for variation, and despite the fact that research on comparative values of motion pictures and filmstrips has not taken these relevant variables into sufficient account, it is possible, nevertheless, to formulate at least two postulates based, in part, on the research evidence.

1. The "superiority" of the motion picture in achieving the greater comprehension, noted in some comparative studies of motion pictures and filmstrips, usual methods, etc., may result from the greater adaptability of movies for portraying interacting events.

2. Where filmstrips are found to be "superior" to motion pictures, this superiority may be due to the slower rate of development used in the actual presentation of the filmstrip to the audience.

CHAPTER VII

AUDIENCE CHARACTERISTICS

INTRODUCTION

The reaction of an audience to a motion picture is intimately related to what the audience brings to the motion picture as well as what the motion picture brings to the audience.

Contrary to rather widely held popular opinion, communication by motion picture is not a mechanical transfer of information. Reactions are dynamic. They involve interaction of the audience with the content and technique of the film.

An audience does not see, hear, understand, accept, or remember exactly, or even approximately, everything the film is intended to present. Instead, it selects and interprets. Sometimes it discounts and disregards. Always it tends to impose its own meanings on the experience.

In this chapter we are concerned with the factors which operate in individuals in the audience to condition their responses to films. These factors are discussed in terms of (1) predispositions brought to the film, (2) the social role or roles of individuals in the audience, and (3) their intellectual abilities, education, and training.

PHASES OF INQUIRY

Part I presents a number of predispositional factors which appear to influence the way individuals in an audience react to motion pictures. These predisposition factors are summarized under: (1) Acceptance and Predisposition to Acceptance; (2) Thresholds of Excitability; (3) Likes and Dislikes; and (4) Appeal of the Movies.

Part II presents evidence on the social factors, and in particular, the social roles which a society or an environment define for the individual. These influences are presented in terms of: (1) Religion Role; (2) Sex Role; and (3) Age Role.

Part III examines the intellectual factors which affect the amount of learning, particularly informational learning, from films. The studies which deal with these factors are summarized under: (1) Intelligence and Educational Level; and (2) Previous Knowledge and Training.

A section at the end of each Part summarizes the experimental evidence and the conclusions suggested by the studies in that Part.

Since this chapter is somewhat long, and the research evidence is often piecemeal and sometimes contradictory, the reader is asked to keep the three major headings in the forefront of his thinking as he reads and reflects on the evidence and our interpretation of it. Briefly, we interpret the research evidence on the audience characteristics that influence responses to motion pictures as somehow related to (1) what the individual wishes or believes things to be, (2) his picture of himself in relation to the groups with which he is identified, and (3) his use of the abilities with which he has been gifted by ancestry and circumstances.

PART I. INDIVIDUAL PREDISPOSITION FACTORS IN AUDIENCE RESPONSE

An individual approaches any motion picture experience with a number of predispositions which may influence his reaction to the film. He may, for instance, be disposed toward or against the bias with which the facts, characters, and situations are presented in the film. Temperamentally and emotionally he may be easily excited by scenes of danger, disaster, love, or politics, or he may be quite dispassionate about the whole subject and all of its parts. His likes and dislikes, his preferences for one kind of film story over another, and his general interest in the topic of the film are part of the mental set with which he approaches a film. Then too, the movie as a medium of communication may be especially appealing, more so than other media or other instructional devices. The problem is the extent to which such audience predispositions influence reactions to films, under what circumstances, and over what period of time. Data bearing on this problem are summarized below.

SECTION 1. ACCEPTANCE AND PREDISPOSITION TO ACCEPTANCE

I. ACCEPTANCE

Logicians have long distinguished between the individual's awareness of a proposition and his assent to it. Such a distinction was implied in P. W. Holaday and G. D. Stoddard's (1933) investigation of reactions to entertainment films, but a categorical difference between acknowledgement and acceptance was not clearly recognized and investigated in film research until World War II, when Hovland, Lumsdaine, and Sheffield (1949) identified the factor of acceptance in the varying influence on opinions produced by the Army's Why We Fight films.

HOLADAY AND STODDARD STUDY

P. W. Holaday and G. D. Stoddard (1933) observed the types of information accepted by motion picture audiences.

Findings

Audiences Accept Both True and False Information

They found that entertainment film audiences of children and adults retained both true-to-fact and contrary-to-fact items. Their "general tests" covered items true-to-fact and contrary-to-fact included in the films. By a "before and after" administration of the general tests, measures of "acceptance" of items contrary- and true-to-fact could be obtained. They reported that "information shown incorrectly in the pictures was largely accepted" (p. 66). Increased misinformation, or, "decreases in general information," ranging from 8 to 38 per cent was reported as resulting from entertainment films which presented both true and false information.

HOVLAND, LUMSDAINE, AND SHEFFIELD STUDY

C. I. Hovland, A. A. Lumsdaine, and F. D. Sheffield (1949) recognized the factor of "acceptance" in their study of the influence of the Why We Fight films on opinions of a military population in World War II.

Findings

Opinion Change Depends on Acceptance

"The extent to which interpretations such as would be represented by changes in men's opinions are influenced by a film obviously depends not only on learning of the material--but also on the acceptance of the material presented. Men might have learned what the film said, but if the film presentation were viewed with skepticism or suspicion they might not accept the interpretation as the correct one" (p. 98).

HOBAN STUDY

C. F. Hoban, Jr. (1942) commented on the reactions of ninth- and eleventh-grade pupils to the film, Work Pays America.

Findings

He pointed out that, in the eighth and ninth grades, "reactions to the film were largely favorable in an undifferentiated way, that is, most students said they now thought WPA a wonderful thing. In the eleventh grade, reactions were much more clearly differentiated: some involved total approval of WPA, some involved new insights into particular aspects of it, others involved a distinctly 'yes - but' attitude. These latter were characterized by such remarks as 'I'd like to see some pictures that were taken when they weren't looking,' and 'I'd like to see how it's working here, not just somewhere else' " (p. 64).

II. PREDISPOSITION TO ACCEPTANCE

In Chapter V, it was pointed out in connection with L. L. Ramseyer's (1938) study, that the effects of films dealing with soil conservation and government responsibility were discriminable in terms of the occupations of the parents of the pupils who saw the films. These discriminable reactions appear to involve a predisposition toward or away from acceptance of the bias of the film, apparently related to socio-economic group identification of the audience.

HOVLAND, LUMSDAINE, AND SHEFFIELD STUDY

The most relevant experimental evidence of the effect of predisposition is contained in the analysis by C. I. Hovland, A. A. Lumsdaine, and F. D. Sheffield of the long-time effects of 15 opinion items "significantly" influenced by the film, The Battle of Britain.

Experimental Design

Recognizing education as one of several possible indices of predisposition to accept a certain interpretation or opinion, the investigators used it as the basis for assigning military trainees into groups, so that education and all its predisposing tendencies would be a common factor. Tabulations were then made of the initial agreement with opinion items within groups having: (1) some college training; (2) high school diplomas; (3) some high school training; and (4) no high school training. The percentage of initial agreement on a particular opinion by a group was regarded as an index of initial "acceptance" of the opinion by that group, and hence an index of its predisposition to accept the film interpretation of that item of opinion, and to be influenced thereby.

The 15 opinion items tested at the four educational levels resulted in 60 quantitative values on initial opinion. These values were arranged in rank order for comparison with the corresponding changes taking place five days (short-time) after the film presentation, in the case of three companies, and nine weeks (long-time) after the film, in the case of two other companies. (Actually, the array of 60 initial-acceptance values was distributed into six class intervals, thus providing a six-interval, rather than a 60-interval scale of most-to-least initial acceptance with which to compare any change in opinion. As a measure of opinion change, the Effectiveness Index* was used.)

Findings

Predisposition Effects Appear on Long-time Tests

The Effectiveness Index showed no intelligible pattern among the six degrees of acceptance, when computed from the tests given five days after the film showing. Figure 7-1 illustrates the Effectiveness Indices for the short-time tests of the six categories of initial acceptance, arranged in decreasing order of initial acceptance. When computed from the test given nine weeks after the film showing, the Effectiveness Index of the six categories fell into the same order as the order of initial acceptance or predisposition. Figure 7-2 illustrates the Effectiveness Indices for the long-time tests of the six categories, again arranged in order of initial acceptance. The rank order correlation of Effectiveness Indices and initial acceptance, or predisposition, was 0.09 for short-time data and 0.41 for long-time data.

Evaluation

Effects Should Appear Immediately

From these results it appears that any effect that this type of predisposition may have on opinion change in relation to data communicated in films, may at times not be immediately evident, but may manifest itself after a longer period of time. There is a clear trend of greater effect with greater initial acceptance for the long-time results, but no such trend in the short-

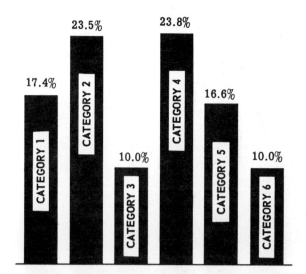

Fig. 7-1. Effectiveness indices from short-time tests of six categories of opinion items categories are arranged in decreasing order of initial acceptance. (Hovland, Lumsdaine & Sheffield, 1949)

time results. But, one would expect that a man, predisposed to accept an idea, would tend to accept that idea more immediately than one which he is predisposed to reject. Thus, the predisposition hypothesis does not seem sufficient to explain the results.

Learner May Forget Incompatible Ideas

It is somewhat optimistic to interpret the correlation between predisposition and general opinion nine weeks after the film exhibition as casually related to the film experience only. A military population in training during World War II obviously had other experiences which related to the general opinion items dealing with the outlook of the war and the strength and activities of our allies and enemies. Were the film the only experience involved, even granting a strong element of reminiscence, a correlation greater than +0.09 might be expected between predisposition and immediate reaction to the film. It is more logical to accept the hypothesis offered by Hovland, Lumsdaine, and Sheffield that "a person soon 'forgets' the ideas he has learned which are not consonant with his predispositions, but that he retains without loss or even with an increment those ideas consonant with his predispositions" (pp. 192-193). We can, however, postulate from the evidence at hand that general opinions tend to increase in the direction of predisposition over a period of time within a milieu of experience related to these opinions, and that the amount of increase appears to be related to the strength or prevalence of the predisposition.

---

* The Effectiveness Index is symbolized by the formula, $\dfrac{P_2 - P_1}{100 - P_1}$ In this formula, P_1 is the percentage of men having a certain opinion on the initial test. P_2 is the percentage of men having this opinion on the post-test. This index, which is a ratio of the measured change to the total possible change, was frequently used by Hovland, Lumsdaine, and Sheffield, to take account of the methodological difficulty that only those individuals who do not initially give the desired response can be influenced in the desired direction. This index seems particularly desirable where items or groups of men with differing initial frequency of responses are compared.

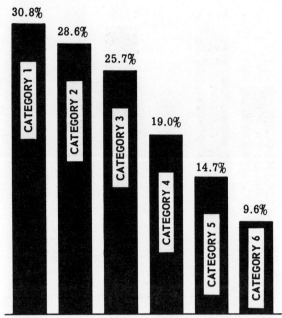

Fig. 7-2. Effectiveness indices from long-time tests of six categories of opinion items. Categories are arranged in decreasing order of initial acceptance. (Hovland, Lumsdaine, & Sheffield, 1949)

Hovland, Lumsdaine, and Sheffield discussed and analyzed three possible explanations of the "delayed effect" of the film, The Battle of Britain, on general opinions: (1) the source of the information, the film, is forgotten more quickly than the material presented in the film; (2) the implications of the content of the film become clearer in the light of relevant new experience; (3) the specific film content is lost in forgetting, and the "general idea" or "substance" is retained in more generalizable form, "so that the individual has a greater tendency to go beyond the facts initially learned" (p. 198).

Motivation or Thought May Aid Acceptance

It was postulated by C. I. Hovland, et al., (p. 165), that two factors enter into a predisposition to accept an opinion related to film content: (1) motivational factors, such as emotional biases and wishes, (2) a rational analysis of the validity of the interpretation on the basis of available factual information. This latter factor is related to intelligence, which, in turn, is related to level of formal education. Since no data were available on motivation as it relates to predisposition, this factor was simply postulated.

SECTION 2. THRESHOLDS OF EXCITABILITY

The experience of watching a motion picture is sometimes accompanied by changes in pulse rate, body temperature, and sweat secretion. Presumably other physical and chemical activities of the body, such as endocrine gland activity and contraction of the smooth and striped muscles, also undergo change. These physical-chemical activities are frequently regarded as evidence of "emotional" activity or excitement, and effects of films on these changes are referred to as "emotional effects" or "effects on emotion."

Physiological Response Indicates "Emotion"

The understanding of "emotional" influences of motion pictures requires an understanding of what is meant by and involved in "emotion" as a psychological phenomenon. Rather than attempting to deal with a confused and confusing concept of emotion, we have summarized the research data relating to the physiology sometimes involved in motion-picture experience in terms of thresholds of excitability. The physiological responses measured in studies of "emotion" are interpreted here as evidence of covert activity, and are, in all probability, indices of the degree of psychological excitement and involvement of the individual.

DYSINGER AND RUCKMICK STUDY

The degree of physiological response of the audience to entertainment motion pictures was investigated by W. S. Dysinger and C. A. Ruckmick (1933) as part of the Payne Fund studies.

Experimental Design

In their experiments they used a modification of the Wechsler psychogalvanograph and an improved model of an electrical pneumocardiograph to measure skin changes and pulse rates respectively. The measurements are indicative of the intensity of physiological reactions from which other psychological activities are inferred. Measurements of physiological responses to specific films were made on a small number of subjects, but the experiment appears to have been carefully conducted and the psychological conclusions are meaningful. The quantitative data were supplemented by the subjects' essays on the films used in the experiment.

Findings

Responses Were Highly Variable

Consistent with the conclusions of Shuttleworth and May, (1935), Dysinger and Ruckmick reported wide individual variation in responses to films. They also reported different degrees of excitement for various ages, for the different sexes, and for various dramatic contents, thus reinforcing our conclusion that reactions to motion pictures are specific with reference both to film content and factors of audience involvement.

Love-scene Responses Strongest in 16-18 Age Group

Physiological responses to the film, The Feast of Ishtar, is a useful example of the method of analysis of

Dysinger and Ruckmick. When the indices of physiological responses of the various age groups to love scenes are averaged, the average index of response rises progressively from the 6-10-year age group to a peak in the 16-18-year age group, and declines in the older age groups in the early twenties. Under 12 years of age, the physiological response to love scenes was slight; there was an increase in response in the 13-15 age group and a larger increase in the 16-18 age group. From the 19-year through the early-twenty group, the response declined to a level approximately that of the 13-15 age group. However, in any age group, greater differences in intensity of response may appear among the individuals of the age group than between the averaged indices of responses of two age groups. No reliability coefficients were computed for group differences in emotional responses.

Six Major Conclusions

The major conclusions of Dysinger and Ruckmick, derived from samples similar to the one described above, may be summarized, with some interjected comments.

1. Individuals differ widely in the degree of physiological responsiveness to a given motion picture.

2. Responses to "pseudo-tragedy, conflict, and danger" are most intense under the age of 12. This intensity decreases among those near the age of 16, and sharply decreases among the 19-year-old group.

3. Responses to love scenes show a different curve of intensity, rising to a peak in the 16-year-old group, and declining among both younger and older groups. The age of 16 appears to mark the peak of excitement from romantic and conflict scenes in entertainment films.

4. An "adult discount" is developed beyond the age of 16, and appears to be well established in adulthood. Artificiality in the pictorial story is more readily perceived among adults than among young children. It is possible that the discounting effect from suspicion of manipulative intent, noted by Hovland, Lumsdaine, and Sheffield, is related to the general factor of "adult discount" reported by Dysinger and Ruckmick, although it does not appear, from the evidence at hand, that the two are identical.

Personal experience with children in late childhood and early adolescence, particularly with those children who have had extensive experience with modern radio, comics, movies, and television, leads the present reviewers to believe that some degree of sophistication with reference to commercial media of communication develops somewhat before the age of 16 among urban and suburban populations.

In a study of comic book reading among 200 subjects sampled from an urban, suburban, and rural population and ranging in age from seven to 17 years, K. M. Wolf and M. Fisk (1949) reported some evidence in support of the hypothesis that excessive excitability and involvement are found among a small proportion of the population and that this excessiveness is related to neurotic tendencies. There is no necessary conflict between this finding and the data reported by Dysinger and Ruckmick on the wide variation of excitability and response to movies within any age group.

5. Excitability decreases with repeated viewing of the same motion picture. This finding in interpreted by Dysinger and Ruckmick as reinforcement of the evidence on "adult discount." It is corroborated by N. Kleitman's (1945) more recent study of temperature variation after movie experience (see Ch. VIII). Interestingly enough, repeated showing of instructional films has been demonstrated in other studies to increase the magnitude and reliability of informational learning from the film. This interposes an interesting problem on the relationship of emotional excitation and effective instruction.

6. Adults report disgust with slapstick comedy. However, in studies of audience evaluation of cartoons used for instruction during World War II, slapstick comedy was high on the list of likes among GI's.

The growth periods in involvement responses reported by Dysinger and Ruckmick correspond roughly to similar patterns of responses reported for choices of reading and radio listening of children, adolescents, and adults, and for choices of comic book reading of children and adolescents.

SECTION 3. LIKES AND DISLIKES

Like or dislike of a film appears to be a fourth factor in individual reactions to instructional films and seems related to the direction of film effects or influences. It is not clear whether the like (or dislike) is a general appraisal which influences the individual's reactions to specific items in the film, or whether it arises as a result of reactions to specific items. The like-dislike reaction may be related in some way to the "pleasantness" or "unpleasantness" of the experience stimulated by the film. If so, the affective tone symbolized by "like" or "dislike" may influence the permanence of the film effect, since affectively toned experiences are generally remembered longer than affectively neutral experiences.

Another way of interpreting a like-dislike reaction is as an indicator of predisposition, and some of the research data on the problem suggest this interpretation. Whatever the significance of the like-dislike reaction, little attention has been given to the effect of this type of audience appraisal on learning from instructional films.

I. EFFECTS ON OPINION CHANGE

HOVLAND, LUMSDAINE, AND SHEFFIELD STUDY

C. I. Hovland, A. A. Lumsdaine, and F. D. Sheffield (1949) investigated the changes in eleven items of opinion after showing The Battle of Britain to soldiers, who indicated on a questionnaire whether they "liked" or "disliked" the film.

Findings

Some Correlation Appeared Between "Like" and Favorable Change

On ten of the eleven items, the opinions of those who "disliked" the film were less positively affected by the film than those who "liked" the film. In seven of the eleven opinion items, the "dislike" group changed negatively in their opinions of the British. On only one item did the "like" group change negatively and this change was minus three per cent. On all eleven opinion items the mean Effectiveness Index (proportion of actual change to maximum possible change in desired direction) was +17 per cent in pro-British opinion among those who "liked" the film, and minus three per cent among those who "disliked" the film. The difference was reliable at the two per cent level of confidence. Hovland, Lumsdaine, and Sheffield pointed out that there were methodological difficulties in the questionnaire technique of these studies, and that it could not be concluded from their data that "likes" and "dislikes" were causal factors in opinion reactions.

They described those who "disliked" the orientation films as tending, on the whole, "to be less well educated, to have foreign-born parents (particularly from Axis countries), to come from smaller cities and towns, and to have isolationist attitudes. In the case of The Battle of Britain the men in the "dislike" group were also more likely to feel that they ought to be civilians rather than in the Army and to blame Britain for our entering the war" (p. 86).

Evaluation

"Like-Dislike" Is Indicative of Other Factors

These studies suggest that predispositional factors may at times influence general approval or disapproval, as expressed in "like" or "dislike," and that the influences on opinion may be related to predispositions. Thus "like" and "dislike" appear to be general reactions indicative of the operation of some other factor or factors.

It would also appear that the classic question, "Did you like this film?", sometimes cited as inappropriate for initiating post-film discussion, may evoke a crude index of degree of emotional involvement and of possible opinion change. Involvement factors, in turn, apparently influence in some degree the individual's perceptual-conceptual reaction to the entire film, or to specific sequences or "meanings" of the film, and affect the degree and direction of opinion change. Much more research is needed, however, to justify this interpretation.

II. EFFECTS ON RATING OF FILM'S VALUE

SACKETT STUDY

The relationship between an individual's dislike of something in a film and his judgment of the educational value of the entire film is evident in data assembled by R. S. Sackett (Hoban, 1942). Sackett analyzed student ratings of 500 films used in the film evaluation project of the American Council on Education.

Findings

Specific Dislike Affects Rating of Entire Film

Sackett reported that, when the students' judgments of the educational value of the films were arranged on a descending scale (excellent, good, fair-or-worse), the percentage of students who indicated they disliked something in the film increased progressively. Among those who rated a film "excellent," 17 per cent disliked something in the film, whereas, among those rating a film "fair-or-worse," 48 per cent expressed a dislike. In other words, approximately half of those who rated a film as fair-or-worse in educational value, indicated a dislike of something in the film. Thus, there appears to be some relationship between a student's dislike of something in a film and his judgment of the value of the film as a whole. How this judgment is related to amount of informational learning from the film was not pursued in this study.

III. EFFECTS ON INFORMATIONAL LEARNING

A somewhat different matter is the relationship between liking or disliking a particular film and the amount of information learned from the film. Collateral questions are the relationship between the amount of informational learning and preference for a particular medium (e.g., films vs. books), and the method of using that medium (e.g., long vs. short film sessions). To date, little research has been done along these lines.

ASH STUDY

P. Ash (1949), in a study conducted under the auspices of the Instructional Film Research Program, touched upon these problems to some extent in investigating the relative effectiveness of massed versus spaced film presentations. This study is discussed in more detail in Chapter VIII in connection with other methods and conditions of the use of instructional films.

Experimental Design

The study included two different populations; one, consisting of 11 classes of undergraduate psychology students, and the other, consisting of ten companies of Navy recruits.

The psychology classes saw two silent-film series of four 15-minute reels each. The first series, The Ape and the Child series, dealt with maturation and learning in a human infant and a chimpanzee. The second series, The Cat Neuroses series, dealt with the induction and treatment of experimental neuroses in cats. Of the 11 classes, three saw each series in a single one-hour session; two classes saw the two series at the rate of two reels per session; and two classes saw the two series at the rate of one reel per session. The remaining four classes served as controls, taking the tests, but not seeing the films.

The Navy recruits were shown two film series, each consisting of three 15-minute sound films. One series dealt with "rules of the nautical road," and the other presented certain principles of elementary hydraulics. One group saw the three reels in a single session of 45 minutes; another group saw them in three sessions, one reel per session; and one company took the tests without seeing the films at all.

An interest rating form was filled out at the conclusion of each film session to ascertain the subjects' degree of interest in the films and their judgment of film quality. The possible scores on this seven-question inventory ranged from zero to 18 points. One or two weeks after a series was shown, the classes were tested on the film content for that series.

Findings (1)

Little Correlation Between Interest and Gains

For The Ape and Child, the mean interest ratings ran high, means of 14 to 15 points out of possible 18, (SD's approximately 1.5 points) with no film getting an interest score of less than 7. Instructors have observed these films to be very popular with the general psychology students and the interest ratings agree with these observations. Correlations were calculated between the interest ratings and the information test scores for the three different lengths of film sessions. None of the correlations differed significantly (five per cent level) from zero, that is, test results appeared to be independent of interest ratings. The skewing and restricted range of the rating distributions may have contributed to reducing the correlations, as Ash points

out. Although a small proportion of the one-hour groups (3.4, 4.5, and 10.5 per cent for each of the three classes) thought the session was too long, this length was not found to have any adverse effect on either reported interest or measured learning.

Higher Correlations Appeared in Second Series

The subject matter of the Cat Neuroses series, which involved more complex concepts, was less appealing, and perhaps presupposed a more extensive technical background than that of the average general psychology student. The distribution of interest ratings spread somewhat more and was skewed toward the low end of the scale, the mean ratings being about two points lower than in the Ape and Child series. When interest ratings were again correlated with information, the majority of the 22 correlations were not significantly greater than zero, but the "picture" presented by the correlations is not entirely the same as that for the Ape and Child series. Two correlations (0.43 and 0.54) are significant at the one per cent level; one correlation of 0.45 was significant at the five per cent level; and six other correlations range from 0.20 to 0.38. In the previous series, the highest correlation is 0.19, and 14 of the 22 correlations are 0.10 or lower. Apparently in some groups or under certain conditions, there may be a fair correlation between interest in the films and amount of informational learning. The question of relationship between interest in the subject of a film and learning from a film is complex, and is not likely to be solved by incidental and peripheral research.

Massed Presentation Was Least Popular in the More Complex Series

In the Cat Neuroses series, when different methods of presentation were contrasted, it was found that the mean interest ratings for the massed-presentation sessions were one to two points lower than for either of the other two types of sessions. Analysis of the answers to the individual questions of the rating form showed that 61 and 81 percent of the two groups subjected to the one-hour session thought the session too long, whereas 13 and 21 percent of the two 30-minute session groups thought them too long. A slightly higher percentage in the one-hour group reported that the films held their interest only "some of the time," or "none of the time," and higher percentages of the massed presentation groups rated the films "useless" than did either of the two spaced-presentation groups.

Spaced-presentation Scores Were Higher in the Complex Series

The author concludes that, even though the one-hour session of the Cat Neuroses series had been rated unfavorably, the one-hour session did not seem to impair learning. However, the data for this series show some trends which are not found in the Ape and Child series. The mean total test scores on the information tests given in the 15-minute sessions are two and three points higher than those in the one-hour sessions. This superiority is due to the higher scores made on the parts of the tests based on the first and second reels, and is more pronounced on tests given two weeks after the films than one week afterward. The F-ratio for Part I of the test (based on reel one) after two weeks is significant at the 0.1 percent level and, for Part II of the test (based on reel two) it is significant at the five percent level. Thus, it would seem for the Cat Neuroses series that we not only have a less favorable interest rating when a one-hour session is used, but that there is, at least an indication of slightly less permanent learning.

It is interesting to note, however, as the author points out, that the class which was most critical of the first series (using four sessions) was also the class which was most critical of the second series, which it saw in a one-hour session. He suggests that the general negative reaction of this class to both film series, regardless of length of showings, was, at least in part, a function of the attitude of the class to films in general.

Findings (2)

Little Relation Found Between Interest and Learning

In the Navy groups which saw the series on Rules of the Nautical Road, the distribution of interest ratings for both groups and all sessions was definitely skewed toward the low end of the scale, the model rating being four points out of 18. The ratings, however, were scattered over almost the entire scale. Personal interviews with some of the trainees confirmed these low interest ratings, their answers indicating that they found the films dull and uninteresting. When the interest ratings were correlated with information test scores, only one of the 12 correlations was significantly greater than zero at the one percent level (an "r" of -.288). The remaining correlations were .16 or lower, mostly with positive signs. Thus, with this group there was no significant relation between interest rating and amount of learning from the film, except for the one-hour session group for which the "r" of -.288 was obtained. (The other hour-session group had a correlation of -.028, practically zero.)

Trainees Had Little Motivation to Learn

In this experimental situation there probably was no intense motivation for the trainees to learn the material, since, although they were required to come to the sessions, it probably was clear to them that these films were not part of their immediate training program. An old problem in the use of training films in the Army and Navy during World War II arose; as Ash says, "--the experimental situation. . .afforded a period for relative relaxation and even sleep." This probably helped to skew the ratings to the low end of the scale and may have affected the correlations. It is one of the few remarks we have been able to find in the experimental literature which approached the very practical problem that film showings in military training often provide a well-known opportunity for sleep on duty.

Similar Results Appeared in Second Series

The results for the Hydraulics series with the Navy groups were similar to those for the Rules of the Nautical Road series, although the Hydraulics series "seemed to win a slightly greater degree of interest than the preceding series." Of the 12 correlations of interest with information test scores, only three were significantly greater than zero. Two of these were for the two companies which had the long film sessions. One of these correlations was plus .248 (significant at the one percent level), and the other was minus .235 (five percent level). No attempt to explain this contradiction was made. One other correlation, plus .164, significant at the five percent level, was for the combined score of the two companies having distributed sessions, and was the one calculated for the part of the test covering their second film session. The remaining nine correlations were .17 or lower, all positive. Thus, for this series, there was no consistent relation between interest rating and amount of learning.

In an analysis of the individual questions which entered into the interest ratings, Ash reports "at least indirect evidence" that the distributed sessions were slightly better received. More of the subjects attending the spaced-film sessions indicated that they would "like to see more films in the series," and that they learned "something" or "a great deal" from the films than did those who attended the massed-film session.

Evaluation

Previous Knowledge Was Uncontrolled Variable

It appears that the study of the relation between interest and informational learning for this series may have been contaminated by the great influence which previous knowledge had upon the amount of learning from the films. Of the personnel who had previous knowledge (a course in physics or hydraulics) and who had seen the films, those in the various experimental groups had mean information scores which were six to 11 points higher than those in the control group. The mean superiority of the no-previous-knowledge film groups over their control groups was only three to five points. This previous knowledge factor was not controlled in the study of interest.

From Ash's study, as it concerned the relationship between interest and informational learning, it is clear that within the conditions of his experimental design, he found no consistent correlation between these two factors. However, he did find that in some groups, under certain inexplicable conditions, there may be a fair correlation (as high as .54) between interest in the films and amount of informational learning. There was no uniform tendency in the four series of films to rate either the long or short film sessions consistently high or low in interest.

In the Cat Neuroses series, there is evidence that the long session received a less favorable rating, and at least an indication of slightly less learning during that session than during the four 15-minute sessions. Also, in the Hydraulics series, there was at least indirect evidence that the distributed sessions were more acceptable to the subjects. Any comparison of this with amount of learning was apparently contaminated by the influence of previous knowledge. This latter factor was found to affect greatly the amount of film learning in this series and was not controlled in the study of interest.

There was some evidence that a given class might show a consistently negative attitude, regardless of the length of film showings, and it is suggested that this might be, in part, a function of the attitude of that class toward instructional films in general, or toward experimental film sessions as such. Also, whether a class will consider an hour session of films too long, it would seem, is affected by the intrinsic difficulty of the subject matter.

HEIDGERKEN STUDY

L. E. Heidgerken (1948) compared the effectiveness of sound films, filmstrips, and films and filmstrips combined, in the teaching of two units of the course in nursing arts to classes of students in 12 schools of nursing. Details of her study are presented in Chapter VI and further mention of it appears in Chapter VIII. She collected some data on the students' opinions on the value of the filmic teaching aids and on the desirability of using similar films in other units of the course.

Findings

Preferred Medium Gave No Better Scores

She found a high agreement among the students that the films used helped them in the units studied and that they would like to see similar films used in other units of the course. The students did not agree about the value of the filmstrips or whether they preferred the filmstrips or the motion pictures, although the latter received the highest average preference rating. Despite the students' feelings that the films had been of value and more should be shown, Heidgerken reports that, on the basis of an analysis of variance technique, there was not significant difference in amount of learning between any of the special-aids groups and the control group that had been taught in the usual way. Thus we find that preference for films and the opinion that they had aided learning are not reflected in higher achievement scores of these student nurses.

VANDERMEER STUDY

A. W. VanderMeer (1948, 1949), in his study of the effectiveness of color films with ninth-grade science students, using five films available in both black and white and color versions, obtained a measure of "liking" for the films as one of his evaluations. More details of this study are given in Chapter VIII in the section on Emphatic Devices.

Findings

Using groups equated on intelligence, pre-test knowledge of the film material, age, and sex, he found that, as measured by the paired comparison method, there was a slight tendency for the students to prefer films in color over identical films in black and white. In the case of two films, the differences were significant at the five percent level, and for the other three, the differences were even less reliable. This not-too-reliable tendency of ninth-grade pupils to prefer color films seems to be reflected in a slight, but consistently greater efficiency in learning. This greater efficiency, which generally is not highly reliable, was most evident on delayed tests.

WESTFALL STUDY

L. H. Westfall (1934) conducted a study of the effectiveness of different types of verbal accompaniment for instructional films. This investigation had as a secondary phase a measure of likes and dislikes for different types of verbal accompaniment.

Experimental Design

In this investigation three silent films, The Harvest of the Sugar Maple, Banana Land, and Cotton, and three sound films, Plant Growth, Beach and Sea Animals, and The Frog, were used in their original form and in five modified versions in the case of the former, and in four modified versions for the latter. Westfall did not correlate preferences with amount of learning, but at the conclusion of his six weeks of film showings (one film per week), each student was asked to answer a short questionnaire, indicating the best and poorest of the six films. In addition, the student was asked to indicate which type of verbal accompaniment he thought best, which poorest, and which helped him most in understanding the picture. In order to obtain more accurate answers from fifth-grade pupils, the various forms of verbal accompaniment were reduced to four classes, without regard to whether the original film from which the modified version was made, had been a silent or a sound film. The four classes of accompaniment were: (1) reading titles from the screen, in the case of regular silent films, or reading inserted titles on the case of sound films with the sound shut off; (2) reading from the screen plus added comments by the teacher, in the case of the silent films; (3) listening to the teacher read a prepared lecture, with captions cut out of silent films, or with sound cut off for sound films; (4) listening to the recorded sound, using a sound-on-disc system.

In measuring the amount of learning, the results for each of the 11 experimental versions were treated separately and compared in two groups, according to whether the original film was (1) sound or (2) silent, but this was not done with the study of preferences for different verbal accompaniments. In the latter case, as just indicated, the students were simply asked to react to the four conditions listed above, and all results were grouped together regardless of whether the film to which the teacher read a commentary had been a sound or silent film originally. His findings on preference are possibly thus affected by this lack of precision in treating the results in this part of the study.

Findings

Recorded-Sound Version Was Preferred

The table that follows presents the preferences of 541 fifth-grade pupils from 18 classes in four different types of communities for the four methods of verbal explanation mentioned above.

Form of Verbal Accompaniment	Percentage Marking Each Form As:		
	Best	Poorest	Most Helpful to Understanding
1. Reading from screen	15	43	16
2. Reading from screen plus listening to teacher	11	25	15
3. Listening to teacher	12	15	21
4. Listening to recorded-sound	62	17	48

More Learning Occurred from Recorded-Sound Version of Sound Films

The experimental design used by Westfall was a modified rotation method, films and methods both being rotated; 25 classes were involved altogether. Raw scores on the information tests were converted to standard scores for comparison. Intelligence was equated by a regression matching technique, in which predicted mean scores were compared with the ob-

tained mean scores. When the mean scores for the five versions of the three sound films were compared, it was found that the sound films with recorded sound resulted in reliably more learning than the other versions (printed titles, identical with commentary and spliced into film; teacher-read commentary; teacher-prepared explanation, given with film; film with no verbal accompaniment, sound off).

Score Differences Were Smaller Than Preference Differences

The superiority of learning from the recorded-sound version was by no means in proportion to the differences in percentages of preference reported in the above table. The sound version, though reliably better (CR of 2.92) than the teacher-read version, was not superior by a sizable score; the difference was only about 0.17 to 0.19 of the SD's of the film-test distributions of the two groups. The superiority of the recorded-sound version to reading the commentary from titles was larger, but still only about one third of the SD's of the test-score distributions, whereas the preference percentages for "most helpful" were 48 and 16 per cent, respectively. Listening to the teacher-read commentary was better to a small degree than reading from the screen, a fact which agrees fairly well with the percentage differences on "helpfulness," but not with the difference in ratings of "best." Reading from the screen and listening to teacher-prepared explanation were about equally effective, a result which does not reflect the high percentage assigning "poorest" to reading from the screen. Perhaps the only consistency between the preference ratings and the achievement was the superiority of the recorded-sound, and that was grossly overestimated by the pupils.

SECTION 4. APPEAL OF THE MOVIES

Motion pictures appear to have an unusual appeal which is strongest among persons between 15 and 20 years old and recedes among older individuals. One measure of this appeal is frequency of attendance at entertainment motion pictures.

Persons Under 20 Attend Most Frequently

E. Dale (1935) reported that peak attendance among children and adolescents was reached between 14 and 20 years of age. In a recent study of movie attendance of high school boys and girls in New Zealand, W. J. Scott (1947) found that the age group attending movies most frequently was 14 to 17 for boys, and 13 to 16 for girls. In their analysis of adult communications habits, P. F. Lazarsfeld and P. L. Kendall (1943) found that there was a progressive decrease in frequency of attendance at entertainment films from 21 to 60 years of age. In the 21 to 29-year range, 19 per cent of the adults attend no movies, and this percentage increases progressivley until, for the age bracket of 60-plus years, it reaches 73 per cent.

Films Appeal to Military-Training Age Group

The attraction of motion pictures, using frequency of entertainment-film attendance as the index of attraction, is nearly maximum among the group of military-training age. Thus, films, at least the dramatic type, appear to be particularly appropriate as a military training device when the factor of popular appeal is considered.

STERNER STUDY

By her analysis of communications habits of high school adolescents, A. P. Sterner (1947) throws some light on the subject of the appeal of movies.

Findings

With reference to radio programs, entertainment movies, comic books, comic strips, and magazines, Sterner concludes that "adolescents seek satisfaction of interests through these media and are indifferent as to the special means of communication. It is the theme, not the medium, which is important to young people" (p. 25).

Sterner reaches this conclusion by correlating the interest scores for the three themes: adventure, humor, and romance, pair by pair, within each medium studied; and then taking the average of these inter-theme correlations within the separate media as a measure of the relationship among interests independent of media. This inter-theme average correlation was .724 (using Fisher's z values for the averaging). She then correlates the interest or activity scores for each of the five media studied, pair by pair, within each of the three themes, and takes the average of these inter-media correlations within the separate themes as a measure of the relationship among media independent of interests. This inter-media correlation was .266. From these two average correlations Sterner concludes, "it is obvious, therefore, that the attraction among interests is greater than the attraction among media" (p. 25).

Evaluation

Films May Have Intrinsic Appeal

Although this conclusion appears to be warranted by the various separate correlations, it tends to obscure the high relationship of the "interest" themes within the medium of motion pictures (as compared, for instance, with radio), and the reasonably high relationship between any of these themes and movies which have not been classified under any of the three "interest" items. Examination of the detailed correlation data leads to the conclusion that the attraction of motion pictures appears to be relatively independent of any one of these three themes. For instance, within movies as a medium of communication, the coefficients of correlation between the themes of adventure and humor, adventure and romance, and humor and romance are all .80 or slightly higher (.83 for adventure and humor, which in the case of the radio is only .61).

Stated in another way, the "interest" themes appear to be so highly related within adolescents' choice of motion picture experiences that it is difficult to conclude that adolescents select motion picture experiences because of any one of these three themes. It appears more probable that they attend the movies with very little discrimination as to whether the particular movie deals with romance, or with adventure, or with humor, and that all three appear to be interchangeable as factors in motion-picture selection. Furthermore, these three themes are typical patterns of adolescent interests.

The correlation coefficients between these three themes are higher for movies than for any of the other media. It is conceivable that Sterner's interpretation can be modified and her data can be interpreted to mean that entertainment motion pictures dealing with romance, adventure, and humor are particularly attractive to adolescents, and that any one of these themes is interchangeable with any other one in the selection of any particular movie experience. If this interpretation can be imposed on Sterner's data, we may be justified in concluding that, for one reason or another, entertainment motion pictures appear to have an unusual attraction for adolescents when humor, adventure, and romance are involved. This is not as clearly evident for any of the other mass media of entertainment.

SACKETT STUDY

The attraction of motion pictures as a communication medium does not appear to be limited to entertainment films.

Findings

R. S. Sackett's (Hoban, 1942) analysis of responses of elementary and high school students to classroom films showed that 59 per cent of the students suggested seeing another motion picture as their choice of activity following a film experience. This preference was highest among a list of ten activities suggested by the students, including all conventional classroom activities such as additional reading, individual reports, and the like.

BECK, KELLY, AND PETERMAN STUDY

The foregoing evidence suggests that the attraction of motion pictures is not entirely dependent on the use of adventure, romance, and humor, but is related, at least in part, to the medium as such. L. F. Beck, F. E. Kelly, and J. Peterman (Hoban, 1946) conducted a study on the frequency with which comparable films and filmstrips were used in the Army training program.

Findings

With approximately the same number of motion pictures and filmstrips available for use in training, films were used five times as often as filmstrips, even when the use of filmstrips was intensively promoted. This finding may be partly due to the fact that many instructors find motion pictures require less effort to use than filmstrips.

SUMMARY

PREDISPOSITIONAL FACTORS IN AUDIENCE RESPONSE

PREDISPOSITION TO ACCEPTANCE

Some experimental evidence is available to support the hypothesis that the predisposition of an audience to accept an attitude or opinion is a factor which operates in the interpretation of experience from a motion picture. The effect of this predisposition may at times not manifest itself immediately, but may appear after a longer period of time.

Theoretically, it is probable that the individual not only tends to forget those items of experience that are inconsonant with this predisposition, but also perceptually rejects experience from any medium either by not "seeing" or by not immediately accepting these items during their initial presentation in communication. Most of us are familiar with people who consistently refuse to "see what they do not want to see." Psychological knowledge and understanding of this process of selective perception is, at present, inadequate.

THRESHOLDS OF EXCITABILITY

We may conclude from the evidence at hand that the threshold of excitement from movies portraying danger, conflict, romance, and humor varies within any age group, and that excitability generally declines as we approach adulthood.

The relationship between excitement, involvement, and acceptance is not clear. Here is one of the major areas for film research. It is basic to the choice of dramatic or narrative technique in instructional films.

LIKES AND DISLIKES

A. EFFECTS ON OPINION CHANGE

The limited evidence at hand suggests that adult-audience "likes" and "dislikes" of a film are related to the direction of the influence of the film on opinion, when such an influence is intended and/or occurs. Those who dislike a film appear to be less positively influenced or influenced negatively in opinions, and those who like a film appear to be influenced positively in opinions. ("Positive" is understood to refer to the direction of the intended influence.)

B. EFFECTS ON RATING OF EDUCATIONAL VALUE

Likes and dislikes of something in a film also appear to be related to student judgment of the educational value of a film, in that few films disliked were highly appraised for their educational or instructional value. Questions for further research are: does this relationship apply to instructors as well? Is this judgment of educational value related to amount of informational learning from the film?

C. EFFECTS ON INFORMATIONAL LEARNING

The limited data available fail to show a consistent correlation between degree of interest in a film and amount of informational learning among certain college classes and armed-forces trainee groups. However, in some of these groups, under certain inexplicable conditions, there may be a fair correlation between interest and amount of learning.

Preferred Teaching Aids Were Not Markedly Superior in Teaching

Even though college-age students seem to prefer motion pictures as a supplementary aid in a unit of instruction, and believe that motion pictures benefit learning, their achievement scores do not always reflect increased learning. On the other hand, some less preferred medium may actually benefit learning more.

Some groups of upper elementary school pupils greatly overestimated the helpfulness of a preferred type of verbal accompaniment with a film and underestimated the helpfulness of a much less preferred type. A limited sample of junior high school pupils was found to show a slight tendency to prefer science films in color to identical prints in black and white. This preference seemed to be reflected in a slightly greater, (though not highly reliable), efficiency in learning which was more evident in delayed tests.

Preferred Session-Length Depends on Material

Certain college classes and armed-forces trainee groups had no consistent tendency to rate either long or short film sessions high or low in interest in the case of four different film series. In one series of films there was evidence that the long session received a less favorable rating, and at least an indication that slighly less learning resulted from the single long session than from the four 15-minute sessions. Apparently, the intrinsic appeal and difficulty of the subject matter in the films are two predominant factors in determining whether an audience feels that a one-hour film session is too long. Also, there was some evidence that a given class might show a consistently negative attitude regardless of the length of film showings, an attitude which that class might have toward instructional films in general.

Thus, the limited evidence at hand suggests that degree of interest is no sure indication of the amount of learning that will result from a film, and that preference for a certain characteristic of a film, or for a certain way of using a film, cannot be taken as an index of greater effectiveness in informational learning.

More extensive investigations and much more exact techniques of measuring interest or preference seem to be called for in regard to informational learning and, in fact, in the whole area of affective and emotional reactions to films and the influence of these factors upon the effectiveness of a given type of film. Nothing said here is meant to imply that it is not psychologically desirable for the student to like the methods and materials used in his instruction.

APPEAL OF THE MOVIES

The studies which have been conducted on the appeal of the movies show that entertainment movies have the strongest attraction for adolescents in the 15-20 year age group. Thus, if popular appeal is a factor to be considered when selecting a medium of communication, motion pictures are particularly appropriate for use with audiences in that age group, a group which approaches and includes some of the military-trainee group.

Some of these studies indicate that adolescents attend entertainment movies because they like movies, rather than because they are attracted by a particular type of theme or story. This preference for motion pictures includes classroom films as well as entertainment films. When the choice is between films and filmstrips, the data indicate that films are the preferred medium.

PART II. SOCIAL FACTORS IN AUDIENCE RESPONSE

SOCIAL ROLES

In his development, the individual gradually assumes or is assigned social roles in terms of sex, age, education, occupation, religion, talent or skill, ancestry, and other group characteristics which define the type of behavior expected of that individual in various social situations. The importance of role assignment in the behavior of the individual is becoming increasingly evident.

Some information is available on the relationship between the individual's social role and his reactions to motion pictures. L. L. Ramseyer's (1938) study suggests that parental occupation may enter into attitudinal influences of films dealing with government activity in the conservation of human and natural resources. C. F. Hoban, Jr. (1942) noted some clinical evidence to the effect that socio-economic and religious roles entered into the reaction of high school students to the film, Work Pays America. Similarly, C. I. Hovland, A. A. Lumsdaine, and F. D. Sheffield demonstrated that educational level entered into opinions influenced by military orientation films. It is not clear whether educational level was more an index of social status (including occupation, income, residence area) or whether it was more an index of intelligence. Probably it is related to both. In general, educational level is likely to be related to some role assignment of the individual in that it is a recognized prestige factor in the hierarchy of social and occupational status.

This section summarizes other research data on this challenging problem of the relationship of social role assignment to reactions to films in terms of (1) religion, (2) sex, and (3) age and grade level.

SECTION 1. RELIGION ROLE

KISHLER STUDY

An experiment by J. Kishler (1950) of the Instructional Film Research Program (described in some detail in Chapter VIII) seems to have some bearing on the audience characteristic of role ascription.

Experimental Design

Kishler investigated the effect of the film, Keys of the Kingdom, starring Gregory Peck, on the attitudes of, and factual information learned by, college-student populations. The subjects selected were persons (1) for whom the occupational role of the main character (Catholic priest) had either a high or a low prestige value, and (2) whose "identification" with the main character could be assumed to be influenced by their institutional affiliation or non-affiliation with the Catholic church. In other words, it was assumed that the student who was a member of the Catholic church would be inclined to assume a certain role, and would show certain characteristic attitudes, and hence would be more influenced in factual learning and attitudes by a film with a Catholic theme than the non-Catholic student. Catholic and non-Catholic groups were equated on sex, percentage previously having seen the film, and scholastic aptitude test scores.

Findings

Role Ascription Had Little Influence

As might have been predicted from a group identification hypothesis, Catholics ranked the prestige role of Catholic priest higher than did non-Catholics on both pre-tests and post-tests. Both Catholics and non-Catholics assigned higher prestige values to the role after the film than before the film, and the differences in these values were significant at the one per cent level. The Catholics showed a slight, but unreliably greater, proportional change (effectiveness index) in prestige value than did the non-Catholics. On a religious tolerance attitude scale no change could be found that was related to the role ascription of Catholic; both groups improved slightly, the non-

Catholics reliably so. On a test of information in the film, there was a slight mean difference in favor of the Catholics, reliable at the six percent level. Thus, this study offers only slight evidence of the influence of role ascription in film learning.

SECTION 2. SEX ROLE

Sexes Differ in Rating Educational Value of Certain Films

C. F. Hoban, Jr. (1942) investigated the differences in mean rating of the educational value of instructional films among boys and girls in analyzing reports of student reactions to films shown in elementary and high schools in connection with the American Council on Education's nation-wide evaluation of motion pictures in general education.

He found a number of instances in which boys and girls assigned contrasting educational value to the films. He related these differences to the film content which could be identified, in one way or another, with (1) activities such as science, machinery, and operations requiring stamina and strength, to which the American culture assigns a particular sex role; (2) activities performed more or less exclusively by one sex; or (3) a male or female protagonist in the film.

Boys Learn More Than Girls From Certain Films on Science and Mechanical Processes

H. R. Brenner, J. S. Walter, and A. K. Kurtz (1949), in their study of the value of questions and statements inserted in a film (discussed in Chapter VIII), found some evidence of sex differences in response to film content and to special learning aids inserted in the films.

Their experimental population consisted of six groups of high school students, each containing 111 boys and 111 girls. The groups which were drawn from six different schools were equated in intelligence. They prepared six different versions of each of the two films, and showed one version of each film to each group. The films used were, Snakes, a color film on the types of snakes found in this country, and The Care and Use of Hand Tools: Wrenches, a film used in the training of mechanical workers. Four versions of each film involved either inserted questions or statements, supposed to facilitate learning. The fifth version was the original film, shown once, and the sixth version, the original film, shown twice in succession.

In this study it was found that the boys learned more from both films than the girls, regardless of the version shown, but the difference in favor of the boys was greater for the film, Wrenches. This is in line with the difference in rating of educational value of films by boys and girls just quoted from Hoban, who interpreted this as due to certain activities typically assigned a masculine or feminine role in our

culture. The typical boys' interest in tools and machinery "explains" higher scores of the boys on the Wrenches film. A reliable mean superiority of 2.8 points for the boys on the Otis Quick Scoring Intelligence Test did not seem to explain completely this sex difference in learning from the film. A sex difference in the effectiveness of the several film versions also occurred and varied with the two different films.

A. W. VanderMeer's (1950) study of exclusive film instruction in general science, (mentioned in Chapter VI), provides data on learning differences between boys and girls. He found that, in all comparisons, the boys learned more than the girls in the same method group, but that the order of effectiveness for the three methods studied was the same for each sex in almost every test. Apparently no sex difference existed between these methods with this type of film. The boys' interest in science probably explains the fact that they learned more from all methods than did the girls.

Films More Beneficial to Boys Than Girls In One Investigation in American History

H. A. Wise (1939), in his study of the Chronicles of America Photoplays, mentioned later in this chapter, found some evidence of a sex difference in the effectiveness of these silent films as aids in teaching American History in senior high schools.

On his comprehensive tests the girls gained more than the boys from both film and non-film teaching, but, as a learning aid, the superiority of the films over the usual method was somewhat reliably greater for the boys than for the girls (CR of 2.5 PE's).

On the Columbia Research Bureau American History Test, the boys knew more than the girls at the beginning, learned more than the girls from either method, and showed a somewhat reliably greater benefit from the films than did the girls (for the latter difference the CR was 2.29 PE's).

As shown by their score on an essay-type test of factual information and by their ability to re-create the spirit and atmosphere of the times, the boys were reliably aided by the films. The films were not reliably beneficial to the girls, except in increasing the number of historical facts correctly stated. Regardless of the teaching method, the girls were definitely more verbose than the boys in their essay tests. What the films accomplished for the boys in these tests was to bring the quality of their essays up to the level of that of the girls. Both the boys and girls who saw the films did more voluntary reading than the control groups, but there was no reliable difference between the sexes.

Some Sex Differences in Physiological Indices of Responses to Films

Some differences in the physiological indices of emotional responses to entertainment films among males and females were reported in the W. S. Dysinger and C. A. Ruckmick (1933) study described in detail in an earlier section of this chapter. With particular reference to danger scenes, they found that male responses exceeded those of females. In regard to response to amorous scenes, their laboratory and theater situation results are conflicting, and do not justify a general statement (p. 109).

In the S. Renshaw, V. L. Miller, and D. P. Marquis (1933) study, described in the early part of Chapter VIII, it was found that on the average, boys showed about 26 per cent and girls about 14 per cent greater hourly motility in sleep after movies than in normal sleep. They also stress greater individual differences among the girls than among the boys (pp. 153, 135).

Some Sex Differences in Testimony Regarding the Effect of Films on Emotions and Attitudes

In H. Blumer's (1933) study of "movie biographies," mentioned in Chapter V and described in the early part of Chapter VIII, some sex differences were found in the 458 high school biographies which he analyzed. Among the 64 per cent who mentioned that they experienced sorrow and pathos at entertainment films, there were about twice as many girls as boys. Fifty per cent of the girls admitted having difficulty in keeping from crying at certain pictures while only 26 per cent of the boys made this admission. Sixty-seven per cent of the girls and only 41 per cent of the boys mentioned being

stirred or thrilled by love pictures. An equal number of boys and girls admitted being made more receptive to love by love scenes, 30 per cent in each case. These differences are interesting as indications of what boys and girls are willing to say in anonymous statements and are quite possibly influenced by the individual's tendency to assume the role ascribed to his sex.

Sex Differences in Film Topic Preferences from the Age of Ten and Older

Among ten to 12 year olds, studies have shown that boys tend to prefer more thrill and excitement than girls, who are more interested in romantic situations in films (e.g., M. V. Seagoe, 1931).

A study of movie topic preferences of high school students in Chicago, conducted by P. Witty, S. Garfield, and W. G. Brink (1941), showed the following differences among 350 members of each sex.

Types of Movie Preferred	Per Cent Boys	Per Cent Girls
Comedy	81.4	81.6
Mystery	72.5	62.0
Western	57.9	32.7
News	53.4	30.3
Cartoon	53.1	40.9
Gangster	52.2	30.3
Educational	45.0	48.6
Love	24.1	70.7

These sex differences in movie topic preferences parallel rather closely the preferences of the two sexes in reading and radio listening in later childhood and adolescence. It is quite possible that some of these differences are due to the individual's tendency to assume the typical role assigned to his sex in our culture.

SECTION 3. AGE ROLE

In our American culture, people, including children, are "age-graded" (treated a certain way because of their age and certain things expected of that age); this social phenomenon of age-grading affects a person's behavior as he assumes an age role.

Ability To Learn Factual Material From Films Varies With Age

As reported by H. E. Jones, H. Conrad, and A. Horn (1928), the ability to learn factual material from films, under ordinary motivation, becomes greater as age increases, until a peak is reached in the early 20's. This ability is maintained nearly at peak level until the age of about 45 when a gradual decline begins, becoming more pronounced after the 50's. The increase up to the peak of the curve appears to result mainly from increased intelligence and accumulation of knowledge, although motivational factors

related to age role may also have an effect. The decline is probably partly a matter of gradual physiological impairment of the senses and the nervous system, although Jones used no subjects over the age of 60. (So many of his cases over 60 pleaded exemption from taking the test, usually on the ground of reading difficulty, that all papers of persons above this age were discarded.) It is conceivable that part of this decline may have been influenced by what adults of that age think is expected of them and what they think they can do. In studies of adult learning from other media, it is surprising to note how much adults could learn if they were physically normal and wanted to learn badly enough (cf., E. L. Thorndike, Adult Learning, 1927).

Film Topic Preferences Vary with Age

Preferences for various types of motion pictures vary with age and tend to parallel those for reading and radio listening and show the same sex differences. One investigation (A. M. Mitchell, 1929A) lists the movie preferences of kindergarten, first- and second-grade children in the following order: animated cartoons (by far the most popular), shorts, travelogues, and feature pictures. Another study (W. E. Blatz, 1936) found that, among Toronto children up to 13 years of age, comedy is the first choice, followed by mystery and musical comedies. The type of comedy having the most appeal is the slapstick variety.

A study of children from grades one to eight (M. V. Seagoe, 1931) found that 53.3 per cent of the children preferred going to the movies to reading a book or playing a game. Within this group, children six to nine years old preferred comedies and cartoons. They also liked films in which children and animals were portrayed, and insisted upon active heroes and pretty heroines. In the ten to 12 age group, both boys and girls wanted adventure films and were less fond of comedy. The boys tended to prefer more thrill and excitement than the girls, who were more interested in romantic situations.

A study of the movie preferences of 350 high school pupils in Chicago (P. Witty, S. Garfield, and W. G. Brink, 1941) found that the first three choices for the boys, in descending order, were comedy, mystery, westerns, with news, cartoons, and gangster films approximately equal for least popularity. In the case of the girls, the order of preference was comedy, love, mystery, with a big drop to cartoon films as fourth choice.

It is quite probable that these changes in movie preferences with age are influenced in part by the individual's attempt to "act his age."

Children Interested in Other Children and Families in Movies

Trying to "play" his role, "act his age," etc., are probably factors in the tendency of the individual to emulate motion-picture heroes or to carry out actions portrayed in films, and in the types of motion pictures preferred by children and adults of different ages. (This influence of motion pictures upon conduct was discussed in Chapter V.)

C. F. Hoban, Jr. (1942) analyzed fifth-grade students' responses to films shown in the classroom. He reported that these pupils were "vitally interested in the activities of children of similar age shown in a film, and their interest expands to the brothers and sisters, fathers and mothers of these children in the film. The students are not nearly as interested in adults if the latter do not assume the father or mother role in the film, or if the adults portray fathers and mothers whose children are much older than the children in the school group viewing the film. Younger children are also interested in older children shown in a film, but older children are seldom as interested in younger children, except as other factors would foster this interest" (p. 46).

Similar observations were made from examination of sixth-grade pupil responses to films dealing with family relationships and activities. Although these observations were made from limited populations and were based on free-response of the pupils, they are indicative of a possible influence of age-role on reaction to motion pictures relating directly to this role.

SUMMARY

SOCIAL FACTORS IN AUDIENCE RESPONSE

Roles Adopted Appear to Influence Some Reactions to Films

There is some evidence that the roles ascribed to an individual, and which are adopted and "played" by him, are related to his reaction to a motion picture. Roles related to socio-economic level, religion, educational status, age, and sex of the individual may at times affect the influence of the film on him. From the scanty evidence available, but based on good theoretical reasons, the following hypothesis may be suggested: the nature and degree of the influence of the motion picture is affected by the extent to which the content of the film is directly related to the behavior and response patterns embedded in one or more of the individual's social roles.

Film Preferences Vary with Age

In considering age differences, we must not lose sight of the importance of intellectual maturation and other physiological factors which change with age and sexual maturity. It seems probable, however, that

some of the age differences are culturally influenced when the individual tries to "act his age" and adopt the group code for that age.

Sex Role and Film Influence

It is difficult to state the extent to which the differences in the way the two sexes respond to the films discussed here can be attributed to the individual's acting in accordance with the sex role which he knows has been ascribed to him by society, his family, and his peer group. Possibly some of these differences are at least partially due to more basic physiological differences between the sexes, but this is hard to demonstrate. Certainly a large number of these differences are influenced to a considerable extent by cultural factors related to our concept of the assumption of a role ascribed to and adopted by that particular individual.

Some Sex Differences in Film Influence Which Are Possibly Related to Role Adoption

There is some evidence of sex differences in responses to films. These differences appear as differences in rating the educational value of films; some emotional and attitudinal differences in reaction to a given film, or part of a film; differences in film topic preferences from at least the age of ten years and upwards; a tendency for boys to learn more than girls from certain films relating to science and mechanical processes.

Social Role and Identification

In theory, at least, social role ascription and adoption, is intimately related to the phenomenon of "identification," which is discussed in Chapter VIII in relation to audience involvement in film experience and its relation to learning from films.

PART III. INTELLECTUAL FACTORS IN AUDIENCE RESPONSE

Perhaps, in emphasizing the dynamic factors of individual predisposition and the social milieu, particularly in the chapter on motivation, attitudes, and opinions, and again in this chapter on personality characteristics of the audience, the impression has been created that the ability or abilities included in "intelligence" are of relatively little importance. When the individual reacts to and/or learns from films, it should be stressed that neither the experimental evidence nor your reviewers' concept of the human being is in accord with any such anti-intellectual impression or interpretation.

Intelligence and level of terminal education are positively correlated, and both are correlated with occupational status, class status in the social structure of the community, and other aspects of social prestige and privilege. This is not to say that intelligence is always or, beyond a minimum point, necessarily causative of status. But, because intelligence is so interwoven into the structure of social behavior, and, as such, is bound up with formal education and training, it is important to know how intelligence influences responses to films. This question assumes even greater importance in light of the twin beliefs that (a) films are especially good for teaching the mentally underprivileged, and (b) films are a waste of valuable time in teaching the mentally gifted.

Training and experience also enter into audience reaction to films. Does, for instance, an individual who already knows something about the subject shown in a film learn more from the film than his less well-informed neighbor? Is it a case of "to him that hath shall be given"? Does seeing many films help one to learn more from films, or does it dull the mind to learning from films? Data on these problems are summarized below.

Deficiencies Exist in Intelligence-Film Learning Studies

Most of the studies of the relationship between intelligence and amount of learning from motion-picture films have been made as a minor or incidental phase of some other research problem and, due partly to this fact, the findings on this relationship are subject to various limitations. Some of these limitations are: (1) correlation of IQ's with gains in learning for a group that was not uniform with respect to age or grade in school; (2) correlation of IQ with percentage gain, which is likely to lead to a low or negative correlation; (3) failure to distinguish in meaning between IQ, MA, and raw score on intelligence tests; (4) careless use of the words "bright" and "dull," when comparing two groups differing in intelligence; and (5) failure to distinguish between the size of the gain in learning and the size of the difference in gain between a film and a non-film group of a certain intelligence level.

Correlations Between Intelligence and Non-Film Learning

Outside the field of film learning many studies show that the relationship between intelligence scores as obtained with typical tests and amount of learning under a given condition is practically always positive. Correlations have varied from close to zero to as high as .70 or .80, with measures of perceptual-motor learning tending to be lower than those for various verbal types of material, and with measures of rational learning and problem solving involving abstract relations, usually having the higher correlations. (J. A. McGeoch, 1942, p. 246 ff.)

Studies have shown at least five characteristics of learning material which influence its correlation with intelligence test scores: (1) amount of meaning or organization in the material; (2) the amount of symbolic activity (responding to verbal symbols, mathematical symbols, or diagrammatic symbols) required in the learning; (3) the difficulty or complexity of the material; (4) amount of insight or rational thinking required; and (5) the amount of overt muscular activity required. The first four of these are positively correlated with intelligence, and the fifth is slightly correlated, if at all. It is undoubtedly true that these same factors operate in the correlation of intelligence and film learning, although little, if any, research to identify them has been done.

SECTION 1. EFFECTS OF INTELLIGENCE AND EDUCATIONAL LEVEL

I. LEARNING BY CHILDREN FROM FORMAL FILM INSTRUCTION

A. CORRELATION BETWEEN INTELLIGENCE AND LEARNING FROM FILMS

SECOR STUDY

C. T. Secor (1931) (see page VI-20) studied the influence of ten films in learning certain units of high school biology.

Findings

He reported six correlations of film learning with intelligence, ranging from .35 to .87, four of them between .70 and .87. When the same two groups were taught other units by usual methods without films, the correlations tended to be lower in most cases, the six correlations ranging from .40 to .68, with five of them between .50 and .68. When test items were not in the same sequence as they were in the film, correlations for both film groups were definitely higher than when the items followed the film sequence. These correlations for the two groups were: .97 vs. .66 for one group and .84 vs. .76 for the other.

SMITH STUDY

H. A. Smith (1948, 1949) studied the use of films and demonstrations in teaching three units of general science to ninth-grade pupils.

Findings

He reported low correlations (.18 to .25) between IQ and gains in the units in which a film was used. These correlations were compared with equated groups who watched demonstrations instead of films, and for these groups correlations were slightly lower (.16 to .19).

Evaluation

In his experiment, the variables of film or demonstration constituted only a relatively small portion of the instructional activities presumably measured by the tests, so that one might not expect much differential in either the size of the correlation with IQ or in mean gains to result from either method. However, this does not explain the definitely lower correlations obtained here, as compared with those in the Secor study reported above.

WITTICH AND FOWLKES STUDY

W. A. Wittich and J. G. Fowlkes (1946) present data (p. 89) which indicate that pupils in both the high and low IQ ranges gain about equally from motion pictures when the films are repeatedly exhibited and when self-administering study guides were interspersed between the repeated exhibitions.

Evaluation

In their scatter diagram the investigators have plotted the IQ and gains on the film tests of the pupils from all three grades together, regardless of the pupils' grades in school or their chronological ages. This involves what appears to be a misapplication of the meaning of the IQ, a misapplication which other investigators have made, and which results in a zero correlation between IQ and gains (actually a -.04 correlation as calculated by the reviewers from the scatter diagram).

An IQ of 120 does not have the same meaning for pupils of all ages. A fourth-grade pupil with that IQ may well have a mental age three to four years below a sixth-grade pupil with the same IQ. Mental age (MA), which indicates the level of the pupil's learning capacity, should be used if three or four grades are going to be thrown together in a correlation table. On the other hand, if the reader will turn to the experimenters' discussion of reading grade level and film test score correlations (p. 71), he will find these correlations reported for each experimental factor by grades and by films, which is the way the IQ's and gains should have been reported.

It seems very reasonable to expect that sizable correlations between IQ and learning gains will be found which are very similar to those between reading grade and gains, especially because of the well-known, high correlations existing between reading scores and IQ's for any one grade level or for any 12-months range of ages.

Accordingly, the conclusion of these investigators that "children of a low IQ and those with a high IQ seem to be motivated equally and to learn to a comparable degree from educational sound films," (p. 99), cannot be accepted as statistically valid or logically reasonable when the data presented are compared with the data for reading age and film test scores.

B. FILM LEARNING BY INTELLIGENCE-STRATIFIED GROUPS

GIBBS STUDY

Another approach to this problem has been to compare the film learning of certain specified upper and lower groups in intelligence. One of the earlier comparisons of this type was by D. Gibbs (1925) who compared the usual textbook-recitation method with two ways of supplementing teaching with a film, in teaching the topic of digestion to seventh-grade pupils of three different cities.

Experimental Design

He divided his subjects into upper and lower fourths in intelligence, the mean IQ's being 114 and 85. These groups were then subdivided into three equivalent groups, each receiving one of the three different instructional methods being tested. The three methods differed in length of time involved, so he calculated the improvement in score per minute of learning time.

Findings

The three upper quarter groups learned more in all three situations than the lower quarter groups. Film groups in both quarters learned more than non-film groups. The ratios of the scores per minute of instruction for the two quarters (lower quarter score divided by upper quarter score) were (1) five periods without the film, .73; (2) two usual periods plus one film period, .82; and, (3) one usual period plus one film period, .76. The use of the film brought the per minute score of the lower quarter up somewhat, but by no means equal to the upper quarter.

HINMAN STUDY

S. T. Hinman (1931) studied the effect of advance warning of a film test in stimulating fifth-grade and sixth-grade pupils to learn more from a film.

He found that the upper quarter in MA was better on all three testings (one immediate and two delayed tests) than the lowest quarter, but no additional differential was created here by knowledge or lack of knowledge that a film test was to be given.

ARNSPIGER STUDY

V. C. Arnspiger (1933) investigated the use of sound films to supplement the usual techniques of instructing fifth-grade pupils in music and science. He reports data for "above average" and "below average" groups in IQ, without further defining the groups.

Findings

The films increased the learning of both groups. In the learning of natural science, the films seemed to produce a greater absolute gain for the below-average group, but in the music units, the absolute gains of both higher and lower groups were approximately the same. The above-average groups, whether in film classes or control classes learned more than the below-average groups.

WISE STUDY

H. A. Wise (1939) studied the Chronicles of America Photoplays as aids in the teaching of American History at the senior high school level. He analyzed his data in terms of three intelligence levels: highest quarter (IQ's, 105 plus), middle half (IQ's 91 through 104), and lowest quarter (IQ's 90 and below).

Findings

On his pre- and post-tests the amount of gain of the three intelligence levels was in direct relation to their intelligence in both the control and experimental groups. Each level showed a greater gain with films than without them. The greatest difference in gain between film and non-film groups was for the lowest quarter, but the films did not bring the lowest quarter up to the achievement level of the middle group without films.

On the Columbia Research Bureau American History Test, the middle group in intelligence made the smallest gain with films, whereas the films brought the gain of the lowest quarter well above that of both other groups, giving that quarter the largest difference between film and non-film learning. The average final test score of the lowest quarter, however, was still below the other groups, with or without films. (See Figs. 7-3 and 7-4.)

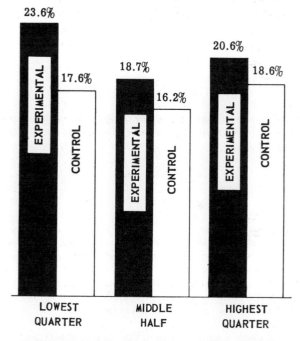

Fig. 7-3. Mean gains of final over initial scores made by three IQ groups on Columbia Research Bureau American History Test. (Wise, 1939)

In the essay test of factual information, the lowest quarter did not do as well as the other groups regardless of whether they had seen films or not. All groups benefited from the use of films. The films were of greatest benefit to the lowest quarter, but did not bring its score up to the level of the other groups which did not see the films.

In the essay test to re-create the spirit and atmosphere of the times, there was a direct relationship between scores and the three levels of ability, both with and without films. The films improved the scores of all groups, but were of most benefit to the highest quarter. It is in the use of historical facts in these essays that the ability of the highest quarter of

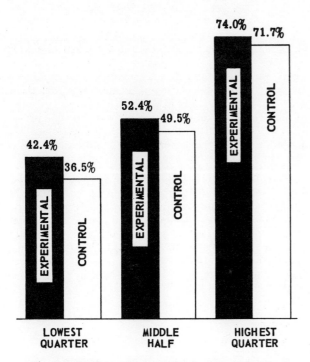

74.0% 71.7%

52.4% 49.5%

42.4% 36.5%

EXPERIMENTAL CONTROL

EXPERIMENTAL CONTROL

EXPERIMENTAL CONTROL

LOWEST
QUARTER

MIDDLE
HALF

HIGHEST
QUARTER

Fig. 7-4. Final mean scores made by three IQ levels of experimental and control groups of Columbia Research Bureau American History Test. (Wise, 1939)

intelligence to learn a greater amount from the usual method plus films than from the usual methods was most evident.

Evaluation

The reader of Wise's study should be warned about his use of the word "superiority" as applied to the lowest quarter, since he uses it in an ambiguous way. In no case is the lowest quarter really superior in achievement to the other two levels when films are used. It is important in research of this sort to distinguish between amount of learning, gain in learning, and difference between gains made by two different groups or with two different methods.

It does seem, however, that in the objective test measures the films were of most benefit in improving scores for those of the lowest quarter in ability. Wise suggests that the greater gains made by the top quarter on the essay test "to re-create the spirit and atmosphere of the times" was due to the stimulation of their imagination by the films and the furnishing of an historical background which "made the people and places of history come alive."

RICHARDSON AND SMITH STUDY

A. C. Richardson and G. H. Smith (1947) in their study of learning from three Disney animated films versus pamphlets dealing with malaria, tuberculosis, and hookworm, stratified their groups into three intelligence levels (IQ's), separately for junior and senior high school.

Findings

At the junior high school level the raw score increase was greater with ascending intelligence levels for both film and control groups. All three levels had greater gains with the films than with the pamphlets. In the senior high school groups all three levels gained more with the films than with the pamphlets; the percentage gain of the low level (IQ below 75) group was 32 per cent compared with 22 and 23 per cent for the other two IQ levels. This percentage superiority was not apparent for the junior high low-level film group. It should be mentioned that when the data are stratified for three levels of IQ, the number of cases for the two extreme levels becomes so small that the reliability of any differences can be questioned. No reliabilities were reported in the article.

MOCK STUDY

A. A. Mock's study (1929) of the relative value of films with "bright" and "dull" children has sometimes been quoted in connection with the other studies we have mentioned.

This study is of doubtful value, since his "bright" group consisted of pupils of IQ 90 and above, and those below 90 were classed as "dull." His "bright" group contained the great bulk of average pupils, as well as the really bright ones. Thus his comparisons are not really comparisons between bright and dull pupils.

* * * * * *

Some other studies which purport to have investigated film learning at three levels of ability fail to make a contribution to the problem since they put the pupils from six to ten grades in one group and classify by IQ levels, leaving mental age and chronological age uncontrolled. As has been pointed out, this makes a rather meaningless comparison.

C. FILM LEARNING BY RETARDED PUPILS AND ILLITERATES

Another phase of this question of intelligence and instructional films is: What, if any, benefit may be derived from the use of films as aids in teaching retarded pupils or illiterate adults?

MAHONEY AND HARSHMAN STUDY

A. Mahoney and H. L. Harshman (1938) studied the value of a sound film as an aid in teaching a unit on transportation to a group of boys in a special class for retarded and handicapped pupils.

Experimental Design

They used two groups of 19 pupils each, matched on the basis of mental age, chronological age and reading age. Both groups were taught by the same teacher; one group saw the film, and the other did not.

Findings

What appears to be a considerable benefit from the film occurred in the mean score differences of the two groups in tests of factual knowledge, new vocabulary used, and concepts learned. Only mean scores without SD's or reliabilities are given.

TILTON AND CHILDS STUDY

J. W. Tilton and A. R. Childs (1933) studied the effectiveness of the Yale Chronicles of America Photoplays in teaching history to three different groups of adults.

Experimental Design

The subjects were mostly mill workers, none of whom had gone beyond the seventh grade, who were attending an opportunity school for four weeks. One group was "illiterate," having an education equivalent to grades I to III; a second group was educated to the level of grades IV and V; the third group was educated to the level of grades VI and VII. Little attempt was made to correlate the films with the course they were taking in the history of North Carolina. The films were shown from 9 to 10 p.m. in the auditorium and the captions were read aloud for the benefit of the "non-readers."

Findings

In this somewhat incidental use of the films, it was found that the gains of the three groups were roughly in direct proportion to their schooling and ability. What the "illiterate" group learned about American history, when compared with the initial testing of the other groups, was shown to be information normally acquired by persons who attend school up through the middle of the fifth grade.

TERRY STUDY

In her study of responses of seventh- and eighth-grade pupils in class discussion of films they had seen in school (rather than of the amount of learning), L. G. Terry (1932) analyzed some of the data from the D. C. Knowlton and J. W. Tilton study (1929) with the Chronicles of America Photoplays.

Findings

She found that bright pupils responded in teacher-led class discussion more frequently than less bright students with four out of six films studies. With the other two films the difference was definitely in favor of the slower pupils. In one instance the slower pupils exceeded the bright pupils in total number of responses and in number of voluntary responses, with no difference in the types of responses made. There is some slight evidence that this latter reaction was more apparent when teacher-dominance of instruction was relaxed, than when it was exerted.

Evaluation

Proper Atmosphere May Stimulate Response

There is reason to believe that when teachers dominate pupil discussion, responses of the pupils who score higher on group intelligence tests are more typically encouraged, whereas the social climate of the classroom is not conducive to free response by the less bright pupils. If these inferences are correct, it is entirely conceivable that variation of intelligence, that is, the quality or characteristic measured by group intelligence tests consisting largely of symbolic items, is of itself less important in influencing responsiveness in class discussion than the social atmosphere of the instruction.

II. ADULT INTELLIGENCE AND LEARNING FROM FORMAL FILM INSTRUCTION

A. INFORMATIONAL LEARNING BY INTELLIGENCE- OR EDUCATION-STRATIFIED GROUPS

JONES, CONRAD, AND HORN STUDY

One of the earliest investigations of intelligence and film learning was by H. E. Jones and his associates, H. Conrad and A. Horn (1928).

Experimental Design

In their attempt to find applicable and reliable indices to adult intelligence, they compared the measures of intelligence on the Army Alpha Test with tests of knowledge obtained from silent motion pictures which were shown as free exhibitions. The population consisted of 800 people of varying ages in rural New England.

Findings

They reported correlations with two different film tests of .69 and .71 for a heterogeneous age group of 10 to 54 years of age. When calculated for the 10 to 16 year-olds, the correlation became .64 in both cases. In other words, Jones and his associates found that specific reactions to the content of motion pictures (presumably informational in nature) were related to the degree of intelligence possessed by the individuals.

VERNON STUDY

P. E. Vernon (1946), in a study previously described, investigated film learning with British seamen.

Findings

He presents data which show that in terms of total amount learned, the men who were above average intelligence of the group learned more from the film than did those who were below average. However, when divided into top, middle, and lowest thirds in intelligence, the percentages of improvement in informational learning from the addition of the film to usual instruction were 3.2, 8.8, and 8.4 respectively, suggesting that the lower two thirds profited more from the addition of the film. However, part of this result may be due to the fact that the test was too easy for the better men (as Vernon points out), creating a "ceiling effect" which prevented them from scoring higher.

HOVLAND, LUMSDAINE, AND SHEFFIELD STUDY

On the adult level, where mental maturation may be presumed to have approached its upper limits, C. I. Hovland, A. A. Lumsdaine, and F. D. Sheffield (1949) established what they identified as a linear relationship between informational learning from motion pictures and both intelligence and level of education, regardless of the difficulty of material.

Findings

In some analyses by C. I. Hovland, et al., the usual percentage procedures were used; in others, an "Effectiveness Index," (see footnote, page 7-3), was employed. On 29 informational items that were significantly affected by the orientation films studied, they reported Effectiveness Indices of 16.3, 36.6, and 54.2 per cent, respectively, for men with grade school, high school, and college training.

Misinterpretation Decreased Among the Better-Educated

Hovland, Lumsdaine, and Sheffield report an interesting exception to the positive correlation which they found between informational learning from films and educational level. In a few instances where a film tended to produce an appreciable increase in the percentage of men choosing an incorrect answer to a factual question, it was the more poorly educated men who misinterpreted the particular point in the film or in the printed test.

Similar Important Points Need Differentiation

These investigators point out the apparent implications of such findings for film production. It is necessary to make extremely explicit distinctions in a film on points which are judged to be important, rather than expect the learners themselves to distinguish between two closely similar implications. Emphatic film techniques should be reserved for use with the important points of the film. If these techniques are used on a minor point, the men may generalize erroneously or acquire a wrong concept.

GIBSON STUDY

Previous mention was made of a study reported by J. J. Gibson (1947) on the use of a film (on position firing) as compared with (1) an illustrated booklet and (2) an illustrated lecture, in training preflight aviation cadets. The individuals in the top 30 per cent and those in the bottom 30 per cent of each group in amount of learning after instruction were compared both with one another and with the two extremes of another group which received no instruction.

Findings

Both extreme sections learned more from the film than from the other two media, but the superiority of the film was much more pronounced for the lowest 30 per cent. After two months the same relationship existed: the high scoring students retained most of what they had learned, dropping back less than 1 point from their previous mean of 21.28 points out of a possible 25. The low achievers who had been taught by the film retained much more than the low achievers taught by the other two media.

B. PERCEPTUAL-MOTOR LEARNING BY INTELLIGENCE-STRATIFIED GROUPS

ZUCKERMAN STUDY

J. V. Zuckerman (1949) in his study, for the Instructional Film Research Program, of variations in types of commentary in an instructional film on knot-tying, (Chapter VIII), calculated a bi-serial correlation between the Navy General Classification Test and actual success in tying the three knots presented in the film.

Findings

Using a large sample of Naval trainees, he obtained the rather low correlation of .14. A similar, but somewhat higher, (.30) correlation was also calculated between knot-tying and the Navy Mechanical Aptitude Test. These correlations are within the usual range of magnitudes found between such tests and tasks of a perceptual-motor nature, such as knot-tying, when the tasks are learned without film presentation.

C. OPINION CHANGE IN EDUCATION-STRATIFIED GROUPS

HOVLAND, LUMSDAINE, AND SHEFFIELD STUDY

C. I. Hovland, et al., report a study of 31 opinion items which were reliably affected by one or more of four films in the Why We Fight series.

Findings

Their data show a slight trend for the effects of the films on opinion to increase with higher educational level. However, when individual items are analyzed, the trend is found to be an algebraic sum of a bi-directional effect, since, in some cases, the strongest influence on opinions was among the better educated, and in others, among those with less education. No simple relationship was found between educational level and the three types of opinion items, those positively, negatively, and not significantly correlated with educational level before film showings took place.

Predisposition Appeared Involved in Opinion Change

One clear finding, however, was that, for the items positively correlated with educational level before film showing, the influence of the film was greater among the men of higher education. Those negatively correlated with education before film showings did not demonstrate the opposite effect. As was brought out in an earlier section, predisposition and acceptance of a certain interpretation appear to be factors that interact with intelligence and operate to influence opinion change. The presumed ability of more intelligent persons to form opinions more rationally from the evidence presented does not appear in these data to be clearly separate from the factors of predisposition and acceptance. Nor are people of different educational levels as different in stability or consistency of opinion as their intellectual differences might lead one to expect.

SECTION 2. EFFECTS OF PREVIOUS KNOWLEDGE AND TRAINING

A. FAMILIARITY AND PREVIOUS KNOWLEDGE

There are theoretical and empirical reasons for believing that familiarity with the subject presented in the film is another factor (in addition to intelligence and education) that influences the amount of learning that results from a film. However, little evidence is available on the factor of familiarity (or previous knowledge) and its influence on reactions to films.

HOVLAND, LUMSDAINE, AND SHEFFIELD STUDY

C. I. Hovland, A. A. Lumsdaine, and F. D. Sheffield (1949) analyzed the effect of educational background on film learning.

Findings

They introduced evidence that the percentage of new material learned from the film increased with the percentage of knowledge of the subject prior to the film showing. However, prior knowledge and film learning were correlated with educational level in their analysis, and no data were presented on the effect of prior knowledge, with educational level and learning ability held constant.

ASH STUDY

P. Ash (1949), of the Instructional Film Research Program, conducted one of his experiments on the effectiveness of massed and distributed exhibition (long and short film sessions).

Findings

Using three films of the Elementary Hydraulics series with Navy trainees, he found highly significant differences in learning scores for those trainees who had had a course in high school physics over those trainees who had not. Differences in favor of trainees with high school physics backgrounds were found in every company used in the experiment.

On the other hand, in his experiment with the Rules of the Nautical Road series in long and short film sessions with Navy trainees, Ash found no significant learning differences between those trainees who reported they had studied relevant chapters in a Navy manual dealing with this subject, and those trainees who reported no study. Ash suggests that the reports of previous study may not have been a reliable index to previous knowledge in this case.

GIBSON STUDY

J. J. Gibson (1947), in his study on teaching position firing, presents some interesting data on the extent of previous knowledge of the topic within a group of aviation cadets awaiting preflight training.

Findings

In a group that had received no training on the topic, but took the same test given to the trained groups, it was found that the 30 per cent making the highest scores knew on the average 40 per cent of the answers in the test without having any training. The 30 per cent making the lowest scores, knew on the average only 6.3 per cent of the answers. Thus, it is obvious that the whole group came to the training with a wide range of information on that special type of aviation gunnery. No study was made of the relation of this information to the amount of learning from the three instructional media used.

B. AWARENESS OF PROPAGANDA

LARSON STUDY

L. C. Larson's (1940) study dealing with resistance to propaganda presented in films was concerned with specific attitudes, but introduced general factors of resistance to specific attitudinal change resulting from propaganda presentation.

Experimental Design

He constructed an attitude scale to measure the propaganda effect of two films, the one biased toward economic conservatism and the other toward economic liberalism. A second test was designed to measure the ability to perceive and analyze the propaganda techniques and appeals used in the two films. Three student groups were used in the study. The first group was enrolled in a science course, the second group in a contemporary affairs course, and the third in a course on the formation of public opinion. It was assumed that a major objective of each of these three courses was, respectively, to teach (1) "scientific thinking," (2) awareness of propaganda, and (3) alertness to current trends, intellectual or otherwise.

Findings

Public-Opinion Students Not Immune to Propaganda

These students enrolled in the course on the formation of public opinion scored reliably higher on the film propaganda analysis tests than did those enrolled in either the contemporary affairs or the science courses. However, when the attitudinal changes arising from the "liberal" and the "conservative" films were analyzed, no reliable differences were found between the various classes. With each film, there was a shift in student attitude in the direction of the film propaganda. Negligible correlations were found between attitude changes and film-analysis test scores, and between scores on a general socio-civic affairs test and shift in attitude.

No evidence was introduced by Larson in support of a relationship between ability to recognize propaganda techniques and the ability to resist the influence of these techniques when employed in propaganda motion pictures. Nor was evidence introduced to support the supposition that a relationship exists between general knowledge of socio-civic affairs and the attitudinal influences of propaganda motion pictures dealing with one phase of socio-civic affairs. Since further analyses of the data are in progress, final results have not been published.

HOVLAND, LUMSDAINE, AND SHEFFIELD STUDY

The problem of the relationship between informational and attitudinal influences of motion pictures, which was raised in connection with the R. Bell, et al., (1941) study, and which appears to be given increased weight by Larson's data, is touched upon in the Hovland, et al., study.

Experimental Design

C. I. Hovland, et al., analyzed the effect on five opinion items [". . .which showed significant over-all effects of the film" (p. 100)] of one of the Why We Fight films in the case of (1) men who regarded the films as propagandistic (in the sense that they believe the intent of the film was to "manipulate" their opinions), (2) men whose appraisal of the film was somewhat between that of propaganda and information, and (3) men whose appraisal indicated no suspicion of anything in the films other than factual information.

Findings

Suspicion Reduced Acceptance

They reported that those men who were skeptical of the film were less influenced in their opinions by

the film than others. There was a gradual improvement in the percentage (Effectiveness Index) of "correct" opinion answers among the men whose appraisals approached the "informational" end of the appraisal scale.

When these results were further analyzed in terms of degree of schooling of the men, it was found that men with less than a high school education tended to be especially resistant to opinion change when they suspected a manipulative intent.

C. LANGUAGE FACILITY

1. READING ABILITY

The studies cited show that there is a considerable correlation between intelligence and amount of informational learning from instructional films. Intelligence, as measured by such tests as the Stanford-Binet (which requires practically no reading on the part of the pupil), correlates, on the average, about .60 with reading ability (Stroud, 1946). Since reading requires knowledge of words, as does learning from instructional films, one would logically expect some, and possibly a fairly large, correlation between reading ability and amount of learning from films. (The fact that learning from instructional films involves the use of language can be readily demonstrated. Project a film containing unfamiliar subject matter with the sound cut off, or with the titles deleted, and note how much less information usually is conveyed.)

Some investigators, assuming this relationship, have used reading or vocabulary tests along with intelligence tests to equate the groups which were to be instructed by films or by other media. This assumption seems to be justified by one of the few studies to attack the problem directly and correlate reading scores with film learning for separate elementary school grades.

WITTICH AND FOWLKES STUDY

W. A. Wittich and J. G. Fowlkes (1946) report 27 correlations, nine for each of the fourth-, fifth-, and sixth-grade groups, each group involving a different Encyclopaedia Britannica film. Eight of these correlations are .70 and above, the highest being .89. Sixteen are above .60, eight are below .50, and only two are below .32, being somewhat aberrant values of .16 and .03.

We can agree with the authors that there is a correlation between reading scores and learning from these films at the three grade levels they studied, and that the highest correlations tend to be with the first experimental factor (showing film without preparatory discussion) and the lowest correlations with the second experimental factor (presenting preparatory material before showing film). See Chapter VIII for details of this study.

2. LISTENING COMPREHENSION

The importance of reading ability in learning from sound films is supported by the fact that several studies have found a sizable correlation between read-ing comprehension and listening comprehension. Among adults ranging in age from 18 to 65 years, H. Goldstein (1940) reports a correlation of .78 between these two types of comprehension. R. P. Larson and D. D. Feder (1940) report a correlation of .68 between two forms of the same reading test, one form presented visually, and the other orally. Another reading test correlated with the oral form to the extent of .53.

I. H. Anderson and G. Fairbanks (1937) investigated the correlation between listening and reading vocabulary, as measured by the same vocabulary test administered both visually and orally to college freshmen. They found a correlation of .80. The reading vocabulary score correlated more highly with reading comprehension and with intelligence than did the listening vocabulary score. The poorer readers had a larger listening vocabulary than reading vocabulary. This is in line with other studies which have found a considerable number of pupils in the elementary grades whose reading comprehension was a year or more below their listening comprehension.

Even though these studies show a fair correlation between reading comprehension and listening comprehension, the correlation is still low enough to permit some persons to be much better reading comprehenders than listening comprehenders and vice versa. The last study suggests a definite reason why sound films, radio and recordings should facilitate learning by pupils whose reading comprehension is lower than their listening comprehension.

3. VOCABULARY ABILITY

PARK STUDY

The only study, to the reviewers' knowledge, in which there was a definite effort to relate some measure of vocabulary ability and amount of learning from films, was that by J. J. Park (1943, 1944, 1945).

Experimental Design

He investigated the vocabulary and comprehension difficulty of eight sound films as used with elementary school pupils and high school pupils. A tabulation of the words in the commentaries of these films was made in terms of their frequency in Thorndike's Teachers Word Book. The words occurring with less frequency in Thorndike's count were considered to be the more difficult words, and a 25-item, multiple-choice vocabulary test of the more "difficult" words was constructed for each film. The score on this vocabulary pre-test was correlated with the score on a test on film content given after the film.

Findings

Large Vocabulary Increases Learning

For 22 different grade groups the correlations clustered around .50, and in 12 groups, they were .50 or above. Thus, there was a definite tendency for those who knew more of the more difficult words before they saw the film to learn more from the film.

The listenability of film narrations or commentaries is a problem for further research. For example, are readability formulae applicable to film commentary, or should some new formula be developed for measuring the "listenability" of commentary? What word-difficulty levels should be used for audiences of certain intelligence or educational levels?

D. FILM LITERACY

Very little is known about the special abilities involved in learning from films which, for want of a better term, we designate as "film literacy." These abilities may relate to sustained observation, to interpretation of such film techniques as dissolves, closeups, intercuts, montages, etc. There is, however, some evidence that film literacy, though not precisely defined, (1) exists, (2) is related to practice in viewing films and practice in learning from films, and (3) influences learning from films. It may be related to, or a manifestation of, what G. Bateson (1951) calls "deutero learning" or, synonymously, "learning to learn," a phenomenon observed by H. E. Harlow (1949) in his study of "learning sets."

AUSTRALIAN COMMONWEALTH OFFICE OF EDUCATION STUDY

In the Australian Commonwealth Office of Education (1950) report on the relative effectiveness of six techniques of using instructional films, the retention of material learned from the films was correlated with frequency of attendance at entertainment movies. In this correlation, the effects of intelligence and prior knowledge of the subjects shown in the films, (both of which contribute to learning from films), were removed. The resulting "residue" of learning was then correlated with frequency of movie attendance.

Findings

The linear correlation between the mean frequency of movie attendance of each class and the residual retention of material learning was +.985--extremely high. The linear correlation between individual movie attendance and individual retention, independent of the causative factors of intelligence and prior knowledge of the subject, may not be as high, but this cannot be ascertained from the study since the computation involved class data only.

HANSEN STUDY

The study by J. E. Hansen (1939), comparing three methods of using sound films in high school biological instruction, involved a second phase which labels it as one of the first studies to recognize that practice in learning from films might transfer to, or improve learning from, additional films---a phase of film literacy---and that the method of practice might affect the transfer. (Hansen's study is described in more detail in Chapter VIII in connection with the grammatical elements of instructional method.)

Experimental Design

His 195 tenth-grade second-semester biology students were divided into three equated groups. A pre-test was given 24 hours before each film presentation, and all groups had a two-minute orientation introduction. Four sound films about plant biology were used with each group. Group A was shown the film with sound-track shut off, but the showing was accompanied by questions and discussion prepared and directed by the teacher. After a ten-minute discussion of film content, the film was shown without sound a second time, with the teacher endeavoring to emphasize the processes which appeared least understood in the light of the ten-minute discussion. The period concluded with a 12-minute test on the film. Group B followed the same pattern, except that the first showing of the film was with the sound; the second showing was silent. Group C followed the same pattern, but the film was projected as a sound film both times, the teacher making no comments during the projections. (As mentioned in Chapter VIII, the Group C method was best in three out of the four films, and was just as good as the Group A method in the remaining film. However, the students had studied most of the material treated in these films in the previous semester.)

The second part of Hansen's study is our concern here. It involved the relative influence of the three methods upon later learning. Specifically, he studied the ability of the students to transfer their knowledge and learning techniques acquired during their experience with the four plant biology films, to new material presented in two Eastman Kodak silent films which described similar processes, but with different types of plants. The two films used were The Green Plant and From Flower to Fruit. The films were shown in the school auditorium to all three groups at the same time with no instruction from the teachers other than a brief orientation about the purpose of the film and a statement that the students would be tested immediately after the showing. A pre-test which had been given 24 hours previously, was also used as the final test.

Findings

In the case of The Green Plant, the Group C method surpassed the other two methods in transfer value to a small, but reliable, degree (below the one percent level). The other two methods were equal. In the

second film, Group C was better than Group A (CR of 2.39), but was only 0.85 of a point better than Group B (CR of 1.03). Group B was 1.27 points better than Group A (CR of 1.56).

From these data it appears that there was more development of "film literacy" from the two sound projections of the four previous films, with an intervening ten-minute discussion, than there was from the two silent projections accompanied by planned questions and comments by the teacher and with a ten-minute discussion intervening. There is a slight indication that the procedure of Group B, following the same pattern, except that the sound track was used in the first film showing and the second showing was silent, might be a better procedure than that of Group A, which had two silent showings with teacher comments. Thus, the Group A method brought about the least development of "film literacy," though the investigator indicated that one might have expected the opposite.

Evaluation

Teacher Commentary May Be Distracting

It may be that the more coordinated and smoother presentation of visual and verbal stimuli to the learner, which probably resulted from the sound projections, leaving special questioning and emphasizing to be done mentally by each student according to his skill and need, would be more likely to develop a greater skill in learning from future films, than would be the case with the other two methods. In the other two methods, the interjected questions and comments by the teacher may have at times served as disturbing and distracting factors, rather than as aids. Indeed, this also seems to be true of some sound commentaries of instructional films.

The transfer effect for pupils who had less prior information in the area of these films is problematic. Also of research interest is the problem of how to teach students to develop effective skills in learning from films.

VANDERMEER STUDY

A. W. VanderMeer (1949) investigated the possibility of learning from films exclusively (see Chapter VI).

Experimental Design

In the experiment, one group of ninth-grade students had been taught four units of general science by means of 44 sound films with no other instruction; another group had used the films with the aid of special study guides, but with no other instruction; and the third group had been taught in the usual way by instructors. To determine the effects of previous instruction by a large number of films upon subsequent learning from films, the investigator showed four films of general information (geography, natural history, etc.) to all three groups and tested them for the content learned.

Findings

Film Experience Aided Subsequent Film Learning

"Preliminary analysis of results indicates that, in subsequent film learning, the group which previously had been instructed by the use of 44 films was con- siderably, and probably significantly, superior to the group which had previously been instructed by cus- tomary means without the use of films. The group which had been instructed with the 44 films plus study guides was in the intermediate position relative to the other two groups" (Instructional Film Research Pro- gram, 1949).

SUMMARY

1. INTELLIGENCE AND EDUCATIONAL LEVEL

INFLUENCE ON INFORMATIONAL LEARNING

1. It appears that, in regard to this learning outcome or objective, there is a fairly high positive correlation between intelligence and learning from films as a pictorial-verbal medium of communication. This relationship seems to exist throughout the public school years and at least into early and middle adult life. (This relationship has not been investigated for persons in their late adult years.)

2. Many of the investigations suggest that "unto him that hath shall be given." The more intel- ligent persons usually know more about the topic when they start, make a greater absolute gain, and maintain their superiority over the lower and average intelli- gence levels at the end of the film learning.

3. In some cases, but certainly not univer- sally, teaching with a film or with the aid of a film, seems to bring about a greater increment in learning among those of lower intelligence than it does among those of higher intelligence. However, this greater increment does not increase their total learning to the extent that it surpasses that of the average or superior groups.

4. The few studies that have been made with retarded pupils and with semi-literate adults indicate that suitable films can bring about a definite increment in learning for these groups.

INFLUENCE ON PERCEPTUAL-MOTOR LEARNING

1. Apparently little research has been done on the relationship between intelligence and perceptual- motor learning from film presentation. The one study quoted found a very low correlation between knot- tying and intelligence, but the correlation was some- what higher when the scores on a pencil and paper mechanical aptitude test were compared with the knot- tying.

INFLUENCE ON OPINION CHANGE

1. The few studies available, made with re- cruits in the U. S. Army, indicate that there is an over-all increase in opinion change with higher educa- tional level.

2. This increase is algebraic and results from three types of relationships: a positive corre- lation between amount of change and educational level; no correlation; and, a negative correlation with educa- tional level. Predispositions and willingness or un- willingness to accept a given interpretation appeared to be factors complicating the relationship.

2. EFFECTS OF PRIOR KNOWLEDGE AND TRAINING

INFLUENCE OF FAMILIARITY AND PREVIOUS KNOWLEDGE

The effect of familiarity of context and previous knowledge of the specific subject requires further investigation. However, it seems likely that the so- called "difficulty" of a given film may not be entirely due to its subject matter. The difficulty of a film de- pends on the learner's intelligence, and is probably related, as well, to the extent of his previous knowl- edge of the subject.

Thus, the amount of learning that results from a single showing and repeated showings of a film ap- pears to depend as much or more on the previous knowledge held by the individuals in the audience than on the density of factual content and the effects of repetition.

INFLUENCE OF PROPAGANDA AWARENESS

There is no evidence that persons who have re- ceived training in the techniques of propaganda are better able to resist propaganda material in films. However, one study does suggest that persons, who suspect that their opinions are being manipulated, are less likely to shift their opinions as a result of film experience.

EFFECTS OF LANGUAGE FACILITY

The studies on this topic suggest three points: (1) That some measures of the reading ability and vo- cabulary knowledge of the individuals in a film audience might serve as a fair indication of the amount of informational learning, and possibly of some other types of learning, which will occur from a film presentation. (2) Though the correlations between reading and listening comprehension are fairly sizable, a given individual may still be a much better comprehender by one or the other sensory channel. (3) Sound films may definitely facilitate the learning of individuals whose reading comprehension is definitely lower than their listening comprehension.

EFFECTS OF FILM LITERACY

The data from the studies of film literacy suggest that some perceptual and other specialized learning abilities develop with increased practice in observing and learning from films, and that this ability helps the individual to learn more from future instructional films.

CHAPTER VIII

THE RHETORIC OF FILM INSTRUCTION:
VARIABLES IN THE PRODUCTION AND USE OF FILMS

INTRODUCTION

Up to this point, we have reviewed research on (1) the objectives which films serve in instruction, (2) the values of films compared with other instructional materials in serving these objectives, and (3) some characteristics of the audience which facilitate or impede reactions to films.

There remains the problem of the variables in the film itself, and/or in its utilization, which increase the effectiveness of any film or series of films in influencing the audience in the desired and intended direction. This brings us to the rhetoric of the film, that is, the actual method of "saying it" in pictures and sound with greatest effectiveness. Aristotle long ago defined rhetoric as "the faculty of discovering the possible means of persuasion in reference to any subject whatever," and it is in this meaning that the term, rhetoric of the film, is used in this chapter. In a real sense, the material presented in Chapter VII on audience characteristics is an integral part of the rhetoric of the film, but for organizational purposes of this report, the term has been reserved for the medium itself and the use of the medium in mass communication.

It is only recently that the rhetoric of the film has been systematically investigated. Much of the earlier film research, particularly with the instructional film, appears to have been dominated largely by a desire to obtain data (1) to convince teachers and administrators that movies were good for teaching, that teachers ought to use films, and that schools and colleges ought to buy films; and (2) to persuade the public and the entertainment-film producers that movies of the sort made during the Jazz, Flapper, and Volstead era were bad for people, and that Hollywood ought to make movies that were good for people, or, at least, not bad for them. Probably both of these purposes were justified by objective conditions and facts of instruction and entertainment existing at that time.

Current Research Trends

However, it is now fairly well established that films do contribute to instruction that they can be

educational in the broad sense and that, frequently, the influence they exert remains with the film observer for a long period of time The research problem then becomes one of discovering the variables or definable processes which increase the instructional effectiveness of films so that better films can be produced and better use can be made of them.

There has been a general increase in the rigor of experimental design and statistical analysis in film research during the past ten years which, at least in part, reflects a somewhat general trend in psychological and educational research.

Recently there have been reports of extensive research on the rhetoric of film instruction. W. A. Wittich and J. G. Fowlkes (1946) investigated the effectiveness of three cumulative procedures of using educational films in grade school instruction. C. I. Hovland, A. A. Lumsdaine, and F. D. Sheffield (1949) reported research during World War II on techniques of using training films and on participation techniques incorporated into a sound filmstrip. A. Sturmthal and A. Curtis (1944) conducted a "film-analyzer" study of audience reactions to propaganda films which indicated some film characteristics which provoke audience response.

Among their various experiments, some not yet published, the Yale Motion Picture Research Project (1947) conducted studies on repetition and audience participation sequences incorporated into the film. Research on techniques of film utilization, conducted by the Commonwealth Office of Education (1950) in Australia, indicates a continuing trend in the investigation of film utilization techniques.

Research on variables involved in the production and utilization of training films has recently been undertaken by the Audio Visual Research Division of The Human Resources Research Laboratories of the U. S. Air Force. (At the time of writing, no reports of this research had been published.)

Instructional Film Research Program

The problem of techniques within the film itself has been attacked most systematically by the staff of the Instructional Film Research Program at the Pennsylvania State College, mutually conducted by the Department of the Army and the Department of the Navy. In addition, research on the techniques of using films has been extended by this Program.

In practice, a film almost always involves the employment of more than one variable. Every film, for instance, has a rate of development, or, actually, several rates of development among its various sequences. Likewise, every film has a dominant camera angle, although a variety of camera angles is possible. In any film which has commentary in its sound track, there is a somewhat constant "level of verbalization," (amount of commentary in relation to the length of the film) but the amount of commentary may vary over a certain range. Some scenes may be repeated and others not. Thus, the study of multiple variables, that is, combinations and interrelations of variables, is an aspect of research that is of considerable importance to film makers.

Multiple-variable analysis is probably the most significant innovation in film research methodology in the thirty-odd years of experimental research in instructional films. If several film variables are to be studied in combination, this form of experimentation generally involves the production of a number of experimental versions of a film to incorporate and test the combinations of variables. Multiple-variable analysis has also been made of audience variables, or of combinations of audience, instructor, and instructional device variables. The problem of multiple-variables in a film is extraordinarily difficult to investigate experimentally and, as mentioned above, is often an expensive process requiring the production of many experimental versions of a film. For example, N. Jaspen's (1948, 1950) studies of combinations of variables involved 17 experimental film versions in one case, and 16 in the other. S. M. Roshal's (1949) study of variables of learner representation involved eight experimental film versions.

The Instructional Film Research Program has studied systematically such film variables as repetition, level of verbalization, phase relationship of picture and narration, prestige of role, rate of development, camera angle, relative importance of picture and narration, showing of errors to be avoided, attention-gaining devices, projective processes in attitude restructuring, audience participation, massed

and distributed screenings, exclusive use of films in instruction, color and black and white films introductions and summaries, action and still representation. As many as 28 different versions of a single film were produced to control and manipulate the variables which, conceivably, influence audience reaction.

Since reports of the Instructional Film Research Program studies are available individually in several versions, the studies are presented in summary form, rather than described in detail, and are related to the results and "hunches" reported in other research studies.

PLAN OF THE CHAPTER

The research on the rhetoric of film instruction is discussed in the two parts of this chapter.

Part I presents studies on the variables in the film which contribute to its influence. The discussion is divided into three sections. The first section describes six factors which appear to involve an audience, or make it take a personal interest, in its film experience. The second section describes five factors in film structure--dealing with the picture and sound relationships in a motion picture. The third section describes three other elements of film structure which also have an important influence on the instructional success of the film.

Part II investigates the influence of variables in the methods of using films and in the physical conditions under which they are used. Since many of the elements which influence learning can be either incorporated into the films or applied during the film showing, some of the rhetorical elements described in Part I are discussed further in the first section of Part II.

The second section of Part II discusses certain other factors, such as room illumination, viewing angle, and spaced or continuous film sessions, which also influence the success of film instruction.

A summary at the end of each Part presents the major conclusions and recommendations suggested by the experimental evidence.

PART I.   ELEMENTS IN THE FILM AFFECTING ITS INFLUENCE

At least five main processes can be identified either in the film content or structure which affect the impact of a film on the audience and contribute to its instructional effectiveness: (1) audience involve-

ment, (2) relation of pictures and sound including verbalization, (3) repetition, (4) rate of development, and (5) orientation and summary. Each of these processes may, and most of them do, have several functions.

SECTION 1. AUDIENCE INVOLVEMENT FACTORS

Description

The process of audience involvement in a film presentation is depicted by a long, but revealing quotation from a recent article of the late Robert Flaherty (1950), describing some of his experiences in producing and distributing <u>Nanook of the North</u>, <u>Moana of the South Seas</u>, and <u>Louisiana Story</u>. In producing Nanook in the Arctic region of Canada, Flaherty brought with him the laboratory equipment necessary for developing "rushes" on location.

"It has always been most important for me to see my rushes -- it is the only way I can make a film. But another reason for developing the film in the North was to project it to the Eskimos so that they would accept and understand what I was doing and work with me as partners.

"They were amazed when I first came with all this equipment, and they would ask me what I was going to do. When I told them that I had come to spend a year amongst them to make a film of them--pictures in which they moved--they roared with laughter. To begin with, some of my Eskimos could not even read a still photograph. I made stills of several of them as preliminary tests. When I showed them the photograph as often as not they would look at it upside down. I'd have to take the photograph out of their hands and lead them to the mirror in my hut, then have them look at themselves and the photograph beside their heads, before suddenly, with a smile that spread from ear to ear, they would understand.

"As luck would have it, the first scene we shot for the film was one of a tug-of-war with walrus. When I developed and printed the scenes and was ready to project them I wondered if the Eskimos would be able to understand them. What would these flickering scenes projected on a Hudson Bay blanket hung up on the wall of the hut mean to them? When at last I told them I was ready to begin the show, they crammed my little fifteen by twenty hut to the point of suffocation. I started up the little electric light plant, turned out the lights in the room, turned on the switch on the projector. A beam of light shot out, filled the blanket, and the show began. At first they kept looking back at the source of the light in the projector as much as they did at the screen. I was sure the show would flop, when suddenly someone shouted, 'Iviuk! (Walrus!) ' There they were -- a school of them -- lying basking on the beach. In the foreground could be seen Nanook and his crew, harpoon in hand, stalking on their bellies toward them. Suddenly the walrus take alarm; they begin to tumble into the water. There was one agonizing shriek from the audience, until Nanook, leaping to his feet, thrust his harpoon. In the tug-of-war that ensued between the walrus now in the water and Nanook and his men holding desperately to the harpoon line, pandemonium broke loose; every last man, woman and child was fighting that walrus, no surer than Nanook

was at the time that the walrus would not get away. 'Hold him!' they would yell, 'Hold him!--Hold him!'" (p. 141).

Unquestionably the Eskimos became <u>involved</u> in the scenes of the walrus hunt, and achieving this condition is the basic problem of all instructional and informational films. Flaherty's quotation illustrates that when an audience becomes completely involved in the subject presented in the film, everybody "gets into the act."

PHYSIOLOGICAL EVIDENCE OF INVOLVEMENT

DYSINGER AND RUCKMICK STUDY

As mentioned in the discussion of <u>Thresholds of Excitability</u>, (Chapter VII), the physiological responses measured in studies of emotional behavior can be interpreted as evidence of covert emotional activity, and are, in all probability, indices of the degree of psychological excitement and emotional involvement of the individual in the stimulating situation. One such study mentioned there in detail was that of <u>W. S. Dysinger</u> and <u>C. A. Ruckmick</u> (1933), who studied the electrical resistance changes of the skin and pulse rate variations while viewing entertainment motion pictures. They worked with 89 subjects in the laboratory and with 61 subjects in the theater situation, the ages ranging from six to fifty years. In numerous instances verbal reports were requested from the individual being studied and were compared with the physiological changes. The specific contribution of this type of study is the fact that here is a technique which will give some indication of excitement or involvement in the child or adult sitting quietly and ostensibly unmoved by the unfolding of the screen drama. Though he may not "get into the act" like Flaherty's Eskimos, nevertheless he may be quite involved emotionally.

Findings

The authors say, "Our records are clear on this point: profound mental and physiological effects of an emotional order are produced" (p. 119). The comments of individual subjects showed that they were largely interested in and moved by specific scenes of conflict, danger, or love rather than by the picture as a whole. These comments corresponded to the readings of the instruments.

Pronounced individual differences in reaction were found at each age level and certain trends of change in average response occurred with age increase. The reader should refer back to Chapter VII for these results. It is interesting to note that the intensity of response to love scenes reached its climax among the 16 to 18 year olds and that apparently none of the subjects studied in this age group were free from the emotional stimulation of such scenes.

RENSHAW, MILLER, AND MARQUIS STUDY

S. Renshaw, V. L. Miller, and D. P. Marquis (1933) conducted a study to determine the extent to which movie attendance affected the motility or restlessness (during sleeping hours) of children and adolescents varying in age from six to 19 years. A representative group of children living in an institution were selected for this experiment. The investigators describe the children as "good" and "bad," "bright" and "dull," and "living under conditions which produced normal happiness." An electrical apparatus was attached to each child's bed and recorded every movement made during sleep. Actual recording was done in an adjacent room, a signal light flashing if a child left his bed during the night. Records were first obtained on the normal sleep habits of each child. In addition to studying the effects of movie attendance, the investigators measured, as controls, the influence of "holiday trips" and of the drinking of coffee and Kaffee Hag at the evening meal or at bedtime. In all, 163 children were used and records were kept for 6650 child-nights of sleep. Fifty-eight different commercial entertainment motion-picture programs were used in the investigation.

Findings

These investigators report a "change in sleep motility which is a consequent of viewing the film and is not due to the 'holiday' effect or to 'normal' periodic variations in motility." This change in motility may be either an increase or decrease; the increases occurred more often than the decreases. These investigators present evidence from the physiological literature on sleep to show that either sort of change in motility represents a state in which the normal recuperative function of sleep is reduced.

Numerous individual differences in the effect of the movies were observed. Some pictures were much more disturbing to sleep patterns than others. Some children were much more affected by some pictures than were other children. The maximum effect seemed to occur at about the age of puberty (when the typical child is in the seventh or eighth grade).

The intensity of the involvement which occurs in some children is indicated by the fact that the movie influence was not necessarily limited to the one night immediately following the viewing of the film. The persistence of this effect varied with age, sex, and particular disposition of a given individual. Also the movie experience was frequently as disturbing to sleep patterns as sitting up till midnight, or, in the case of some pictures and some children, equivalent to the drinking of two cups of coffee in the evening. Surely we have in this study one more clear proof of the profound mental and emotional involvement occurring in children and adolescents as they experience entertainment motion pictures.

KLEITMAN STUDY

Other evidence on involvement in motion picture experience comes from a physiologist. N. Kleitman (1945) studied diurnal temperature changes. His study is based on the assumption that, when the muscles relax, the body temperature falls and, conversely, that an increase in muscular tension leads to a rise in body temperature. By this reasoning, any change in body temperature that can be related to motion picture experience is ostensibly a measure of the muscular tension or relaxation resulting from the motion picture experience.

Findings

Kleitman made an intensive study of two female subjects, one a teen-age girl and the other a young lady in her early twenties. Temperature readings were taken on the day before, immediately after, and the day following various movie experiences.

With the teen-age girl, the average of the temperature readings taken after 55 movie experiences over a period of two years, was 0.93 degrees F higher than the average temperature on days preceding or following the movie experience. In this case, all movies were attended in the afternoon.

The young lady in her early twenties attended movies in the evenings; in some instances she saw one movie, and in others, two. She attended the movies 29 times in two months, and saw 47 feature films. After one movie her average temperature was 0.47 degrees (CR, 6.24) higher than the non-movie average, and after the second movie it was 0.25 degrees (CR, 2.65) higher than the non-movie average.

Movies Are Not Physiologically Relaxing

Kleitman summarized his findings as follows. "In summary, on the basis of occasional data obtained on many subjects, male and female, and through an analysis of multiple readings on two female subjects, it appears that attending motion picture shows, though looked upon as a relaxation in the sense of escape from the humdrum reality of existence, is by no means relaxation in the physiological sense. On the contrary, although the spectator remains in a sitting position for two or more hours, the subject matter of the film evokes an increase rather than a decrease in muscle tension which manifests itself in a highly significant rise in body temperature of one-half to one degree F." (p. 508).

The evidence that muscular tension, rather than muscular relaxation, apparently follows feature-film experience may be interpreted as indicating the involvement of an individual in the movie experience. This study and the two preceding ones indicate, at least, that entertainment motion picture experience is not always as "passive" as might be supposed.

TESTIMONIAL EVIDENCE OF INVOLVEMENT

BLUMER STUDY

H. Blumer's (1933) investigation of reactions to motion pictures, mentioned in Chapter V, is pertinent to the present discussion. His main technique was to obtain autobiographies of motion picture experience, written in narrative form, but following a semi-structured questionnaire which asked questions about effects on emotions, things imitated from the movies, reactions to pictures of love and romance, ambitions and temptations stimulated by the movies, etc. Altogether, 634 university students, 481 college students, 583 high school students, 67 office workers, and 58 factory workers wrote these biographies. Every effort was made to obtain the cooperation of the students and a frank statement of the purpose of the investigation was made. An ingenious technique of using a small class committee who assigned code numbers to each student was employed to keep the biographies anonymous to the teacher, but to enable him to give credit to students who did serious writing.

Findings

Anyone who reads the excerpts from some of these autobiographies quoted in Blumer's book cannot help being impressed by the personal involvement which entertainment motion picture experience has for the child and the adolescent. Though there were great individual differences in the reactions reported, results of an emotional nature were frequently mentioned. In a group of 458 high school biographies, obtained from ten different Chicago high schools, representing different socio-economic statuses, 66 per cent mentioned using movie content in their daydreams; statements of fright or terror occurred in 61 per cent; sorrow and pathos were mentioned in 64 per cent of these case histories; 39 per cent admitted crying frequently including about one-half of the girls and one-fourth of the boys; reactions to romantic love were definitely mentioned in 55 per cent of the cases. General tenseness and excitement, longing to be "good," and resentment at social discrimination or at family interference with an adolescent's ambitions were some of the other involvement reactions mentioned a significant number of times.

As mentioned in our previous discussion of this investigation, Blumer attributes much of the emotional influence of the motion picture to what he calls, "emotional possession." He says, "The psychological characteristics of emotional possession, as we may infer them from the accounts given, are essentially a stirring up of feeling, a release of impulse, and a fixation of imagery. The individual is so preoccupied with the picture that its imagery becomes his own. The impulses, which correspond to the images, are called into play and encouraged, and the individual seems swept by intense feelings" (p. 126).

GALLUP SURVEY

M. Sherif and H. Cantril (1947) report an unpublished survey by Dr. Gallup's organization, from which we quote the following statement regarding adult involvement in motion pictures: "The upshot of the research is that individuals choose as their favorite movie stars those with whom they can most easily identify themselves -- persons of the same sex, of comparable age, and who tend to be cast in roles that represent a person of their income group .... Theatergoers have a tendency to project themselves into the situation portrayed on the screen, to imagine themselves in the place of the star, or (perhaps subconsciously to pretend they are the star)" (p. 351).

ANALYSIS OF THE CONCEPT OF INVOLVEMENT

Before proceeding to discuss some elements in films which seem to facilitate the involvement of the audience, it would seem desirable to examine this concept a little more carefully. Just what seems to be embodied in it? In the light of the studies we have just mentioned and as will be brought out in additional investigations to be mentioned soon, "involvement" seems to include, at a given time, one or more of the following activities or reactions of the individual: (1) being intensely interested in the picture and very attentive to it; (2) taking a very personal interest in the presentation because it relates to his experiences, desires, and needs; (3) being highly motivated toward a certain atttitude portrayed in the film, or toward a certain activity suggested, described, or demonstrated by the film; (4) mentally, or overtly (openly) practicing during the film projection, some material or activity presented in the film; (5) experiencing an emotional reaction to the film presentation, varying in intensity from mild pleasure and excitement to "emotional possession," as described above; (6) "living" in the time and place of the picture, more or less oblivious to surroundings; (7) identification of the self with one or more characters being portrayed, and becoming more or less oblivious to surroundings.

Whether involvement as described above will facilitate learning from a given film will probably depend in part upon which of the above factors are aroused and their intensity; and would seem also to depend upon the learning outcomes desired from that particular film. That is, it would seem to depend on whether the purpose of the film is to teach information, a motor skill, a scientific concept, to start the development of a new social attitude, or to arouse a group to action for a cause. Involvement in which emotional possession was the chief factor might be suitable for the last two outcomes; but might be of no benefit in learning a skilled assembly task or a difficult scientific principle. The importance of the nature of the involvement will become more evident as we proceed to discuss involvement factors and film production.

SIX INVOLVEMENT FACTORS

Research studies indicate that at least six factors enter into the involvement of an audience in a film, but there probably are more yet to be identified. Although some aspects of these factors are not clearly understood at this time, the available experimental and observational evidence indicates that (1) identification, (2) familiarity, (3) subjective camera, (4) anticipation, (5) participation, and (6) dramatic structure and cartoon form are factors which affect the degree to which the audience is involved in a film presentation.

A. IDENTIFICATION

"Identification"* generally means that the individual in the audience sees the characters, institutional affiliations, settings, or situations represented in the film in close personal relationship to himself and to the groups with which he has identified himself. He "experiences" what is represented in the film as his own experiences, his own activities, his own motives, his own aspirations and his own values.

The subject of identification in film experience has been popularly discussed in recent years, but despite the frequently glib discussions, the "mechanism" of identification is not clearly understood -- at least in application to motion pictures. In fact, there is no assurance that identification, as it is popularly understood, has any direct influence on learning from films, especially informational learning.

KISHLER STUDY

An exploratory experimental study of the possible effect of identification in film learning was undertaken by J. Kishler (1950) of the Instructional Film Research Program staff.

Experimental Design

Kishler investigated the effect of the film, Keys of the Kingdom, starring Gregory Peck, on attitudes and factual information learned by college student populations for whom (1) the institutional role of the main character (Catholic priest) had either a high or low prestige value, and (2) an "identification" with the main character could be assumed to exist on the basis of an institutional affiliation with the Catholic Church.

Kishler interpreted the underlying "message" of the film as an appeal for increased religious tolerance, and predicted that audience identification with the film would lead to increased religious tolerance. He hypothesized that those students for whom the institutional role (Catholic priest) had a high prestige value would learn more facts and change their attitudes further in the direction of the film bias than would those for whom the institutional role had low prestige value. In addition, he hypothesized that those who presumably "identified" with the main character in the film because of institutional affiliation with the Catholic Church, would learn more facts and change their at-

titudes further in the direction of religious tolerance than those who were not affiliated institutionally with the Catholic Church.

The population used in the experiment began with 814 students in introductory psychology courses at the Pennsylvania State College; but due to missing data, absences, etc., the original number was reduced to 440. Prestige rating of the vocation of Catholic priest was obtained on a rank order scale of 11 occupations. The information test, based on the film, consisted of 65 multiple-choice items. Religious tolerance was measured by two alternate forms of a Thurstone-type equal-appearing intervals attitude scale, constructed especially for the experiment. High- and low-prestige groups of 100 students each (independent of religious affiliation) were selected from the two extremes of the rating of the prestige value of Catholic priest, every member of the first group having rated priest one or two (high prestige end of the scale), and every member of the second group having rated this occupation ten or 11 (low prestige end of scale). These two groups were equated on sex, percentage who had previously seen the film, and distribution of scores on the Moore-Castore Test of Scholastic Aptitude. Catholic (61 cases) and non-Catholic (379 cases) substratum groups were also equated in the same manner as the high- and low-prestige groups. The alternate forms of the religious tolerance scale and the occupational prestige scale were administered before and after the film showing. The information test was given after the film showing.

Findings

Those Rating Priest Role High Changed Attitude More

Both the high-prestige and the low-prestige groups (neither stratified according to Catholic-non-Catholic affiliation, the high group having 13 more Catholics) changed in the intended direction of more tolerant religious attitudes; but the change of the low-prestige group was very slight (.09 on an 11-point scale) and unreliable. The change of the high-prestige group was greater (.18 on an 11-point scale) and reliable at the two per cent level of confidence. The two groups were practically identical in their pre-test religious tolerance scores. This would seem to indicate that the film had more effect upon the tolerance attitude of those who originally held the role of Catholic priest in high prestige, but that it had little if any effect upon this attitude for those who originally held the role in low prestige. This is the only result in Kishler's study which supports the identification hypothesis with reasonably high reliability. The high-prestige group scored slightly higher in information acquired from the film; but this was just a suggestion of an effect in the same direction as the attitude change, since the information difference was quite unreliable (17 per cent level of confidence).

* This concept was mentioned in the beginning of Chapter V.

Priest Role Rated Higher by Catholics Both Before and After Film

On both pre-tests and post-tests of groups stratified according to religion, Catholics ranked the prestige of Catholic priest higher than did non-Catholics. Both Catholics and non-Catholics assigned higher prestige value to the role after the film, and these higher prestige values were significant at the one per cent level of confidence. The difference between pre- and post-test prestige value assignments was slightly, but unreliably, higher for the Catholic than for the non-Catholic sub-stratum (.10 on an 11-point scale).

Religious Tolerance Effect No Greater for Catholics

On the religious tolerance attitude scale, the Catholic sub-stratum was slightly (.10 on an 11-point scale) but unreliably more tolerant religiously than the non-Catholic sub-stratum on the pre-test. Both Catholics and non-Catholics gained slightly (.17 and .19, respectively), on the religious tolerance attitude scale after seeing the film; but only the non-Catholic gain was reliable (one per cent level). These data failed to support the hypothesis that those who identified institutionally with the Catholic Church would change more in attitude in the direction suggested by the film than those who did not identify institutionally with the Catholic Church. By anyone familiar with Catholic religious doctrine, no such facile prediction would have been made, since religious tolerance is a complex doctrine in the Catholic Church, not susceptible to easy manipulation or solution. Kishler over-simplified his hypothesis.

Informational Gains Slightly Larger for Catholics

On the information test, there was a slight mean difference (1.44 difference, with a mean for Catholics of 46.69) in favor of the Catholic sub-stratum, reliable at the six per cent level of confidence. Kishler interprets the small difference as possibly due to the somewhat limited opportunity provided by the film for informational learning. If this is so, the reliability of the difference increases the importance of the result.

Another factor which may have entered into Kishler's results, and affected the size and reliability of differences in attitude changes, is that the Catholic sub-stratum consisted of only 61 students, whereas, the non-Catholic sub-stratum consisted of 379 students.

YALE MOTION PICTURE RESEARCH PROJECT EXPERIMENT

The implications of the postulated mechanism of "identification" were also studied, (experiment unpublished), by the Motion Picture Research Project at Yale.

Experimental Design

The films used were designed to teach elementary school children the causes of seasonal changes in terms of variations in intensity and duration of sunlight as the earth moves through its orbit. One of the two films (which had been furnished by the Motion Picture Association Pilot Film Project) provided the children an opportunity to identify themselves with the learner-protagonists, since the content was presented in story form with a father explaining the reasons for seasonal change to his two children (a boy and a girl). A parallel version presented the same material in substantially the same way, but in a straightforward, expository manner without the story-protagonist device. Careful experimental tests showed only a minute, wholly unreliable, difference in favor of the story-protagonist version.

B. FAMILIARITY

The data on familiarity as an involvement factor in motion picture experience are not clear-cut. In Chapter VII it was pointed out that the amount of previous knowledge of a subject shown in a film influences the amount of learning from the film. This may be regarded as prima facie evidence that familiarity is a factor in audience involvement. It is supported by some data reported by Holaday and Stoddard (1933) and by the observations of Sturmthal and Curtis (1944).

HOLADAY AND STODDARD STUDY

P. W. Holaday and G. D. Stoddard studied the amount of retention of information from entertainment films.

Findings

They reported that action was remembered best when it concerned activities such as sports, general action, crime and fighting, when it had high emotional appeal, and when it occurred in a familiar type of surroundings, such as the home, school, and tenement. They reported that action was least understood when it concerned unfamiliar activities, such as bootlegging and business, when it had practically no emotional element, and when it occurred in surroundings of an unfamiliar type, such as a cafe or frontier.

STURMTHAL AND CURTIS STUDY

A. Sturmthal and A. Curtis, in their study of audience reaction to Valley Town and What So Proudly We Hail, reported that familiar material was liked by an audience when it had symbolic meaning.

Evaluation

These reports from two studies, which were widely separated in time, film content, and purpose, tend to support the hypothesis that familiarity of setting and familiarity of type of activity influence the degree to which an audience becomes involved in motion picture experience. They also support the qualification that the essential ingredient of involvement is not familiarity itself, but rather the symbolic character (or meaning) of the familiar setting and activity. In other words, the setting and action must not simply be familiar, but they must also have personalized meanings. If this were not the case, familiarity alone in film content would restrict the opportunity for learning, and such effects as would accrue would be largely reinforcing, rather than reorganizational.

C. SUBJECTIVE CAMERA

Before considering the technique of the subjective camera, which gives the audience a learner's eye-view, "realism," as a filmic device, will be discussed.

"REALISM" IN PICTURES

Exact Representation Is Not an Inflexible Principle

The problem of "realism" is basic to the question of the relative influence of pictures presented as a continuous series of actions and interactions, or a series of separate, arrested actions (or "static" situations). It has often been assumed that the more exactly a motion picture represents the situation it portrays, the more "realistic" it is, and, hence, the more effective it is in involving the audience and stimulating audience response. But it is becoming increasingly clear that absolute fidelity of representation may be misleading as a principle of "realism" if it is applied inflexibly to all the decisions and conclusions involved in the production, use, and anticipated influence of films or filmstrips.

Relevant Cues Are Valuable in Learning

C. F. Hoban, Jr. (1949), in discussing concepts of communication, has suggested some implications that relate to the problem of "realism" in motion pictures. Within the concept of communication, motion pictures (like all media of communication and expression) serve to arouse and to pattern the perceptual responses of the audience, rather than to convey or transmit ready-made meanings from the communicator to the audience. This much, at least, is clear from the research bearing on audience characteristics and their relationship to motion picture influence, reviewed in Chapter VII.

The problem of communication via motion pictures and "still" pictures is not to represent exactly every sensory element in the situation portrayed, but to select the relevant cues to reaction and to faithfully represent these relevant cues in picture and or sound. The problem which confronts the film producer is essentially the same as that facing the artist and the sculptor:--to select and represent cues relevant to the meaning the artist is attempting to express. Which cues are relevant, depends, in turn, on the extent and organization of the previous experience of the audience.

When pictures are conceived as a medium of communication, rather than as an exact representation of a social situation, many of the problems of motion pictures vs. filmstrips, or live action vs. simplified

animation, are susceptible to analysis. Decisions may then be based on audience experience and the ability to draw inferences and meanings from cues to experience, rather than on techniques intrinsic to still or motion pictures.

GIBSON STUDY

J. J. Gibson, et al., (1947) studied the effectiveness of the 15-minute animated film, Position Firing in teaching gunnery to aviation cadets (discussed in Chapter VI). The film was compared with an illustrated lecture and a specially prepared illustrated manual. He noted that, "For long passages, the camera takes the position (literally the 'point of view') of the trainee in the learning situation, seeing what he would see, rather than the more conventional position of an on-looker watching someone else in the learning situation. Nearly one-third of the time spent on instruction in the film is devoted to these passages" (p. 252).

Findings

He attributes much of the effectiveness of the film to the "subjective" point of view of the camera, which, he comments, "although relatively little used in American films generally, is highly effective in the film in question" (p. 254). The concept of "rad" was more clearly comprehended by the film group apparently because they had seen how it was used and had vicariously experienced sighting a .50 caliber machine gun.

Since Gibson's study was reported, experimental investigations by S. M. Roshal (1949) and N. Jaspen (1948) of the Instructional Film Research Program staff, have contributed significantly to a better understanding of the importance of the subjective camera, that is, the presentation of the content of the film from the viewing point of the learner.

ROSHAL STUDY

S. M. Roshal designed his study to test the rather widely-held hypothesis that "The learning of a perceptual-motor act, from films, will be more effective as the film presentation approaches an exact representation of the learner himself performing the act or acts to be learned" (p. 7). His data bear out the limitations, pointed out above, of absolute fidelity of representation in producing effective film realism.

Experimental Design

Roshal designed his experiment to test the effectiveness of four variables: (1) camera angle, (2) motion, (3) hands, and (4) participation. His findings on the first three variables are discussed here in reference to "subjective camera"; the fourth variable, "participation," is discussed in a separate section under that heading.

Eight film versions, including various combinations of the four variables, were produced to demonstrate how to tie the three knots, the bowline, the sheet bend, and the Spanish bowline. Each of the three knots was treated separately in each of the eight versions, providing in one sense, twenty-four knot-tying sequences. The experimental population included 3500 Naval trainees at the Great Lakes Naval Training Station, who were tested on their ability to actually tie the knots.

Findings

Roshal found that the 0° (subjective) camera angle was superior to the 180° camera angle for perceptual-motor training. His data indicate that when the camera is placed in the position of someone actually performing the task, rather than opposite him, learning is facilitated.

He also found that the use of motion in portraying the actual tying of the knots was superior to static (still) representation of various stages of the performance. However, he found that the portrayal of the demonstrator's hands in tying the knots (in the static representation) did not facilitate learning. He reported some reasons that led him to believe that the portrayal of hands obscured perception of the actual operations of the rope in tying the knot.*

Evaluation

Crucial Cues Are Important

It is in this last respect that the fidelity-of-representation hypothesis is brought in question, since the necessity for clear perception, rather than details of learner representation seems to assume greater or prior importance. Absolute realism appears to interfere with relevant learning when any of its elements obscure perception of crucial cues.

Thus, Roshal's data appear to substantiate Gibson's hypothesis of the subjective camera angle and to support the hypothesis that motion is desirable in pictures when motion is relevant or crucial to the situation or task represented or portrayed by the pictures. His data also support the hypothesis that absolute realism, that is, fidelity and exactitude of representation, is not essential to motion picture communication, but may, on the contrary interfere with perception. The problem becomes one of discovering the crucial cues. If crucial cues have greater importance than exact duplication of situation and response, Roshal's data achieve importance considerably beyond their purely empirical value with reference to teaching sailors to tie knots.

JASPEN STUDY

N. Jaspen (1948) had extended data on "crucial cues" in two directions.

Experimental Design

In one case he studied the effectiveness of several variables in a series of experimental films designed to teach the assembly of the breechblock of the 40mm antiaircraft gun. Two of the variables introduced were (1) the showing of common errors to be avoided, and (2) nomenclature of the parts of the breechblock.

In Jaspen's study, 17 different versions of the film on assembly of the breechblock were produced, providing various combinations of the six variables under study. The experimental population consisted of 2377 apprentice seamen at the Great Lakes Naval Training Station. Results were tested by actual assembly of breechblocks.

Findings

Depicting Errors Helps Learning

Jaspen found that the showing of potential errors in assembling the breechblock in addition to demonstrating the proper procedure was markedly superior to demonstrating the proper procedure only. This may be interpreted as being similar in effect to the subjective camera, in that the content of the film is presented in terms of the likely behavior of the trainee learning to perform a task. Errors are common forms of human behavior. Elimination of errors is characteristic of almost any pattern of perceptual-motor learning.

Technical Nomenclature May Not Aid Learning

On the other hand, Jaspen found little conclusive evidence that using technical nomenclature in the films increased the efficiency of the performance of the breechblock assembly. Evidently, technical terms served very little, if at all, to involve the learner in the film or in the task, although there is no evidence that the use of nomenclature interfered with learning from the film. Evidently, nomenclature, particularly if it is new or novel (as it apparently was to the trainees in Jaspen's experiment), is not a "crucial cue," and, for all practical purposes reference to "this here piece" or "part" may serve quite as well, if the criterion of learning is specific manual performance, rather than technical literacy.

Evaluation

In the various studies of motion picture influence, it becomes increasingly evident that an instructional film is more likely to be successful when the film con-

---

* An uncontrolled size variable was allowed to be built into the static-no-hands version. This may have affected the results.

tent and, presumably, the film experience are relevant to the specific behavior that the film is intended to influence. Relevance appears to be an important element in the rhetoric of the film.

D. ANTICIPATION

A fourth factor in involvement may be identified as audience anticipation. "Anticipation" means that the individual makes an adjustment for a coming situation, or that he has a state of readiness or expectancy for a coming event and expects certain things to happen in the film. He is on the alert for certain things that he may have been told to look for, and tries to get the "important" points in the film because he has been forewarned of a test following the film, or for the more practical reason that he may need the knowledge when his unit makes its first attack in a few days. On the other hand, he may, on the basis of personal experience, perpare himself for a sequence of events within a film.

Research studies indicate that anticipation may arise either from the instructional activities or procedures which precede the film showing or from the introductory sequence and other comments or sequences presented within the film itself.

A study on the effect of introductory remarks, reported by C. I. Hovland, A. A. Lumsdaine, and F. D. Sheffield (1949), and one on the effect of using pre-screening materials, reported by W. A. Wittich and J. G. Fowlkes (1946), both discussed in connection with conditions and methods of film use, (see Part II), also pertain to this factor of anticipation.

DYSINGER AND RUCKMICK STUDY

The operation of an anticipation factor in influencing emotional response to scenes of danger in entertainment films was noticed by W. S. Dysinger and C. A. Ruckmick (1933).

Findings

Anticipation Influenced Responses

They report that, frequently, anticipation of possible developments in the story seemed to be a factor in the emotional and perceptual experience of children and adults. Depending upon conditions, anticipation appeared to serve as either a deterrent or a stimulant to emotional response. Anticipation of fearful consequences, without "adult discount," increased emotional intensity, but when all developments were expected, because of either "adult discount," or previous experience with similar pictures, emotional response decreased or was entirely lacking.

This may be interpreted to mean that instructional films for some purposes, especially attitudinal development, may be more effective when an instructional stereotype is avoided, when the ending is not

easily predictable and the final answer is not provided in the film. It probably implies that if any set "pattern" is followed too frequently, its instructional effectiveness is likely to diminish.

STURMTHAL AND CURTIS STUDY

A. Sturmthal and A. Curtis (1944) conducted interviews among people who saw the film, Valley Town.

Findings

They found some evidence of an "expected action," or an anticipation of some plot development. They also observed that members of the Valley Town audience (the film dealt with the effects of technological unemployment) who had been unemployed at least three months appeared "to be more wary of committing themselves to positive responses until they know what the slant of the picture is, as a whole, as well as of each new sequence. When they know, they go ahead of the others in their liking. Their liking stands above that of others most clearly in those sequences which show the effect of unemployment upon people" (p. 496). This observation may conceivably be interpreted to mean that the unemployed, in reacting to a film dealing with unemployment and unemployed people, withhold more positive response until they have been assured of the direction of events or circumstances which may be anticipated, but that, once the validity of the anticipation has been established, their emotional response is strong, as measured by frequency of "like" responses on a program analyzer. (The analyzer was a polygraph registering frequency and duration of responses, such as "like" or "dislike," which the audience indicated by means of a push-button mechanism.)

Evaluation

The "wait-and-see" reaction noted by Sturmthal and Curtis may be related to the factor of acceptance identified by C. I. Hovland, A. A. Lumsdaine, and F. D. Sheffield (1949), which was discussed in Chapter V. It is reasonably certain that, although an instructional film audience may be captive in the physical sense, it is not captive in a psychological sense. An audience is most likely to approve in a film those things it approves in real life experiences, and disapprove those things it disapproves in real life. Furthermore, an audience will probably anticipate the sequence of events in a film, and, as these anticipations approach a core of personal reference and importance, the audience will become increasingly involved in the film experience.

E. PARTICIPATION

A fifth factor in audience involvement is overt participation by the learner during the film instruction, or overt practice immediately following the film. The effects of practice after the film were described in Chapters IV and VI. In the present section, the research on audience participation during a film showing is reviewed. W. J. Hall (1936) was possibly the first investigator to grasp the importance of participation during film learning. On testing learning by junior high school science pupils from silent films, he found learning facilitated by questions projected on the screen before and during the film.

During World War II, C. I. Hovland, A. A. Lumsdaine, and F. D. Sheffield (1949) investigated the effect of audience participation in learning from a sound filmstrip dealing with the phonetic alphabet. The same problem was further investigated at Yale University and was also studied in connection with perceptual-motor learning tasks by S. Roshal (1949) and N. Jaspen (1950), and in connection with informational and conceptual learning by H. R. Brenner, J. S. Walter, and A. K. Kurtz (1949), all of the Instructional Film Research Program.

HOVLAND, LUMSDAINE, AND SHEFFIELD STUDY

In the C. I. Hovland, A. A. Lumsdaine, and F. D. Sheffield study (1949), two versions of the sound filmstrip on the phonetic alphabet were prepared for experimental use.

Experimental Design

In one version, review exercises inserted in the filmstrip required the audience to call out the phonetic name of the letter (D — Dog; I — Item, etc.); in the other version the commentator stated both the letter and the phonetic name in the review exercises. The only difference between the two versions was that in one case (standard version) the commentator called out the letter and its phonetic equivalent, and in the other case (participation version) the audience called out the phonetic name. Results were measured both by written tests given to the entire experimental population and by interview tests given to a small sample of the experimental population.

Findings

Participation Version Gave Better Results

In the comparison of the two training groups, one of which saw the standard version and the other the participation version, the participation version produced reliable and reasonably large gains. In percentage of phonetic symbols recalled, the participation version was superior when results were measured allowing both a two-second and a fifteen-second recall period. The average group scores are illustrated in Fig. 8-1, and the differences between them are reliable at better than the one per cent level of confidence.

Participation Aided in Learning More Difficult Material

Results were then analyzed in terms of item difficulty, that is, in terms of phonetic symbols that were found to be relatively easy and relatively difficult to learn. This analysis revealed that the participation version was more influential on difficult items. On the

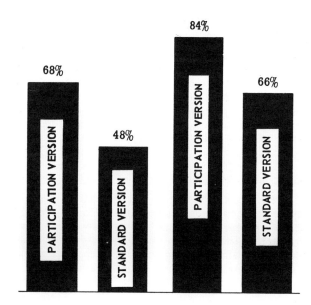

Fig. 8-1. Percent of phonetic symbols recalled from participation and standard film versions. (Hovland, Lumsdaine and Sheffield, 1949)

13 less difficult phonetic symbols, there was only an eight per cent superiority for the participation version, reliable at the seven per cent level of confidence; on the 13 more difficult phonetic symbols, there was a 28 per cent superiority for the participation version, reliable at the one per cent level. Thus, there was a 20 per cent difference in the amount of superiority of the participation version, reliable at the one per cent level, for the more difficult items as opposed to the less difficult ones. From this, Hovland, Lumsdaine, and Sheffield conclude that "active participation is most important when the material to be learned is most difficult" (p. 237).

Announced Test Was Learning Incentive

To measure the influence of participation in relation to motivation, or incentive, before the filmstrip was shown, half of the trainees used in measuring the influence of both the standard and the participation versions were notified that a test on the phonetic alphabet would be given. Care was taken that the announcement of the test did not spread by word-of-mouth to the trainees to whom the announcement of the test was not made in advance. On the standard version, announcement of the test in advance resulted in a 15.4 per cent increase in phonetic names recalled, reliable on the one per cent level of confidence. Significantly enough, there was only a slight difference (2.7 per cent) between those trainees who had seen the participation version of the filmstrip without prior announcement of the test, and those who had seen the standard version with prior announcement of the test. This seems to indicate that announcement of a test in advance produced approximately the same increase in learning as the introduction of vocal participation techniques within the filmstrip.

There was only a small difference between the standard and the participation versions (5.2 per cent in favor of the participation version) when a test was announced in advance of the filmstrip showing. By contrast, the difference which could be attributed to the participation technique when the groups were not motivated by the announcement of a test was 12.9 per cent, reliable at the four per cent level of confidence. These data suggest, as Hovland, Lumsdaine, and Sheffield point out, that active participation is more important when individuals are less motivated to learn.

Participation Benefited Less-Intelligent Most

When the data were analyzed in terms of men with higher and lower scores on a test of mental ability (Army General Classification Test), it was found that the participation version was 20.9 per cent superior for the men with the lower scores on the mental ability test, and only 4.9 per cent superior for those with higher mental ability test scores. Thus, there was a 16 per cent difference in the amount of superiority for participation, reliable at the five per cent level of confidence, for the less intelligent as opposed to the more intelligent trainees. Hovland, Lumsdaine, and Sheffield found that "the less intelligent groups profited most from the increased audience participation" (p. 240).

Participation Challenges Learner

In their theoretical discussion of the effect of vocal participation, Hovland, Lumsdaine, and Sheffield relate this type of participation to ego involvement and to motivation of an individual to learn in order to avoid a feeling of shame for poor performance in the presence of his peers. The participation questions are regarded as a series of examinations "in which the learner is immediately required to show what he had learned" (p. 245). In this way they reconcile the apparently equal results of the announcement of a test in advance of a film showing with the effect of vocal participation during the film showing, and the fact that both of these procedures apparently benefit the men whose scores are relatively low on tests of mental ability. Both devices are apparently less necessary to motivate learning among the men with higher scores on mental ability tests.

YALE MOTION PICTURE RESEARCH PROJECT STUDY

A more recent study (although reported earlier in published form) by the Yale Motion Picture Research Project (1947), was concerned with the effect of both "motivation" and "participation" questions inserted into an existing film dealing with the heart and circulatory system. Among those conducting this study were some of the investigators associated with the preceding study.

Experimental Design

The experimental population consisted of approximately 150 eleventh- and twelfth-grade pupils. The participation questions used here were not the vocal "calling-out" type. After each unit of the film material was presented, a film title directed the pupils to answer the appropriate question contained on a worksheet which the pupils used during the film showing. Shortly afterward, the correct answer was given on the screen. This participation, in contrast with the phonetic alphabet learning, involved a written, rather than vocal, response, and the learner was also informed immediately whether his answer was right or wrong.

Four experimental versions of the film were made with: (1) "motivating" questions preceding each unit of material, (2) "participation" questions, to be answered by pupils after each unit of material, (3) both "motivating" and "participation" questions, and (4) a factual version containing neither "motivating" or "participation" questions, shown once and also shown twice. The time required for the simple factual version was 8.5 minutes, for the participation version, 13 minutes, and for the factual version shown twice, 17 minutes.

Findings

The informational gains, reported in percentages of correct answers, for the various versions are shown in Fig. 8-2. The factual version, shown twice, resulted in approximately the same increment in learning as the single showing of the "participation" version, and a slightly, but probably not reliably, higher increment than the "motivating" question version (reliability not reported).

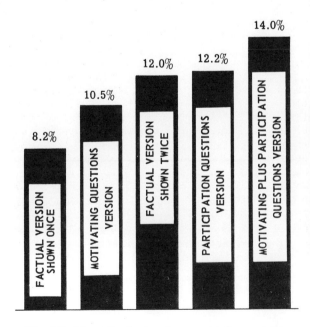

Fig. 8-2. Informational gains, in percent, after presentations of instructional biology film. (Yale Motion Picture Research Project, 1947)

Participation Items Were Learned Best

This study raised another question worthy of further research: What material was affected by the participation questions? It is conceivable that answering questions about particular facts may cause them to be remembered, but this procedure may have a distracting or inhibiting effect on facts not emphasized in this manner. The final test contained some items which had been practiced by the participation questions and others which had not. The scores on the two types of test items were compared for the group who had the participation version and the group who had the factual version. As might be expected, the chief gain from the participation version was on the test items directly covered by the participation questions. The difference between the participation and factual versions on the items not directly covered was too small to be considered by the authors as evidence of a real difference between the two procedures.

GIBSON STUDY

J. J. Gibson (1947) investigated the effectiveness of differences in immediate reinforcement in a learner participation experiment, using aviation trainees who were required to learn to identify airplanes from slides.

Experimental Design

Two methods of using these slides were compared. In the first method, pictures of 20 foreign planes, identified by the instructor before each projection, were exhibited three times. On the fourth trial, the pictures were simply exhibited and the trainees were required to furnish the identification.

In the second method, the reinforced method, the procedure was the same except that the trainees were required to identify the planes on both the second and third trial. Immediately after its second and third showing each slide was repeated and its name announced. Trainees were required to check their written response if it was correct, to correct any wrong name, or to write in the correct name if the plane had been unidentified. In this way, the response elicited was either confirmed, corrected, or completed, and in all cases the correct response was practiced with the knowledge that it was correct. Thus, participation or practice consisted not simply of practice alone, but of practice involving both a knowledge of results and a correct response to the stimulus. This is part of what is meant by the principle, "Practice under favorable conditions is an important factor in learning."

Findings

The trainees who had been instructed with reinforced practice were more than 40 per cent superior to those taught by the unreinforced method. The average scores were: unreinforced, 10.49; reinforced, 14.56.

The critical ratio of this difference was 7.69 -- highly reliable. In the unreinforced group, 2.7 per cent identified all slides correctly on the fourth trial, whereas in the group taught with reinforced practice, 13.7 per cent identified all slides correctly.

Mere Exhibition Does Not Guarantee Learning

Gibson concluded that the results of this experiment "showed clearly that the principle of overt response with reinforcement, the effectiveness of which had been demonstrated many times in learning studies, was applicable to the special form of visual learning required for the successful recognizing of aircraft" (p. 148). He further concluded that visual training materials, "and in fact any other type of material would be of little value if they were presented merely as exhibitions. The great volume of visual training aids being produced could not be expected to yield the most effective result unless they were employed as positive instruments of instruction rather than for display" (p. 148).

Gibson's conclusion regarding mere display as opposed to the use of training materials within the context of well-established instructional principles and procedures is well supported by the research on motivation, participation, and conditions of use.

BRENNER, WALTER, AND KURTZ STUDY

H. R. Brenner, J. S. Walter, and A. K. Kurtz (1949) investigated the differences in learning effects between questions and factual statements inserted in a film.

Experimental Design

Various quantities of (1) multiple-choice questions inserted in the films were projected on the screen and read by the commentator at the same time, and (2) factual statements were simultaneously projected and read by the commentator. Both the questions and the statements were interpolated at the same places in the corresponding film versions, and covered exactly the same facts. The comparison was thus between inserted questions and inserted statements.

Two films were used in the study: (1) The Care and Use of Hand Tools -- Wrenches, a training film dealing with a technical subject, and (2) Snakes, a film on an informational subject, produced by Coronet Instructional Films, Inc.

Six versions of each film were shown: (1) the original film (no inserted questions or statements) shown once, (2) the original film, shown twice in immediate succession, (3) the original film with questions inserted at approximately 32-second intervals, (4) the original film with statements inserted at approximately 32-second intervals, (5) the same as Version 3 except that only the odd-numbered questions were inserted, and (6) the same as Version 4 except that only odd-numbered statements were included. Thus the variables were (1) a single showing of the original film, (2) two showings of the original film, (3) a large number of inserted questions, (4) a large number of inserted statements, (5) a moderate number of inserted questions, and (6) a moderate number of inserted statements. The comparison of statements with questions was based on the hypothesis that questions would stimulate more active participation than statements; hence, the results on the versions with questions were expected to be superior.

The experimental population consisted of 111 boys and 111 girls in the tenth grades in each of six co-operating high schools. Each group was matched person to person on intelligence and sex. The test on the Snakes film consisted of 74 items and the test on the Wrenches film consisted of 71 items. Some of the items on the tests had been covered by the questions and statements in the experimental versions; the other items had not been covered.

Findings

Inserted Questions Are Not Always Effective

Results of this experiment were not conclusive. The only point of general agreement in the results from both films was that the original film shown twice was about as effective as the other special versions. Results varied not only on the effects of statements and questions in the two films, but also between the boys and the girls. What seems apparent from this study is that mere insertion of questions in large or small numbers in any film is not universally effective.

YALE MOTION PICTURE RESEARCH PROJECT STUDY

The foregoing study suggests that we need to know more about how the questions should be inserted. Some additional pertinent evidence on this point, also showing negative results, was obtained by the Yale Motion Picture Research Project (study unpublished) in 1948.

Experimental Design

In this study, involving grammar school children, the exposition of a factual subject (reasons for seasonal change) by purely declarative statements was compared with a presentation using identical visual material, but in which the narrator made liberal use of rhetorical questions. No provision was made for overt answering of these questions, but it was thought that "implicit" participation by the audience might be stimulated by the rhetorical questions.

Findings

The experimental test data showed no significant difference in the amounts learned by the subjects with and without the rhetorical questions.

ROSHAL STUDY

S. M. Roshal's study (1949), discussed under "Subjective Camera," was one of two Instructional Film Research Program studies dealing with the effect of participation in films on perceptual-motor learning.

Experimental Design

Some experimental versions of the films, which illustrate the tying of the bowline, sheet bend, and Spanish bowline knots, instructed the trainees to tie the knots while they were being demonstrated and explained in the films.

Findings

In his analysis of results, Roshal found no reliable differences in favor of the film versions involving audience participation. He attributed these results to the possibility that the film versions did not allow sufficient time for effective participation, particularly in the case of the more complicated knots.

JASPEN STUDY

N. Jaspen (1950) conducted the second Instructional Film Research Program study on the effects of participation in learning perceptual-motor tasks from films.

Experimental Design

He tested the hypothesis suggested by Roshal's study that more time, (slower speed of development of the film), was needed to provide optimum conditions for participation. The same films demonstrating the assembly of the breechblock of the 40mm antiaircraft gun, used in Jaspen's first (1948) experiment, were used in this study. Two versions of the experimental film were employed, one involving a slow rate of development and the other a rapid rate of development. Four groups of naval trainees, equated on age, education, general intelligence, and mechanical aptitude, were each shown a different version of the film: (1) the slow development film with participation (assembling the breechblock during the film showing), (2) the slow development film without participation, (3) the fast development film with participation, (4) the fast development film without participation. All four groups were given a performance test immediately after the film.

Findings

Jaspen found that the slow-rate-of-development film, requiring audience participation was greatly superior to the similar version without audience participation, and that the slow-rate-of-development version with participation was greatly superior to the rapid-rate-of-development version with participation. The latter difference was considerably greater than the former. Both differences were reliable at better than the one per cent level of confidence.

Slow Rate of Development Facilitates Participation in an Assembly Task

From his data, Jaspen concluded that "audience participation is a very effective utilization procedure in teaching this task, when the rate of development of the film is slow enough to permit the learners to view the film and assemble the breechblock without too much loss of attention to either. Conversely, the requirement of audience participation seems to have a negative effect if the film develops rapidly" (p. 16).

F. INFLUENCE OF DRAMATIC STRUCTURE AND THE CARTOON FORM

Little if any experimental research has been conducted on the problem of dramatic and expository structure, and on the related problem of animated cartoons and live photography, as factors which influence the instructional effectiveness of films; or perhaps more correctly stated, influence learning from film experiences.

Emotional Involvement Occurs in Well-Produced Dramatic Films

That there is involvement in well-produced dramatic films which meet an audience at its typical level of background, intelligence, and interests, any thoughtful and observant movie-goer knows full well. The studies mentioned at the beginning of this discussion of involvement, presenting physiological and testimonial evidence, are clear proof of involvement, at least on the emotional level, in dramatic motion pictures. The investigators attributed much of this emotional reaction to the dramatic structure of these films. Whether similar emotional involvement measurements could be obtained from experiencing the expository type of instructional film, is doubtful. No such comparative research has been done.

Dramatic Structure No Guarantee of Involvement

It should not be assumed that dramatic structure alone, guarantees involvement, any more than it should be assumed that the mere existence in a film of subjective camera, participation, or even familiarity, assures involvement. All these are factors that for one reason or another, and under certain conditions, are conducive to involvement.

The hypothesis might be proposed that whether dramatic structure is conducive to involvement or not depends, to a large degree, upon the extent to which the plot and film presentation appeals to, or runs counter to, one or more of the basic motivations and needs (see beginning of Chapter V) or acquired interests and attitudes of the individuals exposed to it.

Under these conditions, dramatic structure may facilitate involvement, assuming that the dramatic presentation is consistent with professional acting and direction of the prevailing mode.

Involvement Through Dramatic Structure Does Not Necessarily Facilitate Learning

As implied in our analysis of the concept of involvement, presented in the early part of this discussion, whether the involvement aroused through dramatic structure will produce the desired learning outcomes appears to depend also upon the particular outcomes desired and upon the nature of the involvement produced.

1. DRAMATIC VS. EXPOSITORY PRESENTATION

Dramatization May Be More Effective for Certain Learning Outcomes Than Text-like Treatment

The films used in the Payne Fund studies were all dramatic treatments produced for theater use. They involved plot, character interaction, conflict, and resolution of conflict. In short, they were film stories or film photoplays rather than film essays or film textbooks. There is some reason to believe that the long-time retention of the effects of these films on informational and conceptual learning observed by P. W. Holaday and G. D. Stoddard (1933) were, in part at least, a function of the dramatic structure of these films. Furthermore, A. W. Reitz (1937) observed that the Yale Chronicles of America Photoplay, Dixie, appeared to produce more informational learning than did the Eastman Teaching film, Wheat, which was text-like in structure. Since the content of the two films is not comparable and since Reitz reported no measures of reliability of his differences, nor of the comparability of his tests, his observations cannot be accepted as experimentally established conclusions. Nonetheless, they fit into what appears to be a coherent pattern of random observations, suggesting that a dramatic, somewhat emotionalized presentation may cause certain facts to persist longer in the individual's memory.

Dramatic Form May Facilitate Identification

The testimonial evidence, cited earlier in this discussion, would seem to demonstrate that some form of identification occurs rather readily in good dramatic films. It remains to be shown experimentally that this identification produces the kind of involvement conducive to a desired learning outcome.

Dramatic Form Possibly More Effective for Attitude Changes

According to the testimonial evidence in Blumer's study of movie "autobiographies," dramatic motion pictures influenced various percentages of his adolescent group from city high schools in acquiring acceptable manners, developing better social adjustments, acquiring love-making techniques, getting a "better" idea of modern society, developing ambition, realizing the value of family life, developing certain religious and moral attitudes, and acquiring a philosophy of life. These are certainly cases of attitudinal learning; but to say that the motion pictures initiated these attitudes would be going beyond the evidence. As suggested in an earlier part of this report, it is probable that most of what the adolescent gets from the movies is mainly a crystallization of points of view, desires, and attitudes already in existence, at least in embryonic form.

Any motion picture presents in dramatic form a large collection of ideas and certain attitudes; each individual is somewhat free to select for himself what he learns, just as he does from any other experience in life. Yet it is quite possible that the technique of good dramatic form with its action, suspense, and emotional appeal may at times have a sort of hypnotic effect upon a certain percentage of an audience, causing them to form certain opinions or attitudes, even though they have not consciously chosen to do so, or are consciously aware that they have done so.

All the studies on attitudinal learning from films, described in Chapter V, used pictures produced in either dramatic or documentary form. To the best of the reviewers' knowledge no study of attitude change from the expository or teaching-type film has been made. Here is an interesting and important type of comparison for research. The following study with recordings has a bearing on this question.

HOVLAND, LUMSDAINE, AND SHEFFIELD STUDY

C. I. Hovland, A. A. Lumsdaine, and F. D. Sheffield (1949) made a direct comparison with Army trainees between a "documentary" recording (involving the acting out of events, with professional actors and musical accompaniment), and a presentation of the events described and interpreted by a commentator only, both programs dealing with the difficult job in Japan after V-E Day.

Findings

They found a slight, though not statistically reliable, difference in "expressed audience interest" in favor of the dramatic presentations. They also found a greater, though unreliable, tendency to accept the dramatic presentations as being more authentic. Thus, in measures of audience "interest" and acceptance of authenticity, the dramatic programs had a consistent, but slight and unreliable, advantage. As the authors point out, there is little reason to expect that these results can be generalized immediately to the film medium or to a comparison between dramatic and textual treatment of content. Nevertheless, this experiment is significant because it makes these comparisons.

Dramatic Form Could Provide a Slower Rate of Development

It is conceivable that dramatic form in teaching some procedures, or a certain process, might be a feasible way of slowing up the development of the film to a rate which would facilitate the learning, provided the dramatic form did not distract attention from the learning of the process itself. This is entirely a speculation for future research.

Unrelated Dramatic Form Might Impair Desired Learning Outcome

A dramatic presentation completely irrelevant to the material being taught might be definitely detrimental to learning, especially if it resulted in considerable emotional involvement. As Gibson (1947) has pointed out, in some training films, where the plot and possibly humor were used only to "dress up" the picture, it can be doubted that they served any instructional purpose, even motivational. The results of the Nelson and Moll (1950) study of the film on desert survival, discussed in Section 2 to follow, suggest that the pictorial treatment of the subject of survival was more or less an example of "window dressing."

Dramatic Form May Create Negative Emotional Involvement

As a sidelight of the Kishler (1950) study of identification factors in relation to the effect of the picture, Keys of the Kingdom, individual interviews were held with a small number of the subjects and a group interview with one of the psychology class sections. In general, the film's theme of religious tolerance was recognized and accepted; but there were several comments of resentment toward what was felt to be a "propaganda" aspect of the picture. One Protestant who rated the prestige value of priest low both before and after the film, stated that she would have rated the priest higher immediately after the film. But with time (6 days) to think it over, she realized that Father Chisholm was not a typical priest and resented the fact that the film had moved her. She actually marked her religious tolerance attitude scale in a more prejudiced way after the film, to demonstrate her resentment of someone's trying to manipulate her attitudes.

Kishler reports the case of another Protestant girl who was apparently so emotionally upset by the picture that, in answering the post-test six days after the film showing, she marked the prestige rating scale and the attitude scale, and then wrote on the information test blank, "May I take this some other time?" It chanced that the experimenter learned that this girl had taken a Rorschach test at the college clinic the day after she refused to fill out the information test. The manifest content of her responses to the "ink blots" of this psychological test was permeated with the locale and situations portrayed in the picture, Keys of the Kingdom. She saw maps of China, pagodas, religious groups in conflict, and paths to heaven and hell.

Apparently the picture had tapped a serious area of conflict for this girl and brought a severe conflict of attitudes to the surface.

These are a few illustrations of the possibility of a dramatic presentation creating a negative emotional involvement in certain types of individuals. By this we mean an emotional involvement aroused by a negation, in the film, of some strong acquired interest or attitude; this emotional reaction then works counter to the informational and attitudinal learning desired from the film. Of course we have no evidence that it was the dramatic form, as such, which aroused these negative reactions and that an expository presentation of the same theme might not have caused similar reactions. This whole area of dramatic versus expository presentation is wide open for research.

2. CARTOON FORM VS. LIVE PHOTOGRAPHY

The postulate that dramatic presentation is more effective because it contains factors of audience involvement may also be applied to the use of animated cartoons and live photography, although no experimental comparisons have been made between these two forms of graphic presentation. However, three studies have been reported in which the animated cartoon was a mode of presentation being used. None of these studies compared two film treatments of the same topic, which are as identical as possible except for the substitution of human characters for cartoon characters. Hence they do not contain experimental evidence on the value of cartooning as a presentation variable.

The previously mentioned study reported by J. J. Gibson (1947), comparing an animated film, an illustrated lecture, and a specially prepared illustrated booklet in teaching position firing to aviation cadets, is relevant here. In addition to the animated diagrams, live action, and commentary, the material was organized around a thread of story providing characterization and humor in the form of a cartoon personage, "Trigger Joe." However, the ideas and rules of the subject-matter itself were the material for "Trigger Joe's" adventures, blunders, and final triumph. He was not allowed to "steal the show."

The film turned out to be by far the best of the three media of presentation, although Gibson makes no effort to attribute its success to the cartoon element. As the reader will recall, Gibson prefers to attribute its success to the dynamic presentation of relationships in action and the use of the subjective camera. He argues that the use of the comic form for emphasis may be valuable; but its use for "relief" or entertainment is beside the point in an educational film.

A. C. Richardson and G. H. Smith (1947) found, as mentioned in Chapter VI, that Disney cartoons in health instruction in junior and senior high school produced much more learning and enthusiasm than did printed pamphlets. There was no attempt, however, to evaluate the cartoon variable as such. The personification of certain abstract ideas by cartoon characters has been used in some instructional films, e.g., the "lift" pushing up on the wings of the airplane and the "electrons" scampering around the electric circuit. Just how effective such techniques are, we do not know; sometimes they may even be an over-simplification which leads to confusion. Here is a subject for further research.

C. I. Hovland, A. A. Lumsdaine, and F. D. Sheffield (1949) reported a study of audience reactions to a cartoon featuring a character named "Snafu," and to four other films involving other cinematic treatments and themes. Audience likes were recorded on a program analyzer and on a questionnaire. The character of "Snafu" differed from that of "Trigger Joe" in that "Snafu" is the continued butt of misfortune, whereas "Trigger Joe" is essentially docile and ultimately a competent, though somewhat non-academic, "Joe." The "Snafu" cartoon rated highest among all five films in the number of "like" reactions made to it on the program analyzer during its projection, but it rated only third in interest on a questionnaire administered after the film. Comments written on the questionnaire suggested that the comic treatment in this cartoon was out of keeping with the soldier's feelings that war is a serious matter.

Evaluation

These three studies raise the question of the influence of cartoons in general, and specifically, the influence of serio-comic elements in cartoons on behavior in contrast with (1) more realistic photographic and (2) more serious treatment of a subject, regardless of the symbol employed.

Possibly the problem of realism and the hypothesis of "crucial cues" also enter into the discussion of the value of animated cartoons in instruction. An animated cartoon contains only the "essential" form and detail in both foreground and background, and makes no attempt to portray a situation with fidelity of representation. Not only is much detail omitted, but the crucial characteristics of appearance and behavior are often exaggerated. If it can be assumed that the instructional effectiveness in the animated cartoon is due, in part, to its adaptability for presenting crucial cues, then the importance of striving for fidelity of representation in instructional films is again open to question.

Use of Crucial Cues May Offer Production Short-Cuts

The new techniques being developed in television, due in part to the small receiving screen and to limitations of studio space, time, and funds, may be and most likely are applicable to instructional film production. Quite possibly, the time, facilities, and expense of producing instructional films can be substantially reduced with little, if any, reduction in the instructional effectiveness of the product, by applying the "crucial cue" hypothesis. Research studies have indicated that lush detail in settings, backgrounds, costumes, furniture, etc., frequently escape the notice of the audience. As large audiences of children, youths and adults become more familiar with the simplified pictorial techniques used in television, the feasibility of reducing fidelity and exactness of situational representation in motion pictures, and the possibility of simplifying procedures and the techniques of studio lighting and of reorganizing the pattern of camera angles, are opened up to instructional film producers.

SECTION 2. PICTURE AND SOUND

The second element in the rhetoric of film instruction is the combined use of picture, visually presented language, and sound (in a typical instructional sound film the sound is mostly oral language), or of picture and visually presented language (in a silent film). The research on this topic is summarized under (a) visual and auditory channels, (b) pictorial and verbal presentation, (c) emphatic devices, (d) verbalization, and (e) music and sound effects. Paradoxically, there is very little direct research on this topic, even though the topic is of great importance to the most effective use of sound motion pictures for instruction.

SENSE MODALITY EFFECTS ON LEARNING RATE

In this inquiry there arises the general psychological question of the relation between the particular sensory channel (sense modality) through which the material is presented to the learner, and his rate of learning that material. Specifically, is material learned more rapidly when presented visually or auditorily?

To begin with, it should be kept in mind that when the amount of learning from any two sense modalities is compared, the comparison is relevant only when the material to be learned can be effectively transmitted by the modality in question. For example, it would be pointless to study the effectiveness of teaching the assembly of the 40mm breechblock by means of narration alone, without any sort of visual presentation, and to compare this presentation with one which gives the assembly procedure in a completely visual manner, with no narration or printed visual symbols in the picture. It should also be stressed that the sense organ is only the starting point and that it alone does not determine the nature of the learner's response. The learner may translate pictorial presentation into verbal symbols and similarly, he may translate auditory presentation into visual images, subvocal speaking, or implicit wiring or drawing movements. Recall our discussion in Chapter IV of what may happen in the learner who is viewing a film of a perceptual-motor skill which is to be learned.

Most of the psychological studies which have compared the learning of materials presented either visually, auditorily, or kinesthetically, or learning by a combination of two or all three of these modalities, have used disparate serial lists of verbal material (lists of unrelated words, nonsense syllables, etc.) The findings of these studies apply directly only to such material, but there is evidence that they also hold in some instances for connected meaningful material.

The basic psychological studies of this problem are reviewed by J. A. McGeoch (1942) and by J. B. Stroud (1946).

Their discussions of these studies lead to the following generalizations regarding the learning of serial verbal material when presented through different sense modalities:

1. The differences in amounts learned through the different modalities usually have been small and irregular in direction.

2. No one sense modality, or mode of presentation, can be said to be generally most advantageous. (However, someone with a special interest can usually select evidence favoring his mode, e.g., the movie, or the radio.)

3. In some experiments, auditory presentation has been rather consistently better than visual, whereas in other studies, the opposite results have been obtained.

4. The use of both visual and auditory presentation in combination has usually been better than the poorer of the two used separately, and in some cases, superior to either one used alone.

5. When kinesthetic stimulation in the form of vocal articulation has been added to visual presentation, auditory presentation, or to the two combined, in most cases there has been an increase in rate of learning.

6. This superiority of kinesthetic stimulation plus either visual or auditory presentation is more uniformly effective, and usually to a larger degree than is the combination of visual and auditory presentation.

7. The particular mode of presentation that results in more rapid learning is a function of several possible accompanying conditions, of which the following have been identified:

   a. The Learner's Experience. If the learner is accustomed to use or is more practiced with a particular method, that form of stimulation may be superior.

b. The Learner's Age. Auditory presentation of verbal materials is usually more effective for younger children, tending to become less effective as age increases.

c. The Type of Material. Meaningful material is less affected by the mode of presentation than is the learning of separate or discrete items in a series.

d. The Learner's Response to the Presentation. The mode of stimulating the learner does not wholly determine the mode by which he apprehends the material. For example, material received through auditory presentation may be immediately translated by the learner into visual images of words, spoken subvocally, or into implicit movements of writing or drawing, instead of mere auditory images of the orally-presented words. In studying spelling many pupils utilize visual imagery, regardless of the perceptual sense to which the words are presented.

e. The Learner's Ability to Utilize Cues. Individual differences in ability to use cues from different sensory modalities do seem to exist and affect rate of learning from various modalities.

8. Meaningfulness seems to be a more important factor in influencing learning than others, such as the sense modality stimulated, and the size, intensity, and color of the stimulus. These other factors seem to be most influential when they increase meaningfulness or motivation, direct the learner's attention, or operate in some way other than through their particular stimulating characteristics, per se (e.g., relative size influencing learning through novelty).

FIVE PRODUCTION FACTORS

A. VISUAL AND AUDITORY CHANNELS

Definitions

In discussing the effects of picture and sound in the motion picture film some terms should be defined.

Verbal material refers to words, numbers, and mathematical symbols. These can be presented to the learner orally from the sound track, or in printed form in the film, or by simultaneous or alternating use of both the oral and visual forms.

Pictorial material refers to all non-verbal material in the film, depicting such things as places, actions of people, operations of machines, art sketches, animated drawings, etc. Mechanical drawings and maps are largely non-verbal, though they may involve a combination of the two presentations, since verbal labels are frequently placed upon various parts of the map or drawing. Natural or simulated sound effects and music for background and affective setting used to make the film picture appear more realistic, are nonverbal materials from the sound track, coming to the learner through the auditory sense modality. The point to keep clear is that the producer's terms, "picture" and "sound" are not synonyms for "non-verbal" and "verbal" material. Both latter types of material can come to the learner from either the picture or the sound track.

Observing these distinctions, this review discusses the visual and auditory elements of the sound motion-picture, or, more familiarly, the "video" and "audio" element or channels.

H. E. Nelson (1949) and H. E. Nelson and K. Moll (1950) conducted the only experimental research that deals directly with the relative contributions to learning made by (1) the visual channel, (2) the auditory channel, and (3) the visual and auditory channels combined, in instructional films. These studies, conducted as projects of the Instructional Film Research Program, bear directly on some of the problems of sound films in instruction and provide some necessary background for the study of verbalization.

Two films dealing with aerodynamics, Theory of Flight and Problems of Flight, were used in the Nelson study. In the Nelson and Moll study, a film entitled, Land and Live in the Desert, dealing with desert survival, was used. Presumably these films were selected for study because it appeared that the narration carried the burden of the instruction and that the visual presentation was somewhat incomprehensible without the narration. Under these circumstances, the narration alone might have the same instructional effectiveness as the motion picture with the sound.

NELSON STUDY

Experimental Design

The experimental population for Nelson's (1949) aerodynamics films study consisted of 430 ROTC students at the Pennsylvania State College, randomly divided into eight groups averaging 54 to a group. Learning was tested by a 65-item multiple-choice test covering the content of both films. Some items were based on the information contained in the pictures, others, on the information in the commentary, and the remainder upon information contained in both visual and auditory channels. Some of the test items were pictorial, others verbal.

The groups were as follows:

Group A (control group)---did not see nor hear either film.

Group B---------------saw and heard <u>Theory of Flight</u> only.

Group C---------------saw and heard <u>both</u> films.

Group D---------------saw and heard <u>Theory of Flight</u>, but only <u>saw</u> <u>Problems of Flight</u>.

Group E₁---------------saw and heard <u>Theory of Flight</u>, but only <u>heard</u> <u>Problems of Flight</u>, in the <u>dark</u>.

Group E₂---------------saw and heard <u>Theory of Flight</u>, but only <u>heard</u> <u>Problems of Flight</u>, in the <u>light</u>.

Group F---------------only <u>heard</u> both films (in the dark).

Group G---------------only <u>saw both</u> films.

Findings

Figure 8-3 illustrates the mean scores on a 65-point test for Groups A, C, F, and G. The 4.2-point superiority of the saw-only group over the heard-only group was significant at the five per cent level. The poor results for the heard-only group in comparison with these other experimental groups is interesting because the test was biased in favor of the heard-only group, since the majority of the items were based on the information contained in the narration.

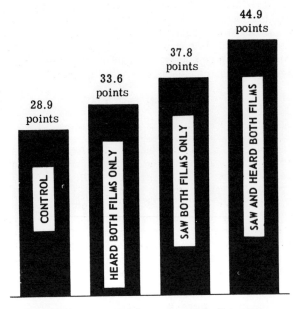

Fig. 8-3. Mean scores of groups instructed by various presentations of the films, "Theory of Flight," and "Problems of Flight." (Nelson, 1949)

A "least squares" analysis of seven factors accounting for the total scores on the test was made. The factors were: a video factor in each film; an audio factor in each film; a "both" factor in each film, indicating the proportion of the effectiveness which cannot be attributed to either the video or audio elements alone, but which must come from the operation of the two factors <u>together</u>; and a constant factor, K, which takes into account the effect of previous knowledge prior to the film showing. (The control group knew 28.9 of the 65 items, on the average.)

In the <u>theory</u> film the video factor was much more important than the audio factor but in the <u>problems</u> film the audio factor was somewhat the more important. The "both" factor was positive for each of the two films, indicating that a <u>combination</u> of audio and video was essential for the imparting of certain items of information included in the test.

NELSON AND MOLL STUDY

Experimental Design

The experimental population for the desert survival film study (Nelson and Moll 1950) consisted of 388 college students divided at random into five groups as follows:

Group C------- Control group, did not see or hear the film.

Group AL------Only <u>heard</u> the film in the <u>light</u>.

Group AD------Only <u>heard</u> the film in the <u>dark</u>.

Group V------- Only <u>saw</u> the film.

Group B------- Both <u>saw</u> and <u>heard</u> the film.

Findings

As in the preceding study, the control group obtained the lowest mean score on a 76-point test and the group which both saw and heard the film obtained the highest score. (See Fig. 8-4.) The means for the audio group (AL and AD combined) and the video group are reliably higher (0.1 per cent level) than that of the control group; and the mean of the saw-and-heard group is reliably higher (0.1 per cent level) than the mean of either the audio or video group. The 1.8-point superiority of the audio group (CR of 2.46, almost the 1 per cent level) is a fairly reliable, though slight, advantage over the video group. In addition, the group AD had a 2.2 point (CR of 2.36) superiority over group AL.

A "least squares" analysis showed that the audio factor was slightly more important in this film than the video factor. For this film the "both" factor was negative, indicating that the audio and video factors overlapped, that is, certain items were taught by each medium, and not by the two media working together, as in the aerodynamics films.

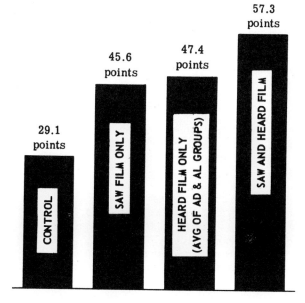

57.3
points

45.6
points

47.4
points

29.1
points

CONTROL

SAW FILM ONLY

HEARD FILM ONLY
(AVG OF AD & AL GROUPS)

SAW AND HEARD FILM

Fig. 8-4. Mean scores of groups instructed by various presentations of the film, "Land and Live in the Desert." (Nelson & Moll, 1950)

Evaluation

There is thus some evidence that even in films in which the narration apparently contains the greater part of the material to be learned, the visual element is almost as effective in communicating the material as the narration, provided the audience has a certain minimum acquaintance with the subject matter. The control groups in the Nelson study and the Nelson and Moll study knew 45 and 38 per cent, respectively, of the items on the tests without having either seen or heard the films. Thus, the experimental groups started with a substantial knowledge of the subject.

If the three films are carefully compared, it is apparent a person viewing Theory of Flight, without the sound, is definitely aided by a number of verbal labels, diagrams, and animation sequences in the film. Note that it was in this film that the video factor was definitely more prominent than the audio factor. This is definitely not true of the other two pictures without their sound tracks; yet, as mentioned above, the films without sound track were not greatly inferior to the sound track alone, with learners who had some initial knowledge of the material. It would be most interesting to see the audio and video differences in cases where the learners had practically no initial knowledge of the material in the film.

Video and Audio Channels Are Most Effective When Combined

The one clear-cut finding, borne out by all three films, is that both the audio and video channels working together, are much more effective than either one alone,

provided the original production was not planned so that either channel would be independently effective in presenting the material. The relative contributions of the visual and auditory media seem to depend on the particular film, its content, the photographic techniques used, and probably the characteristics of the learners who view it.

Nelson and Moll point out the difficulty of making an exact study of the relative efficiency of the video and audio elements in a motion picture film. Such a study would require experimental films containing equal numbers of visual and auditory items of information, of equated difficulty. To have unequal numbers of video and audio items, they point out, would be unsatisfactory, because it is probably easier to learn a high proportion of a small number of items than a high proportion of a large number of items of equal difficulty.

STURMTHAL AND CURTIS STUDY

Another approach to this problem of video and audio effectiveness was taken by A. Sturmthal and A. Curtis (1944) in their analysis of audience likes and dislikes of the two films, Valley Town and What So Proudly We Hail.

Findings

They reported that "the visual part of the film presentation seems to be by far the most important element in determining the trend of likes and dislikes as the film is seen. The variations in the charts of reactions seem to depend much more on changes in visual than auditory stimuli (sound track). And the reasons given during interviews on the likes and dislikes recorded are much more concerned with visual elements than anything in the commentary or sound" (p. 502).

B. PICTORIAL AND VERBAL PRESENTATION

Several other studies have shed some light on a related problem, namely, the relative effectiveness of pictorial versus verbal modes of presentation. In these studies, the pictorial and verbal modes both involve a visual presentation and should be distinguished from those making comparisons of visual and auditory modes of presentation.

YALE MOTION PICTURE RESEARCH PROJECT STUDIES

Two, as yet unpublished, studies conducted by the Motion Picture Research Project at Yale should be cited here.

Experimental Design (1)

The first experiment studied (1) the presentation of the phonetic alphabet to Army trainees in a sound filmstrip which used pictorial cartoon material and accompanying sound effects, and (2) a contrasting presentation in which no cartoon pictorialization (or special sound effects) were used--only the unadorned verbal material, presented both visually in the picture and orally in the sound track.

Findings (1)

In this case, the simple, non-pictorialized presentation, was actually somewhat more effective than the elaborate pictorial and auditory presentation. This result suggests that the "pictorial" elements may have distracted the audience from learning the verbal material.

Evaluation (1)

It should be noted that, in this study, the visual-verbal material (e.g., Able, Baker, etc.), in the simple version appeared in the center of the picture and in much larger letters than was the case in the fancier cartoon version, where the word was usually at the bottom of the picture and in smaller type. The size variable of the visual material was therefore not controlled.

Experimental Design (2)

The second Yale Motion Picture Research Project study, unpublished, was conducted by A. A. Lumsdaine (1949) on this problem.

He investigated "rote" learning of the "names" of randomly-paired objects by college and grade school students from a series of 16-minute film-o-graphs.* The paired objects were presented in four different combinations: picture-picture, picture-word, word-picture, and word-word. In all cases the subjects (audience) had to learn to name, after repeated responses to the pairs, the second ("response") object of each pair when the first member of the pair ("stimulus") was shown on a test. The objective was to determine the relative amounts of learning when the stimulus object was presented first in word form and then in picture form, and when the response object was similarly presented.

Findings (2)

The results of the study showed conclusively that the use of pictures to represent the first object of the pair was better than verbal presentation, but that verbal presentation (printed words) was definitely superior to pictorial presentation for the second ("response") term of the pair. These results were obtained both for college and grade school subjects, for individual as well as classroom presentation, for brighter learners as well as the slower ones, and were consistent despite a number of systematic variations in the conditions of presentation.

VANDERMEER STUDY

A. W. VanderMeer (1950A), under the auspices of the Instructional Film Research Program, also studied this problem of pictorial versus verbal presentation of material in films and filmstrips. Vander-Meer points out that the proponents of filmstrips claim that filmstrips are advantageous because, in presenting visual material to students, the filmstrips can be shown at a pace which permits all the students to analyze the visual details presented. Yet he notices a growing tendency to put the greater part of the learning material in the verbal element of the filmstrip (the titles and the teacher's notes or guide to explain the material), while the pictorial material serves merely as an approximate illustration of the verbal content.

Experimental Design

VanderMeer set up an experiment with The Birth of Our Freedom, a filmstrip which seemed to represent this trend toward verbal emphasis. Of the 46 frames which comprised this filmstrip, 36 were drawings or photographs with superimposed captions, and ten were almost completely verbal. A teaching guide provided the remaining verbal material which was to be spoken or read with 32 of the frames in the filmstrip.

The comparison was made between the filmstrip and an essay composed of the filmstrip captions and notes, with minor changes made to make for smooth reading. With the total instruction time kept constant, the essay was presented to one half of the randomly divided sample population, and the filmstrip to the other half. The experimental population consisted of 147 eleventh-grade, second-semester American history pupils and 64 eighth-grade "core curriculum" classes.** In presenting the filmstrip, the teacher read aloud all the words that appeared on the screen, as well as the appropriate material in the teaching guide. To keep the conditions of the experiment constant, no discussion nor questions were permitted. The time for presentation was 15 minutes.

In the case of the essay, the presentation was both auditory and visual. Each student was given a double-spaced mimeographed copy of the essay which the

---

* A film-o-graph is made by photographing still pictures on motion picture film, using dissolves, some camera movement, narration and sound effects.

** Classes studying broad areas of experience required for all pupils and related to personal and social problems, rather than to any one subject-matter area.

teacher read aloud after telling the students to read silently along with him. After this reading, which required nine minutes, the students were told to spend six more minutes to reread and study the material. Both groups had been told that this was an experiment and that there would be a test on the material. Immediately after the teaching, both groups were given a 45-item multiple-choice test. Three weeks after the experiment the same test was repeated to measure delayed recall.

VanderMeer assumed that if the learning attributable to the verbal element could be measured and subtracted from the learning due to the pictures of the filmstrip, the difference would represent the teaching contribution of the pictorial element. To keep the instruction times equal, VanderMeer unfortunately introduced a factor of repetition into the verbal part of his experiment by having the students reread the material for six minutes. His results, however, are still of some significance with regard to this question of pictorial versus verbal presentation.

Findings

On immediate test results for both grades eight and eleven, he found no real difference between the filmstrip and the essay group (CR's of 0.59 and 0.43) in total test score.

Individual test items were analyzed to determine whether there were learning differences between filmstrip and essay groups on specific items. For the eleventh grade, 15 items met a CR of 2.0, of which eight favored the filmstrip group, and seven, the essay group. (Similar results were obtained for the eighth-grade groups.) In every case in which the reading group did better, it seemed to the investigator that the pictorial element of the filmstrip contributed little or nothing of value in the learning situation, and in some cases the pictorial presentation seemed so deficient in detail or clarity that it may actually have served to inhibit learning.

The filmstrip gave better results on eight items, but one of these was inadvertently omitted from the essay material, thus leaving seven items for comparison between the filmstrip and essay groups. In the case of two, and possibly four, of these seven items, it seemed that the pictorial element made a definite contribution by illustrating or delineating a significant term or concept. But, in the rest of the seven items, apparently a weakness of the reading material caused the difference in favor of the filmstrip, since the point was hidden in a descriptive phrase or clause or near the end of the paragraph.

On the three-week delayed recall test, there were also no real differences in mean scores for the filmstrip and the essay groups.

Evaluation

Thus, the same results were obtained with the mimeographed material as with the filmstrip, with the instruction time kept constant, but with the essay material reread once. The disappointing results for the filmstrip are attributed to faulty production technique. The instruction proceeds from words to pictures, a sort of psychological reversal from real life where, it is pointed out, the learner typically proceeds in concrete situations from observation to description, abstraction, generalization, and application. An attempt to reverse completely this process with pictorial material will probably result in decreased teaching effectiveness.

SUMMARY DISCUSSION:

VISUAL VERSUS AUDITORY PRIMACY

The question of visual versus auditory primacy is still far from being settled. It may well be a complex question which cannot be answered by a single generalization, such as the oft-repeated saying, "One picture is worth 1000 words." Studies, such as those of Nelson and Moll, show that when the visual and auditory elements are used together, they may supplement each other and result in greater learning than from either one alone.

The question of the importance of the visual element in instructional motion pictures is not a problem of absolute primacy of a single mode of presentation. Rather it is a problem of relative primacy. In other words, to what extent should one mode be emphasized over another under various (and as yet ill-defined) conditions, and how well does that emphasis relate to the behavioral objectives of the instruction?

Films Should Rely on Visual Presentation

Nevertheless, it seems that the effectiveness of a motion picture should depend primarily on the strength of the visual presentation (that is, by means of objects, processes, symbols, and words portrayed in the pictures), and secondarily, on the accompanying oral language. If the emphasis is not visual, or if the pictorial presentation does not add materially to the learning, why, as VanderMeer's filmstrip study implies, take the trouble and expense of producing a filmstrip or motion picture?

Our eyes, when we are not reading, are used to perceive the world around us. Language may direct and facilitate that perception, but the real visual perception occurs only when the learner arranges visual impressions into a pattern that means something to him. Once the pattern is formed, language, again, may help us to articulate our discovery and communicate it to others. But language is not always helpful, since as some studies have shown, certain types of film commentary may actually interfere with rather than facilitate learning from pictures. More will be said about the role of language later in this chapter.

The implications of the principle of the relative primacy of the visuals are of greater importance in film production than in utilization. For example, this principle implies that no motion picture should be approved for production unless the subject lends itself to fluent visual presentation that can be well specified. Secondly, visual thinking should predominate over verbal thinking in the over-all production process. For this purpose, the story board is likely to be more useful and efficient than the purely verbal script. In planning a film, we should continually ask ourselves, "What do we want to show visually?"

C. EMPHATIC DEVICES

This topic is concerned with (1) general emphasis, (2) special attention-gaining devices of either a visual or auditory nature, and (3) the use of color for emphasis.

1. GENERAL EMPHASIS

HOVLAND, LUMSDAINE, AND SHEFFIELD STUDY

C. I. Hovland, A. A. Lumsdaine, and F. D. Sheffield (1949) examined "wrong" (contrary to intent) influences on learning of factual information presented in the Why We Fight films.

Findings

They pointed out a provisional implication of "the necessity of making extremely explicit distinctions in a film on points which are judged to be important, rather than relying on the men themselves to distinguish between two closely similar implications. It is also suggested that the spectacular and impressive presentation techniques should be appropriately chosen in relation to the importance of the point to be made; when used on a minor point the men may generalize in ways which are clearly incorrect" (p. 160).

2. SPECIAL ATTENTION-GAINING DEVICES

NEU STUDY

These devices were experimentally investigated by D. M. Neu (1950) of the Instructional Film Research Program. Neu's experiment is of considerable importance to motion picture production particularly because, as far as it goes, his evidence on the effect of attention-gaining devices is negative, and secondarily, because he introduces some evidence relevant to the hypothesis of visual primacy.

It should be remembered that the devices studied by Neu are designated as "attention-gaining," not as "attention-directing" devices. The distinction is obvious but may be easily overlooked in interpreting the significance of Neu's findings for film production techniques.

Experimental Design

Neu's study was designed to test three hypotheses:

"1. Device relevancy. The hypothesis is that film-mediated learning will be facilitated by the use of relevant attention-gaining filmic devices, and inhibited by irrelevant attention-gaining devices.

"2. Device medium. The hypothesis is that film-mediated informational learning will be equally facilitated by visual and sound devices of the same relevance.

"3. Device recall. The hypothesis is that recall of the devices themselves is relatively independent of learning of the factual information content of the film" (p. 18).

To test these hypotheses, five versions of an introductory film on machine shop measuring instruments were produced and tested on populations consisting of 1576 Army trainees at Fort Dix and 1055 Navy trainees at the Great Lakes Naval Training Station.

The basic version of the film was a clear, straightforward treatment of the subject, without any special attention-gaining devices. A second version added "relevant" visual attention-gaining devices, and a third version "irrelevant" visual attention-gaining devices. The fourth and fifth versions added "relevant" and "irrelevant" sound attention-gaining devices, respectively. The "relevant" visual attention-gaining devices were such techniques as extreme closeups, spotlighting, stop motion, pointing finger, zooms, and unusual camera angles. The "relevant" sound devices consisted of alternating the commentators' voices, giving such directions as "Now hear this," slow emphatic reading of the commentary, supplying sound effects, such as ratchet sounds and machine shop noises, where appropriate. In general the "irrelevant" visual and sound devices were, as indicated, attention-gaining in their own right but unrelated to the meaning of the pictures or narration; for example, a picture of a pretty girl, athlete in frozen motion, or the use of unusual sounds such as train whistles, pistol shots, etc.

Neither the "relevant" or "irrelevant" devices were intended to add information to the picture, but were used solely to gain attention and, presumably, to reinforce the instructional material.

Findings

In this experimental study there was no evidence that the relevant attention-gaining devices as used in these experimental films added to the instructional effectiveness of the film. Irrelevant sound attention-gaining devices, as might be expected, were found to detract from film effectiveness. To some degree, there was evidence that any of the attention-gaining devices, visual or sound, relevant or irrelevant, may detract from instructional effectiveness.

With the Army trainees, the basic version with no special attention-gaining devices yielded the highest score, significant at the one per cent level of confidence. With the Navy trainees, the basic film was superior to the versions with irrelevant visual and irrelevant sound devices and was approximately as effective as the versions with relevant visual and relevant sound devices.

No significant difference was found between the effects, on learning, of visual and sound attention-gaining devices.

As might be expected from the fact that none of the devices was intended to add information to the film, there was little relationship between the ability to recognize and remember the devices and learning from the film.

Interestingly enough, however, the visual irrelevant devices seemed to call attention to themselves to a greater extent than did any other type of attention-gaining device. This finding indirectly supports the hypothesis that the visuals have primary impact in a motion picture, and the sound has secondary impact.

Two Recommendations for Film Producers

From the data of his experiment, Neu makes two pointed recommendations to film producers.

"1. Where instruction is the principal aim, and cost a consideration, producers of training films should present the subject matter in a simple, straightforward way and avoid the use of such fancy and expensive devices as spotlighting, zooms, extreme magnification, and stop motion, to gain the learners' attention.

"2. If it seems necessary, in an instructional film, to use devices to attract or direct the learners' attention, use a technique which will emphasize something already in the film -- some special treatment of indigenous materials related to the subject content -- rather than introduce extraneous or irrelevant materials" (p. 35).

3. USE OF COLOR FILM

There have been several studies of the relative effectiveness of color films versus black and white films. Some of these studies have provided insights into the value of color for emphasis in films.

LONG STUDY

A. L. Long (1944) compared color and black and white films in grades 5, 6, 11, and 12.

Findings

On four and one-half months retention tests, reliable differences in favor of color films were reported for grades 11 and 12. On immediate tests, color films were reliably superior in the sixth and twelfth grades.

For the eleventh-grade group, black and white films were unreliably superior on immediate testing, and color was superior on delayed testing. It is difficult to generalize from these results, since no uniform trend is apparent.

McLEAN STUDY

W. McLean (1930) reported a study on the use of colored still pictures which may be applicable to the problem of the use of color in motion pictures.

Findings

He found that, on free-recall tests, high school seniors recalled colored geography prints in a ratio of five to three over black and white prints. He also reported that, in some cases, color distracted from central scenes, but that, in other cases, color contrast appeared to increase clarity of detail.

VANDERMEER STUDY

The problem of color vs. black and white was further investigated by A. W. VanderMeer (1948, 1949) in connection with the Instructional Film Research Program.

Experimental Design

Five films, available in both black and white and color versions, were selected for study: Snakes, How Man Made Day, Maps Are Fun, Rivers of the Pacific Slope, and Properties of Sulphur.

These particular films were selected to determine the effectiveness of color both in general terms and in relation to four specific points:

1. How well the learners like the films.

2. How much more of the general factual content of a film is learned when such facts have no obvious relation to color.

3. How many more facts are learned when color seems to be an important learning cue, such as in the identification of biological specimens.

4. How many more facts are learned when color is not necessarily a vital learning cue, but is used to make certain parts of a diagram or map stand out.

The experiment was first conducted in 1948 with two groups totalling about 325 ninth- and tenth-grade science students who were equated on intelligence, scores on a pre-test of material covered in the film, age, and sex. The study was duplicated a year later using a rotation technique among approximately 200 ninth-grade science students.

Findings (1)

As measured by the paired-comparisons method, there was a slight tendency for the students to prefer films in color over identical films in black and white. In the case of two films, the differences were significant at the five per cent level of confidence; for the other three, the differences were even less reliable.

Findings (2)

In the first experiment, "paper and pencil" tests of a multiple-choice type were given immediately after the showing of each film and repeated six weeks later. On four of the immediate tests, the group seeing the films in color had slightly higher mean scores than the group seeing the films in black and white. None of these differences was significant at the five per cent level of confidence. However, when these same tests were repeated six weeks later, the color-film group retained more than the black-and-white group in every case, so that the differences in favor of color were more significant, two at the one per cent level of confidence and one at the five per cent level.

Findings (3)

Two tests of identification were given. One test required the learners to identify snakes by matching the name of a snake with its pictures in (1) black and white and (2) colored slide form. The other required the learner to select the allotropic forms of sulphur from a collection of samples in small glass vials. On both these tests the group that saw the black and white films had higher mean scores (for sulphur at the one per cent level of confidence) than those of the color-film group. However, this superiority was lost on the delayed-recall test given six weeks later.

Findings (4)

Similar findings on identification tests resulted from the 1949 replication of the experiment. Immediate tests were given on film items whose portrayal in color was thought to be an important learning aid. The mean scores, treated separately for males and females, were higher for the black and white than for the color films. But for items based on diagrams in which color was used to emphasize certain parts, the mean scores were higher for color than for black and white.

Evaluation

The most conclusive finding of the study is that color may be more of a help in reducing the amount of forgetting than in increasing the amount of immediate learning.

Color May Be Distracting

Secondly, color seems to contribute least to learning in cases where it might logically be expected to contribute most, that is, it seems least effective in promoting the learning of those facts for which color seems to be an important learning cue. The author suggests that this may well be explained by the hypothesis that color may be such an overpowering attention director that it may distract the learner from other equally or more important learning cues. But this hypothesis still must be verified.

Finally, subjects in the age group being tested tend to prefer color films. This preference seems to be consistently reflected in a slightly, though often not reliably, greater efficiency in learning, which shows up most when measured by delayed tests.

Color May Be Crucial Cue

VanderMeer's findings on the effect of color in presenting information pictorially are not inconsistent with the hypothesis of visual primacy. There is some evidence that, under certain conditions, the color medium increases the effectiveness of the visual presentation, and, perhaps reinforces the effect of the picture. By this same line of reasoning, it is conceivable that color may distract attention from other important learning cues, for example, material in the commentary or other visual cues in the picture. In the final analysis, it is probably a question of determining what are the crucial cues for learning. If color provides crucial cues in some learning situations then it should be used. Much research remains to be done in this area.

D. VERBALIZATION

With the growing use of the sound film in instruction, the problem of verbalization, that is, narration and/or commentary in the sound track, has assumed increased importance. Actually, the problem existed in silent films, because of the use of both printed titles and narration or commentary by the instructor while the film was shown.

Considerable experimentation was undertaken on the relative values of sound and silent films, but most of the findings are questionable since the relevant variable of verbalization as such was seldom, if ever, isolated and studied systematically.

The controversy over the comparative value of sound and silent films in instruction still rages. The argument, which is often conducted with great vigor in the British Isles and continental Europe, is also being carried on, though somewhat less strenuously, among some visual educationists in the United States. Fundamentally, the controversy appears to arise from the supposed challenge of the sound film to the authority, competence, and prerogative of the teacher as the master of the classroom and the source of knowledge and enlightenment. Since we have defined the function of the teacher or instructor in much broader and more responsible terms (in Chapter I), both the controversies and the research on sound versus silent instructional films seem somewhat misdirected. The research on sound and silent films will be discussed briefly, prior to the discussion of more recent research which has explored the problem of verbalization more systematically.

1. STUDIES OF SILENT AND SOUND FILMS

McCLUSKY AND McCLUSKY STUDY

F. D. and H. Y. McClusky (1924) compared silent motion pictures, slides, and photographic prints, with and without oral accompaniment, in grades five through eight. In all comparisons, oral accompaniment added to the effectiveness of the presentation.

EINBECKER STUDY

W. F. Einbecker (1933), using two silent films in high school physics, compared the regular silent film with the same film accompanied by oral commentary prepared by the teacher. In the case of both films he found that the commentary increased the film's effectiveness.

Using two sound films, he compared the regular film with the film without sound track, but accompanied by a specially prepared teacher commentary. In five out of six comparisons the teacher-prepared commentary was as effective as the sound track.

One group viewed one "sound film" with no sound, no comments, and no captions in the film. This group learned about 64 per cent as much as corresponding groups who saw the film with either of the two verbal accompaniments. The title of this film was, The Romance of Power.

HANSEN STUDY

J. E. Hansen (1936), using four high school biological science films, compared the regular sound film with sound-track commentary and with the teacher reading the identical commentary. He found that, in three out of the four films, in two different schools, the teacher-read commentary was either equal to or superior to the sound-track. In the fourth film, which was the same for both schools (Fungus Plants), the commentary coming from the sound track was superior, but not to a highly reliable degree.

GOODMAN STUDY

D. J. Goodman (1942) investigated the relative effectiveness of (1) sound motion pictures, (2) silent motion pictures, (3) sound filmstrips and (4) silent filmstrips with printed titles, in teaching four safety topics in sixth-grade classes.

In the case of both media the silent versions contained the same pictorial material as the sound versions, with caption frames inserted to give the verbal material, the latter being identical in the case of the filmstrips (or film slides; it is not clear which he used).

In tests of immediate learning he found small but reliable differences in favor of the silent motion picture over the sound motion picture and sound filmstrip; and slightly smaller, but statistically reliable differences in favor of the silent filmstrip over the sound motion picture and the sound filmstrip. No differences were found between the two silent media, nor between the two sound media on immediate tests.

However, in retention tests, administered 30 days later, the size and reliability of the differences in favor of the silent motion picture over the sound motion picture and sound filmstrip, were reduced. The silent filmstrip lost its advantage over the sound motion picture and sound filmstrip. The silent motion picture was slightly better than the silent filmstrip. No difference was found between the two sound media.

The silent media, both films and filmstrips, had a longer running time; and in the case of the sound film, more verbal material was presented. The slower rate of development and somewhat lower frequency of verbalization would tend to favor the silent motion picture in this comparison, as results of other studies to be discussed soon indicate.

SCOTTISH FILM COUNCIL STUDY

A study, reported by the Scottish Film Council (1948), compared the effectiveness of teacher commentary with that of various film versions without teacher commentary.

Findings

It cites some evidence that the silent film with teacher commentary was equally and possibly more effective than either the sound film version or the silent film version. The caution accompanying this conclusion is interesting: "the silent film becomes a more effective aid to teaching when reinforced by the teacher's commentary, provided the teacher has a sufficient knowledge of the film and his commentary is well prepared beforehand . . ." (p. 27). In one of two experimental comparisons, the sound film was superior in delayed measures of learning.

Evaluation of These Studies

Type, Not Mode, of Verbalization Is the Problem

From these various studies conducted over a period of 24 years, we can conclude that, in the type of instructional films used, verbal commentary increases the effectiveness of the films, but no clear-cut advantage can be assigned specifically to the mode

of the commentary. Thus, the subject narrows down
to the relevant variable of verbalization, rather than
the variables of the voice on the sound track, the voice
of the teacher, or printed words in the "picture."

2. STUDIES OF VERBALIZATION

PARK STUDY

The problem of verbalization was explored by
J. Park (1943, 1944, 1945) in his study mentioned in
Chapter VII.

Experimental Design

This study was concerned with the difficulty of
the vocabulary as it affected comprehension of the
commentary in eight sound films used with elementary
school pupils and high school pupils. He tabulated the
words in the commentaries of these films in terms of
their frequency in Thorndike's Teachers Word Book.
The words occurring in the less common frequencies
of Thorndike's count were considered to be the more
difficult words.

Findings

Park reports (1944) the percentage of words at
various Thorndike levels for each film and the mean
vocabulary level of each film. (For the relation between the vocabulary knowledge of the learner and the
amount of film learning, see the reference to Park in
Chapter VII.) The mean sentence length of each commentary was also computed and varied from 9.71 words
to 20.35 words. He found, in general, a greater amount
of learning occurring from the films with shorter
sentence lengths.

JASPEN STUDY

Systematic investigation of levels of verbalization
was undertaken in the Instructional Film Research
Program in two studies by N. Jaspen (1948, 1950).

Experimental Design (1)

In his first study of experimental films in teaching
the assembly of the breechblock of the 40mm gun,
Jaspen (1948) used two levels of verbalization: a small
number of words per minute of film and a large number
of words per minute of film.

Findings (1)

No significant differences were found in the effectiveness of the high and low levels studied. However,
the possibility remained that some intermediate level
of verbalization might be more effective than either
of these two levels.

Experimental Design (2)

In his second study, Jaspen (1950) systematically
studied high (142 words per minute of film), medium
(97 words per minute of film), low (74 words per
minute of film), and very low (45 words per minute
of film) levels of verbalization in film versions. These
versions included a slow rate of development, and
showed common errors to be avoided in assembling
the breechblock.

Findings (2)

From this study he concluded that "the relationship between level of effectiveness of the film and
level of verbalization (amount of narration used to
describe the action), appears to be curvilinear, with
the apex of the curve at the medium level of verbalization (approximately 100 words for each minute of
film)" (p. 16).

Evaluation

It should be borne in mind that this experiment
dealt with perceptual-motor-learning -- the assembly
of the breechblock of an antiaircraft gun -- and cannot
necessarily be generalized to all films. Nonetheless,
the result fits into the emerging concept of interfering
and facilitating elements in instructional motion pictures.

ZUCKERMAN STUDY

J. V. Zuckerman (1949), also of the Instructional
Film Research Program, investigated high, medium,
and low levels of verbalization in experimental films
designed to teach trainees how to tie the bowline, sheet
bend, and Spanish bowline knots.

Findings (1)

His results are consistent with those reported in
Jaspen's second study, that is, a medium level of
verbalization is superior to either a low or high level.
He concluded that, in the films he used, "verbal descriptions of acts and relationships assisted the learners, but a very detailed description given within a
short time interval interfered with and actually reduced learning" (p. 31).

Findings (2)

Zuckerman also investigated the effectiveness of
various types of instructional statements using the
first person active, the second person active, the third
person passive, and the imperative.

For the perceptual-motor learning involved in
knot-tying, he concluded that "with a military population
directive statements in the film commentary which
used the imperative mood, or the second person active,

were more effective in promoting learning than the third person passive type of statements" (pp. 31-32). Results on the first person type of statement were inconclusive.

Findings (3)

Zuckerman investigated a third variable, phase relationship, which is the time relationship between the appearance of an item on the screen and mention of the item in the sound track.

He concluded that "leading" commentary (action is mentioned before it is shown) "seemed to promote more learning than a 'lagging' commentary" (action shown before it is mentioned) (p. 32). Synchronous commentary was not studied in this experiment.

E. FILM MUSIC

There is no conclusive experimental evidence that a musical background in instructional films affects factual learning or the development of attitudes. The subject is one that is argued in Sunday newspapers, in film and music journals, and among film producers.

One unpublished study of the Instructional Film Research Program reported inconclusive results on the contribution of music in instructional films.

NUCKOLS AND ABRAMSON STUDY

R. C. Nuckols and R. Abramson (1949) investigated the effect of two versions of the film, We Make a Fire.

One version had a continuous musical accompaniment and the other had music only during introductory and final titles. The study was conducted with pupils in the third, fourth, and fifth grades, ranging in age from seven through 11 years.

Findings

Apparently, the subject of the film was already fairly familiar to the pupils, and relatively little "new" learning was gained from either version. No difference was found in informational learning or in expressed attitudes between either version. Only 55 per cent of the pupils who saw the "music" version recognized afterwards that music had accompanied the film throughout, and 62 per cent of those who saw the version with introductory and end music only recognized later that music was absent throughout the main part of the film.

Evaluation

It is generally accepted by those who write and perform music for entertainment films that the audience should be unaware of background music. The results of the study by Nuckols and Abramson, though inconclusive, indicate that, in effect, a considerable proportion of the learning audience was unaware of the presence or absence of background music. The question remains unanswered as to whether or not music of which the audience is "unaware" actually facilitates learning.

SECTION 3. OTHER ELEMENTS OF FILM STRUCTURE

A. REPETITION

Repetition has been shown to be an important factor in film instruction. The effect of repeated exhibition of a film was discussed in Chapter VI and was briefly mentioned earlier in this chapter in connection with the Yale studies of participation. It is discussed further in Part II of this chapter in connection with conditions and methods of film use. In this section, we are concerned with identifying repetition as a factor in film learning and with the use of repetition in the film itself.

JASPEN STUDY

N. Jaspen (1948) of the Instructional Film Research Program conducted an experiment on the use of repetition which showed that repetition (together with slow rate of development), is one of the most critical factors in films dealing with perceptual-motor learning. This was his first study using experimental versions of a film on breechblock assembly.

Experimental Design

In some experimental versions, Jaspen included the main breechblock assembly sequence once, twice, three times, and four times. The repetitions of the main assembly sequence were not identical, but involved small variations in camera treatment and, in general, proceeded at a faster rate than the first assembly sequence.

Findings

Jaspen found that the film versions with the greater number of repetitions were the more effective, and that the film with the assembly sequence shown four times "was in every respect the best film of the group of seventeen variations. Although it appeared to 'drag' there was no doubt regarding its efficiency for teaching the task."

Evaluation

Jaspen's results are consistent with results reported in the Yale experiment in which repetition was used, with C. L. McTavish's (1949) study reported in

Part II of this chapter, and with results reported in Chapter VI in studies dealing with comparative values of films.

Repetition Is Important Instructional Device

Although repetition may be distasteful to instructional film producers from an aesthetic, artistic, or filmic point of view, and may be contrary to the prevailing practice of producing films to amuse an audience, the experimental fact seems to be that repetition, in a film or of a film, is a major factor of instructional effectiveness.

From a production point of view, repetition within the film involves little additional time or expense. There is room for considerable imagination when using repetition in films to avoid stereotyped patterns of production. Repetition in exhibition is sometimes complicated by problems of projector supply, room illumination, class periods, and a general reluctance on the part of the instructor and audience to sit through the same film twice.

B. RATE OF DEVELOPMENT

Another critical factor in instructional effectiveness of a motion picture is the rate (speed of development) at which the subject is presented. C. F. Hoban Jr. (1942) reported that one of the frequent criticisms of instructional films used in elementary and high schools is that they moved too quickly.

JASPEN STUDY

N. Jaspen's (1948) study was mentioned in our discussion of participation and repetition.

Findings

He found that slow rate of development in a film is superior to rapid rate of development.

In his second study, Jaspen (1950) studied the effectiveness of a "succinct treatment," consisting of a rapid three-minute presentation of the disassembly and assembly of the breechblock taken from an existing film. While this extremely succinct treatment was reliably better than no film at all, it was the least effective of all the 14 versions used in this experiment.

VINCENT, ASH, AND GREENHILL STUDY

The problem of rate of development was further explored by W. S. Vincent, P. Ash and L. P. Greenhill (1949) with somewhat inconclusive results.

Experimental Design

Four versions of an introductory film, The Weather, were made up from five films on aerology, produced by the Walt Disney Studio for the U. S. Navy.

In these four versions, fact density and length of time of presentation were varied. The long versions ran 30 minutes; short versions ran 15 minutes. The heavy versions included twice the number of facts as did the light versions. The four versions were: (1) long heavy, (2) long light, (3) short heavy, (4) short light. The commentaries of all four versions were of equal verbal difficulty on the Dale-Chall formula of readability. The experimental populations consisted of 324 college students, 434 high school students, and 503 Air Force trainees.

Findings

From the analysis of results, it was tentatively concluded that within certain limits, the more information included in a film, the greater the amount of information learned. But the investigators state that "the data suggest that, as more and more information is presented, interferences are set up that result in less efficient learning of any particular part. . . . Finally, it seems clear that packing more and more information into a film yields only very slight increments in total measured learning" (p. 24). In other words, increasing the absolute amount of film content tends to decrease the proportional amount of learning of film content.

Evaluation

The lack of clear-cut results is due, presumably, to a fatigue or boredom factor in the audience caused by taking a long and difficult test and perhaps to the fact that the audiences had little background or interest in the subject of the films.

The various studies of rate or speed of development in films indicate that when a film containing a large amount of information presents that information to the audience at a rapid rate, the audience learns relatively little from the film.

C. INTRODUCTORY AND SUMMARY MATERIAL

In this section we are concerned with the effect of introductions (or orientation material) and summaries contained within the films themselves on audience learning from a film. The effects of introductions and summaries, as applied to the condition of using the films, are discussed in Part II. There, the studies of methods of film utilization reported by Hovland, Lumsdaine, and Sheffield (1949), by Wittich and Fowlkes (1946), and by the Australian Office of Education (1950), indicate that an introduction or orientation, supplied by the instructor or other instructional materials, increases learning from films.

LATHROP STUDY

C. W. Lathrop (1949) investigated, as part of the Instructional Film Research Program, the contributions to learning of introductions contained in film presentations.

Experimental Design

Two experimental versions of each of three instructional films were compared. In one version, the introduction used in the original film was retained. In the other version, it was omitted. The three experimental films used were Sulphur and Its Compounds, Mammals of the Rocky Mountains, and Rivers of the Pacific Slope. Multiple-choice tests (four-choice) of 50 to 60 items each were administered to the experimental and control groups to measure learning gains from the various versions of each film. The experimental population consisted of 500 ninth-grade students.

Findings

Small differences in favor of the film-plus-introduction groups were found for Sulphur and Its Compounds (+1.14 points) and Rivers of the Pacific Slope (+1.81 points), reliable on the six per cent and one per cent levels of confidence, respectively. However, a larger (+2.55 points) and more reliable difference (0.2 per cent level of confidence) was found in favor of the version of Mammals of the Rocky Mountains from which the introductory sequences were deleted. Apparently, the introductory sequences of this film had an adverse or interfering effect on learning of the main content which followed the introduction.

NORFORD STUDY

C. A. Norford (1949) of the Instructional Film Research Program made a similar study of the effect of summary sequences in films.

Experimental Design

The experimental films were The Cell: Structural Unit of Life, Magnetism, and Rivers of the Pacific Slope. The experimental population consisted of 561 ninth-grade pupils.

Findings

Very small differences (+.57, +1.92, and +.30 points) were found in favor of the versions which included the summaries. Only one of these differences, (for Magnetism), was reliable at better than the five per cent level of confidence.

Evaluation

Irrelevant Introduction May Impede Learning

These two studies, which are exploratory in nature, indicate that some introductions and summaries, used as instructional techniques in films, may increase learning from films at least slightly. But they also indicate that every introduction and summary does not result in either large or reliable learning gains. On the contrary, there is evidence that at least some introductions may set up interferences with the learning of subsequent material. Presumably, an orientation or introduction must be relevant to the scenes that follow, otherwise the irrelevant material may interfere with learning from the following scenes.

Norford offers an alternate explanation of the slight effectiveness of summaries in the three experimental films, based on the factual density and high speed of development of these films. "As a final comment it might be observed that the failure of the summaries to have any noticeable effect on learning in this experiment, could perhaps be a result of the fact that these films are so tightly packed with factual information (a 60-item test was constructed on each ten-minute film with comparative ease). Thus, the level of learning was comparatively low, and it is possible that the summaries could add little" (p. 45).

Presumably two psychological principles of learning are involved in film introductions and summaries: (1) orienting the audience by pointing out the importance of the material to be learned and its relation to previous learning, and motivating the audience to learn it, and (2) repeating major concepts in the introduction, the body of the film, and the summary. If this is so, introductions and summaries are special applications of the elements of involvement and repetition. If orientation is an involvement factor, it may operate intrinsically to clarify the broader meaning of the main content of the film, or it may operate to show that the film content is important from the audience's point of view.

Repetition in the summaries, or the main body of the film following the introduction, is not simply verbatim repetition, but varied presentation of the major concepts or meanings. Thus, in introductions and/or summaries, the broader conceptual meanings may be repeated.

SUMMARY

INFLUENCE OF VARIABLES IN THE FILM

1. AUDIENCE INVOLVEMENT FACTORS

Six factors were identified as contributing to the involvement of an audience in a film experience. The evidence on the existence and influence of these factors may be summarized as follows.

IDENTIFICATION

As yet there is only weak unsatisfactory experimental evidence to support the theory of identification as a factor of audience involvement in motion picture experience, which results in an increment in various types of learning from the film. Much more exploration and experimentation are required on the relationship between identification and learning of various types.

FAMILIARITY

When an audience is familiar with the setting and the type of activity shown in a film, it tends to become involved in the film. This conclusion is supported by both the Holaday and Stoddard, and Sturmthal and Curtis studies. But this conclusion must be qualified because familiarity alone does not inevitably involve an audience in the film. The things which are familiar must also have a personal meaning for the audience. If this were not the case, familiarity in film content would restrict the opportunity for learning and the results would have more of a reinforcing than a reorganizing effect on the individual's experience. While familiarity of material may result in a pleasant and satisfying experience, it may also result in very little more than nostalgic reminiscence.

SUBJECTIVE CAMERA

When an instructional film gives its audience a learner's eye view, rather than a bystander's view, more learning is likely to take place. The studies which support this conclusion suggest some qualification of the widely-held belief that more perceptual-motor learning occurs when the film presentation shows an exact representation of the learner himself performing the task. Roshal, in his study of knot-tying, found that when the camera pictured the learner's hands in a way that obscured the audience's view of the actual knot-tying operation, audience learning was impaired. Hence it appears that crucial cues, that is, cues which give the learner the important steps that guide him through the operation, are of greater instructional value than exact representation. Further, the data from Jaspen's study indicate that technical terminology is not necessarily one of the crucial cues.

ANTICIPATION

Anticipation of situations in a film seems to govern the intensity of audience response. For example, when the audience anticipated fearful consequences in a film, it had a more intense reaction when it actually witnessed the event in the film. However, when "adult discount" is combined with anticipation, the emotional response may be less intense.

PARTICIPATION

It is clear that audience participation, properly used, is effective when it involves practice of the behavior which a film is intended to influence. It is probably most effective when used in such a way, and at such time, that a sufficient amount of learning has accrued to make practice feasible, as was done in the filmstrip on the phonetic alphabet. Furthermore, when actually teaching a motor skill in a film, participation is most effective when the task is not too complex or the speed of development of the film is not too rapid to interfere with practice.

In the available studies of informational learning from films, such as the Yale experiment and the Instructional Film Research Program studies of the films on snakes and wrenches, questions and statements inserted in a film had little more practice value than a second showing of a film. In all cases, it is apparent that such practice as is involved in audience participation under favorable conditions is most likely to be effective when the behavior practiced is relevant to the objective of instruction.

The research data on audience participation have implications for both the producers and users of instructional films. Judicious use of participation techniques effectively incorporated into films, and employed after some initial learning has taken place, may increase the effectiveness of a film which is likely to be exhibited only once to its audience.

DRAMATIC STRUCTURE AND CARTOON FORM

1. Dramatic vs. Expository Presentation

    There is evidence of emotional involvement resulting during showing of well-produced dramatic films; whether similar involvement can be obtained from the expository type of film, remains to be demonstrated, but is doubtful. Dramatic structure is no guarantee of involvement. Many factors seem to interact in producing involvement.

    Whether the involvement aroused through dramatic structure will facilitate learning appears to depend upon the desired learning outcomes and upon the nature of the involvement produced. Dramatic structure may be more effective for certain learning outcomes than expository presentation, although this remains to be demonstrated. For instance, dramatic structure may be more effective for changing attitudes. All the studies on attitudinal changes from films have used either dramatic or documentary form, so the question is not answered. Expository treatment may be equally or more effective for informational learning.

2. Cartoon Form vs. Live Photography

    Since none of the studies on this topic made a direct comparison between a cartoon and live photographic presentation of the same material, it is difficult to generalize on the effectiveness of cartooning as a presentation variable.

Cartooning omits all except the essential detail and often exaggerates the crucial characteristics of appearance and behavior. The cartoon thus seems to be an adaptable medium for presenting crucial cues.

If these cues are proved to be an effective learning aid, then cartooning and other simplified pictorial techniques now being developed for television may relieve film producers of the tedious and expensive process of striving for exact representation.

2. PICTURE AND SOUND

VISUAL AND AUDITORY CHANNELS

There is some evidence that even in films in which the narration appears to contain the greater part of the instructional material, the visual element is almost as effective in communicating the material as the narration, provided the audience has some prior acquaintance with the subject matter. The visual and audio elements have a much greater combined effect than either one alone. The relative contributions of the visual and auditory channels seem to depend on the particular film, its content, the techniques used, and probably on the characteristics of the learners who view it.

PICTORIAL AND VERBAL PRESENTATION

The studies comparing the effectiveness of pictorial and verbal presentation do not give conclusive evidence in favor of either presentation. Rather, they suggest that the problem involves the amount of emphasis to be placed on one or the other presentation. But it is evident that since the motion picture is primarily a visual medium, it should be used to portray that material which can be conveyed to best advantage by visual means.

EMPHATIC DEVICES

The study on general emphasis indicates that the film should make an expressed distinction between items having similar implications, and that the differentiation should not be left to the judgment of the learner.

Attention-gaining devices apparently add little to an otherwise well-made instructional film. Devices which call attention to irrelevant materials may interfere with the learning of more important items. However, it seems probable that devices which direct attention to visual elements which may otherwise be overlooked, may serve a useful purpose in facilitating learning.

Similarly, color appears to have been a distracting influence under some of the conditions studied, possibly because it distracts the learner from more important learning cues. Probably the steps involved in using color most effectively are to determine what the crucial learning cues are, and then to emphasize these cues by the color medium.

VERBALIZATION

Research on the comparative instructional value of silent and sound films shows no clear-cut advantage for either medium. From this we conclude that how the commentary is presented is less important than what is said in the commentary itself.

These various experiments indicate that: (1) commentary facilitates film learning; (2) an intermediate amount of talk in the film commentary or narration is more effective than too little or too much talk; (3) direct statements are generally preferable in instructional films to the third-person passive voice; and (4) commentary which alerts the audience and orients it to some forthcoming action is preferable in "how-to-do-it" films to commentary which lags behind the action.

FILM MUSIC

There is little experimental evidence to suggest that musical background has any marked effect on learning from instructional films.

3. FILM STRUCTURE

REPETITION

The evidence comparing the amount of learning resulting from repeating certain sequences within a film shows that some repetition definitely increases the teaching and training effectiveness of a film.

RATE OF DEVELOPMENT

The various studies of rate or speed of development in films indicate that when a film containing a large amount of information presents that information to the audience at a rapid rate, the audience learns relatively little from the film. A slower rate of development definitely increases the efficiency of learning from such a film.

INTRODUCTIONS AND SUMMARIES IN FILMS

The studies cited present some evidence that introductory and summary material may increase the amount of learning from films. However, there were no large learning gains to support this conclusion, due partly to instructional shortcomings of the films studied.

Thus, it is evident from the research on the rhetoric of film instruction (how to "say it" effectively with films) that an audience responds to a film and learns from it more effectively when (a) the audience becomes involved in the subject presented on the screen; (b) the story of the film is told visually, and verbalization at an optimal level is integrated with the visual presentation; (c) crucial sequences are repeated in the film; (d) the rate of development is adjusted to the rate of learning of the audience; and (e) the audience is oriented to the story or task represented in the film. It is also clear that any or many of these factors, if improperly employed in a film, may interfere with learning rather than facilitate or contribute to it. Too much talking, irrelevant introductions, unwieldy audience participation, fast rate of development, high density of facts, a too-literal representation which obscures the audience's perception of the crucial cues -- all appear to detract from the effectiveness of films in instruction.

There is no evidence that the motion picture as a medium of communication is exempt from the rhetoric of instruction. As was pointed out in previous chapters, learning involves "suffering and undergoing." In a sense, films do not make learning, itself, "easier." But, if they skillfully employ these elements of the rhetoric of instruction they can facilitate learning, and thus make the instruction more efficient. It is axiomatic that instruction facilitates learning and that instructional films should be produced which will further facilitate the process.

PART II. VARIABLES IN THE METHODS AND CONDITIONS OF FILM USE

Once the variables or factors in the rhetoric of film instruction have been identified, it is possible to deal with the methods of using instructional films in terms of these characteristics or factors, rather than simply in terms of specific techniques or routines. Research on the methods of film use reveals that the rhetorical elements, which were found to increase learning when incorporated into films, also increase learning when they are applied to the use of the film by the instructor, as might be expected.

The research studies on the use of films, in addition to the rhetorical elements, have investigated certain conditions, both physical and psychological, of using instructional films. Other research data are available on administrative practices which make possible the most economical use of films in instruction. The research on film use is summarized under (1) elements of instructional method, and (2) physical conditions of film use.

SECTION 1. ELEMENTS OF THE INSTRUCTIONAL METHOD

The research on utilization will be summarized under six topics: (1) rhetorical elements, (2) integration of films in instruction, (3) massed and distributed exhibition, (4) range of film use, (5) influence of the instructor, and (6) effects of administrative organization. As we mentioned earlier in this chapter, the data on some of the techniques of film utilization are not plentiful, since the research on this subject was undertaken fairly recently.

A. RHETORICAL ELEMENTS

The rhetorical elements of film utilization will be reviewed under (1) repeated showings of films, and (2) combinations of films with other instructional elements. The studies on repetition are clear cut, while the studies involving other elements involve a combination of variables, often including repetition.

1. REPEATED SHOWINGS

The effect of repeated exhibition of a film on learning was discussed in Chapter VI on the comparative effectiveness of instructional films. In a preliminary study, P. J. Rulon (1933) compiled student preferences on the number of times some experimental films should be shown in a science-teaching experiment, and decided that each reel should be shown three times. L. K. Eads and E. M. Stover (1936) found that two showings of an experimental film were necessary to

obtain critical differences in results, and V. C. Arnspiger (1933), showed each film three times to his experimental groups.

In both the Yale (1947) and H. R. Brenner, J. S. Walter, and A. K. Kurtz (1949) experiments, reported in Part I, an experimental version with two copies of the film spliced together and shown in succession, was found to be better than a single showing of the original film and approximately equal in effectiveness to the experimental versions into which audience participation techniques had been built.

McTAVISH STUDY

The most systematic study of the effect of repetitive showings of a film was made by C. L. McTavish (1949) in connection with the Instructional Film Research Program.

Experimental Design

He studied the learning gains by means of pre-tests and post-tests, from one, two, three, and four showings of each of four films, Atomic Energy, Electrochemistry, Colloids, and Food and Nutrition. The experimental population consisted of 319 college freshmen enrolled in a required science survey course at a Pennsylvania State Teacher's College. All repetitive showings were completed within a single class period for each film.

Findings

When results from all four films were combined in sigma scores, the mean gains in score points for the second, third, and fourth showing, respectively, were 4.2, 1.2, and 0.2. Percentage gains in mean score attributable to each additional showing were 35.0, 7.4, and 1.1 for the second, third, and fourth showings, respectively. The only reliable difference in mean score gains among the second, third, and fourth showings was the substantial gain of the second showing over a single showing (0.1 per cent level of confidence). The mean gains of the third over the second showing, and of the fourth over the third showing were both small and unreliable.

From this study, McTavish concluded that "for factual films of the kind used in this study, showing them twice results in appreciably more learning; showings after the first two contribute little more to learning, and the drop-off is very rapid" (p. 48).

Evaluation

Two Showings Give Greatest Learning Increment

In a sense, McTavish conducted a somewhat idealized experiment, because he studied repeated showings as an isolated variable. He made no attempt to utilize the instructional procedures normally employed in teaching with films. The films were merely exhibited and those students who had to sit through four showings of some of the particularly abstruse films expressed some salty reactions to the experimenter in private. Nonetheless, as McTavish stated, in a curriculum crowded for time, one repetition reliably and substantially increases the amount of learning from films of that type. But further repetitions under these conditions add relatively little to factual knowledge.

2. COMBINED INSTRUCTION TECHNIQUES

HANSEN STUDY

Apparently feeling that the sound motion picture is not the best possible teaching technique, or that it gives the teacher too little opportunity to guide the learning, J. E. Hansen (1939) designed, for his doctoral study, a comparison of three ways of using four Encyclopaedia Britannica sound films.

Experimental Design

He investigated the teaching of information on plant biology to second-semester, tenth-grade biology students. The films used were: Plant Growth, Plant Roots, Leaves, and Work of Flowers. A total population of 195 students was divided into three equated groups on the basis of chronological age, mental age, IQ, and apparently, knowledge of plant biology. The students had studied much of the subject matter of these films during their first semester's work.

All three groups received a two-minute orientation introduction. Then, Group A saw the film with the sound-track shut off, but accompanied by questions and comments prepared by the teacher to direct attention to certain points. Relatively few questions and comments were used to avoid distracting the pupils. A ten-minute discussion of film content then followed from a prepared set of questions. After that, the film was again shown without the sound track, and this time the teacher asked more detailed questions and emphasized the processes that appeared to be least understood in the preceding ten-minute discussion period. The period was concluded by a 12-minute test on the film content.

Group B saw the film as a sound film, had the ten-minute discussion, which was followed by a silent showing of the film. During this second showing the teacher emphasized processes that appeared least understood during the discussion. The 12-minute final test was then given.

Group C followed the same procedure as A and B, but the film was projected as a sound film both times.

The investigator points out that a sound film projected without the sound is ordinarily not equivalent to a silent film, since good silent films use captions and animation. But he felt that, in this case, the four films made good use of animation, words and arrows in the pictures, etc., to identify the parts of plants and the biological processes occurring. A test on the film content was given 24 hours before the film was shown and the same test was used as the final test, the learning being measured in terms of gains from pre- to final-test.

Findings

With the film, Plant Growth, methods A and C were both, and equally, superior to method B. With the film, Plant Roots, method C, (sound track, twice), was the best method; method B, (first projection sound, second projection silent), was slightly better than method A (two silent projections). With the film, Leaves, methods B and C were equally superior to method A. In the case of the fourth film, Work of Flowers, method C was best, with a slight tendency for B to be better than A.

The over-all results were: (1) all three groups gained to a reliable degree from the instruction; (2) the three most reliable comparisons were those involving the superiority of method C over method A in two films and of method C over B in the first film (one per cent level); all but one of the remaining differences were reliable at less than the five per cent level; (3) method C was better than method A with three of the four films and just as good as A in the first film; (4) method A was the least effective with three of the four films, though Hansen thought that one might have expected it to be the best method.

Evaluation

It should be borne in mind that the pupils used in this investigation had studied in the previous semester much of the subject matter presented by these films. Their pre-test scores were 65 to 75 per cent of the possible score of 100 points. The fact that all groups made reliable gains, six to 18 points on the various topics, from the instruction is rather remarkable in the light of these facts. How well groups having little or no specific pre-knowledge of these topics would have done under the three methods is problematical and worthy of further research.

A second part of Hansen's study investigated the transfer of the knowledge and the film learning techniques acquired by the three groups to learning from two silent films covering similar topics, but involving different plants. This is discussed in Chapter VII under Film Literacy.

* * * * * *

Three studies dealing with other instructional variables, and with cumulative effects of variables used in combination have been reported during the past five years.

HOVLAND, LUMSDAINE, AND SHEFFIELD STUDY

C. I. Hovland, A. A. Lumsdaine, and F. D. Sheffield (1949) report a study of the use of introductory and review exercises in teaching military trainees from a film on map reading. Two instructional procedures were used: (1) discussion of the film content by the instructor prior to the film showing; and (2) review by means of a 15-item true-false test, scored immediately, and discussed by the instructor.

Findings

Both methods resulted in small, but reliable, increases in informational learning. The introductory exercises were a more effective learning aid, but unreliably so, than the review exercises. Both instructional procedures were effective for both high and low intelligence groups, and interestingly enough, the increased learning resulting from the introductory remarks was found not only on the items covered both in the introductory remarks and the film, but also on items covered only in the film.

Evaluation

This study lends support to the theory that relevant introductory remarks have an anticipational or motivational effect, as well as to the theory that learning results from the practice effect of repeating material in different symbolic forms.

WITTICH AND FOWLKES STUDY

The effects of casual presentation of films, anticipatory introduction, practice after a film showing, and repeated film showings were investigated by W. A. Wittich and J. G. Fowlkes (1946) in their study of the use of 27 Encyclopaedia Britannica films.

Experimental Design

Three instructional methods of using these films were compared on their effectiveness in bringing about informational and conceptual learning among 264 children in grades four through six: (1) a casual presentation of the films without any specific anticipational or preparatory activities, followed by an information test; (2) introductory material consisting of reading matter which presented the film content in story form, studying and defining the technical vocabulary, discussing a list of questions generally related to the film content, finally, the film showing and an information test; (3) the same procedure as (2), but, in addition, 24 hours later, there was another set of discussion questions, a second showing of the film, and a second administering of the same information test. There were three rotations of each of the classes on each of the grade levels.

Findings

Scores on the informational test increased progressively on all grade levels and on all rotations with anticipation, practice, and repetition. Anticipation plus film plus discussion, plus the test, plus a second showing (method 3) resulted in higher mean scores than anticipation only (method 2). In grades four and five, the mean difference between the casual presentation of a film and method 2 and method 3 increased with each successive rotation, but, in grade six, these differences decreased in magnitude with each rotation. This decrease with each successive rotation, that is, with increased experience with a particular method or routine of instruction, may indicate a saturation or "over-instruction" of a limited amount of material among more mature audiences. All mean differences reported by Wittich and Fowlkes were considerable in magnitude and highly reliable, thus increasing the likelihood that the material learned would be retained.

Evaluation

To decide whether we are justified in using more elaborate instructional procedures and in going beyond formally preparing an audience on what to expect from a film, we probably must determine what the additional instruction will involve; that is, will the additional instruction have the same content as the film, or other content?

COMMONWEALTH OFFICE OF EDUCATION STUDY

The most recent study of film utilization methods is that reported by the Commonwealth Office of Education (1950) of Australia.

Experimental Design

Six films were used in the experiment: <u>Market Town</u>, <u>Water Cycle</u>, <u>Water Power</u>, <u>City Water Supply</u>, <u>Latitude and Longitude</u>, and <u>Expansion of Germany</u>. Six classes of boys in a junior technical school were used, with the same instructor teaching all classes. Each class saw all the films at the rate of one film a week.

Six instructional methods were used with the films: (1) an introduction preceding the film; (2) an introduction, the film, and then a ten-minute discussion; (3) an introduction followed by two successive showings of the film; (4) an introduction, the film, and a ten-minute discussion during one class period, followed the next day by a second showing of the film; (5) an introduction plus the film during one class period, followed the next day by discussion and a second showing of the film; and (6) an introduction, plus the film, plus discussion during one class period, followed the next day by a second showing of the film and a second discussion of the same set of questions used the previous day.

Each of the six classes saw each film with a different instructional method. Six tests, totalling 120 objective items covering all six films, were administered approximately a month prior to the first film showing. The appropriate test was administered immediately after the film lesson, and the over-all test was again administered approximately three weeks after the screening of the last of the six films. Data were treated by analysis of variance and the "t" test of significance of mean differences.

Findings

In this experiment, some of the conclusions suggested by the Wittich and Fowlkes (1946) and the McTavish (1949) studies were verified. It was found, for instance, that "the effectiveness of a method may not be directly proportional to the time spent using it" (p. 16). While the sixth method (introduction, two showings of the film and two discussion periods, distributed through two class periods) was superior in measures of immediate learning, the fourth method was superior on delayed tests of learning. The fourth method consisted of an introduction, the film, and discussion during the first class period, followed the next day by a second showing of the film.

Four variables were found to be superior in aiding the pupils to retain the material learned: (1) introduction or orientation prior to the film showing, (2) discussion, that is, participation or practice in dealing with the film content in terms of concepts and facts, (3) repetition of the film showing, and (4) distributing the activity over a period of two days, rather than condensing all the activity into one class period. This last variable, distribution of screening, will be discussed in a later section of this chapter.

B. INTEGRATED INSTRUCTION

The problem of the close integration of films into the instructional procedure, that is, the use of the "right" film, at the "right" time, in the "right" place, in the "right" way, is prominent in the lore of instructional film method, but is relatively unexplored in film research.

Only one study is reported which directly attacks the problem of close integration of film instruction and application of routine techniques, such as those just discussed.

WILSON AND LARSON STUDY

E. C. Wilson and L. C. Larson (1940) studied the influence of a series of films in teaching current history at the General College, University of Minnesota, in terms of extreme differences in integration.

Experimental Design

In the one group, films related to the subject were simply projected during the appropriate class period without a direct follow-up discussion or reference to the film in the lecture. The films, however, were carefully selected so as to correspond closely to the lecture material.

In the other group, each film was introduced with remarks before it was shown, summarized afterward, and referred to in the subsequent lecture.

Findings

No reliable differences were found in the informational tests of each group. However, on a scale of ease and difficulty of the course, the integrated-film-group rated the course reliably easier than the non-integrated-film group, and students with high initial information seemed to gain more from the integrated use than did those with low initial information. Students with low initial information and high interest in the subject appeared to gain more from the non-integrated use.

Evaluation

This study suggests several cautions about film use: (1) rigid routines of film instruction can be profitably followed only under limited circumstances; (2) the value of film instructional routine varies with the characteristics of the audience; and (3) film instructional routines may influence learning other than that measured by purely informational tests.

C. MASSED AND DISTRIBUTED EXHIBITION

The problem of massed (continuous) and distributed (spaced) exhibition of films appears to be related to the problem of rate of development and density of content. It is difficult to control the rate of development and content density under practical conditions of instructional film use, because both of these variables may vary between any two or more films which an instructor may exhibit successively during a single instructional session. The problem is further complicated by the fact that the films may be "dull" or "interesting" to the audience.

The two experimental studies dealing directly with this problem reported results which, on the surface, do not appear to be entirely consistent.

U. S. ARMY STUDY

A study conducted during World War II by the Information and Education Research Branch of the U. S. Army (1944), mainly by D. A. Grant and B. Smith, investigated the learning differences resulting from consecutive vs. spaced showing of two films.

Findings

It was found that two films shown successively resulted in no percentage difference of learning from either film among Army trainees of higher intelligence, but among those of lower intelligence there was a decrease of learning from the second film shown consecutively in contrast to the second film shown the second day.

ASH STUDY

P. Ash (1949) conducted a study on massed and distributed showings in connection with the Instructional Film Research Program

Experimental Design

Two experimental populations were used one consisting of undergraduate psychology students, and the other of Naval trainees. With each group, two different film series were used. The college population saw four silent films of the Ape and Child series and four silent films of the Cat Neuroses series. The Navy population saw three sound films in the Elementary Hydraulics series and three sound films in the Rules of the Nautical Road series.

In massed-showing presentations of all four series of films to both populations, all films were projected in succession during a single instruction period (varying from 45 minutes to one hour).

In the distributed presentation to the groups of psychology students, two films were shown in a 30-minute period, and the remaining two films were shown separately in additional class periods. In the Navy groups, the three films of each series were shown during one instructional session to one group, and separately in three instructional sessions to another group.

Findings

In over-all results, no significant differences were found which could be attributed to either massed or distributed exhibition methodology. From his study, Ash concluded:

1. "When a typical hour-long series of instructional motion pictures is used as the sole teaching tool, students learn about the same amount from the series whether they are shown all the reels comprising the series in one long training session, or one reel at a time in several short training sessions.

2. "Increasing the length of the training session to one hour does not seem to result in a diminution of interest on the part of the learners. Furthermore, a learner's test performance is practically independent of his rated interest in the films.

3. "Long massed film sessions are about as effective in ensuring long-term (two-week) retention of the film content as short spaced sessions are" (p. 73).

Evaluation

As we mentioned above, there seems to be a disagreement in the research findings on this problem. The collateral evidence is somewhat in favor of distributed showings. However, Ash's study involved a sufficient number of films and sufficient diversity of populations to support the conclusion that, under the instructional and physical conditions sometimes found in practice (where the instructor plans no immediate discussion of the film), one-hour film sessions may be conducted without substantial loss in over-all group learning. This conclusion applies to film sessions involving a subject divided into three or four major and self-contained sequences. Rate of development and content density probably also enter into the problem of long and short film sessions to influence the result.

D. RANGE OF FILM USE AND EFFECTIVENESS

HOBAN STUDY

C. F. Hoban Jr. (1942) investigated the average range of use of instructional motion pictures in the schools participating in the American Council on Education evaluation program.

Findings

He found that the average range of use for these films was seven school grades. The full range of use reported for 250 films was fifteen grades.

RUMMEL STUDY

P. L. Rummel (1940) studied the results from ten educational film shorts produced for commercial theaters and released to schools for educational use. The films were shown to 2100 pupils from grades three through twelve.

Findings

He reported that optimum learning from these films had a mean range of 4.4 grades, with single films having an optimum learning range of from two to seven grades. Grades six through eleven were the grades where reliably higher learning scores from this type of film were most frequently found.

Evaluation

Film Producer Should Consider Audience Level

Although it is not possible to generalize from these two studies, it appears that while films have a relatively wide range of grade-level usefulness, the optimum range is narrower than the range of use found in actual practice. Studies of film effectiveness in which results were analyzed in terms of terminal education and intelligence scores (see Chapter VII) confirm the principle of optimum placement of films, or rather of optimum learning in terms of mental growth. The data imply that films will be most effective instructionally when they are produced for a somewhat narrow range of audience age and ability.

E. INFLUENCE OF THE INSTRUCTOR

In Chapter VI dealing with comparative effectiveness of films, the subject of exclusive use of films as a means of instruction was introduced and discussed. This subject has also been investigated from the practical point of view of training of large numbers of troops. It becomes necessary, here, to define "exclusive use" somewhat more clearly, particularly with reference to the role of the instructor.

"Exclusive use" of films means that films are used as the sole instructional material during any or several class periods, thereby excluding the textbooks, manuals, lectures, discussions, and other procedures ordinarily utilized for teaching and study purposes. But it does not mean that films provide the entire curriculum without the aid of teachers, practice, application, discussion, etc. In a sense, this point of view was presented in Chapter I in the discussion of the process of instruction and the role of the teacher. It is restated here for review and clarification, and as background for the research findings on the role of the instructor in film instruction.

VERNON STUDY

The effect of the instructor on group learning from film instruction was pointed out in the review of P. E. Vernon's (1946) study of a film and filmstrip used to teach the taking of soundings to British naval trainees in World War II.

Findings

Quality of Instructor Is Important Influence

He found that the quality of the instructor was one of the four significant variables in instruction. Furthermore, he found that excellent instructors were critically effective in promoting learning, and that their influence "carried over" even though they were not present during the projection of the film or filmstrip. "Classes taught by good instructors show a definite superiority over those taught by weak ones, regardless of the type of instruction. One of the most striking findings of the experiment is that the improvement is not confined to classes undergoing normal instruction, but is just about equal in extent in the filmstrip classes, where the instructors had been told to do little but read the captions, and even in the film-alone classes, which were not taught soundings by their instructor at all. Presumably the reason is that classes with good instructors have better morale and are more alert and attentive, so that they learn better even when they are not personally instructed" (pp. 156-157).

Insecurity May Explain Some Opposition to Films

Another quotation from Vernon's report sheds light on what seems to be a subconscious basis for the opposition of some instructors to instructional films -- the fear that the use of films threatens the status and employment of the teacher. Describing the procedure of the experiment, Vernon comments as follows:

"The psychologist was much struck by the differences between instructors, which usually more than confirmed the assessments previously made by the training commander. As he put it: 'There is more difference between the best and worst instructors than between the top and bottom ten per cent of seamen in intelligence.' The better ones made excellent use of the filmstrip, interjecting occasional explanations, keeping their classes attentive, both asking, and obtaining from the recruits, numerous questions and answering the latter clearly. The weakest ones were completely muddled and unadaptable. Often they had to be told to read out the captions. Relatively few questions were asked, and they were often unable to answer them because they were not within the scope of the conventional recitation. For example:

> Qu. -- What is the difference between the hand line and the sounding machine?
>
> An. -- Both serve the same purpose.

"While all the instructors were guarded in their approval of the new device, it was only the three poorest ones who expressed thorough dissatisfaction, and saw no advantages in it. An almost invariable comment was that practical work is needed in addition. One or two other objections were that the pictures in this particular strip were poor, and that recruits will not attend to any kind of film unless it is amusing" (p. 153).

REED STUDY

The recent study by P. C. Reed (1950) supplies more insight into the role of the instructor and on "good" use of films.

Experimental Design

Reed's problem was to discover the ways teachers were using sound motion pictures in classroom instruction, and to gather factual material as a basis for improving audio-visual administrative service to teachers. He selected all fifth-grade teachers in the Rochester, New York, public school system, and used twenty-five instructional sound films, chosen on the basis of teacher advice, in the fifth-grade course of study about our nation. Five sources of data were utilized: (1) records of films ordered by the fifth-grade teachers; (2) teacher-personnel data and grade-organization; (3) direct observation of teaching situations in which films were used; (4) reports from principals based on their observation of film use by teachers; and (5) a questionnaire sent to all fifth-grade teachers.

Reed selected 13 teachers at random in different schools for direct observation, most of whom made relatively frequent use of films in their teaching procedure. Four criteria were used in the observations: (1) clarity of purpose of film use, (2) knowledge of film content and plan for its use, (3) "readiness" of the pupils for film observation, and (4) "follow-through" after film exhibition.

Findings

From his and from the observations of school principals, Reed drew, among others, the following conclusion: "In terms of the criteria that have been used for 'good' utilization, the evidence collected by this observer and by the principals seems to indicate that the teachers who are using sound films are making 'good' use of them. In only a very few instances was there evidence of failure to follow the principles of 'good' film usage.

"This does not mean, however, that there was not variation in the quality of the film teaching. There was; but this variation did not seem to be caused by the degree of understanding of the medium and the way to use it in teaching, nor was it caused by the degree of skill in manipulating the equipment. Rather the variations between 'good' and 'best' seemed to be caused by those factors that cause variation in teaching regardless of materials and equipment used. The teacher's fundamental concept of what learning is, her understanding of children and the way they learn, her skill in living and working with them, are the kind of factors that go beyond basic principles of film usage and are of most importance in bringing about the best possible classroom utilization of films" (pp. 85-86).

Evaluation

This conclusion is consistent with the main weight of experimental evidence which indicates that principles of teaching are important. Routine techniques are perhaps more characteristic of mediocrity than of excellence.

F. INFLUENCE OF ADMINISTRATION

REED STUDY

P. C. Reed (1950) also investigated the degree to which films were used by the fifth-grade teachers in the Rochester public schools.

Findings

He found that the use of films was not uniform. One-third of the teachers ordered three-fourths of the films, and most of the teachers ordered either few films or none at all. Furthermore, even though new sound films were made available, the older silent films continued to be widely used, and the new sound films were not ordered in quantity or to the extent anticipated.

The situation in the Rochester schools probably is duplicated in other organizations and institutions where, because facilities have been established for the supply and use of instructional films, it is assumed that these films are therefore used by most, if not all, teachers.

BECK, PETERMAN, WINER, AND KELLY STUDY

During World War II, a study of the effectiveness of Visual Aids Coordinators assigned to film libraries was made by Beck, Peterman, Winer, and Kelly, and reported by C. F. Hoban Jr. (1946). The function of the Visual Aids Coordinator in the Army's film instructional program, in addition to administering the supply and maintenance facilities of the film library, was to keep training officers informed of appropriate films, arrange previews, and, in general, to operate the film library service at a high level of efficiency. The study examined the operation of 36 Army film libraries from June to December, 1943, in comparable training centers, 18 of which had Visual Aids Coordinators, and 18 of which did not.

Findings

The data indicate that the film libraries with Coordinators were considerably more efficient in terms of (1) print stock (number of individual prints of films), (2) showings per print, (3) number of troops served, and (4) total number of film showings. In print stock, the libraries without Coordinators had approximately the same number of prints in December as in June, whereas the libraries with Coordinators decreased their print stock from a gross total of approximately 12,300 prints to approximately 10,300 prints. Meanwhile, the showings per print per month increased in film libraries without Coordinators from

1 to nearly 1.5 and in libraries with Coordinators from approximately 1.3 to approximately 2.9.

The number of troops actually served by films in camps without Coordinators and in those with Coordinators increased approximately 40 per cent, and 75 per cent, respectively, and the number of showings increased by approximately 40 per cent and 68 per cent, respectively. In other words, libraries with Visual Aids Coordinators served more troops more frequently and with fewer prints than did libraries without Visual Aids Coordinators.

Evaluation

It seems evident from Reed's study and from the U. S. Army study of film library administration that, without administrative "push," films are not used to the optimum extent in the teaching and training situations for which they were planned and produced. On the contrary, local promotion of film use both increases the extent of film use and the efficiency of film supply. The problem of film use, as Reed pointed out in his recent study, is not so much that of "better" use of films among teachers and instructors who are using the films available to them. He found that teachers who used films, on the whole used them well. Vernon's report suggests this same characteristic of instructors who willingly use films. The problem is that of increasing the use of films among the majority of instructors who use few films or none at all, and, perhaps, assisting this majority to use films well when they do use them.

SECTION 2. PHYSICAL CONDITIONS OF FILM USE

Research on the effect on learning of the physical conditions under which films are used compares auditorium with classroom use, and considers the viewing angle and the amount of illumination.

A. AUDITORIUM VS. CLASSROOM USE

The difference in learning from projecting film in an auditorium and a classroom has had very little serious investigation. Teachers have usually assumed that classroom projection was more practical from the standpoint of good teaching, probably basing their judgment on incidental observations of some of the results of showing instructional films in an auditorium. It might be pointed out, however, in this connection that in the Wittich and Fowlkes (1946) experiment, all the films were projected in the school auditorium, although only the front rows were occupied during any one showing. Auditorium projection was used in their study to reduce to a minimum environmental variations resulting from projection in different classrooms.

KNOWLTON AND TILTON STUDY

D. C. Knowlton and J. W. Tilton (1932) reported a study whose purpose was to compare auditorium and classroom projection.

Experimental Design

The investigators used 11 of the Chronicles of America Photoplays which they had previously used in their earlier study (1929) on the effects of motion pictures in teaching history. Each of three teachers taught two matched classes of seventh-grade pupils. One group was taught in an auditorium where the projected picture was 9 by 12 feet, and the other in a regular classroom where the image on the screen was 16 by 24 inches. In addition to this great difference in the stimulus value of the size of the projected pictures, the instructional activities accompanying the films also differed. For instance, no questions were asked by the auditorium groups, and other visual aids were used to fill out the remaining time in the period; whereas in the classroom groups, the teachers had time before and after each showing and between reels to answer and discuss the pupils' questions.

Findings

Small, statistically reliable, differences in favor of the classroom groups, were obtained in six out of ten comparisons in immediate tests; in four of these six, a difference was still evident the following September.

Evaluation

Unfortunately, because of the differences in instructional activities in the two situations, the differences found may be just as easily accounted for by the variation in instructional techniques as by the difference between classroom and auditorium projection.

STODDARD STUDY

A. J. Stoddard (1934), while superintendent of schools at Providence, R. I., reported a study which bears indirectly on the relative merits of classroom and auditorium projection.

Experimental Design

Three groups, of about 150 sixth-grade pupils each, were taught three science units and three music units in an auditorium with the aid of sound films. Three other groups, of the same size and matched on intelligence and achievement, were taught these units in the auditorium without the aid of films, but with all other possible aids. Finally, three other groups, of about 40 pupils each, were taught in classrooms without the aid of films. The nine participating teachers each taught every type of group twice and in every one of the nine schools.

Findings

The largest gain between pre-test and post-test was for the auditorium groups with films, whose mean gain was 5.5 points more than that of the auditorium groups without films. The scores of the classroom groups were between those of the other two groups; the mean gain was two points below that of the auditorium groups with films. No measures of variability were reported by the author, but, considering the size of his groups, at least the difference of 5.5 points (where the mean gain is around 42 points) is probably reliable. The other differences may be reliable also.

Evaluation

Unfortunately Stoddard did not include the fourth variation, namely, classroom groups with films. However, he was only interested in learning if large classes, with the aid of films, could learn as well as small classes taught without films. Accordingly, he was not concerned with the two conditions of projection.

KRASKER STUDY

One part of A. Krasker's study (1941, 1943) of the use of motion pictures was concerned with the effectiveness of six silent films shown in the auditorium and classroom to groups of eighth- and ninth-grade pupils, with intermittent projection in both cases. Intermittent projection involved stopping the film to permit questions, note taking, and discussion, but it was not considered a variable in this study.

Findings

The 1943 article presents results for the six films, showing two comparisons where there was no real difference in means (83.35 vs. 83.13 and 70.88 vs. 69.67). On two films, small and possibly unreliable differences in favor of the classroom are found--the article gives no reliabilities, (50.00 vs. 44.38 and 76.78 vs. 72.82). Two films did show sizable differences in favor of the classroom (61.05 vs. 39.00 and 77.25 vs. 63.15).

Evaluation

Krasker's study is often referred to as evidence that, within the scope of his investigation, the size of the class or group being taught affects the amount of learning by the students. But, on the basis of the above results, the present reviewers cannot agree with this interpretation. These findings do not constitute an "every instance" argument for classroom projection.

Thus the problem of the relative contributions of auditorium and classroom projection, regardless of its feasibility, is a question for further investigation. The data from Gibson's study on the viewing angle and the viewer's distance from the screen, reported in the next section, add some weight to the following

hypothesis: whether a film is projected in an auditorium or a classroom may not, by itself, be a highly important factor in influencing the amount of learning, but other instructional procedures combined with it may be the really crucial factors. D. C. Knowlton and J. W. Tilton (1932), however, attribute a difference in learning in favor of classroom projection "to the difference in pupil attitude and activity which differentiate classroom and auditorium periods" (p. 670). If this is so, the problem is primarily one of pupil attitude, rather than one of the physical size and arrangement of audience viewing conditions.

B. ILLUMINATION, VIEWING ANGLE, AND DISTANCE FROM THE SCREEN

The only experimental data on the effects of room illumination, and of angle and distance from the screen were reported by J. J. Gibson (1946).

GIBSON STUDY

Findings

Out of some 20 motion-picture test situations with Air Force trainees, he found only three that appeared to involve learning effects reliably related to either distance or viewing angle, and all three of these were test films making extreme demands on visual acuity. Except where acute visual perception is involved, the differences in distance and viewing angle (up to at least 45 degrees) within the range of the ordinary classroom or small theater, while presumably related to the audience's comfort and ease of perception, seem to have little reliable effect on test-film performance. Presumably the same findings would apply to learning from instructional films.

Experimental studies of room illumination show no highly reliable differences in test-film performance which can be attributed to the amount of light in a room during film projection. No reliable difference (.30 in mean scores with CR of .80) was found between "blackout" and dim lighting. A difference in test performance reliable on the five per cent level of confidence, was found to result from screenings when the room lighting level was approximately 0.1 foot candle (dim) and when it was approximately 1.4 foot candles (full illumination).

Evaluation

From these data Gibson concluded that films may be shown in a room with sufficient illumination to permit note taking or written response to questions without obviously reducing the learners' ability to see the film. "The simple expedient of low-wattage ceiling lights is fairly sure to be satisfactory" (p. 59) for the use of films requiring audience participation. This suggests a way of combatting the "spectator attitude" of the movie theater and aiding in setting up a situation that is more conducive to active learning.

SUMMARY

1. VARIABLES IN THE METHODS AND CONDITIONS OF FILM USE

ELEMENTS OF INSTRUCTIONAL METHODS

Film User Should Observe Instructional Principles

It is evident that at least some of the same variables of instruction which were isolated in the research on film techniques, are critical variables in film use. From these studies we can infer that the effective use of films is not so much a matter of applying a "formula" of instructional method to film utilization, as it is a matter of applying the principles of instruction to methods of film use.

Over-instruction Wastes Effort

McTavish found that the greatest learning increment results after a second showing of a film, and thereafter, additional showings have relatively little effect. This finding was extended in the Australian study to apply to "over-instruction" in other film methods. When we use retention of learning to judge the effectiveness of an instructional method, we observe that over-instruction not only consumes time and effort without compensating increments of learning, but also apparently "interferes" with retention.

INTEGRATED INSTRUCTION

The information about the close combination of films with other instructional methods is limited. The study cited suggested some cautions about using films: (1) adopting a rigid routine for using films and following it unvaryingly may decrease the usefulness of films in certain learning situations; (2) the appropriate combination of films and other instructional methods often is dictated by the audience's characteristics.

MASSED AND DISTRIBUTED EXHIBITION

There is some evidence, though not decisive, that a massed (one-hour) film session does not substantially reduce over-all group learning, especially when the instructor does not plan to discuss the individual films. However, such film characteristics as the rate of development and the density of content, also have an important influence in determining when a film session is too long.

RANGE OF FILM USE AND EFFECTIVENESS

It appears that, although films are used over a fairly wide range of school grades, the films are effective within a more limited range. As a result, it may be possible to increase the instructional value of films by "tailoring" them for audiences of definite age and ability levels.

INFLUENCE OF THE INSTRUCTOR

The influence of a good instructor is an important one in a learning situation. A class which has a good instructor frequently has better morale and is more alert and attentive than a class whose instructor is mediocre or poor. Sometimes this influence carries over into learning situations where the instructor is relatively inactive or is not present at all.

Even in cases where teachers use the same instructional materials, there are variations in the quality of teaching. These differences reflect the teacher's concept of the learning process and his (or her) understanding of the pupils and ability to work with them. Routine instructional techniques probably more often characterize the mediocre teacher than the excellent teacher.

INFLUENCE OF ADMINISTRATION

The fact that a film library is available does not ensure that teachers and instructors will take best advantage of the facilities. A study of one school system revealed that a minority of the teachers were responsible for a major share of film circulation and use. An active library organization can be helpful in promoting the use of films among instructors who might otherwise seldom or never use them.

2. PHYSICAL CONDITIONS OF FILM USE

It appears, on the basis of available evidence, that physical surroundings and conditions of projection, except, of course, when the room is fully illuminated, are not likely to be critical factors in affecting factual learning from motion pictures. Most likely instructional procedures, which are relatively independent of room illumination, viewing angle and distance from the screen, are the more important factors of audience response, as far as factual learning is concerned. It may be that the realism of the film projected in the darkened room, as compared with projection in a dimly lighted room, is a factor to consider in the influencing of emotional attitudes. This is a question for further investigation.

CHAPTER IX

PRINCIPLES OF FILM INFLUENCE

INTRODUCTION

In concluding this review of instructional film research we shall (1) summarize the values of instructional motion pictures as indicated in the research studies, (2) present a series of principles which appear to govern the influence of films, and (3) present some general observations. Although these instructional values, principles, and observations may be widely known and accepted (or perhaps disagreed with, in some cases), they are often overlooked in the planning, production, and use of motion pictures in instruction.

We offer this summary and these observations

in somewhat the same spirit expressed by Granville Hicks (1946) in his concluding chapter of Small Town.

"What I have learned," he wrote, "will seem commonplace enough to many persons, and I am aware that I have said and can say little that hasn't been said before. It seems to me, however, that there are certain ideas that many persons profess to accept but that few act upon. One way of disposing of an awkward fact is to say, 'Everybody knows that.' Perhaps everybody does, but what difference does that make if nobody takes the knowledge into account?" (p. 271).

PART I.   VALUES OF INSTRUCTIONAL FILMS

"What good are movies in teaching, anyway?" In answer to this blunt, but pertinent question, film research studies suggest five major values of motion picture instruction.

VALUE 1: People learn from films.

They can learn factual knowledge, concepts, motor skills, attitudes, and opinions. Probably, films are useful in achieving other educational objectives, such as appreciations and creative imagination, but there is little evidence available on these outcomes.

VALUE 2: When effective and appropriate films are properly used, people learn more in less time and are better able to retain what they have learned.

When a film satisfies, to a fair degree, the majority of the ten principles of film influence (see Part II), it frequently results in more factual learning than comparable reading materials or lecture presentations, and requires less instructional time. Moreover, when films are used and integrated with other instructional procedures and materials, more learning results from the combination than from either medium alone.

Films used alone, or combined with other instructional methods are in many cases superior to purely verbal methods of presenting facts, as measured by both immediate and delayed tests of effectiveness, and especially by the delayed measures. Occasionally, an audience has even been found to know a higher percentage of certain facts presented in a film or to have stronger film-directed opinions several weeks after the film than did a comparable audience a few hours or days afterward.

Nevertheless, the statement of Value 2 must be qualified. As we pointed out at the end of Chapter III and substantiated in Chapter VI, "there is nothing in a motion picture presentation, per se, that guarantees better learning." Some films have turned out to be no better than other methods, except that they make it possible to instruct a larger group simultaneously, and some films may even promote less learning than usual methods.

What is implied in proper use is outlined in Part II under Principles nine and ten of film influence. The meaning of effective and appropriate is sketched, as far as our present insights enable us to go, in Principles one to eight on film influence.

VALUE 3: Instructional films may stimulate other learning activities.

Several research studies indicate that certain instructional films are likely to stimulate such activities as discussions, voluntary reading, investigations, art work, and the like. How much of this type of activity is stimulated probably depends on the nature of the film, the permissive or domineering attitude of the teacher, and the accessibility of reading materials, as well as other factors.

VALUE 4: Certain films may facilitate thinking and problem solving.

Thinking is a process of using what a person knows. If this thinking leads to problem solving or becomes critical thinking, the person must comprehend new relationships or patterns in the perceptions and ideas he is using. The experimental evidence from at least four carefully controlled studies indicates that films aid in promoting comprehension, or understanding to a greater extent than they do the learning of specific facts of a rote memory nature.

One study found that general science classes taught with text and supplementary films were better able to apply their learning than classes taught only with textbooks and other usual methods. A recent study indicates that films which merely repeat what text and teacher present may not aid in problem solving.

VALUE 5: Appropriate films are equivalent to at least an average teacher, and sometimes even to an excellent instructor insofar as the instructor's function is communicating the facts or demonstrating the procedures presented in the film.

This finding is supported by several studies, mostly involving high school, college, and armed-service trainee populations. In at least three studies, the film presentation gave better results than a "good" lecture that utilized charts and other aids.

This value has at least three important applications: (1) good films may improve the effectiveness of poor teachers in instructing classes; (2) films can substitute for the instructor in certain demonstrations and lectures, thus making it possible to teach certain topics when a qualified teacher is not available to present those topics (as in small schools, large groups, televising to several schools, home study, etc.); (3) the wise use of film instruction can, to some extent, save the teacher's time and energy for situations where face-to-face leadership, individual instruction, and personal guidance are required.

PART II. PRINCIPLES GOVERNING THE INFLUENCE OF FILMS

It is often assumed that a motion picture provides a common experience for the group that sees it. A given picture does not vary physically in the content presented from one showing to another or from one group to another, but it does not follow from this that all individuals who observe the film have the same experience. Motion picture experience is a common experience in that it is shared, but this experience always has a somewhat different meaning (sometimes the difference is considerable) for the individuals who see the film.

The difference in the meaning of film experience and, consequently, in the learning by the individuals in the audience, may be understood, at least partially, in terms of ten major principles or postulates of film influence. The principles of film influence presented here are tentative generalizations derived by the authors of this review from the data reported in published studies. In a sense, these principles or postulates represent our attempt at creative synthesis of present knowledge of film influence, insofar as this knowledge is reflected in the published literature of experimental film research. Future research results may require their extension, reformulation, or revision, and future developments in systematic psychology may require their reorientation and modification. Within the limits of the available data, and the insights of the reviewers, these principles are presented here so as to facilitate more accurate prediction of film results, better methods of film planning and production, and more effective ways of using films in instruction.

It is clearly evident in the mass of film research data that the influence of motion pictures on behavior is dynamic, rather than exclusively inherent in the medium of the motion picture. Film influence depends not only on (1) the content and the treatment of the film, but also on (2) the psychological make-up of the audience, and (3) the social and instructional characteristics of the situation in which the film is presented.

When the influence of films is accepted as dynamic in nature, and when the dynamics of film influence are understood, even if imperfectly, the mystery of the influence of motion pictures on human behavior begins to disappear, and with it the exaggerated hopes and fears of "movie magic."

No one principle or postulate can satisfactorily or completely "explain" film influence. The ten major principles of film influence are interrelated. Quite certainly, other principles can be formulated and applied to the production and use of motion pictures in instruction. For example, the principle of closure (especially as it relates to the tendency to remember and complete an interrupted act or sequence) appears to be highly important to instruction in general, and to instructional films in particular. But there is no evidence that this principle has been satisfactorily or systematically applied in either the production or use of instructional films. What is perhaps unique about the proposed principles of film influence is that they have direct application to the motion picture as a medium of communication and direct implications for instructional film production and use. The ten principles and some of their implications follow.

I: PRINCIPLE OF REINFORCEMENT

Films have greatest influence when their content reinforces and extends previous knowledge, attitudes, and motivations of the audience. They have least influence when previous knowledge is inadequate, and when their content is antagonistic or contrary to the existing attitudes and motivation of the audience.

This principle takes on meaning when we remember that the motion picture is a medium of communication, and not an independent determinant of behavior. A person responds to a film in terms of what he already knows, what he can do, how he feels, and what he wants at that time in that situation. A film helps to change the person in the sense that it helps to change his way of looking at things, including himself, and presents a model of new responses that he can make in that or similar situations.

The influence of any one film is likely to be limited, just as the influence of any ordinary experience lasting less than an hour, or an hour or two at most, is likely to be limited. However, the influence of several related films is likely to be cumulative. Two or more films with similar bias on the same or similar subjects, each of which has little measurable effect on audience learning, may have a measurable effect when used consecutively in instruction.

There is experimental evidence that the influence of any motion picture depends to a very great extent on the reinforcing experiences that occur before, after, or during the film showing. The effectiveness of a given film in implementing any instructional objective is likely to decrease if, at any point during its production, distribution, and utilization, the film departs from the context of instructional and educational experience in which it is intended to be used. Unfortunately, many instructional and informational films are produced without adequate consideration of the context of their use, and without due recognition of other instructional materials and instructional procedures which are required in organized teaching, and in organized training and information programs.

IMPLICATIONS

The principle of reinforcement has implications for both the production and use of films. It implies that whether the purpose of a film is to (1) extend and reinforce behavior, or (2) reorganize and redirect behavior, it will probably be most effective when it is planned, distributed and used as one of a series of related and cumulative experiences all of which operate in the same direction. This means that films should be produced and used as part of a package of instructional materials, not as unique instruments of total instructional power and influence. The principle of reinforcement does not imply that films have no influence in reorganizing and redirecting behavior, that is, in helping the audience to understand and to respond in a new way.

The concept that a motion picture is an independently effective experience is likely to be wishful thinking. When the objective of instruction is reorganization and redirection of behavior, it becomes more necessary to reinforce film instruction with supporting instructional materials and experiences and a related social environment, conducive to the learning which films are intended to stimulate.

II: PRINCIPLE OF SPECIFICITY

The influence of a motion picture is more specific than general.

This holds true for all instructional objectives. We cannot expect an audience to have a broad general attitude, a general motivation, a general increase in knowledge, or a general improvement in perceptual-motor skills after seeing a single film, especially when these objectives are not treated directly in the film. The cumulative effect of related films, shown over a period of time and reinforced by the social environment and by other instructional experiences may be more general, but, even in this case, the general influence is limited to the broad area of the film content.

IMPLICATIONS

The principle of specificity implies that the sponsoring agencies must define in very specific terms the instructional objectives which a film is intended to serve. The failure to define film objectives specifically in the planning stage of production handicaps film producers severely, and reduces the likelihood that the film will be as influential as it might otherwise be.

III: PRINCIPLE OF RELEVANCE

The influence of a motion picture is greater when the content of the film is directly relevant to the audience reaction that it is intended to influence.

The validity of this principle is immediately apparent when stated in abstract terms but, in the production and use of specific films and in the prediction of audience reactions, it is frequently overlooked and disregarded. There is evidence that some producers, users, and research workers expect a film to influence behavior even though the film content is not directly relevant to the anticipated or predicted behavior. For example, instructors sometimes expect the quality of students' handwriting to improve after showing a film which demonstrates the correct arm and finger position for handwriting. In other cases, instructors expect to find an improvement in arithmetic computation as a result of a film portraying the social applications of arithmetic; or, increased skill in manipulating machinery from a film which explains the operating principles of the machine. Such expectations lead to disappointment.

IMPLICATIONS

The principle of relevance has three implications for film producers.

1. If motion pictures are to have specific influences on the behavior of their intended audiences, the instructional objectives must be defined in terms of specific behaviors.

2. After, and only after, the desired behavior changes in the intended audience have been defined and described, can the producer select the relevant film content and its treatment. In a motion picture, subject matter content is purely instrumental, and within any given subject matter there is a wide range of possibilities for selection and treatment.

   The selection of proper film content is the general responsibility of the project officer or the technical advisor, and is the immediate responsibility of both the writer and director. A film producing agency cannot develop a precision instrument for influencing behavior if the intended influence is defined for the creative artist in terms of subject matter and not in terms of desired audience response and change of audience behavior.

3. A third implication of this principle is that only those things which are relevant to the behavior pattern which the film is intended to affect are relevant to a film produced to influence that behavior pattern. For example, if a film is intended to demonstrate the firing of the bazooka, then the history of the research on and the process of manufacture of the bazooka is irrelevant. The relevant content of the film is the operations involved in firing the bazooka.

   The efficiency of film production is likely to be increased by omitting content that is not relevant to the specific behavior desired. For example, one study definitely established that some "how-it-works" sequences in a film had little, if any, influence in teaching the assembly of a part of a complicated piece of equipment. In this instance, "how-it-works" was irrelevant to the behavior involved in actual assembly. Production time, facilities, and expense, as well as training time, can be reduced by omitting irrelevant content without impairing the instructional effectiveness of the film.

IV: PRINCIPLE OF AUDIENCE VARIABILITY

Reactions to a motion picture vary with most or all of the following factors: film literacy, abstract intelligence, formal education, age, sex, previous experience with the subject, and prejudice or predisposition toward the subject.

It is often assumed that a motion picture has the same effect on every individual of the audience. Actually, there is a wide range of individual differences in any audience; the more heterogeneous the audience, the greater the range. Moreover, the range of these differences increases as the individuals in the group approach maturity. These differences in individual characteristics cause people to respond differently to instructional films.

Six variables that affect differences in individual response to motion pictures have been thus far identified in research studies.

1. Film Literacy

   Film literacy is an ability to learn from films, ostensibly developed by practice in observing entertainment films, instructional films, or both. The psychological nature of this ability is not clearly understood at this time, but probably, as an individual becomes more familiar with the motion picture medium (as measured by the number of movies he has seen), his ability to learn from a film tends to increase also. However, viewing habits appropriate for entertainment films may not be entirely appropriate for instructional films and re-teaching may be necessary.

2. Intelligence
3. Level of Formal Education

   A high level of intelligence is usually accompanied by an extensive formal education in the general population, and both influence the amount of factual learning from films. Intelligence also affects the validity of the interpretation of the material presented (opinions formed). The notions that the motion picture is best utilized for instructing an audience that is inferior in abstract intelligence (the so-called "dull"), and that films waste the time and talents of the mentally-gifted, are not supported by the experimental evidence. Students of below-average intelligence learn more from films than from verbal materials, but students of above-average intelligence often learn proportionately more in terms of possible learning and, perhaps, different kinds of responses than do the below-average students, provided, of course, that the films do not impose a ceiling on the amount of learning possible.

4. Age

   Intelligence and formal education increase with age up to a given point, but age itself is a variable in the way people react to films. As a variable, age is important to the extent that breadth of experience, interests, resistance to excitability, and the leveling and declining of mental alertness vary in different ways with age in an otherwise rather homogeneous group. The ability to perceive and to retain motion picture content seems to reach its peak somewhere in the late teens or early adulthood, and then gradually declines. Moreover, excitability and resistance to excitability, that is, "emotional discount," appear to be rather well established in the late teens, although there is probably some change during later ages.

5. Sex

In some cases, persons of different sex have been found to respond differently to films. Most likely, sex differences in responses to films are largely the result of the values, activities, occupations, and other social norms assigned in the American culture to males and females. Whatever their origin, sex differences may affect the attitudes and information gained from films, and they do affect attendance of teen-agers, at least, at entertainment motion pictures.

6. Predisposition

A person's predisposition, or prejudice, toward the subject of a film influences the degree to which he accepts the point of view and interpretation of the film, and the direction of the effect of the intended influence of the film. In general, the influence of the film will be in the direction in which the film content is slanted, but this influence is likely to vary in degree and durability according to the predisposition of the individual. As a result of predisposition, individuals vary in the direction and degree of their response to films, and any one individual may respond differently to single items in a film. Boomerang effects (reinforcement of the individual's prevailing mind-set) may occur when the bias of the film is contrary to the individual's predispositions. Other things being equal, predisposition is likely to have a stronger effect than the immediate intended influence of the motion picture if its bias is contrary to the individual's predisposition.

IMPLICATIONS

One implication of this principle is that the effectiveness of a film or films cannot be assured unless the audience characteristics which influence the nature and extent of response to the film (1) and known, (2) are carefully described, and (3) the film presentation is appropriate to them. Therefore, if film production is to have a scientific basis, as well as artistic treatment, a considerable amount of pre-production research on audience characteristics must be done. This research requires more than a pre-release testing of a given film on a sample of its target audience, although this procedure probably helps to improve specific films. It involves knowing, insofar as possible, the distribution of ages and learning abilities, the previous knowledge and training of the audience in the particular subject, and the predispositions of the audience (or, at least their dominant direction) on attitudes, opinions, interests, and motivation. After the target audience

has been described in terms of these variables of response, the producer can plan more effectively and develop the appropriate film content and organization.

A second implication of the principle of audience variability as applied to film production is that, for a target audience with a relatively narrow range of ability, a single film, produced for a level slightly below the average level of intelligence and education of the audience, is likely to be effective. But, if the audience has a rather wide range of ability, two or more film versions, each presented on a different level of complexity and instructional technique, may be and probably are necessary for most effective learning. There is no experimental evidence that film instruction techniques designed for pupils of average intelligence interfere with or impede learning among pupils of above-average and superior intelligence. A fact that military-film producers have apparently overlooked in the present emergency is that the level of formal education of the current draftee population has increased over that of the draftee population of World War II. The majority of today's draftees have completed high school, and one out of five has had some college training.

The use of audience participation techniques and film introductions are apparently effective under certain circumstances in increasing learning of the below-average individuals in the audience. They are not as positively effective among above-average individuals, but, as far as is known at this time, they at least do not interfere with learning by the above-average individual and probably make some contribution to it. Furthermore, (1) limiting the amount of film instruction in a session of a given length, and (2) showing films at intervals rather than consecutively, do not interfere with the learning of the above-average individuals, but packing or crowding of film instruction into a long film session and showing films consecutively may have an adverse effect on an average or somewhat below-average audience.

For film users, the principle of audience variability implies that there is no one method of using films which is appropriate to all audiences or to every person within an audience. The instructional procedure for using a film must be adapted to suit the abilities and backgrounds of the majority of a particular audience. As implied in the Principle of Reinforcement, instruction becomes more difficult as the variability of the audience increases.

V: PRINCIPLE OF VISUAL PRIMACY

The influence of a motion picture is primarily in the strength of the visual presentation, and secondarily, in the narration or commentary. It is relatively unaffected by "slickness" of production as long as meaning is clear.

This principle may profane some sacred cows of the film industry, but its validity for instructional films* is becoming increasingly clear from comparisons of the relative instructional effectiveness of: visual and auditory elements; various levels of verbalization; attention-gaining devices; and color and black and white film.

The primacy of the visual factor is further suggested in film-analyzer studies of audience like-dislike reactions to the visual and auditory elements of sound motion pictures. It is consistent with the hypothesis that all learning involves individual discovery, that discovery itself is in some degree non-communicable, and that communication serves only to facilitate discovery. The picture (still or motion) makes individual discovery possible, as does the actual situation it portrays. Language puts this discovery into words, or alerts the audience to it. Film commentary can actually interfere with, as well as facilitate, learning from the pictures. There apparently is a golden mean of amount of verbalization in an instructional film commentary, somewhere between the "blamable extremes" of too little and too much.

Many of the visual and auditory usages characteristic of the entertainment film and radio industries seem to have little direct influence when applied to instructional films. For instance, unless the color provides crucial learning cues (e.g., as in identifying colored signal flags), color film does not give better instructional results than black and white film for many kinds of content. There is some evidence to suggest that visual or sound attention-gaining devices do not add significantly to the instructional effectiveness of an otherwise well-made film. Musical background, which has been studied very little, was found in one small study to have little effect on the instruction of elementary school pupils. Possibly, music may serve to announce some particular sequence or underscore a mood, and its effect probably depends on its familiarity and symbolic significance to the individual.

IMPLICATIONS

The implications of this principle are more apparent in relation to the production than to the utilization of instructional films. For one thing, it suggests that a motion picture should not be approved for production unless the subject lends itself to fluent visual presentation that can be well specified. The basic criterion for deciding to produce a motion picture is not the importance of the subject, as such, but the suitability of the subject for communication by motion picture.

A second implication is that the production staff should continually remember that it is producing a motion picture, and not an illustrated lecture. The story-board, although more exacting and more time consuming in the pre-photographic stages of planning and production is likely to be more useful and efficient than the purely verbal script. Story-board treatments may require closer teamwork and less specialized division of labor in the pre-production stages between artists, writers, directors, and technical advisors.

A third implication is that the amount of language (commentary, narration, and dialogue) used in a motion picture should be limited, and that it be used either to express or integrate the meanings of the pictures or to alert the audience to these meanings.

A fourth implication is that the production cost of instructional motion pictures in time, facilities, and personnel may be substantially reduced with little, if any, sacrifice of instructional effectiveness by reducing the emphasis on filmic devices and "slickness," and increasing the emphasis on straightforward use of the camera and integrity of presentation.

The implication for the film user is that when motion pictures are produced as motion pictures, rather than as pictorial backgrounds or illustrations for the verbal lessons presented in the sound track, the effect on the audience is more likely to be stimulating: discussion, analysis, re-showing, and other independent activities are likely to be a natural consequence of film use, rather than a routine and sometimes painful requirement.

VI: PRINCIPLE OF PICTORIAL CONTEXT

An audience responds selectively to motion pictures, reacting to those things which it finds familiar and significant in the pictorial context in which the action takes place.

It is wishful thinking for film producers and film users to assume that everything shown and said in a motion picture will be seen and heard, learned and remembered by everybody in the audience. People respond to motion picture selectively, not photographically, and it is apparent that audience variables affect the selectivity of response. The question is, "What factors in the motion picture influence the selection of responses and the nature of the responses selected?"

The most important factor determining response selection in a motion picture seems to be the pictorial context or surroundings in which the action is presented. Moreover, it is important for the context to be (1) familiar, and (2) significant in terms of audience values. Therefore, the condition that apparently determines the perception and retention of specific scenes in the film by an audience, is not the action itself, but the importance or meaning of the action; not the close-ups themselves, but the significance of the object in the close-ups; and not the performance of the task, but the meaning of the task to the audience. What an audience sees in a film depends on the answer, in the film, to the individual's question, "What does this mean for me?"

IMPLICATIONS

This principle suggests that alternative structures of film form and treatment, such as cartoon or live photography, and dramatic or "straight" treatment, may not be effective in themselves. Rather, the effec-

---

* Those which are truly films, and not lectures combined with some more-or-less related pictures.

tiveness of any structural form or treatment depends on the way the context of action is developed in the film. The crucial cues for learning a particular subject or task should be identified and "built into" a film using a suitable treatment. Important scenes or interpretations must be made to appear important to the audience. A priori decisions on structural form and treatment, based entirely or primarily on artistic, aesthetic, dramatic, or entertainment preferences, are likely to involve time and expense in film production out of proportion to instructional results.

VII: PRINCIPLE OF SUBJECTIVITY

Individuals respond to a motion picture most efficiently when the pictorial content is subjective for them.

This principle applies to the camera position from which the content is photographed, to the roles characterized in the film, and to the treatment of the content of the picture. The subjective camera angle, that is, photographing the action from the eye-position of the learner, makes for better learning than photographing the action from the opposite position. The influence on attitudes, exerted by the prestige role of the principal character in a film and by audience identification with the social institution involved, such as a religious denomination, have been suggested in film research. Similar influence on factual learning has also been suggested, but the evidence is less reliable.

IMPLICATIONS

The principle of audience subjectivity emphasizes that it is desirable to show the errors the learner is likely to make in learning to perform a task. This application is contrary to the somewhat widely accepted doctrine that wrong methods ("negative instruction") should never be shown in instructional films.

For the film producer, the principle of audience subjectivity implies that the instructional content of a film be presented much the same way as the audience would normally view the actual subject, and in such a way that it can see itself in the film. An audience probably sees the subject and itself in terms of variables indicated in the Principle of Audience Variability. Creative film artistry requires not only a clear, workmanlike representation of the subject or lesson in a film, but also a representation of the subject or lesson that causes the audience to become involved in the subject and accept, with some degree of enthusiasm, the lesson of the film.

Theoretically, at least, an audience becomes involved in a motion picture to the extent it can identify itself with some or all of the following factors: the role of the protagonist or principal characters, the personality of the actors, the situations portrayed, the obstacles encountered, the mistakes to be avoided, and the successful resolution of the problem or task portrayed in the film.

A second implication has to do with the final approval of an instructional film for distribution or use. A film, acceptable on the basis of accuracy of subject matter and excellence of technical production, may be ineffective for the audience for which it is intended. The "expert" who has the authority of approval is likely to be "expert" in subject matter or photographic technique, rather than in a knowledge of the intended audience and the suitability of the instruction in the film for that audience. This latter type of "expertness" is a prerequisite for legitimate evaluation of a film prior to its release for distribution.

VIII: PRINCIPLE OF RATE OF DEVELOPMENT

Rate of development influences the instructional impact of a motion picture on its audience.

There has been a tendency on the part of film producers and film users to regard more learning in less time from films as an absolute goal, and, accordingly, to put a large amount of instructional material into a relatively short film. An audience's liking for entertainment films packed with fast action is often generalized and applied to instructional films. However, one of the differences between entertainment and instructional films is that the former is designed to please, whereas the latter is designed to instruct.

A slow rate of development in an instructional film is greatly superior to a rapid rate of development; in fact, a succinct (condensed) treatment of instruction material, particularly in perceptual-motor learning, may be very ineffective. It is clear from the research that learning from films takes time and effort, and that some of this time must be provided by the film itself.

IMPLICATIONS

This principle implies that instructional material must be presented in a film at a rate that is geared to the learning capabilities of the intended audience. In general, the rate of learning from instructional films is somewhat slower than is popularly believed.

IX: PRINCIPLE OF INSTRUCTIONAL VARIABLES

Established instructional techniques, properly built into the film or applied by the instructor, substantially increase the instructional effectiveness of a film.

Instructional motion pictures have been produced and used as if the traditional instructional techniques either did not apply to the motion picture as an instructional medium or were nothing more than the eccentricities of "old maid" teachers. But these techniques do apply, and the following is a list of the instructional techniques, which, if properly used, significantly increase learning from films:

1. Orienting an audience on what it is going to see or summarizing what it has seen.

2. Announcing that a check-up or test on learning will be given after the film.

3. Repeating the important points (with variation) _within_ the film. Showing the film more than once.

4. Conducting audience-participation (or practice) exercises during or after a film showing.

5. Informing the learner of how much he has learned. Giving test results or correct answers as soon as possible, or during the film if the practice is conducted during the film.

Research indicates that there is a cumulative effect in the combined use of some of these procedures. The two instructional procedures which have been repeatedly shown to have a critical effect on the amount of learning from a film are: (1) repetition, and (2) participation or practice of the relevant behavior, either during a film showing or following it. Discussion after a film and taking a test on the film material are both forms of practice or participation.

IMPLICATIONS

This principle implies that the instructional effectiveness of films can be increased during both the production and utilization stages by the deliberate inclusion and insightful application of well-known and proven instructional methods. But, these procedures should not be applied in a dull, dreary, or "stuffed-shirt," manner when making a film or using one. Without creative artistry, learning, which involves "suffering and undergoing" even under the best of circumstances, becomes a more difficult process.

This discussion suggests two ways of improving the structure and use of films: (1) insert the appropriate instructional techniques and methods directly into instructional films, especially when the instructor or the conditions of instruction are likely to be poor; and (2) train instructors in effective instructional techniques, and how to apply them to film instruction.

X: PRINCIPLE OF INSTRUCTOR LEADERSHIP

The leadership qualities of the instructor affect the efficiency with which his class will learn from the film or filmstrip.

The instructor is a leader of the group under instruction. As a leader, he plans, arranges, and manages instructional situations, materials, and procedures in a way that creates a favorable atmosphere for learning and stimulates the performance of the group. Instructors vary in their ability to create this atmosphere.

One of the most significant findings of film research is that the amount of learning from an instructional film depends not only on the film and on the audience, but also on the motivation and morale that result from the leadership qualities of the instructor. In one study this motivation and morale appeared to carry over to film learning when the instructor was actually not present during two or three separate showings of the films.

IMPLICATIONS

The principle of instructional leadership implies that films do not and cannot substitute completely for the good instructor, especially in the exercise of leadership functions, and that a well-trained instructor is one of the essential elements of effective film instruction. There is no evidence that the instructional methods or procedures used with films are any different from the methods used with other instructional media.

PART III. IN CONCLUSION, SOME OBSERVATIONS

The _five instructional values_ of appropriate films were clearly indicated in the research literature reviewed. The _ten principles of film influence_ have been suggested by and are at least partially supported by the accumulated film research of the past thirty-odd years. As research continues, as better techniques of observation and analysis are developed, and as theoretical systems provide new insights, these principles can be extended and modified as necessary. More creative and courageous minds may be attracted to the field of research as the interest in and uses of audio-visual media increase. Eventually, the paralyzing fear of imperfection that obstructs pioneer thinking and deprives research of the derring-do of scientific inquiry will diminish.

In drawing this review to a close, a few general observations on the influences of motion pictures and on ways of improving films so as to capitalize on this influence appear to be in order. These observations are made on the basis of our review of film research and our experiences in actual situations of instructional film planning, production, and use.

1. When NECESSARY and DESIRED learning is dependent upon a background of experience possessed to only a slight degree by the learner, the advantage of the film over other media, especially for rapid mass instruction, may be most evident.

A good film, with its subjective presentation designed to create involvement, can give the learner clear-cut notions of unfamiliar objects and actions in the world about him better than other methods of instruction, with the possible exception of television. This seems especially true in those situations where the individual must learn a series of motions in performing a complex skill; or where he must acquire a concept of certain action sequences such as might be involved in physical or chemical processes, biological development, social behavior, or tactical maneuvers; or where it is desired that he feel the atmosphere and spirit of the situation or "times" being portrayed.

2. The actual influence of a given motion picture is frequently less than its anticipated influence.

This holds for a single motion picture, and it holds for the influence of this one motion picture on information, opinions, attitudes, skills, and other behavior patterns. The effect upon information is likely to come closer to expectations than will that of the other types of learning outcomes. A notable exception was the pronounced success of certain versions of the 40mm breechblock films in teaching a somewhat puzzling assembly task (Jaspen, 1948).

There is very little or no evidence that the experience of a motion picture, in and of itself, is a sole determinant of certain thoughts, feelings, or actions. Instead, the evidence indicates that prior knowledge, attitudes, dispositions, and values relating to the subject of the film enter into the individual's interpretation of the message of the film and its meaning. Motion picture experiences, to be effective, generally require reinforcement by other related experiences and by appropriate social and psychological rewards.

The "adult discount" noted in connection with the Payne Fund studies of entertainment film influence in the early 1930's, may have increased during the past twenty years as defense against overstimulation from radio, movies, and more recently, television. The triviality of much of the content of these three media, plus the "entertain-me" attitude with which an audience approaches these media, may also tend to militate against optimum influence of even the best-made film.

It is evident from the research data that if strong attitudes are to be changed, information is to be understood, skills are to be taught, and action patterns aroused and structured, it is not enough simply to make and show one movie on the subject. The concept of a motion picture as a unique determinant of human behavior is a contradiction of the American concept of the dignity and integrity of the human personality.

3. If motion pictures are to teach, they must be made as tools of teaching, rather than merely as examples of cinema art.

Whatever the origin and whatever the explanation, it is evident in some instructional films that the concept of teaching and the role of the "teacher" have not dominated their production. Sooner or later, it seems that the making of an instructional film turns into a major movie production. Deep in the soul of many producers of films, including instructional films, is the bright hope of recognition and award at some Film Festival or by some Academy dedicated to the Art of the Cinema.

The solution to the problem of the Art of the Cinema probably does not lie in abortive attempts to eliminate the hope for recognition and award, but rather to base recognition and award on the effective performance of the teaching mission of the documentary, informational, training, and educational film.

4. If the effectiveness of motion pictures in instruction is to be increased, improvement must be made by all involved, not simply by the producer.

This observation assumes that effectiveness of motion pictures in instruction, i.e., in teaching, can be improved. The research evidence demonstrates that film effectiveness can be substantially improved at both the production and the use levels.

Two things are required to effect this improvement. First, the concept of the ultimate use of the film must dominate the entire planning, production, and distribution of the film. In turn, the concept of organized instruction, organized information, or organized training must constitute the frame of reference for thinking on the use of the film. If and when this is done, the motion picture can and will be accepted as a tool of teaching, rather than a determinant of human behavior. The emphasis is shifted, then, from the film as a movie production, to the film as one of the several instruments, devices, and procedures to be employed to achieve a desired change or enrichment of the behavior pattern of the target audience.

Second, much more and much better staff work in pre-production planning is required. An effective film is not likely to be produced unless and until its performance requirements are spelled out, its audience defined, and the use situation carefully described. There is not enough genius and sheer talent in the film production field to compensate entirely for inadequate staff work in pre-production planning and analysis, and for inadequate training in utilization.

GLOSSARY

(Simplified explanation of the technical terms used in the text)

ANALYSIS OF CO-VARIANCE---a statistical technique frequently used for the purpose of adjusting initial differences in means between experimental groups for relevant variables such as intelligence, age, etc. This makes valid comparisons possible when groups have not been matched beforehand.
See MATCHED GROUPS.

ANALYSIS OF VARIANCE---a statistical technique for evaluating the significance of differences among a set of means. The test of significance is generally made in terms of F-ratio (q.v.).

Analysis of variance enables the experimenter to determine the significance of differences between several interacting variables. The interaction is the measure of the joint effect of two variables. For example, if an experiment used two versions of a film as its first variable and two levels of intelligence as its second variable, a significant interaction might mean that the learning increment from a given film version was higher for one particular level of intelligence than for the other, while a reverse result might be true for the other film version. Thus, one of the film versions might result in a high learning increment for high level intelligence and a lower learning increment for low level intelligence, whereas the other film version might result in a high learning increment for low level intelligence and a lower increment for high level intelligence.

BI-SERIAL CORRELATION---See CORRELATION COEFFICIENT

CORRELATION CCEFFICIENT---a measure of the relationship between two variables. Correlation coefficient values approaching plus one indicate a high positive relationship; values approaching minus one indicate a high inverse relationship; values near zero indicate "no" relationship.

For example, a correlation coefficient of .88 between scores on an intelligence test and scores on a test of learning would indicate a very close positive relationship between levels of intelligence and amount of learning.

Different kinds of correlation coefficients are used depending on the nature of the variables. The most common include:

1. PEARSON PRODUCT-MOMENT CORRELATION (r)---where the variables are measured on a continuous scale and are linearly related; for example, scores on an intelligence test and scores on a test of learning.

2. BI-SERIAL CORRELATION---where the relationship between a two-category variable and a continuous variable is being measured. For example, a measure of the relationship between scores on a mechanical aptitude test and classification of workers as "satisfactory" or "unsatisfactory" could be established by use of a bi-serial correlation coefficient.

3. RANK ORDER CORRELATION---where the two variables are ranked in order of merit, rather than on a continuous scale. For example, a measure of the agreement between two judges' rankings of a series of films could be established by use of a rank order correlation coefficient.

CRITICAL RATIO (CR)---the difference between two comparable statistics divided by the standard error of that difference.

For example, critical ratio may be used to measure the significance of the difference between two means. In such a case, the critical ratio would be the ratio of the difference between the two means to the standard error of the difference.

Ordinarily, a critical ratio of 1.96 (or larger) would indicate that a difference between two means would occur by chance only five times (or less) out of 100. Therefore, a critical ratio of 1.96 or larger is usually considered as evidence that the difference did not occur by chance.
See LEVELS OF CONFIDENCE.

F-RATIO---a test of significance which is more general than the t-ratio (q.v.). Whereas t-ratio is used to test the significance of difference between two means, F-ratio is an over-all test of significance of differences among any number of means. (F-ratios are evaluated in Snedecor's Tables of Distributions.)

LEVELS OF CONFIDENCE---statistical evaluations of the results of an experiment. For example, a difference between two mean scores which is significant at the five percent level of confidence would occur by chance only five times in 100; a difference significant at the 1.0 percent level of confidence would occur by chance only one time in 100; and a difference significant at the 0.1 percent level would occur by chance only one time in 1000.

In general, results are considered significant if they reach the five percent level of confidence or better.
See CRITICAL RATIO.

MATCHED GROUPS---groups which have been equated on the basis of one or more independent variables which are believed to be relevant to the variable being investigated. For example, in experiments comparing different methods of teaching, groups may be matched on the basis of age, intelligence, sex, etc.

When groups are matched with regard to a given variable, each of the matched groups will have the same mean and the same standard deviation on the measure of the variable.
See STANDARD DEVIATION.

PERCEPTUAL-MOTOR SKILL---a performance involving sensory-motor processes and their coordination in executing an action or series of actions; for example, typing, handwriting, driving, athletic skills, etc. The concept of perceptual-motor skill is used to replace the more conventional term "motor skill" which fails to signify adequately the sensory-perceptual processes which are parts of performance learning.

r-----symbol for correlation coefficient (q.v.).

RANK ORDER CORRELATION---See CORRELATION COEFFICIENT

RELIABILITY OF RESULTS---Differences are generally assumed to be reliable when their statistical significance reaches a five percent level of confidence or better.
See LEVELS OF CONFIDENCE.

REMINISCENT EFFECT---an improvement in learning with the passage of time without intervening intentional practice.

RETROACTIVE INHIBITION---the tendency for recent learning to impair recall of previous learning.

STANDARD DEVIATION (SD or Sigma)---a measure of the variability, or spread, of individual scores from a mean. (The square of the standard deviation is known as variance.) For large samples, normally distributed, the range of measures is usually from 3 SD's below the mean to 3 SD's above the mean. For example, if the mean intelligence test score were 100 for a large normally distributed sample, and the SD were 15, we would expect very few, if any, scores to be above 145 or below 55.

Values which are 1.96 SD's (or more) removed from the mean (in a normal distribution) will occur with a relative frequency of five times (or less) in 100.

STANDARD ERROR (SE)---a measure of the variability of a statistic (q.v.) from sample to sample. Standard error enters into the calculation of critical ratio. Sometimes the significance of the difference between two statistics is expressed in terms of the standard error of the difference between the two statistics. For example, instead of calling his statistic a critical ratio, an investigator may simply report that the difference is greater than, say, 2.5 SE's. Differences which exceed 1.96 SE's are usually considered statistically significant.

STATISTIC---any measure computed from a sample; for instance, a mean, standard deviation, per cent, etc.

STATISTICAL SIGNIFICANCE---See LEVELS OF CONFIDENCE

TEST RELIABILITY---the consistency with which a test measures something. Test reliability is often measured in terms of the correlation coefficient (q.v.) between the scores made on two administrations of the same test or between scores on two comparable forms of the same test.

TEST VALIDITY---the extent to which a test measures what it is designed to measure. Ordinarily, test validity is measured by the correlation coefficient between a test and some outside criterion. For example, the validity of a test to select efficient truck drivers may be established by comparing scores on the test with the accident rates of the individuals taking the test.

t-RATIO---a measure of the significance of the results of an experiment. t-ratio was developed for a situation where the number of cases is small. As the number of cases becomes indefinitely large, t-ratio becomes identical with critical ratio (q.v.).

VARIANCE (SD^2)---See STANDARD DEVIATION

REFERENCES

ABBOTT, MARY A. 1937. A sampling of high school likes and dislikes in motion pictures. Sec. Educ. 6, 74-76.

ADAMS, T. 1939. Motion pictures in physical education: teaching the tennis serve with school-made films. New York: Bureau of Publications, Teachers College, Columbia Univ.

ADLER, M. J. 1937. Art and prudence. New York: Longmans, Green.

ALBERTSON, F. W. & REED, H. B. 1931. The relative value of the motion picture film as a teaching device in the field of agriculture. Internat. Rev. educ. Cinematography, 3, 859-865.

ALEXANDER, V. W. 1950. The contribution of selected instructional motion pictures to achievement in varying school situations. Unpublished Doctoral thesis, University of Nebraska.

AMERICAN COUNCIL ON EDUCATION, COMMITTEE ON MOTION PICTURES IN EDUCATION. 1942. Selected educational motion pictures: a descriptive encyclopaedia. Washington, D. C.: American Council on Education.

AMERICAN COUNCIL ON EDUCATION, COMMITTEE ON MOTION PICTURES IN EDUCATION. 1943. Films for America at war: supplement #1 to selected educational motion pictures. Washington, D. C.: American Council on Education.

AMERICAN EDUCATIONAL RESEARCH ASSOCIATION. 1948. Psychological research in the armed forces. Rev. Educ. Res., 18, 525-655, Whole No. 6, (Special Edition).

ANDERSON, I. H. & FAIRBANKS, G. 1937. Common and differential factors in reading vocabulary and hearing vocabulary. J. educ. Res., 30, 317-325.

ARNOLD, R. W. 1932. A study of the effectiveness of motion pictures in teaching industrial arts in junior high school. Unpublished Master's thesis, A & M, College of Texas.

ARNSPIGER, V. C. 1933. Measuring the effectiveness of sound pictures as teaching aids. Teachers College Contributions to Education, No. 565. New York: Teachers College, Columbia Univ.

ASH, P. 1949. The relative effectiveness of massed versus spaced film presentation. Technical Report SDC 269-7-3. State College, Pa.: Pennsylvania State College, Instructional Film Research Program.

BAKER, W. K. 1940. An experimental study of effectiveness of motion pictures in teaching general science. Unpublished Master's thesis, Wittenberg College.

BARTRUFF, H. L. 1938. The use of slow motion pictures in teaching tumbling. Unpublished Master's thesis, Univ. So. Calif.

BATESON, G. & RUESCH, J. 1951. Communication: the social matrix of psychiatry. New York: W. W. Norton & Co., Inc.

BELL, R., CAIN, L. F., & LAMOREAUX, LILLIAN A. 1941. Motion pictures in a modern curriculum. A report on the use of films in the Santa Barbara schools. Washington, D. C.: American Council on Education.

BENTLEY, R. R. 1949. An experimental evaluation of the relative effectiveness of certain audio-visual aids in vocational agriculture. J. exp. Educ., 17, 373-381.

BLATZ, W. E. 1936. What do children think of movies? N. W. G. PERIMAN (ED.), The Movies on Trial. New York: Macmillan.

BLUMER, H. 1933. Movies and conduct. New York: Macmillan.

BLUMER, H. & HAUSER, P. M. 1933. Movies, delinquency, and crime. New York: Macmillan.

BODE, BARBARA. 1941. An experiment in propaganda. J. adult Educ., 13, 365-370.

BOLES, J. M. 1946. A study of visual aids in teaching safety to railway maintenance of way employees. Unpublished Doctoral thesis, Univ. Ky.

BRECHBILL, EDITH. 1941. A study of a microprojector as a teaching aid. Sci. Educ., 25, 215-218.

BRENNER, H. R., WALTER, JEANETTE S., & KURTZ, A. K. 1949. The effects of inserted questions and statements on film learning. Progress Report No. 10. State College, Pa.: Pennsylvania State College, Instructional Film Research Program.

BROOKER, F. E. 1946. Training films for industry: final report on the war training program of the Division of Visual Aids for war training. U. S. Office of Education, Bull. No. 13, 1946. Washington, D. C.: Government Printing Office.

BROOKER, F. E. & HERRINGTON, E. H. 1941. Students make motion pictures. Washington, D. C.: American Council on Education.

BROWN, H. E. 1928. Motion picture or film slide? Sch. Sci. and Math., 28, 517-526.

BROWN, H. S. & MESSERSMITH, L. 1948. An experiment in teaching tumbling with and without motion pictures. Res. Quart. Amer. Ass. Hlth., 19, 304-307.

BROWN, J. W. 1947. A comparison of verbal and projected verbal-pictorial tests as measures of ability to apply science principles. Unpublished Doctoral thesis, Univ. Chicago.

BRUMBAUGH, W. D. 1940. The use of motion pictures in teaching current events. Unpublished Master's thesis, Univ. Colo.

BUEGEL, H. F. 1940. The effect of introducing ideational elements into perceptual-motor learning. J. exp. Psychol., 27, 111-124.

BURKHARD, SISTER M. WENDELINE, O.S.B. 1939. Primary school children's interest in the content of pictures. Unpublished Master's thesis, Univ. Notre Dame.

BUSWELL, G. T. 1935. How people look at pictures. Chicago: Univ. of Chicago Press.

CAMERON, V. E. 1933. A comparison between the use of motion pictures and the question-discussion method in teaching high school physics. Unpublished Master's thesis, Univ. So. Calif.

CANTRIL, H., GAUDET, HAZEL, & HERZOG, HERTA. 1940. The invasion from Mars. Princeton, N. J.: Princeton Univ. Press.

CARPENTER, C. R. 1948. Requirements of research on instructional films. Hollywood Quarterly, III, 3, 262-266.

CARPENTER, C. R. 1948. Challenge for research. Educ. Screen, 27, 119-121.

CARPENTER, C. R. & GREENHILL, L. P. 1950. Using instructional films effectively. Educational Screen XXIX, 8, 331-333.

CARSON, D. 1947. "The American Way of Life" as portrayed in filmstrips: an experiment in visual education. Research Publication No. 2. Scottish Educational Film Association. Glasgow, Scotland.

CHARTERS, W. W. 1933. Motion pictures and youth. New York: Macmillan.

CLARK, C. C. 1932. Sound motion pictures as an aid in classroom teaching. Unpublished Doctoral thesis, New York Univ.

CLARK, C. C. 1933. Effectiveness of sound films as aids in classroom teaching. Educ., 53, 337-342.

CLARK, C. C. 1933. The talking movie and students' interests. Sci. Educ., 17, 312-320.

COCHRAN, B. 1940. Films on war and American policy. Washington, D. C.: American Council on Education.

COCKRUM, A. E. 1932. An experimental study of the motion picture film as an aid to teaching general science. Unpublished Master's thesis, Univ. Ill.

COMMISSION ON HUMAN RELATIONS, PROGRESSIVE EDUCATION ASSOCIATION. 1939. The human relations series of films. New York: Progressive Education Association.

COMMONWEALTH OFFICE OF EDUCATION. 1950. Research report number 4: the effective use of sound films. Sydney, Australia: Commonwealth Office of Education.

CONRAD, H. & JONES, H. 1929. Psychological studies of motion pictures: III, fidelity of report as a measure of adult intelligence. Univ. Calif. Publications in Psychology, Vol. 3, 245-276.

CONSITT, FRANCES. 1931. The value of films in history teaching. London: G. Bell & Sons, Ltd.

DALE, E. 1935. Children's attendance at motion pictures. New York: Macmillan.

DALE, E. 1935. The content of motion pictures. New York: Macmillan.

DALE, E., DUNN, F. W., HOBAN, C. F. & SCHNEIDER, E. 1937. Motion Pictures in Education. New York: H. W. Wilson Co.

DALE, E., FINN, J. D., & HOBAN, C. F., JR. 1949. Research on audio-visual materials. Nat. Soc. for the Study of Educ. 48th Yearb., Pt. 1. Audio-visual materials of instruction. Chicago: Univ. of Chicago Press.

DALE, E., FINN, J. D., & HOBAN, C. F., JR. 1950. Audio-visual materials. Summary in Encyclopedia of Educ. Research. New York: Macmillan.

DALE, E. & HOBAN, C. F., JR. 1941. Visual education. Summary in Encyclopedia of Educ. Research. New York: Macmillan.

DALY, G. M., BRUGGER, H. E., & ANDERSON, K. E. 1947. America: an experiment. J. educ. Res., 41, 222-229.

DASH, A. J. 1935. Effectiveness of sound film in changing knowledge of and interest in chemistry. Unpublished Master's thesis, College of the City of New York.

DAVIS, HELEN C. 1932. Specific values of educational films used as supplementary aids. Unpublished Doctoral thesis, Univ. Chicago.

DAVIS, R. L. 1923. The application of motion pictures to education. Unpublished Doctoral thesis, New York Univ.

DEVEREUX, F. L. 1933. The educational talking picture (esp. Ch. VI). Chicago: Univ. of Chicago Press.

DOLLARD, J. 1943. Fear in battle. New Haven, Conn.: Institute of Human Relations, Yale University.

DOOB, L. W. 1948. Public opinion and propaganda. New York: Henry Holt.

DUNKERLEY, G. 1941. An experiment with films: Parts I and II. J. Educ., 73, 306-308, 348-349.

DYSINGER, W. S. & RUCKMICK, C. A. 1933. The emotional responses of children to the motion picture situation. New York: Macmillan.

EADS, LAURA K. & STOVER, E. M. 1936. The educational talking picture in teacher training. Unpublished report, Erpi Picture Consultants, Inc., (now Encyclopedia Britannica Films, Inc., Chicago, Ill.)

EATON, REBA E. 1929. Motion picture preferences of Passaic High School. On file in English Seminar Room, Teachers College, Columbia Univ.

EDMAN, M. 1940. Attendance of school pupils and adults at moving pictures. Sch. Rev., 48, 753-763.

EICHEL, C. G. 1940. Experiment to determine the most effective method of teaching current history. J. exp. Educ., 9, 37-40.

EINBECKER, W. F. 1933. Comparison of verbal accompaniments to films. Sch. Rev., 41, 185-192.

ELLIOTT, G. M. (ED.). 1948. Film and education. New York: Philosophical Library.

EVANS, C. F. 1942. Studies in visual education: Effects of title and immediate test responses. Unpublished Master's thesis, State Univ. Iowa.

EXTON, W. 1947. Audio-visual aids to instruction. New York: McGraw-Hill.

FLAHERTY, R. 1950. Robert Flaherty talking. In R. MANVELL (ED.), The cinema 1950. Harmondsworth, Middlesex, England: Penguin Books, Pp. 11-29.

FORD, W. E., JR. 1947. Is note taking when viewing motion pictures effective in high school science? Educ., 68, 125-127.

FORMAN, H. J. 1933. Our movie-made children. New York: Macmillan.

FREEMAN, F. N. (ED.). 1924. Visual education. Chicago: Univ. of Chicago Press.

FREEMAN, F. N. & HOEFER, CAROLYN. 1931. An experimental study of the influence of motion picture films on behavior. J. educ. Psychol., 22, 411-425.

FREEMAN, F. N., REEDER, E. H., & THOMAS, JEAN A. 1924. An experiment to study the effectiveness of a motion picture film which consists largely of tables, maps, and charts, as a means of teaching facts or giving abstract information. In F. N. FREEMAN (ED.), Visual education. Chicago: Univ. of Chicago Press. Pp. 258-274.

FREEMAN, F. N., SHAW, LENA A., & WALKER, D. E. 1924. The use of a motion picture film to teach position and penholding in handwriting. In F. N. FREEMAN (ED.), Visual education. Chicago: Univ. of Chicago Press. Pp. 282-309.

FREEMAN, G. L. 1931. The spread of neuro-muscular activity during mental work. J. gen. Psychol., 5, 479-494.

GATES, GEORGIANA S. 1923. An experimental study of the growth of social perception. J. educ. Psychol., 14, 449-461.

GATTO, F. M. 1933. Experimental studies on the use of visual aids in the teaching of geography. Pittsburgh Schools, 8, 60-110; (excerpts in Elem. Sch. J., 1934, 34, 494-495.)

GIBBS, D. 1925. An experiment as to economy of time in instruction by use of motion pictures. Educ. Screen, 4, 520-526.

GIBSON, J. J. (ED.). 1947. Motion picture testing and research, Report No. 7, Army Air Forces Aviation Psychology Program Research Reports. Washington, D. C.: Government Printing Office.

GIBSON, J. J. 1950. The perception of the visual world. Boston: Houghton Mifflin.

GOLDSTEIN, H. 1940. Reading and listening comprehension at various controlled rates. Contributions to Education, No. 821. New York: Teachers College, Columbia Univ.

GOODMAN, D. J. 1942. Comparative effectiveness of pictorial teaching aids. Unpublished Doctoral thesis, New York Univ.

GOODMAN, D. J. 1942A. Comparative effectiveness of pictorial teaching materials. Educ. Screen, 21, 358-359, 371.

GRAY, H. A. 1940. Pupil evaluation of sound film components. Elem. Sch. J., 40, 507-517.

GREENHILL, L. P. 1950. Research programme. U. S. A. Visual Education (London), I, II.

GREENHILL, L. P. & TYO, J. 1949. Instructional film production, utilization and research in Great Britain, Canada and Australia. Technical Report SDC 269-7-1. State College, Pa.: Pennsylvania State College, Instructional Film Research Program.

GUITZEIT, C. L. 1937. Teaching an abstract concept in science by means of the motion picture. Educ. Screen, 16, 147-148, 150-151.

HACKETT, R. J. 1931. An experiment with motion pictures in learning zoology. Unpublished Master's thesis, Univ. Pittsburgh.

HALL, W. E. & CUSHING, J. R. 1947. The relative value of three methods of presenting learning material. J. Psychol., 24, 57-62.

HALL, W. J. 1936. A study of three methods of teaching science with classroom films. Sch. Sci. Math., 36, 968-970.

HALSEY, J. H. 1936. An experiment in geography teaching. Educ. Screen, 15, 137-140.

HANSEN, J. E. 1933. The effect of educational motion pictures upon the retention of informational learning. J. exp. Educ., 2, 1-4.

HANSEN, J. E. 1936. The verbal accompaniment of the educational film; the recorded voice vs. the voice of the classroom teacher. J. exp. Educ., 5, 1-6.

HANSEN, J. E. 1939. A study of the comparative effectiveness of three methods of using motion pictures in teaching. Unpublished Doctoral thesis, Univ. Wis.

HANSEN, J. E. 1940. A study of the comparative effectiveness of three methods of using motion pictures in teaching. Educ. Screen, 19, 55-57, 74-77, 97-98.

HARAP, H. 1943. The motion picture as communication. Social Educ., 7, 19-21.

HARLOW, H. E. 1949. The formation of learning sets. Psychol. Rev., 56, 51-65.

HEIDGERKEN, LORETTA E. 1948. An experimental study to measure the contribution of motion pictures and slide films to learning certain units in the course, Introduction to Nursing Arts. Unpublished Doctoral thesis, Univ. Ind.

HENNEN, LOUISE R. 1936. A study of the effect on children's choices of adding color to illustration. Unpublished Master's thesis, West Virginia Univ.

HICKS, G. 1946. Small town. New York: Macmillan.

HINMAN, S. T. 1931. The value of pre-knowledge of tests in stimulating pupils to observe and retain facts presented in motion pictures. Unpublished Master's thesis, New York Univ.

HIRSCH, R. S. 1949. Using motion pictures in teaching English drama. Unpublished Master's thesis, Stanford Univ.

HOAR, F. B. 1932. An experiment with motion pictures in health instruction. Unpublished Master's thesis, Univ. Pittsburgh.

HOBAN, C. F., JR. 1937. Experimental research in instructional films. Part V in DALE, DUNN, HOBAN, SCHNEIDER, Motion Pictures in Education. New York: H. W. Wilson Co.

HOBAN, C. F., JR. 1942. Focus on learning. Washington, D. C.: American Council on Education.

HOBAN, C. F., JR. 1946. Movies that teach. New York: Dryden Press.

HOBAN, C. F., JR. 1949. Some aspects of learning from films. Incidental Report No. 2. State College, Pa.: Pennsylvania State College, Instructional Film Research Program.

HOBAN, C. F., JR. & VAN ORMER, E. B. 1950. Practical principles governing the production and utilization of sound motion pictures. Special Report No. 1. State College, Pa.: Pennsylvania State College, Instructional Film Research Program.

HOEFER, CAROLYN & KEITH, EDNA. 1924. An experimental comparison of the methods of oral and film instruction in the field of health education. In F. N. FREEMAN (ED.), Visual education. Chicago: Univ. of Chicago Press. Pp. 346-376.

HOLADAY, P. W. & STODDARD, G. D. 1933. Getting ideas from the movies. New York: Macmillan.

HOLLINGSHEAD, A. B. 1949. Elmtown's youth. New York: John Wiley & Sons.

HOLLIS, A. P. 1924. The effectiveness of the motion picture used as an introduction or as the summary. In F. N. FREEMAN (ED.), Visual education. Chicago: Univ. of Chicago Press. Pp. 275-281.

HOLLIS, A. P. 1924A. The effectiveness of the motion picture, demonstration by the teacher, and oral instruction in teaching cooking. In F. N. FREEMAN (ED.), Visual education. Chicago: Univ. of Chicago Press. Pp. 339-341.

HOLLONQUIST, T. & SUCHMAN, E. A. 1944. Listening to the listener. In P. F. LAZARSFELD and F. STANTON (ED.), Radio research 1942-43. New York: Duell, Sloan & Pearce. Pp. 266-274, 307-334.

HOUGHTON, G. H. 1931. The effect of the use of motion picture titles on pupil's study of general science material. Unpublished Master's thesis, Univ. Pittsburgh.

HOVLAND, C. I., LUMSDAINE, A. A. & SHEFFIELD, F. D. 1949. Experiments on mass communication. Princeton, N. J.: Princeton Univ. Press.

INSTRUCTIONAL FILM RESEARCH PROGRAM. 1949. Progress Report No. 11-12. State College, Pa.: Pennsylvania State College, Instructional Film Research Program.

IRWIN, W. E. 1936. An experiment with auditorium motion pictures in the junior high school. Unpublished Master's thesis, Univ. Pittsburgh.

JAMES, H. W. 1924. The relative effectiveness of six forms of lesson presentation: film, lecture, still picture, film-lecture, film-music, and reading, with particular emphasis on the suitability of different types of material for film presentation. In F. N. FREEMAN (ED.), Visual education. Chicago: Univ. of Chicago Press. Pp. 190-228.

JARDINE, A. 1938. The experimental use of visual aids in teaching beginning reading. Educ. Screen, 17, 220-222.

JASPEN, N. 1948. Especially designed motion pictures: I. assembly of the 40mm breechblock. Progress Report No. 9. State College, Pa.: Pennsylvania State College Research Program.

JASPEN, N. 1950. Effects on training of experimental film variables, study II: verbalization, "how-it-works," nomenclature, audience participation, and succinct treatment. Progress Report No. 14-15-16. State College, Pa.: Pennsylvania State College, Instructional Film Research Program.

JAYNE, C. D. 1944. A study of the learning and retention of materials presented by lecture and by silent film. J. educ. Res., 38, 47-58.

JOHNSON, D. A. 1949. An experimental study of the effectiveness of films and filmstrips in teaching geometry. J. exp. Educ., 17, 363-372.

JONES, H. E., CONRAD, H., & HORN, A. 1928. Psychological studies of motion pictures: II. observation and recall as a function of age. Univ. Calif. Publ. Psychol., 3, 225-243.

KINDER, J. S. 1942. Visual aids in education. Rev. Ed. Res., 12, No. 3, Ch. VI.

KISHLER, J. P. 1950. The effects of prestige and identification factors on attitude restructuring and learning from sound films. Progress Report No. 14-15-16, State College, Pa.: Pennsylvania State College, Instructional Film Research Program.

KLEITMAN, N. 1945. The effect of motion pictures on body temperature. Science, 101, 507-508.

KNOWLTON, D. C. & TILTON, J. W. 1929. Motion pictures in history teaching. New Haven, Conn.: Yale Univ. Press.

KNOWLTON, D. C. & TILTON, J. W. 1932. Auditorium versus classroom showing of motion pictures in history teaching. J. educ. Psychol., 23, 663-670.

KRASKER, A. 1941. A critical analysis of the use of educational motion pictures by two methods. Unpublished Doctoral thesis, Boston Univ.

KRASKER, A. 1943. A critical analysis of the use of educational motion pictures by two methods. Sci. Ed., 27, 19-22.

KURTZ, A. K., WALTER, JEANETTE S. & BRENNER, H. R. 1950. The effects of inserted questions and statements on film learning. Technical Report SDC-269-7-16. State College, Pa.: Pennsylvania State College, Instructional Film Research Program.

LACY, J. V. 1919. The relative value of motion pictures as an educational agency. Teach. Coll. Rec., 20, 452-465.

LAPP, C. J. 1939. Some experiments on the teaching value of sound films in college physics. Amer. Physics Teacher (now Amer. J. Physics), 7, 172-173.

LAPP, C. J. 1939A. The effectiveness of a sound motion picture in college physics. Amer. Physics Teacher (now Amer. J. Physics), 7, 224-230.

LAPP, C. J. 1941. Teaching effectiveness of the sound motion picture, The Electron. Amer. J. Physics, 9, 112-116.

LARSEN, B. P. & FEDER, D. D. 1940. Common and differential factors in reading and hearing comprehension. J. educ. Psychol., 31, 241-252.

LARSON, L. C. 1940. The relation of cognitive and affective factors to suspend judgment. Unpublished manuscript, Univ. Minn.: Committee on Educational Research.

LASHLEY, K. S., & WATSON, J. B. 1922. A psychological study of motion pictures in relation to venereal disease campaigns. Washington, D. C.: United States Interdepartmental Social Hygiene Board.

LATHROP, C. W., JR. 1949. Contributions of film introductions to learning from instructional films. Progress Report No. 13. State College, Pa.: Pennsylvania State College, Instructional Film Research Program.

LAZARSFELD, P. F. & KENDALL, PATRICIA L. 1948. Radio listening in America. New York: Prentice Hall.

LINDSAY, W. F. 1949. The film and composition, Research Publication No. 4, The Scottish Educational Film Association. Glasgow, Scotland.

LOATS, H. A. 1942. The effect of one and two showings of educational films. Unpublished Master's thesis, State Univ. Iowa.

LOCKHART, JEANNE A. 1942. The value of the motion picture as an instructional device in learning a motor skill. Unpublished Doctoral thesis, Univ. Wis.

LOCKHART, JEANNE A. 1944. The value of the motion picture as an instructional device in learning a motor skill. Res. Quart. Amer. Assoc. Health, Rec., and Phys. Educ., 15, 181-187.

LONG, A. L. 1945. Recent experimental investigations dealing with effectiveness of audio-visual modes of presentation. Educ. Adm. Supervis., 31, 65-78.

LONG, A. L. 1946. The influence of color on acquisition and retention as evidenced by the use of sound films. Unpublished Doctoral thesis, Univ. Colo.

LUCKIESH, M. 1944. Light, vision, and seeing. New York: Van Nostrand.

LUMSDAINE, L. L. 1947. Experimental research and the improvement of teaching films. Educ. Screen, 26, 254.

LUMSDAINE, A. A. 1949. Ease of learning with pictorial and verbal symbols. Unpublished Doctoral thesis, Stanford Univ.

McCLUSKY, F. D. 1924. Comparisons of different methods of visual instruction. In F. N. FREEMAN (ED.), Visual education. Chicago: Univ. of Chicago Press. Pp. 83-166.

McCLUSKY, F. D. & McCLUSKY, H. Y. 1924. Comparison of motion pictures, slides, stereographys, and demonstration as a means of teaching how to make a reed mat and a pasteboard box. In F. N FREEMAN (ED.), Visual education. Chicago: Univ. of Chicago Press. Pp. 310-334.

McCLUSKY, F. D. & McCLUSKY, H. Y. 1924A. Comparison of six modes of presentation of the subject-matter contained in a film on the iron and steel industry and one on lumbering in the north woods. In F. N. FREEMAN (ED.), Visual education. Chicago: Univ. of Chicago Press. Pp. 229-257.

McCLUSKY, H. Y. 1924. An analytical study of the content of educational motion picture films. In F. N. FREEMAN (ED.), Visual education. Chicago: Univ. of Chicago Press. Pp. 377-388.

McCOWEN, M. C. 1940. A controlled experiment in visual education in general science. Educ. Screen, 19, 143-146, 172-173.

McGEOCH, J. A. 1942. The psychology of human learning. New York: Longmans, Green.

McINTOSH, D. M. 1947. A comparison of the efficacy of sound and silent films as teaching aids. Research Publication No. 3 Scottish Educational Film Association, Glasgow, Scotland.

McLEAN, W. P. 1930. A comparison of the effectiveness of colored and uncolored pictures. Unpublished thesis, Univ. Chicago.

McNEMAR, Q. 1946. Opinion-attitude methodology. Psychol. Bull., 43, 289-374.

McNEMAR, Q. 1949. Psychological statistics. New York: John Wiley & Sons.

McTAVISH, C. L. 1949. Effect of repetitive film presentations on learning. In Progress Report No. 13, State College, Pa.: Pennsylvania State College, Instructional Film Research Program.

MAHONEY, A. & HARSHMAN, H. L. 1938. Sound-film experiment with handicapped and retarded pupils. Educ. Screen, 18, 359-360, 373.

MANEVAL, R. V. 1939. The relative value of sound motion pictures and study sheets in science teaching. Sci. Educ., 23, 83-86; also unpublished Doctoral field study, No. 1, 1940, Colo. State Coll. of Ed., with same title.

MANEVAL, R. V. 1939A. The relative value of sound motion pictures and study sheets in science teaching (Field Study No. 2). J. exp. Educ., 8, 39-43; also unpublished Doctoral field study, No. 2, 1940, Colo. State Coll. of Ed., entitled, A further study of the relative value of sound motion pictures and study sheets in science teaching.

MANEVAL, R. V. 1940. The relative value of sound and silent motion pictures in science teaching. Unpublished Doctoral field study No. 3, Colo. State Coll. of Ed.

MANEVAL, R. V. 1940A. The relative value of sound and silent motion pictures in science teaching. Sci. Educ., 24, 361-364.

MARCHANT, J. (ED.). 1925. The cinema in education. London: G. Allen & Unwin, Ltd.

MASON, W. L. 1934. A study of the status of motion picture films in education. Unpublished Master's thesis, Univ. Va.

MAY, M. A. 1946. The psychology of learning from demonstration films. J. educ. Psychol., 37, 1-12.

MAY, M. A. 1947. Educational projects, Educational Screen, 1947, 26, 200-201, 232.

MEAD, C. D. 1927. Visual vs. teaching methods - an experiment. Educ. Adm. Supervis., 13, 505-519.

MENDENHALL, J. E. & MENDENHALL, MARCIA E. 1933. The influence of familiarity upon children's preferences for pictures and poems. Lincoln School Research Studies. New York: Teachers College, Columbia Univ.

MIHALKO, MADELINE M. 1942. The use of films in musical education. The School (Secondary Edition), 31, 222-223.

MILES, J. R. & SPAIN, C. R. 1947. <u>Audio-visual aides in the armed services</u>. Washington, D. C.: American Council on Education.

MILLER, J. M. 1932. Visual education experiments give tangible results. <u>J. Engineering Educ.</u>, 22, 721-722.

MITCHELL, ALICE M. 1929. <u>Children and movies</u>. Chicago: Univ. of Chicago Press.

MITCHELL, ALICE M. 1929A. Movies children like. <u>Survey</u>, 63, 213-216.

MOCK, A. A. 1929. The relative values of the use of motion pictures with bright and dull children. Unpublished Master's thesis, Univ. So. Calif.

MOLEY, R. 1928. <u>Are we movie made?</u> New York: Macy-Masius.

MOLYNEAUX, MARY LOUISE. 1939. A content evaluation of motion picture films for use in the teaching of elementary science. Unpublished Master's thesis, Univ. Pittsburgh.

MONTELBANO, D. 1941. The production and experimental evaluation by the teacher of a series of 16mm. silent films for teaching mathematics in grade 7A as outlined in the syllabus for the New York City junior high school. Unpublished Doctoral thesis, New York Univ.

MOUNT, J. N. 1931. The learning value of motion pictures in high school physics as compared to the use of supplemental textbooks. Unpublished Master's thesis, Univ. Wash.

NATIONAL COUNCIL FOR SOCIAL STUDIES. 1947. 18th Yearb. Audio-visual materials and methods in the social studies. Washington, D. C.: National Education Association.

NATIONAL COUNCIL OF TEACHERS OF MATHEMATICS. 1945. 18th Yearb. Semi-sensory aids in the teaching of mathematics. Washington, D. C.: National Education Association.

NATIONAL SOCIETY FOR THE STUDY OF EDUCATION. 1949. 48th Yearb. Pt. I, Audio-visual materials of instruction. Chicago: Univ. of Chicago Press.

NELSON, H. E. 1949. The relative contributions to learning of video and audio elements in films. In <u>Progress Report No. 13</u>. State College, Pa.: Pennsylvania State College, Instructional Film Research Program.

NELSON, H. E. & MOLL, K. R. 1950. Comparisons of the audio and video elements of instructional films. <u>Technical Report SDC 269-7-18</u>. State College, Pa.: Pennsylvania State College, Instructional Film Research Program.

NEU, D. M. 1950. The effect of attention-gaining devices on film-mediated learning. <u>Progress Report No. 14-15-16</u>. State College, Pa.: Pennsylvania State College, Instructional Film Research Program.

NOEL, F. W. 1940. <u>Projecting motion pictures in the classroom</u>. Washington, D. C.: American Council on Education.

NORA, F. F. 1941. The effect of a liberal persuasive film in shifting attitudes of a group of journalism students. Univ. of Minn., Studies in Higher Educ., Biennial Report of the Committee on Educ. Res. for 1938-40. Pp. 96-97.

NORFORD, C. A. 1949. Contributions of film summaries to learning from instructional films. In <u>Progress Report No. 13</u>. State College, Pa.: Pennsylvania State College, Instructional Film Research Program.

PARK, J. J. 1943. A study of the vocabulary and comprehension difficulties of sound motion pictures. Unpublished Doctoral thesis, Univ. Mich.

PARK, J. J. 1944. Analysis of the verbal accompaniment to classroom films. <u>Sch. Rev.</u>, 52, 420-426.

PARK, J. J. 1945. Vocabulary and comprehension difficulties of sound motion pictures. <u>Sch. Rev.</u>, 53, 154-161.

PARK, J. J. & STEPHENSON, RUTH. 1938. A teaching experiment with visual aids. Education, 58, 498-500.

PERKINS, L. N. 1939. A comparative study of teaching rote songs with the use of visual aids as compared to the method now used. Unpublished Master's thesis, Okla. A & M.

PERRY, C. A. 1923. The attitude of high school students toward motion pictures. New York: National Board of Review of Motion Pictures.

PETERS, C. C. & VAN VOORHIS, W. R. 1935, 1940. Statistical procedures and their mathematical bases. New York: McGraw-Hill.

PETERS, FLORENCE M. 1938. Are visual aids and other enriched materials superior to the textbook methods in teaching geography? Unpublished Master's thesis, La. State Univ.

PETERSON, J. A. 1950. The effectiveness of selected motion pictures in changing the beliefs of Nebraska secondary students relative to the United Nations and its activities. Unpublished Doctoral thesis, University of Nebraska.

PETERSON, RUTH C. & THURSTONE, L. L. 1933. Motion pictures and the social attitudes of children. New York: Macmillan.

PHILLIPS, B. E. 1941. The relationship between certain phases of kinesthesis and performance during the early stages of acquiring two perceptuo-motor skills. Res. Quart. Amer. Ass. Hlth. Phys. Educ. & Rec., 12, 571-586.

PHILLIPS, H. W. 1930. An experimental study in the use of motion pictures in the classroom. Unpublished Master's thesis, Univ. Pittsburgh.

POLAND, E. I. 1933. The efficiency of the motion picture program in a junior high school: Part VI. Unpublished Master's thesis, Boston Univ.

PORTER, ELFA McW. 1930. The curve of retention in moving pictures for young children. Unpublished Master's thesis, State Univ. Iowa. (cf. Holaday & Stoddard, 1933, where some of the data are reported.)

POTTHOFF, C. J., LARSON, L. C. & PATTERSON, D. O. 1940. The motion pictures as an aid in teaching human biology. Unpublished manuscript, Univ. Minn.: Committee on Educational Research.

PRIEBE, R. E. & BURTON, W. H. 1939. The slow motion picture as a coaching device. Sch. Rev., 47, 192-198.

PROGRESSIVE EDUCATION ASSOCIATION. COMMISSION ON HUMAN RELATIONS. 1939. The human relations series of films. New York: Progressive Ed. Assoc.

RAMSEYER, L. L. 1938. A study of the influence of documentary films on social attitudes. Unpublished Doctoral thesis, Ohio State Univ. (cf. idem, 1939.)

RAMSEYER, L. L. 1939. Measuring "intangible" effects of motion pictures. Educ. Screen, 18, 237-238.

REED, P. C. 1950. A study of the use made of a group of sound motion pictures in relation to the administration of the Department of Visual and Radio Education, Rochester public schools. Unpublished Master's thesis, Syracuse Univ.

REEDER, E. H. & FREEMAN, F. N. 1924. A comparison of the teaching value of film and of oral instruction in the case of two short projects and one longer project. In F. N. FREEMAN (ED.), Visual education. Chicago: Univ. of Chicago Press. Pp. 167-189.

REID, S. & DAY, D. 1942. Radio and records in education. Rev. of Ed. Res., 1942, 12, No. 3, Ch. VI.

REITZ, A. W. 1937. The relationship of acquired information or knowledge obtained from certain educational motion picture films to the intelligence, grade, age, sex, and type of educational training of the pupil. Unpublished Doctoral thesis, New York Univ.

RENSHAW, S., MILLER, V. L. & MARQUIS, DOROTHY P. 1933. Children's sleep. New York: Macmillan.

RICHARDSON, ADELINE C. & SMITH, GERTRUDE H. 1947. Movies vs. reading - pupils taught with moving pictures score big gains over those using only text material. *The Clearing House*, 22, 15-19.

ROLFE, E. C. 1924. A comparison of the effectiveness of a motion picture film and of demonstrations in instruction in high school physics. In F. N. FREEMAN (ED.), *Visual education*. Chicago: Univ. of Chicago Press. Pp. 335-338.

ROSENTHAL, N. H. 1945. *Films in instruction, Part I, Films -- their use and misuse*. Melbourne, Australia: Robertson & Mullens.

ROSENTHAL, S. P. 1934. Change of socio-economic attitudes under radical motion picture propaganda. Arch. Psychol., No. 166

ROSHAL, S. M. 1949. Effects of learner representation in film-mediated perceptual-motor learning. *Technical report SDC 269-7-5*. State College, Pa.: The Pennsylvania State College, Instructional Film Research Program.

RUFFA, E. J. 1936. An experimental study of motion pictures as used in the teaching of certain athletic skills. Unpublished Master's thesis, Stanford Univ.

RUGER, H. A. 1910. The psychology of efficiency. Arch. Psychol., 19, No. 15.

RULON, P. J. 1933. *The sound motion picture in science teaching*. Cambridge: Harvard Univ. Press.

RUMMEL, P. L. 1940. Theories of grade placement of motion picture film material. Unpublished Doctoral thesis, Boston Univ.

SCOTT, G. 1949. A study of the contribution of motion pictures to the educational achievement in Nebraska high schools. Unpublished Doctoral thesis, University of Nebraska.

SCOTT, W. J. 1947. Reading, film and radio tastes of high school boys and girls. Christchurch, New Zealand: New Zealand Council for Educational Research, Educational Research Series No. 28.

SCOTTISH FILM COUNCIL & SCOTTISH EDUCATIONAL FILM ASSOCIATION. 1948. *Sound films in education*. Glasgow, Scotland: Scottish Film Council.

SEAGOE, M. V. 1931. The child's reactions to the movies. *J. juv. Res.*, 15, 169-180.

SECOR, C. T. 1931. A comparative study of the effectiveness of the motion picture followed by oral discussion and a combination of the lecture, laboratory, and recitation methods of teaching certain units in high school biology. Unpublished Master's thesis, New York Univ.

SENGBUSH, GERTRUDE A. 1933. An experiment with the use of lantern slides in the teaching of typewriting. Unpublished Master's thesis, Univ. So. Calif.

SHAFFER, L. C. 1930. *Children's interpretations of cartoons*. Teachers College Contributions to Education, No. 429. New York: Columbia Univ.

SHEPHARD, J. W. 1922. The teaching efficiency of the film. Educ. Screen, 1, 176-180.

SHERIF, M. & CANTRIL, H. 1947. *The psychology of ego-involvements: social attitudes and identification*. New York: John Wiley & Sons.

SHERMAN, M. 1940. Using visual aids to correlate a first-grade subject - "Gray Squirrel." Educ. Screen, 19, 11-13, 24-25.

SHUTTLEWORTH, F. K. & MAY, M. A. 1933. *The social conduct and attitudes of movie fans*. New York: Macmillan.

SKINNER, C. D. & RICH, S. G. 1925. Visual aids in geography: an experiment. Elem. Sch. J., 25, 700-705.

SMITH, H. A. 1948. A determination of the relative effectiveness of sound motion pictures and equivalent teacher demonstrations in ninth-grade general science. Unpublished Doctoral thesis, Univ. Neb.

SMITH, K. R. & VAN ORMER, E. B. 1949. A classification in terms of learning theories of some areas for research on instructional films. In Progress Report No. 11-12. State College, Pa.: Pennsylvania State College, Instructional Film Research Program.

SMITH, K. R. & VAN ORMER, E. B. 1949A. Learning theories and instructional film research. Technical Report SDC 269-7-6. State College, Pa.: Pennsylvania State College, Instructional Film Research Program.

SNYDER, H. A. 1930. Historical motion pictures in the junior high school. Unpublished Master's thesis, Univ. Pittsburgh.

STENIUS, A. C. 1945. Auditory and visual education. Rev. educ. Res., 15, 243-255.

STERNER, ALICE P. 1947. Radio, motion picture, and reading interests. New York: Bureau of Publications, Teachers College, Columbia Univ.

STILLWELL, R. R. 1939. A study of the effects of motion pictures on the attitudes of seventh-grade students. Unpublished Master's thesis, Ohio State Univ.

STODDARD, A. J. 1934. Will sound pictures tend to increase class size? The Nation's Schools, 14, 16-19.

STOUFFER, S. A., SUCHMAN, E. A., DEVINNEY, L. C., STAR, S. A. & WILLIAMS, R. M. JR. 1949. The American soldier: adjustment during army life. Princeton, N. J.: Princeton Univ. Press.

STRICKLER, G. M. 1939. The effect of the film slide as a teaching aid in general science. Unpublished Master's thesis, La. State Univ.

STROUD, J. B. 1946. Psychology in education. New York: Longmans, Green.

STURMTHAL, A. 1941. Research in educational film. Release No. 2. Inst. for Econ. Educ. Pp. 32-53. New York: Bard College.

STURMTHAL, A. & CURTIS, ALBERTA. 1943. A study of audience reactions to two educational films. Educ. Screen, 22, 306, 314-315.

STURMTHAL, A. & CURTIS, H. 1944. Program analyzer tests of two films. In P. F. LAZARSFELD & F. STANTON (ED.), Radio research, 1942-1943. New York: Duell, Sloan & Pearce. Pp. 485-506.

SULLENGER, T. E. 1930. Modern youth and the movies. Sch. & Soc., 32, 459-461.

SUMSTINE, D. R. 1918. A comparative study of visual instruction in the high school. Sch. & Soc., 7, 235-238.

TERRY, LAURA G. 1932. Types of children's responses to the Yale Chronicles of America Photoplays. Unpublished Master's thesis, New York Univ.

TILTON, J. W. & CHILDS, ARNEY R. 1933. The use of the Yale Photoplays in an elementary school for adults. Educ. Method, 13, 71-75.

TOWER HILL SCHOOL STAFF. 1940. A school uses motion pictures. Washington, D. C.: American Council on Education.

THOMPSON, LOUISE. 1944. The role of verbalization in learning from demonstrations. Unpublished thesis, Yale Univ. (cf. ref. to M. A. May, 1946.)

TWINING, W. E. 1949. Mental practice and physical practice in learning a motor skill. Res. Quart. Amer. Ass. Hlth. Phys. Educ. & Rec., 20, 432-435.

U. S. WAR DEPARTMENT, ARMY SERVICE FORCES, SPECIAL SERVICE DIVISION, RESEARCH BRANCH. 1942. Prelude to war; report on experimental study of 1st film in "Why We Fight" series. Washington, D. C.

U. S. WAR DEPARTMENT, ARMY SERVICE FORCES, INFORMATION AND EDUCATION DIVISION, RESEARCH BRANCH. 1943. Relative amounts learned from sound film and filmstrip instruction on map reading. Washington, D. C.

U. S. WAR DEPARTMENT, ARMY SERVICE FORCES, MILITARY TRAINING DIVISION, RESEARCH BRANCH. 1943. Value of introductory and review exercises in supplementing training films. Washington, D. C.

U. S. WAR DEPARTMENT, ARMY SERVICE FORCES, INFORMATION AND EDUCATION DIVISION, RESEARCH BRANCH. 1945. Value of an audience-participation technique in filmstrip presentation. Washington, D. C.

VANDELL, R. A., DAVIS, R. A. & CLUGSTON, HELEN A. 1943. The function of mental practice in the acquisition of motor skills. J. gen. Psychol., 29, 243-250.

VANDERMEER, A. W. 1943. The economy of time in industrial training: an experimental study of the use of sound films in the training of engine lathe operators. Unpublished Doctoral thesis, Univ. Chicago.

VANDERMEER, A. W. 1945. The economy of time in industrial training: an experimental study of the use of sound films in the training of engine lathe operators. J. educ. Psychol., 36, 65-90.

VANDERMEER, A. W. 1948. Relative effectiveness of color and black and white in instructional films. Progress Report No. 9. State College, Pa.: Pennsylvania State College, Instructional Film Research Program.

VANDERMEER, A. W. 1949. Relative effectiveness of exclusive film instruction, films plus study guides and typical instructional methods. Progress Report No. 10. State College, Pa.: Pennsylvania State College, Instructional Film Research Program.

VANDERMEER, A. W. 1950. Relative effectiveness of instruction by: films exclusively, films plus study guides, and standard lecture methods. Technical Report SDC 269-7-13. State College, Pa.: Pennsylvania State College, Instructional Film Research Program.

VANDERMEER, A. W. 1950A. Relative contributions to factual learning of the pictorial and verbal elements of a filmstrip. Sch. Rev., 58, 84-89.

VERNON, P. E. 1946. An experiment on the value of the film and filmstrip in the instruction of adults. Brit. J. educ. Psychol., 16, 149-162.

VINCENT, W. S., ASH, P. & GREENHILL, L. P. 1949. Relationship of length and fact frequency to effectiveness of instructional motion pictures. Progress Report No. 13. State College, Pa.: Pennsylvania State College, Instructional Film Research Program.

WALTER, JEANETTE S. & BRENNER, H. R. 1949. The effects of inserted questions and statements on film learning. Unpublished Master's thesis, Pennsylvania State College.

WATKINS, R. K. 1931. The learning value of some motion pictures in high school physics and general science as an illustration of a simplified technique in educational experimentation. Educ. Screen, 10, 135-137, 156-157.

WEAVER, G. G. & BOLLENGER, E. W. 1949. Visual aids: their construction and use, (esp. Chap. XIX). New York: Van Nostrand.

WEBER, J. J. 1922. Comparative effectiveness of some visual aids in seventh-grade instruction. Chicago: Educational Screen, Inc.

WESTFALL, L. H. 1934. A study of verbal accompaniments to educational motion pictures. Teachers College Contributions to Education, No. 617. New York: Teachers College, Columbia Univ.

WILLIAMS, DOROTHY M. 1945. A study of the relative effectiveness of selected teaching procedures in the modification of children's attitudes toward the negro. Unpublished Doctoral thesis, New York Univ.

WILLIAMS, FLORENCE. 1924. An investigation of children's preferences for pictures. Elem. Sch. J., 25, 119-126.

WILSON, E. C., LARSON, L. C. & LORD, F. 1940. Use of films in teaching current history: (1) The motion picture as an aid; (2) Methods of use of motion pictures. A study for the Committee on Motion Pictures in Education of the American Council on Education. Unpublished manuscript, Univ. Minn.: The Committee on Educational Research.

WILSON, GERTRUDE E. 1939. Educational effectiveness of specially designed motion pictures in selected areas of child development. Unpublished Master's thesis, State Univ. Iowa.

WISE, H. A. 1939. Motion pictures as an aid in teaching American history. New Haven, Conn.: Yale Univ. Press.

WISE, H. E. 1949. Supplementary contributions of sound motion pictures in high school biology. Sci. Educ., 33, 206-213.

WITTICH, W. A. & FOWLKES, J. G. 1946. Audio-visual paths to learning. New York: Harper.

WITTY, P., GARFIELD, S. & BRINK, W. G. 1941. Interests of high school students in motion pictures and radio. J. educ. Psychol., 32, 176-184.

WOLF, KATHERINE & FISKE, MARJORIE. 1949. The children talk about comics. In P. F. LAZARSFELD & F. N. STANTON (ED.), Communications research 1948-1949. New York: Harper. Pp. 3-50.

WOLFE, H. G. 1930. An experimental evaluation of the motion picture as an aid in classroom teaching. Unpublished Master's thesis, Univ. Rochester.

WOOD, B. D. & FREEMAN, F. N. 1929. Motion pictures in the classroom. New York: Houghton Mifflin.

WOODBURN, L. O. 1936. An experimental study of the effectiveness of silent motion pictures in ninth-grade general science. Unpublished Master's thesis, Univ. Cincinnati.

YALE MOTION PICTURE RESEARCH PROJECT. 1947. Do "motivation" and "participation" questions increase learning? Educ. Screen, 26, 256-259, 274-283.

ZUCKERMAN, J. V. 1949. Commentary variations: level of verbalization, personal reference, and phase relations in instructional films on perceptual-motor tasks. Technical Report SDC 269-7-4. State College, Pa.: Pennsylvania State College, Instructional Film Research Program.

ZYVE, CLAIRE. 1932. An experimental study of the teaching of arithmetic combinations. Educ. Meth., 12, 16-18.

TECHNICAL REPORTS OF THE INSTRUCTIONAL FILM RESEARCH PROGRAM

SDC 269-7-1. Instructional Film Production, Utilization and Research in Great Britain, Canada and Australia, by L. P. Greenhill and J. H. Tyo.

SDC 269-7-2. Music in Motion Pictures: Review of Literature with Implications for Instructional Films, by J. V. Zuckerman.

SDC 269-7-3. The Relative Effectiveness of Massed Versus Spaced Film Presentation, by P. Ash.

SDC 269-7-4. Commentary Variations: Level of Verbalization, Personal Reference, and Phase-Relations in Instructional Films on Perceptual-Motor Tasks, by J. V. Zuckerman.

SDC 269-7-5. Effects of Learner Representation in Film Mediated Perceptual-Motor Learning, by S. M. Roshal.

SDC 269-7-6. Learning Theories and Instructional Film Research, by K. R. Smith and E. B. Van Ormer.

SDC 269-7-7. Relationship of Length and Fact Frequency to Effectiveness of Instructional Motion Pictures, by W. S. Vincent, P. Ash and L. P. Greenhill.

SDC 269-7-8. Contributions of Film Introductions and Summaries to Learning from Instructional Films, by C. W. Lathrop and C. A. Norford.

SDC 269-7-9. The Effect of Attention-Gaining Devices on Film-Mediated Learning, by D. M. Neu

SDC 269-7-10. The Effects of Prestige and Identification Factors on Attitude Restructuring and Learning from Sound Films, by J. P. Kishler.

SDC 269-7-11. Effects on Training of Experimental Film Variables, Study II: "How-It-Works," Verbalization, Participation, Succinct Treatment, by N. Jaspen.

SDC 269-7-12. Effect of Repetitive Film Showings on Learning, by C. L. McTavish.

SDC 269-7-13. Relative Effectiveness of Instruction by: Films Exclusively, Films Plus Study Guides, and Standard Lecture Methods, by A. W. VanderMeer.

SDC 269-7-14. The Classroom Communicator, by R. Eggleton, C. R. Carpenter, F. T. John, and J. B. Cannon Jr.

SDC 269-7-15. The Film Analyzer, by R. Eggleton, C. R. Carpenter, F. T. John, and J. B. Cannon Jr.

SDC 269-7-16. The Effect of Inserted Questions and Statements on Film Learning, by A. K. Kurtz, J. S. Walter and H. R. Brenner.

SDC 269-7-17. Effects on Training of Experimental Film Variables, Study I: Verbalization, Rate of Development, Nomenclature, Errors, "How-It-Works," Repetition, by N. Jaspen.

SDC 269-7-18. Comparison of the Audio and Video Elements of Instructional Films, by H. E. Nelson and K. R. Moll.